Everyday Peace

How So-called Ordinary People Can Disrupt Violent Conflict

ROGER MAC GINTY

OXFORD
UNIVERSITY PRESS

Oxford University Press is a department of the University of Oxford. It furthers the University's objective of excellence in research, scholarship, and education by publishing worldwide. Oxford is a registered trade mark of Oxford University Press in the UK and certain other countries.

Published in the United States of America by Oxford University Press
198 Madison Avenue, New York, NY 10016, United States of America.

© Oxford University Press 2021

All rights reserved. No part of this publication may be reproduced, stored in a retrieval system, or transmitted, in any form or by any means, without the prior permission in writing of Oxford University Press, or as expressly permitted by law, by license, or under terms agreed with the appropriate reproduction rights organization. Inquiries concerning reproduction outside the scope of the above should be sent to the Rights Department, Oxford University Press, at the address above.

You must not circulate this work in any other form
and you must impose this same condition on any acquirer.

Library of Congress Cataloging-in-Publication Data
Names: Mac Ginty, Roger, 1970– author.
Title: Everyday peace : how so-called ordinary people can disrupt violent conflict / Roger Mac Ginty.
Description: New York, NY : Oxford University Press, [2021] | Includes bibliographical references and index.
Identifiers: LCCN 2021010356 (print) | LCCN 2021010357 (ebook) | ISBN 9780197563397 (hardback) | ISBN 9780197563410 (epub)
Subjects: LCSH: Peace-building. | Peace. | Conflict management.
Classification: LCC JZ5538 .M327 2021 (print) |
LCC JZ5538 (ebook) | DDC 303.6/9—dc23
LC record available at https://lccn.loc.gov/2021010356
LC ebook record available at https://lccn.loc.gov/2021010357

DOI: 10.1093/oso/9780197563397.001.0001

1 3 5 7 9 8 6 4 2

Printed by Integrated Books International, United States of America

Everyday Peace

STUDIES IN STRATEGIC PEACEBUILDING

Series Editors

R. Scott Appleby, John Paul Lederach, and Daniel Philpott
The Joan B. Kroc Institute for International Peace Studies
University of Notre Dame

STRATEGIES OF PEACE
Edited by Daniel Philpott and Gerard F. Powers

UNIONISTS, LOYALISTS, AND CONFLICT
TRANSFORMATION IN NORTHERN IRELAND
Lee A. Smithey

JUST AND UNJUST PEACE
An Ethic of Political Reconciliation
Daniel Philpott

COUNTING CIVILIAN CASUALTIES
An Introduction to Recording and Estimating Nonmilitary Deaths in Conflict
Edited by Taylor B. Seybolt, Jay D. Aronson, and Baruch Fischhoff

RESTORATIVE JUSTICE, RECONCILIATION, AND PEACEBUILDING
Edited by Jennifer J. Llewellyn and Daniel Philpott

QUALITY PEACE
Peacebuilding, Victory, and World Order
Peter Wallensteen

THE PEACE CONTINUUM
What It Is and How to Study It
Christian Davenport, Erik Melander, and Patrick M. Regan

WHEN POLITICAL TRANSITIONS WORK
Reconciliation as Interdependence
Fanie Du Toit

This book is dedicated to my brother, Manus Mac Ginty, 1967–2019

Contents

List of Figures and Table   ix
Acknowledgements   xi
Abbreviations   xiii

Introduction   1
1. The Everyday, Circuitry, and Scalability   25
2. Sociality, Reciprocity, and Solidarity   51
3. Everyday Peace Power   80
4. Parley, Truce, and Ceasefire   104
5. Everyday Peace on the Battlefield   136
6. Gender and Everyday Peace   161
7. Conflict Disruption   190
Conclusion   212

Bibliography   223
Index   255

List of Figures and Table

Figure 1.1.	Circuitry in a conflict-affected country.	46
Figure 2.1.	Everyday peace continuum.	55
Table 6.1.	Percentage of female representation in post-peace-accord lower chambers at five-year intervals.	170

Acknowledgements

Completion of this manuscript is about seven years late, a fact not unrelated to having a seven-year-old daughter, Flora. The book is dedicated to my brother, Manus Mac Ginty, who died much too young. He loved his family, the outdoors, and storytelling. I miss him very much.

Many debts were incurred in writing this book. Alex Bellamy, John Brewer, Nemanja Džuverović, Pamina Firchow, Marsha Henry, Laura Mcleod, Eric Lepp, Ben Rampton, Oliver Richmond, Tom Rodwell, and Mandy Turner all read sections of the book or provided help with literature. Conversations with Tatsushi Arai, Séverine Autesserre, Christine Bell, Morten Bøås, Roddy Brett, Kris Brown, Christine Cheng, David Ellery, Larissa Fast, Landon Hancock, Chip Hauss, Stefanie Kappler, Walt Kilroy, Sung Yong Lee, Alp Özerdem, Michelle Parlevliet, Jan Pospisil, Gearoid Miller, Sarah Njeri, Stefano Ruzza, Elena Stavrevska, Anthony Wanis St. John, Gëzim Visoka, Birte Vogel, Andrew Williams, and Susan Woodward also helped clarify thinking and provided encouragement. At Durham, a "Conflict +" seminar spent an invaluable few hours discussing chapter 6; thanks are due to Emil Archambault, Olga Demetriou, Elisabeth Kirtslogou, and Nayanika Mookherjee. My wonderful PhD students, and successive Masters classes, also provided a great sounding board. Alex De Waal provided access to African Union data on security incidents.

Much of the stimulus for this book came from the Everyday Peace Indicators project, and I have been fortunate to work alongside the indefatigable and ever supportive Pamina Firchow for many years. I have been privileged to learn from Everyday Peace Indicators colleagues Peter Dixon, Naomi Levy, Lindsay McClain Opiyo, Jessica Smith, and Zach Tilton. The Carnegie Corporation of New York has provided patient and generous support to the Everyday Peace Indicators project, and I am particularly grateful to Aaron Stanley and Stephen Del Rosso. I also acknowledge support from the Economic and Social Research Council in the form of a grant to work on peacekeeping data.

Ideas in the book were honed at papers given at the universities of Amsterdam, the Arctic, Belgrade, Bradford, Bristol, Durham, George Mason, Kent State, King's College London, Leeds Beckett, Queen Mary, Manitoba, Newcastle, Notre Dame, St. Andrews, Turin, and York. I am grateful for the hospitality and the questions.

I benefited enormously from encouragement and advice from the editors of the Oxford University Press series Studies in Strategic Peacemaking—Scott

Appleby, John Paul Lederach, and Daniel Philpott, all at the Kroc Institute for International Peace Studies at the University of Notre Dame. I am very grateful to David McBride and Holly Mitchell at Oxford University Press for their guidance. The anonymous reviewers managed to perfect the balance between encouragement and gently pointing out the holes in the argument.

I am also grateful to the community I live in and the distractions it provides. I appointed myself "writer in residence" in the cafe bus at the Chain Bridge Honey Farm. Not a word of this book could have been written without the support of Mrs. Mac Ginty. Everyone needs a Mrs. Mac Ginty. Thanks are also due to Patrick, Edward, and Elisabeth Mac Ginty.

This is the book I wanted to write, and I am grateful for having the opportunity to do so.

Abbreviations

CVE	countering violent extremism
DUP	Democratic Unionist Party
EPI	Everyday Peace Indicators
EPP	Everyday Peace Power
IFI	international financial institution
IHL	international humanitarian law
INGO	international non-governmental organisation
IRA	Irish Republican Army
ISAF	International Security Assistance Force
LRA	Lord's Resistance Army
POW	prisoner of war
SGBV	sexual and gender-based violence
SS	Schutzstaffel
UNAMID	United Nations African Union Mission in Darfur

Introduction

During the height of its violent campaign, the Lord's Resistance Army (LRA) abducted and brutalised thousands of children in northern Uganda, Sudan, and the Democratic Republic of Congo. Many of these children were turned into child soldiers and sex slaves. Over time, and especially as the LRA suffered from battlefield setbacks, many of the former child soldiers and sex slaves returned to their villages. Naturally, many of the villagers were suspicious, even fearful, that people responsible for atrocities would be living in their midst. But as research conducted by the Everyday Peace Indicators (EPI) project has indicated, many villagers were sanguine and pragmatic. According to one male focus group participant, 'We need help for the formerly abducted persons. They have returned home but they have nowhere to start from. If possible, they should be helped to start their life afresh'.[1] A female in another focus group remarked, 'You forgive because it was not their will to be abducted',[2] while a participant in a youth focus group showed remarkable understanding: 'Formerly abducted persons are being stigmatised . . . because some of them have AIDS that they acquired while in captivity'.[3] This quiet acceptance at the level of individuals or groups of individuals can be regarded as everyday peace, or a way in which community members use their own agency to navigate through potentially awkward situations.

Attitudes and actions like those described above lie at the heart of everyday peace and are the focus of this book. The peace forged between a villager and a returning child soldier is unlikely to rely on ministrations by civil society organisations or on the peacebuilding theories found in a book like this one. Instead, they depend on common sense, pragmatism, and an understanding that if space is to be shared, then accommodations have to be made. Importantly, these forms of peace are demonstrable and help us illustrate the varieties and texture of peace. Another example of everyday peace comes from Sudan in April 2019, when protesters against long-term Sudanese ruler Omar al-Bashir came under attack from a government militia. A small group of soldiers—just a handful—stepped in to protect the civilians from attack.[4] The actions of the soldiers were not sanctioned

---

[1] Male focus group, EPI project, Attiak, northern Uganda, 4 October 2013.
[2] Female focus group, EPI project, Attiak, northern Uganda, 12 November 2013.
[3] Youth focus group, EPI project, Attiak, northern Uganda, 4 October 2013.
[4] Borzou Daragahi, 'Clashes between Rival Sudan Armed Forces Risk "Civil War", Protesters Warn,' *Independent*, 10 April 2019, https://www.independent.co.uk/news/world/africa/sudan-civil-war-omar-al-bashir-khartoum-bouteflika-a8863881.html.

from above. Instead, the soldiers acted on the spur of the moment, showing humanity and a concern for the rights of fellow citizens. This small act had enormous repercussions in that it showed that the military was not completely loyal to al-Bashir and that some members, if made to choose between their fellow citizens and an autocrat who had been in power for thirty years, would choose the former. The micro-action, just a small act in the midst of a wider situation, was pivotal in the ousting of al-Bashir. It showed the capacity of a micro-act to scale up and have implications far beyond the original act.

Or take a third example. In the midst of a battle in World War II, a British infantryman found himself face to face with a German tank: 'I turned to see a Mark IV tank only a few yards behind us with his machine gun still aimed and smoking. I tensed myself for the inevitable, but he held his fire . . . he released the trigger and I lived to tell the tale'.[5]

The surviving soldier had been saved by a split-second decision by the machine-gunner in the tank. The incident did not change the course of the war, but it did change the soldier's life, allowing him to live for another seventy years, have a family, and set up a flourishing business.[6] Although it was momentary, the spontaneous act of compassion was pro-peace and pro-social and can be categorised as everyday peace in the context of war.

This book is about the capacity of so-called ordinary people to disrupt violent conflict and forge pro-social relationships in conflict-affected societies. It is concerned with small acts of peace, termed here *everyday peace*, that have the capacity to disrupt conflict and possibly grow into something more substantial. It is interested in the scaling-up potential of grassroots actions and stances by individuals and groups of individuals whose actions can have a ripple effect—and just possibly a tsunami effect. The book argues that there is often a precursor stage to conflict management, resolution, and transformation: *conflict disruption*. The book investigates the disruptive and pacific potential of so-called ordinary people in situations of conflict and division. It unpacks—conceptually and empirically—the everyday peace that so-called ordinary people use to navigate through life in societies affected by violent conflict. It is interested in the 'peace' that is on display when Catholics and Protestants in Northern Ireland share the same workplace or when Christians and Muslims in northern Nigeria use the same marketplace. This everyday peace is far removed from the 'big peace' of peace accords and symbolic gestures by political leaders.[7] Instead, it

---

[5] Ray Ellis, *Once a Hussar: A Memoir of Battle, Capture and Escape in the Second World War*, Kindle ed. (Barnsley: Pen and Sword, 2013), chap. 11.
[6] Melissa Hills, 'Last Hero of the WWII Battle of Gazala in Libya Dies at Age 94', *Daily Express*, 24 February 2014, https://www.express.co.uk/news/uk/461440/Last-hero-of-the-WWII-Battle-of-Gazala-in-Libya-dies-at-age-94.
[7] Herbert V. Evatt, 'Risks of a Big-Power Peace', *Foreign Affairs* 24 (1946): 195–209.

is the stuff of everyday life—the actions and thoughts that constitute how we embody and live life as individuals, families, and communities. Rather than occurring in diplomatic capitals in front of the world's media, it occurs at tram stops, in the stairwells of apartment buildings, and in the line at the bakery in societies in which there may be conflict or intergroup tension. It can even occur on the battlefield with combatants showing mercy and compassion to apparent enemies. As these examples show, this book is concerned with interpersonal and small-group peace that occurs at the level below civil society organisations and formally organised pro-peace groups. Thus, the book is interested in levels below excellent works on peacebuilding—such as Séverine Autesserre's *Peaceland* or Oliver Richmond's *Failed Statebuilding*—which tend to concentrate on international interveners and organised peacebuilding.[8] It is also the level below the 'middle range leadership' identified by John Paul Lederach as often crucial in peacebuilding endeavours.[9] This book is anxious to break through the 'concrete floor' to see a level that is often overlooked by many analyses: the individual, the family, the friendship network, neighbours, or work colleagues, rather than peace groups or civil society organisations. As a result, the book moves beyond political science and international relations analyses and draws on more sociological views of peace and conflict. Thus, it looks beyond an orthodox gaze on states and formal institutions in order to take note of the personal, the informal, the hyper-local, and the relational. While international relations and political science have made attempts to tackle their ethnocentrism, sometimes we have to move on.[10] Crucially, as is argued in this book, a top-down peace can only reach its potential if it is given life through bottom-up enactments and embodiment. Capturing these acts and embodiments requires lenses inflected by sociology, anthropology, and gender studies.

For understandable reasons, top-down peace receives much attention. In the right circumstances, it is capable of providing the physical, psychological, and legal security that enables other types of peace to take root. For this top-down peace to become real or meaningful, however, it must be reflected in how people live their lives—in the routes they take to school, in their cultural activities and friendship networks, and in how they navigate through the awkwardness and potential dangers of a society transitioning away from violent conflict. As a result, this book is very much interested in issues of scale and how top-down

---

[8] Séverine Autesserre, *Peaceland: Conflict Resolution and the Everyday Politics of International Intervention* (Cambridge: Cambridge University Press, 2014); Oliver P. Richmond, *Failed Statebuilding: Intervention, the State and the Dynamics of Peace Formation* (New Haven, CT: Yale University Press, 2014).

[9] John Paul Lederach, *Building Peace: Sustainable Reconciliation in Divided Societies* (Washington, DC: United States Institute of Peace Process, 2002), 39.

[10] George Lawson and Robbie Shilliam, 'Sociology and International Relations: Legacies and Prospects', *Cambridge Review of International Affairs* 23, no. 1 (2010): 69–86.

and bottom-up approaches to peace (and all the approaches in between) might interact.[11]

The notion and practice of everyday peace provokes three questions: Is it really peace? How can everyday peace deal with and confront power? Can everyday peace be scaled up? This book attempts to answer those questions. The first, question—is it really peace?—can be answered in the affirmative. Christians and Muslims in Ambon Province in Indonesia may live side by side, but they may do so in grudging toleration—apparently a mere coexistence or negative peace.[12] This is far removed from effusive and emancipatory forms of peace, and it is understandable if everyday peace faces questions regarding its pacific nature. Yet the circumstances of conflict and deep societal divisions often do not allow for anything more than tolerance or the acceptance that individuals from 'the other side' have a right to coexist in a shared space. While this might be a very limited form of peace, it often requires considerable bravery on the part of those who engage in it, and so it is a mindset and behaviour worthy of serious study. Moreover, this everyday peace has the capacity, under certain circumstances, to disrupt conflict and develop into something more significant. It can be thought of in terms of the first and last peace. It is the first peace in the sense of the first tentative steps towards accommodation as a violent conflict comes to a close, and it is the last peace in terms of the last intergroup contact to survive as societies slip towards violent conflict. For example, it might take the form of a Guji farmer retaining, or re-establishing, links with a Gedeo trader in southern Ethiopia in the midst of wider communal unrest. Such links may not sound significant, but they do deserve labels associated with the word *peace*.

Moreover, the argument of this book is that everyday peace has the capacity, under certain circumstances, to scale up. Cumulative small acts often can have larger outcomes in terms of preventing conflicts from escalating and in saving or protecting lives. By disrupting the narrative and logic of conflict, small acts of everyday peace can create space for civility, reciprocity, solidarity, and possibly more expansive concepts such as reconciliation. They can become agonistic peace in the sense of a positive societal dynamic in which problems can be acknowledged and possibly dealt with.[13]

---

[11] Maire A. Dugan, 'A Nested Theory of Conflict', *A Leadership Journal: Women in Leadership* 1: 15.

[12] As Patrick M. Regan makes clear, the concepts of positive and negative peace originated with Quincy Wright and Fred Cottrell. Patrick M. Regan, 'Bringing Peace Back In: Presidential Address to the Peace Science Society', *Conflict Management and Peace Science* 31, no. 4 (2014): 346. See also Fred Cottrell, 'Men Cry Peace', in *Research for Peace* (Oslo: Institute for Social Research, 1954), 99–164; and Quincy Wright, 'Criteria for Judging the Relevance of Researches on the Problems of Peace', in *Research for Peace* (Oslo: Institute for Social Research, 1954), 3–98.

[13] Karin Aggestam, Fabio Cristiano, and Lisa Strömbom, 'Towards Agonistic Peacebuilding: Exploring the Antagonism-Agonism Nexus in the Middle East Peace Process', *Third World Quarterly* 36, no. 9 (2015): 1736–1753.

The second question—how can everyday peace confront power?—poses a serious challenge to the notion and practice of everyday peace. A Sinhala and a Tamil may live next to each other in Sri Lanka and have good neighbourly relations. Yet would this micro-level relationship be able to survive a worsening of political relations and a deteriorating security situation at the national level? The criticism is made that everyday peace is unable to offset the tremendous structural power that underpins conflict, nor can it offset the proximate power of men with guns. A friendship or working relationship between an Israeli Jew and a Palestinian may seem inconsequential in the context of much broader conflict and its power imbalances. Such critiques of everyday peace are indeed valid, and it is often the case that everyday peace occurs on the margins of society or under the radar. Yet it is argued in this book that everyday peace can be significant. Fundamentally, it can be seen as a form of power in its own right: *Everyday Peace Power* (EPP). It can disrupt dominant narratives and modes of thinking that normalise the sense of superiority that one group might have over another. Everyday peace might show that alternative approaches to intergroup behaviour are possible. As chapter 3 in particular will demonstrate, the notion of everyday peace requires us to think differently about power and move beyond coercive and material ideas of power to consider more sociological and positive views of power such as power from, power to, and power with.

The third question facing everyday peace—can it be scaled up?—is perhaps the most common question I face when giving talks on everyday peace. What happens to grassroots initiatives if they only stay at the grassroots? Everyday peace initiatives and stances may be so heavily localised that they have no wider significance. Certainly, this book focuses on the micro-processes that constitute everyday peace: the encounters in a workplace shared by Serbs and Croats, the studiedly neutral conversations between a Catholic and a Protestant in Northern Ireland, or the split-second battlefield decision to take a prisoner rather than pull the trigger. Yet all of these highly localised encounters take place in wider contexts. A key task facing this book is to connect the hyperlocal (a peace between neighbours in a specific place) with large-scale spaces such as the state, the international, and all levels in between. While a Shia and a Christian in Beirut might have good relations, clearly this relationship is nested with a much more complex set of political, economic, and cultural dynamics. Everyday peace may appear to occur within a localised ecosystem, but this is likely to be shaped by state, regional, international, and transnational contexts. These linkages—between the hyperlocal and all the other levels—are often difficult to see. A major part of this book aims to highlight the connectivities between the very local and other levels. To do this, the notion of circuitry is developed as an analytical device. It is argued that hyperlocal everyday peace acts and thinking can be conceptualised as micro-circuits that occur in larger circuits. Thus, while acts of everyday peace and conflict disruption might be seen as hyperlocal and seemingly unconnected with wider events and processes, they are actually part of wider dynamics. More than this, EPP co-constitutes the wider circuits. It can disrupt them, provide alternatives to dominant narratives, and offer a means of escaping the logic of conflict and violence.

The central mission of this book is to explicate the concept and practices of everyday peace. It is argued that everyday peace constitutes the social glue that prevents fragile societies from tipping over the edge. It might be the first and last peace. As such, it has the capacity to disrupt violent conflict and create the space in which something more significant—such as conflict management, conflict resolution, or conflict transformation—can take place. Tolerance, coexistence, intergroup friendship, and recognition of minimal rights for the other side may not sound like an expansive peace, but they may constitute major advances given the violent ruptures that might have occurred. Importantly, while there is academic and practitioner focus on 'scaling up', everyday peace is often likely to 'scale out'. That is, rather than directly scaling up and encountering power in the form of institutions, everyday peace is likely to scale out, or replicate horizontally and at localised levels. Scaling out can reach critical mass, or a level of participation or acknowledgement that shapes society and may make political and community leaders take note and possibly change behaviour.

Three Innovations

This book makes three claims to originality. Of course, it is worth questioning if any ideas can be novel on a planet occupied by humans for about two hundred thousand years. It is also worth noting the enormous debt owed to the peace practitioners and scholars who have provided the foundation for many of the ideas in this volume. These caveats aside, the first claim to originality is that the book unpacks the meanings of everyday peace in a sustained and detailed way. Key here is the identification of three core concepts that constitute everyday peace: *sociality*, *reciprocity*, and *solidarity*. Not all of them are present in all instances of everyday peace, but they form a repertoire that is drawn upon as circumstances permit. The concepts, which are explored in detail in chapter 2, remind us that everyday peace is a mode of reasoning as well as a series of actions and postures.[14] Everyday peace can be considered as a way of sense-making and

---

[14] See work by John Brewer on everyday peace as a mode of thinking as well as actions. Brewer's work on the value of sociology to peace and conflict studies has been very influential in the writing of this book. See, for example, John D. Brewer et al., *The Sociology of Everyday Life Peacebuilding* (Basingstoke, UK: Palgrave Macmillan, 2018); and John D. Brewer, 'Towards a Sociology of Compromise', in *The Sociology of Compromise after Conflict*, ed. John D. Brewer (Basingstoke, UK: Palgrave Macmillan, 2018), 1–29.

reasoning that allows individuals and groups to accept (and even respect) those from the out-group. It involves emotional intelligence and may entail overriding the groupthink and hegemonic narratives that dominate the in-group. Everyday peace relies on 'reading' social situations, making judgements on whether it is safe to engage in particular activities, and pursuing a course of everyday diplomacy. The concepts of sociality, reciprocity, and solidarity help us understand the contingent nature of everyday peace and how it depends on the structural and proximate context. This, in turn, underscores the importance of power and how everyday peace—like other forms of peace—is subject to 'power over' or the ability of actors to exert power and influence over others. Yet, as explained above and explored in detail in chapter 3, everyday peace is a form of power in its own right, EPP. The conceptual exploration of the notion of everyday peace draws heavily on the EPI project and its findings from local communities in Colombia, Uganda, South Africa, and Zimbabwe.

A second innovation in the book is the use of *circuitry* as an analytical tool to understand the connections between the everyday peace that occurs at the hyperlocal level and other dynamics occurring at the levels above. Drawing on network theory and literature on biological and engineered circuits (for example, plant root systems and electronic circuit boards), the concept of circuitry allows us to see how everyday peace can be nested within, and can contribute to, a wider series of structures and processes. Circuits help explain the multi-scalar nature of peace and conflict and how apparently local, isolated, and one-off events fit within much broader patterns. This ties in with notions of conflicts as interlocking systems in which both actors and issues 'can be connected through convergence of complex conflict dynamics'.[15] Importantly, these networks or circuits are relational and embedded in a cultural context.[16] One of the findings in the book is the hyperlocality of everyday peace as it follows the contours of everyday life; everyday peace is forged and maintained at the local level. The local level is embodied and enacted and thus takes form in the home and the immediate vicinity of the home, the commuting routes one might take, and the habitual and convenient spaces that one might frequent such as particular cafes, shops, or places of worship. Circuitry is a way of capturing the local as part of a series of wider networks and political economies. It allows us to address the issue of scaling up or the question of what happens if grassroots everyday peace just stays at the grassroots level. Circuitry encourages us to think of how power and information might flow (or be blocked) between different levels of our social and political ecologies. It also allows us to conceptualise how linkages might be

---

[15] Ho-Won Jeong, *Understanding Conflict and Conflict Analysis* (Thousand Oaks, CA: Sage, 2008), 122.

[16] Mark Granovetter, 'Economic Action and Social Structure: The Problem of Embeddedness', *American Journal of Sociology* 91, no. 3 (1985): 481–510.

hidden, tenuous, and contingent. Here it is useful to go back to the example of the Sudanese soldiers who took a stand in favour of the protesters and against the militia. The soldiers were member of multiple circuits. Some of these circuits, most obviously the Sudanese armed forces, will be formal, but others, such as clan, family, or friendship networks, will be informal and not always visible. As will be developed later in the book, everyday peace does have the potential to scale out and scale up. Obviously, this is context-dependent, but, importantly, everyday peace is co-constitutive of contexts, and the notion of circuitry will help demonstrate how scaling out has the potential to develop into scaling up; scaling out became scaling up. A recurring question in this book is whether everyday peace, for example, acts of intergroup civility or kindness, can become 'societalized'[17] or generalised in the civil sphere.

The third innovation in the book is to unpack the notion of *conflict disruption*. At first glance, conflict disruption may seem of minor importance, especially if compared to more ambitious concepts such as conflict resolution or conflict transformation. Yet disrupting the narrative and calculus of violence and prejudice is an essential step in moving towards forms of peace. Everyday peace thinking and acts have the capacity to disrupt, not merely interrupt, conflict and create spaces in which other forms of peace may take root. The notion of conflict disruption, mentioned throughout the book but explored in detail in chapter 7, draws on literature from business and management that shows how orthodox business models are disrupted by start-ups that seek to develop new modes of operation. In a similar way, everyday peace can be seen as a disruptive force—indeed, a form of power EPP—that can circumvent existing modes of thinking and action that suggest that conflict is totalising or unavoidable. A good example of conflict disruption comes from the mutinous actions of substantial numbers of soldiers in the German, French, and Russian militaries towards the end of World War I. Their actions were important in making the existing mode of warfare unsustainable. Importantly, multiple small-scale acts had a cumulative impact.

What Is Everyday Peace?

Everyday peace is a series of actions and modes of thinking that people utilise to navigate through life in deeply divided and conflict-affected societies. It works at the intra- and intergroup levels and relies on emotional intelligence to 'read'

---

[17] This is a more positive view of societalization than found in Jeffrey C. Alexander, 'The Societalization of Social Problems: Church Pedophilia, Phone Hacking, and the Financial Crisis', *American Sociological Review* 83, no. 6 (2018): 1049–1078.

social situations and act accordingly. In many ways, everyday peace is a coping mechanism and a survival strategy that may become internalised and naturalised into everyday life. It is a form of tactical agency that is enacted and embodied into how people behave, present themselves, and go about their daily business. It is socially learned behavior, with the family and close peer group often playing a significant role in this learning process. Importantly, and as argued by John Brewer and colleagues, everyday peace is not merely the actions and performativity that are found in daily interactions, but it is also a mode of reasoning.[18] Everyday peace is a way of seeing the world, of 'reading' a social environment, and of rationalising a situation that might involve violence or the threat of violence. It relies on the deft use of a social infrastructure or a series of cultural, social, and economic networks that we use in our daily existence. These networks, and how we use and constitute them, are highly political.

Everyday peace is heavily context-dependent. In some circumstances, it will be impossible for individuals or groups to engage in everyday peace. There may be physical barriers to prevent intergroup contact (for example, as in Israel–Palestine or Georgia and South Ossetia), or levels of violence may mean that intergroup relations more or less evaporate. In such circumstances, showing friendship or familiarity with out-group members might attract the attention of gatekeepers and disciplinarians within one's own community. There should be no expectation that individuals will be consistent in their everyday peace activities and thinking. Everyday peace may be a one-off 'moment' of compassion or empathy to an out-group member in a specific circumstance—even on the battlefield, as illustrated in chapter 5. It can be an enduring intergroup friendship or relationship that is singular. Those involved may hold generally negative views of other out-group members. It may take the form of self-realisation and self-actualisation over the long term, whereby an individual moderates his or her opinions. As interview material later in the book shows, some individuals who were radicalised during the Lebanese civil war came to regret their involvement and to interpret the world in a different way.

Everyday peace involves a series of social practices such as avoidance, a system of manners, telling and blame deferring that, taken together, constitute a survival strategy that individuals and groups use to avoid difficult situations.[19] It involves a fleetness of foot, quick calculations, and a good deal of dissembling. That is, people might believe one thing but say another simply to avoid or defuse a tense situation. This indicates insincerity, but if the insincerity is for socially good purposes, then it can be justified. Indeed, all societies have scripted

---

[18] Brewer et al., *Sociology of Everyday Life*.
[19] Roger Mac Ginty, 'Everyday Peace: Bottom-Up and Local Agency in Conflict-Affected Societies', *Security Dialogue* 45, no. 6 (2014): 548–564.

social interchanges (just think of interactions with the waitstaff in a restaurant). In a deeply divided society, however, the script becomes important as individuals pursuing everyday peace strategies will avoid contentious topics in conversation and rely on the script of manners and civility to chart a way through interchanges. While individuals and groups may use a modulated and restrained script in their intergroup interchanges, they may fall back on the hidden transcript when interacting with members of the in-group—or certainly more zealous members of the in-group.[20] The picture that emerges is of individuals and groups who draw on a wide repertoire of social skills and are adept at matching the social skill to the situation. The notion and practice of everyday peace encourage us to think of so-called ordinary people as skilled diplomats who are adaptable and alert to a changing environment. While many everyday peace activities are rational and based on self-preservation, some are pro-peace and pro-social. They might even hold the promise of disrupting conflict.

One can think of a Serb living in an apartment building in a town in Bosnia. In the morning, he may comment to his wife, who also identifies as Serbian, on something he hears on the radio news. The comment may be pejorative towards Bosnian Muslims, but as it is a comment made in the private space of the home, it can be considered part of the 'hidden transcript'. Five minutes later, he may then meet a Bosnian Muslim neighbour on the shared stairwell of the apartment building and greet him convivially. The two may have known each other for years and realise that as they live in close proximity, cordial relations are prudent. The man may work as a bus driver. Here he must be 'on guard' and try—as far as possible—to keep his politics, identity, and opinions to himself. Thus, rather than risk offending a passenger, he will keep any conversations to neutral issues such as the weather or the heavy traffic. After work, he may meet up with fellow bus drivers for a drink. As this is likely to be a mixed-identity group, the conversation will again be modulated and will avoid, to the extent possible, issues that would make anyone in the group uncomfortable. On the way home, he might stop off at his brother's apartment for a last drink. His brother might hold extreme sectarian views, but the man—simply wanting an easy life and not wishing to have a row with his brother—laughs at his sectarian jokes. The picture that emerges is of a social chameleon, an individual who is socially adept and capable of drawing on a repertoire of multiple modes of behavior depending on the circumstances.

In one reading, the activities of the man are contradictory and do not constitute peace. They are, at best, ambivalent and possibly even cowardly. The man is far removed from an activist or campaigner who wants to address the absence of intergroup reconciliation following the Dayton Accords. His actions and stances

---

[20] James C. Scott, *Domination and the Art of Resistance: Hidden Transcripts* (New Haven, CT: Yale University Press, 1990).

are, however, deeply embedded in the everyday and its 'situational constraints'.[21] They show a good deal of emotional intelligence and an ability to shift between modes of behavior and thinking. Importantly, and why they deserve the term *peace*, the man's actions are not inflammatory. They recognise the tensions of a deeply divided society and the potential of injudicious actions and words to contribute to a worsening of relations between communities. The man's behaviour is not an expansive type of peace, yet it shows social maturity and contributes to the functioning of society (albeit a society with considerable dysfunctions). In an optimum scenario, it could be that the man engages in more expansive intergroup activity as circumstances allow. His act of living—peacefully—in the same apartment block as Bosnian Muslims might encourage other Serbs to move in. Intergroup social mixing will involve multiple micro everyday actions and stances. It may not constitute a peace revolution, but for a society emerging from violent conflict, it may be significant. Again, in an optimum scenario, there may be a scaling out of everyday pro-social activities that may, over time, become more significant.

Why Is Everyday Peace Important?

There is no shortage of publications on peace and conflict. But works that drill down to understand the meanings and forms of peace are relatively rare. This book seeks to contribute to the relatively small corpus that unpacks the meanings of peace.[22] It concentrates on a specific form of peace—everyday peace—that is more prevalent and significant than much of the extant literature would lead us to believe. With good reason, there is much attention on formal approaches to peace through peace processes, peace accords, and the actions of political leaders, states, and institutions.[23] There is also significant, and deserved, attention to the work of civil society organisations, activists, and peacebuilding professionals who work to foster reconciliation and cement peace accords.[24] This

---

[21] Mark Granovetter, 'Economic Action and Social Structure: The Problem of Embeddedness', *American Journal of Sociology* 91, no. 3 (1985): 481–510.

[22] See, for example, Gordon L. Anderson, 'The Elusive Definition of Peace', *International Journal on World Peace* 2, no. 3 (1985): 101–104; Paul Smoker, 'Small Peace', *Journal of Peace Research* 18, no. 2 (1981): 149–157; Royce Anderson, 'A Definition of Peace', *Peace and Conflict* 10, no. 2 (2004): 101–116.

[23] See, for example, I. William Zartman and J. Lewis Rasmussen, eds., *Peacemaking in International Conflict: Methods and Techniques* (Washington, DC: United States Institute of Peace Press, 1997); Stephen J. Stedman, Donald Rothchild, and Elizabeth M. Cousens, eds., *Ending Civil Wars: The Implementation of Peace Agreements* (Boulder, CO: Lynne Rienner, 2002); Chester H. Crocker, Fen Osler Hampson, and Pamela Aall, eds., *Herding Cats: Multiparty Mediation in a Complex World* (Washington, DC: United States Institute of Peace Press, 1999); and John Darby and Roger Mac Ginty, eds., *The Management of Peace Processes* (Basingstoke, UK: Macmillan, 2000).

[24] See, for example, Maria O'Reilly, *Gendered Agency in War and Peace: Gender Justice and Women's Activism in Post-Conflict Bosnia-Herzegovina* (Basingstoke, UK: Palgrave Macmillan, 2018); Roberto

book is interested in the layers beneath formal peacebuilding. It is interested in the informal and the everyday, in civil society rather than civil society organisations. Civil society and civil society organisations may overlap considerably, but the former tends to be organic and unencumbered by logframes, annual reports, and the necessity to please donors. It operates through family and friendship networks and informal cultural and social gatherings. By focusing on everyday peace, the intention is to explore how peace, or situations approximating peace, are lived, enacted, embodied, and experienced in everyday life.

This section will restrict itself to six reasons everyday peace is important, although the list could be more extensive. The first reason, previously alluded to, is that everyday peace can be regarded as the first and last peace. It may be the first peace to follow a conflict or upsurge in violence. Local-level intergroup interaction may take the form of the resumption of trading or social relations between villagers in Rakhine State in Myanmar. Such relations may be tentative and possibly occur under the radar lest they are observed by the authorities or more militant members of the in-group. But such forms of everyday peace might be the beginning of wider intergroup relations that may pave the way for a normalisation of intergroup relations, and thus disrupt the conflict. They may be experimental confidence-building measures that give confidence to other individuals and groups. In other words, they might scale out. In time, intergroup relations may stabilise and normalise. Everyday peace may also be the last form of peace, in that some social, economic, and cultural relations between friends, business associates, and colleagues from differing identity groups may survive a worsening of tensions. The actions and voices of political and militant leaders, ethnic agitators, and mobs may work to increase violence and tension. Established cross-community patterns of social and economic relations may become unsafe or unwise as individuals retreat back into their own single-group contexts. Yet, depending on circumstances, some individuals and groups may be able to persist in having intergroup contact. This contact will most likely be fragile and contingent, but it may be the social glue required to prevent the total collapse of intergroup relations.[25] It also helps puncture the notion, often favoured by political and military elites, that conflict is totalising and all-consuming and that there can be no dissent. As this book will reveal, charismatic community leaders are often able to dissuade 'hotheads' from inflammatory acts and disrupt

---

Belloni, 'Shades of Orange and Green: Civil Society and the Peace Process in Northern Ireland', in *Social Capital and Peace-Building: Creating and Resolving Conflict with Trust and Social Networks*, ed. Michaelene Cox (London: Routledge, 2009), 5–21.

[25] Indeed, the positive impact of surviving intergroup social capital is a major finding of Adam Moore, *Peacebuilding in Practice: Local Experience in Two Bosnian Towns* (Ithaca, NY: Cornell University Press, 2013).

the narratives of political leaders who might seek to paint the out-group as irredeemable.

A second reason everyday peace is an important concept and practice is that it encourages us to look beyond formal, institutional, elitist, and male forms of peace. Given its very nature, everyday peace involves individuals and groups of individuals in all contexts and all stations of life. Formal and institutional approaches to peacemaking are usually dependent on male-dominated political and military elites. These are often exclusive forms of peacemaking that involve relatively small numbers of people—often based in the capital city or urban centres. Formal peace processes and peace accords are often based on the hope that the peace process will create a context that will allow individuals and groups to get on with life. In a sense, it is 'trickle-down peace'. There is a hope that peace forged at the elite level will trickle down to the levels of society below and provide security and economic opportunities. Just like trickle-down economics,[26] trickle-down peace is based on the hope that macro-level activities (such as reaching a peace accord) will stimulate and enable micro-level peace. In many cases, everyday peace will be dependent on top-down elite-level peace. But in many other cases, it is independent, or relatively independent, from the elite-level peace. As Daniel Philpott observed in relation to justice processes after violent conflicts, we should be wary of any axiomatic link between elite-level peacemaking and results at other levels: 'It is far from inevitable that the judicial punishment of war criminals will build stability, and peace, and give popular legitimacy to the rule of law, as the rehabilitation rationale claims it will'.[27] Indeed, everyday peace may occur despite elite-level activities designed to encourage division. Everyday peace encourages us to look beyond elites, whether in-country political and militant elites or the peace professionals who work for international organisations and international non-governmental organisations (INGOs).[28] It also encourages us to look beyond peace events, such as peace accord signing ceremonies or symbolic acts by political leaders, and instead focus on the multiple small acts of tolerance, coexistence, and even reconciliation that constitute social processes.[29] As such, to focus on everyday peace can be regarded as part

---

[26] It is worth noting that trickle-down economics has been subject to considerable critique. See, for example, Dierk Herzer and Sebastian Vollmer, 'Rising Top Incomes Do Not Raise the Tide', *Journal of Policy Modelling* 35, no. 4 (2013): 504–519.

[27] Daniel Philpott, 'Peace after Genocide', *First Things* (2012): 41.

[28] Vivienne Jabri refers to this as an 'international civil service' in *The Post-Colonial Subject: Claiming Politics/Governing Other in Late Modernity* (London: Routledge, 2003), 121.

[29] On the difference between events and processes, see Róisín Read and Roger Mac Ginty, 'The Temporal Dimension in Accounts of Violent Conflict: A Case Study from Darfur', *Journal of Intervention and Statebuilding* 11, no. 2 (2017): 147–165, esp. 152–156; and Roger Mac Ginty, 'Political versus Sociological Time: The Fraught World of Timelines and Deadlines', in *Building Sustainable Peace: Timing and Sequencing of Post-Conflict Reconstruction and Peacebuilding*, ed. Arnim Langer and Graham K. Brown (Oxford: Oxford University Press, 2016), 15–31.

of the critique of orthodox approaches to peace.[30] It can be seen as part of the 'local turn' in the study of peace and part of a move to put people at the centre of approaches to peace.[31] It moves us beyond Newtonian logics of a peace deal automatically ushering in peace and instead encourages us to think of the agency of individuals and communities.

A third reason for the focus on everyday peace is that it encourages us to think about our levels of analysis. Everyday peace is enacted at the local or very local levels of the commute to work, the school playground, the cafe, or the beauty parlour. It encourages us to examine individuals, small groups, families, and communities. But clearly, these micro-levels of analysis are only one part of the equation. Everyday peace occurs within, and co-constitutes, wider contexts and spaces. Thus, our focus on the everyday recommends that we develop an awareness of how the everyday might be connected with the substate, national, international, and transnational levels and all levels in between. Work on multiscalar politics is well advanced in the field of political geography but less so in international relations and political science.[32] This book argues that insights from biological and engineered circuitry offer a useful analytical tool with which to visualise and understand the connections between the hyperlocal and the everyday on the one hand and the national, international, transnational, and all levels in between on the other. Particularly helpful is the notion of circuits within circuits, and different orders of circuits, something that allows us to envisage how the hyperlocal might be located in wider systems. The notion of circuits allows us to think that everyday peace might be scaled up or out. Grassroots peace is significant in its own right, but what if it is restricted to the very local level? An argument in this book is that everyday peace matters, especially in terms of the quality of peace that develops; it can scale up and out and shape the character of the wider peacemaking context. While much of our focus is on the level below civil society, this should not be interpreted as a lack of concern with structures, institutions, and actors, such as states and international organisations, that might wield considerable power. The concept of circuitry allows us to see the

---

[30] The critique of the liberal peace has spawned a substantial literature. Examples include David Roberts, *Liberal Peacebuilding and Global Governance: Beyond the Metropolis* (London: Routledge, 2011); Gerald Knaus and Felix Martin, 'Lessons from Bosnia and Herzegovina: Travails of the European Raj', *Journal of Democracy* 14, no. 3 (2003): 60–74; Oliver P. Richmond, *The Transformation of Peace* (Basingstoke, UK: Palgrave Macmillan, 2005).

[31] Hanna Leonardsson and Gustav Rudd, 'The "Local Turn" in Peacebuilding: A Literature Review of Effective and Emancipatory Local Peacebuilding', *Third World Quarterly* 36, no. 5 (2015): 825–839; Roger Mac Ginty and Oliver P. Richmond, 'The Local Turn in Peace Building: A Critical Agenda for Peace', *Third World Quarterly* 34, no. 5 (2013): 763–783; Roger Mac Ginty, 'Where Is the Local? Critical Localism and Peacebuilding', *Third World Quarterly* 36, no. 5 (2015): 840–856.

[32] Rachel Pain, 'Everyday Terrorism: Connecting Domestic Violence to Global Terrorism', *Progress in Human Geography* 38, no. 4 (2014): 531–550; and Jussi P. Laine, 'The Multiscalar Production of Borders', *Geopolitics* 21, no. 3 (2016): 465–482.

connections between levels and thus pursue avenues of critique beyond the local or the immediate subject of our gaze.

A fourth reason the study of everyday peace is important is that it suggests that we should take seriously highly localised and vernacular understandings of peace (and conflict).[33] Experiences of peace and conflict are contextualised and personalised. As the research underpinning this book shows, these experiences often relate to the family and the home or the immediate vicinity of the home (see chapter 6). The social sciences and much policy work seek to understand social phenomena through abstraction and generalisation. While this has many sense-making advantages, it does iron out local variance, colour and granularity. A country or region deemed to be 'at war' may contain areas characterised by explicit violent conflict. It might also contain areas that are relatively peaceful and apparently removed from the conflict. There is a danger that the 'at war' narrative becomes hegemonic and masks a heterogeneity of experience. A focus on the everyday reminds us of the need to concentrate on aspects of life that might be mundane, hidden, and hard to access. Some aspects might be pacific or be uninvolved/uninterested in the conflict and the dominant narratives that reinforce it.[34] It is worth remembering that many of those affected by violent conflicts are based in the global south, and so the local is likely to be subaltern and very probably equipped with minimal material resources.

A fifth reason to champion the study of everyday peace is that it encourages us to think about the methodologies we use, and the data sources we draw on, in order to understand how peace is actually enacted and embodied in the mundane interactions and thoughts that make up life. Peace and conflict studies is a well-tilled field, and the range of data and resources available has been growing. Yet accessing the everyday and hyperlocal can be difficult. Many dimensions of everyday peace operate behind closed doors, and in what might be thought of as the 'private sphere'. It can take the form of a hidden transcript[35] within the family or a small group of friends or of a one-off compassionate act in the midst of violent conflict. Finding the methodological tools to access such types of peace is difficult,[36] and while attempts to decolonise our research are under way, they face immense structural barriers.[37] Moreover, when everyday peace is conceptualised as a mode of reasoning—a stance or a position that might translate into

---

[33] Roger Mac Ginty and Pamina Firchow, 'Top-Down and Bottom-Up Narratives of Conflict', *Politics* 36, no. 3 (2016): 308–323.

[34] Roger Mac Ginty, 'Between Resistance and Compliance: Non-participation and the Liberal Peace', *Journal of Intervention and Statebuilding* 6, no. 2 (2012): 167–187.

[35] Scott, *Domination*.

[36] Pamina Firchow and Roger Mac Ginty, 'Including Hard-to-Access Populations Using Mobile Phone Surveys and Participatory Indicators', *Sociological Methods and Review* 49, no. 1 (2020): 133–160.

[37] Linda Tuhiwai Smith, *Decolonising Methodologies: Research and Indigenous Peoples* (London: Zed, 2012).

action only if circumstances allow—then it becomes difficult to access. This book is able to draw on data from the EPI project and a number of other projects (explained below) in an attempt to access the less obvious manifestations and narrations of everyday peace. While the everyday is everywhere, it is not always easy to access. The book also draws on war memoirs and personal diaries—a resource used with surprising rarity in peace and conflict studies—to access how people think through and rationalise everyday peace.

A final reason to take seriously the notion of everyday peace is that it entreats us to examine the concept of power and how it is operationalised in terms of how peace is enacted, embodied, and experienced. Peace, like other social phenomena, needs to be subject to a power analysis to ascertain who holds power, how it operates, and whether it can be transferred or shared. A power analysis allows us to understand the extent to which power operates in different ways and is gendered. Orthodox approaches to peace, perhaps through a peace process that results in a peace accord, might depend on quite traditional forms of power such as electoral power and the ability of the state or other actors to impose their will or order via a mix of coercion and incentives. Everyday peace, on the other hand, might rely on alternative sources of power that are embedded within society. Thus, for example, the power of family, elders, or charismatic individuals may come into play. This power might operate through the networks and social infrastructure that constitute everyday life in the cultural, economic, social, and familial domains. Such sources and types of power may not always be visible to outsiders, and innovative research methodologies may be required to access them. The key point is that our analyses of everyday peace are very much about power. As such, this is a potentially subversive research agenda that looks beyond traditional (overwhelmingly male and statist) forms of power to examine hidden and less obvious forms of power.

Origins, Sources, and Methodologies

With the benefit of hindsight, this book is the third in a trilogy I've written. The first book, *No War, No Peace: The Rejuvenation of Stalled Peace Processes*, examined top-down peace processes whereby conflicting parties, and interested international actors, collaborate to reach a peace accord and manage the conflict.[38] The second book, *International Peacebuilding and Local Resistance: Hybrid Forms of Peace*, looked at the interface between top-down and bottom-up forms of

---

[38] Roger Mac Ginty, *No War, No Peace: The Rejuvenation of Stalled Peace Processes and Peace Accords* (Basingstoke, UK: Palgrave, 2006).

peace.[39] It was concerned with how no actor—local, national, or international—could act unilaterally to forge peace. Instead, actors constructed hybrid political orders that sometimes approximated peace. This book, the third in the retrospectively identified trilogy, is focused on bottom-up forms of peace and conflict disruption. It seeks to identify and conceptualise forms of everyday peace and consider the extent to which they are scalable and can be placed in a wider context.

The book draws on a number of research projects I have been working on over a number of years. Crucially, these projects, and particularly the EPI project, allow us to *demonstrate* everyday peace in action. They help lift everyday peace out of conceptualisation and show how it is embodied and enacted and how it can—in certain circumstances—make a difference. Taken together, these projects have sought to understand the meanings and forms of peace. They have benefited from a broadening disciplinary perspective that draws not only on international relations and political science but also on sociology, history, anthropology, and gender studies. Certainly, no single discipline is able to account for the complexities of peace and conflict. I am convinced that more people-focused perspectives—particularly evidenced in sociology and gender studies—are the best route through which to access everyday peace.

The main project that has informed this work has been the EPI project directed by myself and Pamina Firchow at Brandeis University.[40] Initially funded by the Carnegie Corporation of New York, the project began by piloting the crowdsourcing of meanings of peace, security, and change in local communities in Colombia, South Africa, South Sudan, Uganda, and Zimbabwe. The project allowed the collection of significant amounts of data and analysis of how communities see peace and conflict in their own lives. One major finding from the project was that many people interpret peace and conflict through extremely local lenses. For many, the local level does not constitute the municipality or the subregion. Instead, it is the home and the immediate vicinity of the home. This level of localism, perhaps hyperlocalism, requires us deploy research tools that can grapple with detail that is personalised and granular. Thus, we need to move beyond simplistic three-layer models of the local, the national, and the international and embrace more complex models that acknowledge the varieties of the different levels and the complexity of interactions between them.

The book also draws on a major Economic and Social Research Council project, which I led. The 'Making Peacekeeping Data Work for the International

---

[39] Roger Mac Ginty, *International Peacebuilding and Local Resistance: Hybrid Forms of Peace* (Basingstoke, UK: Palgrave, 2011).
[40] Everyday Peace Indicators, 'About', https://everydaypeaceindicators.org/about/.

Community' project examined how UN peacekeepers collect and utilise data.[41] In particular, it was interested in how they used data to 'see' and respond to the conflict environment in which they were operating. At the heart of the project was the question: Do peacekeepers see the same conflict that people on the ground live through? The question is an important one. If peacekeeping operations do not respond to the concerns and threats experienced by populations in areas hosting peacekeepers, then there is a danger that the protection mandate will not be fulfilled and local needs will not be addressed. The project was useful for this book project in that it 'lifted up the hood' on how a major international organisation (in this case the United Nations) understands and narrates the environment in which it operates. The project was also able to conduct multiple interviews with those who experienced a UN peacekeeping mission and so sought to understand how peace or protection was 'received'.

Another major source for this book was the personal diaries and memoirs of participants in, and witnesses of, violent conflict. These sources are largely overlooked in peace and conflict studies. Part of the reason is that contemporary peace and conflict studies concentrates on contemporary conflicts and international interventions and so has limited interest in historical cases. I would argue that this constitutes a major blind spot in the study of peace and conflict. There is a tendency in much analysis of contemporary peace and conflict to concentrate on the post-Cold War period. Yet human history is rich with examples of conflict and peacemaking. As a result, this book draws on sources well before the end of the Cold War. While personal diaries and memoirs have a number of methodological shortcomings (further explained in chapter 4), they are a wonderful firsthand resource and open up a window on the personalised everyday nature of violent conflict. Much of this book concentrates on the 'hard cases' or instances in which everyday peace (and any form of peace) is difficult to conceive. Thus, chapter 5 in particular looks at everyday peace (or cases of empathy and compassion) on the battlefield. In order to capture these, war memoirs and personal diaries proved to be the best sources.

Structure of the Book

This introduction is followed by three conceptual chapters that seek to help unpack the notion, operation, and context of everyday peace. Chapter 1 explores two concepts that are central to the book: the everyday and circuitry. The notion of the everyday is highly political and is the antithesis of approaches that

---

[41] UK Research and Innovation, 'Making Peacekeeping Data Work for the International Community', Project ES/L007479/1, https://gtr.ukri.org/project/494E4AD1-F7A2-4AD3-B474-FEAC43CA18B8.

privilege elites and the notion that peace and conflict are the concern of political and military leaders. It encourages us to think about issues of scale (top-down or bottom-up) and the connections (or lack of them) between all the different levels interested in peace. The everyday also forces us to think about how peace is embodied and enacted in the mundane tasks that constitute life. This book advocates circuitry as a way of understanding the links between the hyperlocal and the national, international, and transnational and all levels in between, and so chapter 1 unpacks the concept. This book is convinced of the multi-scalar nature of peace and conflict and how what might appear as somehow isolated behavior (such as everyday peace) is, in fact, part of much larger assemblages and political economies. The chapter illustrates how the concept of circuitry— both biological and engineered—can be used as an analytical tool to understand the connections between the apparently hyperlocal and other levels. While circuitry is concerned with the connectedness of the everyday to other levels, scalability is concerned with the possibility of everyday or grassroots peace scaling up and having greater significance than the initial act or stance. Thus, the chapter unpacks the concepts of scaling up and scaling out, or vertical and horizontal scaling. Subsequent chapters then utilise the concepts of circuitry and scalability in an attempt to understand the chains of connection and implication that tie together small acts of compassion and toleration with wider, systemic-level, political economies.

Chapter 2 further unpacks the notion of everyday peace and seeks to understand the rationality behind it by exploring the concepts of sociality, reciprocity, and solidarity. The concepts help illustrate how everyday peace is contingent on circumstances and how it depends on emotional intelligence and the ability of individuals and groups to read social situations and make decisions. It inhabits structuration or the melding of structure and agency.[42] Also apparent from an interrogation of these concepts is the inconsistent nature of everyday peace and those who engage in it. It is often fragmentary and episodic, on display at particular moments but not necessarily a permanent fixture in life.

Chapter 3 examines a central factor in this book: power. On the one hand, everyday peace is a form of power—one with the capacity to interrupt and contradict orthodox narratives that might emphasise division and the incompatibility between groups. On the other hand, everyday peace, like other forms of peace, is subject to power. It operates in permissive environments and so is often dependent on actors with power to allow it to act. The chapter distinguishes between 'power over' and 'power to' and finds that everyday peace is subject to the former but belongs to the latter. Crucially, everyday peace constitutes a form

---

[42] Anthony Giddens, *The Constitution of Society: Outline of the Theory of Structuration* (Cambridge: Polity, 1986).

of power: Everyday Peace Power (EPP). This requires us to think about power in alternative ways. So rather than seeing only the material and political power that we associate with states and military organisations, it is prudent to also see the power of emotional intelligence, remarkable intergroup friendships, the ability to seize opportunities, and local-level legitimacy systems.

Having explored the key concepts that lie behind everyday peace, the next four chapters illustrate everyday peace and conflict disruption in action. In particular, they are alert to the criticism that everyday peace might be seen as somehow 'marginal' and only occurring under the most optimal circumstances. A contention of this book is that everyday peace is possible even in the 'hard cases' of ongoing violent conflict. As a result, chapters 4 and 5 deliberately concentrate on the hard cases of war and largely focus on the world wars. The chapters can be read side by side and offer a perspective on how everyday peace can operate in the midst of war. Chapter 4 sets the scene by illustrating the unpropitious nature of war for everyday peace and outlining how traditional and top-down approaches to peace are often uninterested in the everyday, 'organic', and spontaneous approaches to peacemaking. Based on evidence from war memoirs and personal diaries, chapter 5 shows that everyday peace and conflict disruption can take place even in the most unlikely of circumstances. The hard cases of warfare show that everyday peace was often opportunistic and momentary, but it also shows that narratives of total war and the irredeemable nature of 'the other' require re-evaluation.

Chapter 6 examines the gendered nature of everyday peace. All forms of peace are gendered. As everyday peace often occurs at the quotidian level, it seems appropriate that we examine it in relation to the family—a highly gendered site. The family is often overlooked in institutionalist approaches to peace and conflict. Yet the family is, arguably, the most significant institution that many of us will have contact with during our lives. Familial dynamics and relationships are crucial in relation to everyday peace. The family can be a site of radicalisation, but it can also be a site of restraint, the encouragement of toleration, and a safe space away from incitement. The chapter is careful not to essentialise the role of women or to axiomatically equate females with the family, but it finds the family a useful space in which to investigate how everyday peace is subject to gender calculations and practices. Women are often the driving force behind familial activities and rituals of care, eating, visiting, worship, and leisure. These spaces allow for moderation, supervision, and guidance—all of which might promote everyday peace.

The final substantive chapter explores the concept of conflict disruption. Everyday peace can be regarded as a way of contradicting the dominant narrative and modes of thinking and acting in deeply divided and conflict-affected societies. The chapter begins by detailing three remarkable intergroup friendships that went against the grain. These friendships, or 'unusual pairs', to use Marc Gopin's phrase, were problematic at the in-group level and extraordinary at the intergroup level.[43] They show, however, the ability of everyday peace and the small actions it involves to disrupt the 'conflict norm'. Drawing on literature from business and management, the chapter unpacks the notion of bottom-up conflict disruption and its potential to leverage everyday peace for wider change. This is in keeping with the notion of multi-scalar peace in which actions and thinking at the hyperlocal level can have consequences at other levels of society. The chapter then goes on to examine the potential of charismatic individuals in breaking the conflict cycle. While formal community violence-reduction schemes do operate, the main focus here is on informal actions by self-starting individuals. They tend not to be part of programmes, projects, or funded attempts to make peace or manage tension. All of this connects with the sustainability agenda and the need for all levels of society to be engaged in, and to benefit from, peace. The notion of sustainable peace has become a major policy concern in recent years, and this book seeks to speak to that agenda.[44]

A Note on Language, Terminology, and Context

This book depends on terms such as *bottom-up* and *local* that are much more complex than they might originally seem. The terms mask enormous variance, and they might also bring with them assumptions about our starting point. For example, by using the term *local*, are we making assumptions about the place of the local in relation to other spheres, such as the national or the global? Are we assuming that the local might be somehow peripheral or secondary? Might some of our assumptions betray ethnocentrism and other indicators of our positionality?[45] Moreover, many of the terms used in the book might be seen as part of binaries: *top-down/bottom-up, global/local, everyday/extraordinary,*

---

[43] Marc Gopin, *Bridges across an Impossible Divide: The Inner Lives of Arab and Jewish Peacemakers* (Oxford: Oxford University Press, 2012), 4.

[44] Sustaining and sustainable peace has been adopted as a major policy goal by the United Nations: United Nations, Report of the Secretary-General: Peacebuilding and Sustaining Peace, New York18 January 2018, https://www.un.org/peacebuilding/content/report-secretary-general-peacebuilding-and-sustaining-peace. As a consequence of the UN adoption, the concept has been embraced as a research and policy theme by a number of practitioner, policy, and academic organizations. See, for example, Stockholm International Peace Research Institute, Sustainable Peace, 2019, https://www.sipri.org/research/peace-and-development/sustainable-peace; or a major peacebuilding conference hosted by the Kroc Institute for International Peace Studies at the University of Notre Dame in November 2019, 'Building Sustainable Peace: Ideas, Evidence, and Strategies', https://kroc.nd.edu/news-events/events/building-sustainable-peace-ideas-evidence-and-strategies/.

[45] Meera Sabaratnam, 'Avatars of Eurocentrism in the Critique of the Liberal Peace', *Security Dialogue* 44, no. 3 (2013): 259–278.

peace/war, orthodox/unorthodox, global north/global south, and so on. A major aim of this book is to emphasise the intersectionality of life or the connectedness of social phenomena (as illustrated through circuits). In other words, this book rejects binaries as overly simplistic and as contradicting the strong evidence of relationality between actors in peace and conflict situations. The terms *bottom-up* and *top-down* state with great certainty a direction of travel. Yet the real world is not made up of the straight lines that these terms suggest. The social world is, of course, made up of norms, but there are also exceptions, outliers, and complexity. In keeping with this complexity, everyday peace and conflict disruption are regarded as part of wider assemblages or complex adaptive systems[46] in which peace is hybrid, messy, and incomplete.

Standing against these deficiencies with the language employed in this book (and indeed the entire field of peace and conflict studies), there is also the need to be understood. Terms such as *local* and *bottom-up* are readily understandable and serve as a useful shorthand for much more complex concepts. In order to be understood, this work will persevere with such terms in the knowledge that they are not perfect but they have a utilitarian functionality. As far as possible, terms will be discussed and caveats will be applied, and there will be an attempt to reach a balance between conveying the complexity of social phenomena and the need for accessibility. The scholarly and practice worlds do not always aid comprehensibility. Scholars manufacture and use terminology that is useful for scholarly debate but can be exclusionary to non-academics. For example, there has been wonderful scholarship around the term *ontological security*,[47] but the term is not immediately understandable. At a basic level, the term simply means 'comfort' or a feeling of security. It is probably no exaggeration to say that the term *ontological security* has never been uttered in any focus group or interview involving a non-academic, yet it appears in hundreds of academic articles (some produced by myself) based on fieldwork. The key point is that scholars should be aware of the language they use and the danger that they engage in an exercise of conceit.[48] They may be writing about everyday phenomena but feel the need to scaffold their writing with bewildering terminology.

A final point concerns the need to reflect on the positionality of the field of peace and conflict studies and those who constitute it. The academic study of

---

[46] Cedric de Coning, 'Complexity Thinking and Adaptive Peacebuilding', *Accord*, no. 28 (2019), https://www.c-r.org/accord/inclusion-peace-processes/complexity-thinking-and-adaptive-peacebuilding.

[47] See, for example, Catarina Kinnvall, 'Feeling Ontologically (In)secure: States, Traumas and the Governing of Gendered Space', *Cooperation and Conflict* 52, no. 1 (2017): 90–108; Brent J. Steele, 'Organisational Processes and Ontological Security: Torture, the CIA and the United States', *Cooperation and Conflict* 52, no. 1 (2017): 69–89.

[48] Patrick Chabal, *The End of Conceit: Western Rationality after Postcolonialism* (London: Zed, 2012).

peace and conflict is dominated by scholars and institutions located in the global north. This is despite the fact that the majority of the violent conflicts studied are in the global south. The dominance of global north scholarship means that a series of biases and assumptions attend peace and conflict studies. The author of this book and, therefore, this book are not immune from these biases. The reader is encouraged to think of issues of power, positionality, race, gender, and positionality when reading the work. It is also worth thinking about the balance between the emic (insider) and etic (outsider). Can a white, Irish, middle-aged man based in the global north really understand the experiences and perspectives of those living in different polities, economies, timescapes, and conflict contexts? As Swati Parashar notes, 'it is important to pay attention to language. Eurocentrism . . . means that International Relations has not actively pursued an interest in resources beyond English texts in original or translations'.[49] As a result, peacemakers such as Abul Kalam Azad, Abdul Ghaffar Khan, the Dalai Lama, Desmond Tutu, and many other non-white scholars and activists deserve to be in our conceptualisations of peace.[50]

Conclusion

This book's focus on everyday and bottom-up peace should not be read as a statement that top-down or formal and institutional approaches to peace are unimportant. Nor should it be read as in some way absolving international actors of their responsibilities in terms of peace and conflict. Instead, it can be read as a corrective to shallow treatments of the local level and the possibilities of everyday peace. I believe that there is much to recommend in relation to everyday peace but that everyday peace is only one part of the equation; everyday peace must be contextualised within wider systems that shape peace and conflict. The book's emphasis on circuitry is an attempt to do that.

While I regard everyday peace as an important type of peace, and one worthy of serious analysis, I am careful not to romanticise this approach to peace. As should be clear in the coming chapters, everyday peace is not always peace in the sense of an emancipatory and expansive peace. We should not regard the everyday and the local as somehow naturally pacific spaces that are polluted only by top-down militant and political actors. The everyday and the local can be spaces of exclusion, patriarchy, extremism, and danger. While violent conflict

---

[49] Swati Parashar, 'Interview—Swati Parashar', *E-International Relations*, 8 March 2020, https://www.e-ir.info/2020/03/08/interview-swati-parashar/.

[50] See, for example, Ramin Jahanbegloo, *The Gandhian Moment* (Cambridge, MA: Harvard University Press, 2013); A. B. Rajput, *Maulana Abul Kazam Azad* (Lahore: Lion, 1957); Abdul Ghaffar Khan, *My Life and Struggle: Autobiography of Badshah Khan* (New Delhi: Hind Pocket, 1969).

must be seen in the context of its wider political economies, it will also have local-level dynamics, agitators, and protagonists.

Yet, in the spirit of appreciative theory,[51] it is worth stressing the potential of everyday peace stances, acts, and thinking to disrupt violent conflict. It requires bravery, emotional intelligence, good judgement, and—very probably—a good deal of luck and circumstance. So-called ordinary people can display a resilience, persistence, entrepreneurialism, and sheer humanity and goodwill that can change conflict outcomes. This can be seen as a form of power that can disrupt dominant narratives and modes of thinking that normalise the sense of superiority one group might have over another and that can be factored up and out.

---

[51] Hugo Slim, 'Wonderful Work: Globalizing the Ethics of Humanitarian Action', in *The Routledge Companion to Humanitarian Action*, ed. Roger Mac Ginty and Jenny H Peterson (London: Routledge, 2015), 14.

1
The Everyday, Circuitry, and Scalability

Introduction

This chapter unpacks two concepts that lie at the heart of this book: the everyday and circuitry. The everyday, or the daily acts and thinking that constitute our existence, needs to be placed in context. It is not an end in itself. Instead, it is part of, and helps constitute, much broader systems that might seem very far removed from routine and quotidian activities and ways of thinking. The notion of circuitry allows us to make these connections and to think about the scalability of local level and grassroots actions. Daily regimes and activities that occur at the individual, family, or local levels may not seem to be immediately or obviously connected to other types and scales of activity—such as elite political dealmaking. It is the contestation of this book that the concepts of the everyday and circuitry are crucial to our understanding of many forms of contemporary peace. They encourage us to look beyond the 'big peace' of peace accords and the activities of political and military leaders who operate on national and international stages. By focusing on everyday peace, we explore an important, but often overlooked, aspect of peace. We are able to expand the notion of peace to encompass how peace is embodied and enacted in daily life and how it might disrupt conflict and possibly lead to something more than highly localised toleration.

While the chapter is mainly conceptual, it does not lose sight of the fact that peace and conflict (and all stages in between) happen to, and are constructed by, real people. Indeed, the focus on the everyday is a useful way of grounding peace and conflict studies and retaining an emphasis on the prosaic and often highly localised ways in which spaces for peace, toleration, and conciliation are carved out. These spaces and activities happen alongside, and within, other daily activities that may seem dull or mundane: commuting, grocery shopping, caring for children and elders, and sourcing firewood, water, or Wi-Fi. Importantly, these activities—however routine and matter-of-fact—need to be seen as part of wider systems. They reside in, and help co-constitute, wider contexts. The notion of circuitry allows us to see these connections and realise the extent to which seemingly isolated, personal, and sometimes dull tasks are part of larger political economies and worldviews. The concept of circuitry can be read as an extension of literature on networks and complexity and extends to evolved (biological) and constructed (electronic and technological) circuitry.[1] These literatures are rarely consulted in peace and conflict studies, but they help us think through the possibilities of using circuits as an analytical device to better understand the connectivities between the everyday and dynamics that are seen as exceptional or elite.

Crucially, the concept of circuitry allows us to think about the possibility of scaling up and scaling out everyday peace to other levels. It allows us to consider the extent to which highly localised and interpersonal pro-peace and pro-social acts and stances might influence the wider polity and society. This involves a process of 'societalization' whereby 'civic sensibility' might spread horizontally through society or sections of it.[2] It has echoes of John Paul Lederach's notion of 'middle out' whereby middle-range actors and leaders are able to have an amplified influence on peace.[3] In the case of everyday peace, though, we are interested in the level below mid-range leaders; our focus is on the informal and hyperlocal. Again, literature from outside of peace and conflict studies is useful here in pointing us towards the notion of scaling out as well as scaling up. Small pacific acts can, under certain circumstances, have significant ramifications. As we will see in later chapters, localised charismatic actors, and isolated pro-peace actions and stances can influence wider spheres. This particularly works in terms of scaling out, or horizontal influence, imitation, or inspiration. These actors, actions, and stances can affect the wider environment, and seemingly isolated or singular events can coalesce to produce something more significant.

Circuitry allows us to see the connections between the mud-stained Rohingya refugee sheltering in Bangladesh and the suave diplomat in Paris. More than this, it allows us to see where we—the student, the practitioner, the professor who might be reading this—fit into the equation. What emerges from the use of circuitry as an analytical device is a better view of the webs of implication and imbrication that link apparently unconnected actors. This helps us transcend the tendency to exoticise violent conflict and humanitarian situations as phenomena that happen 'over there' and apparently have little to do with us.[4] Circuitry shows the complex networks and connectivities around political economies, capital, ideas, and aspirations that are shared by those involved in violent conflict and those who might be many thousands of miles away and consider themselves uninvolved in the conflict.

---

[1] Roger Mac Ginty, 'Circuits, the Everyday and International Relations: Connecting the Home to the International and Transnational', *Cooperation and Conflict* 54, no. 2 (2019): 234–253.

[2] Enrique Peruzzotti, 'The Societalization of Horizontal Accountability', in *Human Rights, State Compliance and Social Changes: Assessing National Human Rights Institutions*, ed. Ryan Goodman (Cambridge: Cambridge University Press, 2011), 244.

[3] Lederach, *Building Peace*, 39.

[4] Amy S. Rushton, 'A History of Darkness: Exoticising Strategies and the Nigerian Civil War in *Half of a Yellow Sun* by Chimamanda Ngozi Adiche', in *Exoticising the Past in Contemporary Historical Fiction*, ed. E. Rousslet (London: Palgrave Macmillan, 2014), 178–195.

The Everyday

In recent years, there has extensive academic discussion of the concept of 'the everyday'.[5] Much of this discussion is sophisticated and largely conceptual. With that in mind, it is worth beginning this consideration of the everyday with a reminder that, beneath the multitude of academic writings, the everyday is quite a basic concept. It is simply the tasks and thought processes that one undertakes on a daily basis to navigate through life. Yet such a basic concept requires one to step back—especially if one comes from a political science or international relations background. While disciplines such as sociology and anthropology are long used to analysing the everyday and of seeing the individual, the family, or other social groups as a primary unit of analysis, most mainstream political science and international relations is not. For those coming from the latter disciplines, some painful disciplinary unlearning may be required to see beyond a world in which states and formal political institutions dominate the conceptual horizon. Manuela Picq points to how the discipline of international relations 'perpetuate[s] the imaginary of the state system as modern and global'.[6]

This is not to say that state- and institution-centric lenses have little to offer our analyses. Nor is it to say that states and formal institutions (such as military organisations) do not wield considerable power in the real world. It is to say, however, that there are benefits from complementing traditional views of politics and international relations with views that are able to recognise the importance of human agency, highly localised processes, and the spaces that individuals and groups carve out for themselves in terms of subversion, resistance, and alternatives.[7] As the discussion on circuitry and scalability later in this chapter, and indeed throughout this book, will show, we need to explain the extensive relations between top-down and bottom-up dynamics. Moreover, in unpacking this multi-scalar world, we need to move beyond the notion that there are binaries (such as indicated by shorthand phrases such as *top-down* and *bottom-up*) and become cognisant of a complex, dynamic, and messy assemblage of politics, economics, and society. The vertical axis of top-down and bottom-up needs to be seen alongside horizontal and other dynamics that confound neat conceptualisations.

---

[5] Alasdair Jones, 'Everyday without Exception? Making Space for the Exceptional in Contemporary Sociological Studies of Street Life', *Sociological Review* 66, no. 5 (2018): 1000. See also Annika Björkdahl, Martin Hall, and Ted Svensson, 'Everyday International Relations: Editors' Introduction', *Cooperation and Conflict* 54, no. 2 (2019): 123–130.

[6] Manuela Lavinas Picq, 'Critics at the Edge? Decolonizing Methodologies in International Relations', *International Political Science Review* 34, no. 4 (2013): 452.

[7] John Harald Sandie Lie, 'Challenging Anthropology: Anthropological Reflections on the Ethnographic Turn in International Relations', *Millennium* 41, no. 2 (2012): 201–220.

A further introductory point to make about the everyday is to puncture the notion of hierarchies connected with levels of analysis. We could very easily think of the international and national levels as being more important than the everyday levels of the bottom-up, grassroots, and local. Certainly, states and international organisations can mobilise immense power and can shape the everyday experiences of billions on the planet. Often this power is material in the form of economic, military, and formal political resources. It can also be immaterial in terms of symbolism, rhetoric, and legitimacy. Yet it would be inaccurate to think of a hierarchy in which state- and international-level dynamics are somehow superior to those at the everyday. Rather than a hierarchy, it is prudent to conceive of an assemblage in which no level operates independently. Instead, the everyday helps constitute state and international level dynamics, with citizens in some contexts ceding rights and sovereignty to states or giving consent to rule from above. The connections between the different levels that constitute a social system may not always be obvious or might, at best, seem circuitous (given the focus on circuits, the pun is intended). But all elements of an assemblage will, to some extent, be engaged in co-production.

When thinking about 'hierarchies', it is important to note that for many people, the everyday is the most important level of life. The state may be remote and irrelevant. It may play little role in the provision of basic (or more sophisticated) needs. Here it is worth thinking about post-conflict contexts in which state capacity may be low. The international level may also seem irrelevant, especially in terms of how it shapes daily routines. As the discussion of circuitry later in the chapter should make clear, international and transnational dynamics usually have substantial importance, but they may not seem apparent in the midst of everyday life. The pressing exigencies of getting food on the table, getting the kids to school, and looking after relatives mean that the family and the setting of the family are often the primary focus for many people (as will be discussed in chapter 6). Certainly, the national, international, and transnational will shape much of this, but these are spheres on which individuals and groups of individuals may have little influence. This bottom-up perspective is a useful corrective to the temptation to reinforce top-down hierarchies in our analyses. By embracing everyday-ness, and the sociological and anthropological literature that lies behind it, we engage in an intellectual pivot that regards the individual as important, recognises the individual's social nature, and further recognises that the small acts that constitute everyday life are important. As well as accepting the state and other formal political institutions as a level of analysis, we must also accept the family, the friendship group, work colleagues, and classmates as other worthy levels of analysis.

A final introductory point to be made in light of the voluminous literature on the everyday is that academics, students, and political leaders have everydays as well.[8] There is a tendency in some of the peace and conflict literature to exoticise the everyday and regard it as something that only research subjects, especially those living in conflict zones, might have. We all have an everyday. This is an important point to take on board, as it enables us to think through how our everydays might be connected to the everydays of those in a conflict zone and those who we might be tempted to think are far removed from our own lived experiences.

So how do we define the everyday, especially given that the term is somewhat fuzzy and 'familiar and under-considered at once'?[9] The everyday can be regarded as the practices, logics, and spaces that constitute life. At a very basic level, we can see the everyday as the repetitive and often dull tasks that fill our lives and are often taken for granted.[10] While we should not lose sight of this entry-level definition of the everyday, it is worth noting that the concept opens up to us important ways of seeing the social world. Rather than seeing the everyday as mere background to more important or prominent activity, it is useful to see it as significant in its own right.[11] In this view, the notion of the everyday allows us to see everything and everywhere as political.[12] Thus, the everyday helps us transcend the tendency to compartmentalise the everyday as domestic, insubstantial, or secondary. This point has been reinforced by feminist scholars who have explored the home and everyday activities within the home (often seen as of second-order importance by politics and international relations scholars who foreground formal institutions) as a site of power, patriarchy, consumption, and production.[13] Many everyday activities take place in what might be considered the private realm, but again, feminist scholars have been prominent in breaking down this artificial distinction between the public and the private.[14] In this view, and one shared in this book, the private, the personal, the routine, and the

---

[8] Gëzim Visoka makes the very good point that diplomats have an everyday existence, too, in 'Metis Diplomacy: The Everyday Politics of Becoming a Sovereign State', *Cooperation and Conflict* 54, no. 2 (2019): 167–190.

[9] Andrew Smith, 'Rethinking the "Everyday" in "Ethnicity" and Everyday Life', *Ethnic and Racial Studies* 38, no. 7 (2015): 1137.

[10] Matteo Capasso, 'Sketches of the Everyday', *Middle East Critique* 27, no. 3 (2018): 221.

[11] Smith, 'Rethinking', 1138.

[12] Olga Demetriou, 'Counter-conduct and the Everyday: Anthropological Engagements with Philosophy', *Global Security* 30, no. 2 (2016): 218–237.

[13] Laura Sjoberg, 'Gender, the State and War Redux: Feminist International Relations across "Levels of analysis"', *International Relations* 25, no. 1 (2011): 108–134; Maria Mies, *Patriarchy and Accumulation on a World Scale: Women in the International Division of Labour*, 2nd ed. (London: Zed, 2014); Seema Narain, 'Gender in International Relations: Feminist Perspectives of J. Ann Tickner', *Indian Journal of Gender Studies* 21, no. 2 (2014): 179–197.

[14] Linda Åhäll, 'The Dance of Militarisation: A Feminist Security Studies Take on "the Political"', *Critical Studies on Security* 4, no. 2 (2016): 164; Johanna Kantola, 'The Gendered Reproduction of the State in International Relations', *British Journal of Politics and International Relations* 9, no. 2 (2007): 276; Jill Steans, 'Engaging from the Margins: Feminist Encounters with the "Mainstream" of International Relations', *British Journal of Politics and International Relations* 5, no. 3 (2003): 428–454.

quotidian are all political and important. The lens offered by the everyday allows us to view women and gender as central to our studies of peace and conflict and not just as 'add-ons'.[15]

Everyday activity might be difficult to see, and occur, outwith the surveillance of the state.[16] Here we can think of the everyday as occurring in the home, or in the intimate chat with a work colleague confidant, or in the discreet greeting that one gives to a member of a different group in a deeply divided society. Certainly, the everyday can be a space for resistance, subversion, experimentation, and alternatives. But we must be careful not to see the everyday in stark terms of either passivity and compliance with power on the one hand or resistance on the other.[17] Some people simply are not terribly interested in politics, and we should be careful not to shoehorn their lack of interest in politics into narratives of oppression and exclusion.[18] Alongside 'routine actions whose repetition brings stability, order and submission to institutional authorities',[19] there can be space for alternatives and resistance but also space for in-between situations and flux. As Pérez notes, there is an 'irreducibility of everyday life to the dichotomous frame of resistance and oppression'.[20] As the examples of everyday peace in this volume will show, everyday peace manifests itself in inconsistent, opportunistic, and messy ways. It is not the case that individuals and groups are stuck in path-dependencies. Instead, they react, create, ignore, forget, don't give a damn, conform, rebel, and do more—often within the space of a day or an hour.

The chief point to take from this discussion is that the notion of the everyday encourages us to think about power (the topic of chapter 3) and how individual and group acts and stances fit into broader societal and political frames. The everyday reveals how people interact with power. The notion of 'tactics', as described by de Certeau, captures how people are adaptable and use a repertoire of skills to pilot a path through everyday life.[21] Important here, too, is Bourdieu's notion of 'habitus' or the contexts that guide how people live.[22] These sites are often durable but flexible. In keeping with the notion of everyday peace, they are spaces for initiative, emotional intelligence, rule-following, and rule-breaking.

---

[15] Sarah Arnd-Linder, Ayelet Harel-Shalev, and Shir Daphna-Tekoah, 'The Political Is Personal—Everyday Lives of Women in Israel', *Women's Studies International Forum* 69 (2018): 76.
[16] Smith, 'Rethinking', 1138.
[17] Frances Thirlway, 'Everyday Tactics in Local Moral Worlds: E-Cigarette Practices in a Working Class Area of the UK', *Social Science and Medicine* 170 (2016): 107.
[18] Mac Ginty, 'Between Resistance and Compliance'.
[19] Capasso, 'Sketches', 221.
[20] Michael Vicente Pérez, 'The Everyday as Survival among Ex-Gaza Refugees in Jordan', *Middle East Critique* 27, no. 3 (2018): 277.
[21] Michael de Certeau, *The Practice of Everyday Life* (Berkeley: University of California Press, 1984).
[22] Pierre Bourdieu, *Distinction: A Social Critique of the Judgement of Taste* (London: Routledge, 1984).

These spaces are gendered, may be episodic and dynamic, and are very context-specific.

While the everyday encourages us to think about the level of analysis (the everyday at the level of the street or the diplomatic chamber), it also encourages us to think about the unit of analysis. The everyday, and particularly quotidian actions of hygiene, laundry, and cooking, points us towards actions and logics of the individual, the family, and the small group. In this gaze, the interpersonal becomes as important as the international.[23] At the same time, however, it is worth avoiding homogenising members of collectives.[24] Not all Israeli Jews or Northern Ireland Protestants are the same. Instead, we need to be aware of in-group differences in terms of race, gender, class, and age and of the 'everyday situated intersectionality' that locates people in specific times and places.[25] One such place that requires to be taken seriously in our studies is the home and the immediate vicinity of the home.

Research from the Everyday Peace Indicators (EPI) project underscores the extent to which many people experience and narrate peace, security, development, and change in terms of the home and its immediate surroundings. In multiple locations where the EPI research was undertaken (two communities in Colombia and three each in South Africa, South Sudan, Uganda, and Zimbabwe), focus group respondents used the hyperlocal level as their frame of reference. They referred to security for themselves and family members in terms of safety in their own homes at nighttime or how safe it was for their children to walk to school. Thus, for example, members of a female focus group in Mbare, a suburb of Harare in Zimbabwe, discussed peace in terms of 'peace of mind and without any disturbances in the neighbourhood', 'the ability to walk around freely without any interference by the police', 'not [being] afraid of housebreakings and robberies', and 'when children are able to go to school freely'.[26] All of this points to the ordinariness and hyperlocalism of what is at once location-specific but also applicable quite widely. This sameness, or generalised applicability, is worth thinking about in terms of the scalability of everyday peace, especially on a horizontal plane.

There has been a 'local turn' in the peace and conflict studies literature, and this has been reflected in policy literature and stances with, for example, a localisation agenda seeking to make the Sustainable Development Goals relevant to local contexts. But it is not entirely clear if national and international actors (and

---

[23] Josephine Mylan and Dale Southerton, 'The Social Ordering of an Everyday Practice: The Case of Laundry', *Sociology* 52, no. 6 (2018): 1134–1151.
[24] Nira Yuval-Davis, Georgie Wemyss, and Kathryn Cassidy, 'Everyday Bordering: Belonging and the Reorientation of British Immigration Legislation', *Sociology* 52, no. 2 (2018): 232.
[25] Yuval-Davis, Wemyss, and Cassidy, 'Everyday Bordering', 232.
[26] EPI project female focus group, Mbare, Zimbabwe, 21 May 2014.

indeed many academics) fully comprehend just how local the local is to many people. NATO, for example, has adopted the language of the local in some of its documents and policies, but it is not clear that it understands the local to be anything other than in-country suppliers of resources.[27] This rather shallow and non-specific understanding of the scale of the local is very different from that held by the participants in the EPI study. For them, the local was a very small area made up of the home and its immediate surroundings, and it was also made up of familiar routes to school, shops, and work. A number of focus group participants in Zimbabwe, for example, mentioned the need to urinate and defecate inside at night because they felt unsafe using outdoor latrines. This reminds us of the habitual nature of the everyday and how it is embodied and enacted through routine activities. It is connected with the micro-geographies of our existence. Male youths in a focus group in Gudele, South Sudan, emphasised the relational and highly local nature of peace and security through repeated references to neighbours, community, the marketplace, and home.[28] It is worth reminding ourselves—students, scholars, and practitioners—that we all live very local lives, often centred around a very few places: home, work, school, university library, relatives' houses, and cultural meeting places. Although many of us may travel extensively and have significant transnational aspects to our lives, many of us have favourite coffee and grocery shops and have family or work commitments that mean that we must travel along particular routes on a near-daily basis. Anyone who owns a dog will understand that the same few routes are walked day in, day out. The essential point is that for many of us, the everyday occurs on a very local scale. This, in turn, raises a question for researchers: do we have the skills and resources that make us able to access the hyperlocal? Here the disciplines of sociology, anthropology, and gender studies offer much of value, especially with their concentration on people and their ability to draw out intersectionalities or the different roles people play, and the identities they project, in life.[29]

A key point about the notion of the everyday is that it can play an important role in making, maintaining, and possibly changing identity. Through everyday actions and micro-social practices, individuals and communities employ and develop cultural repertoires.[30] In a deeply divided society, the simple acts of reading a newspaper, listening to the radio, and getting dressed in the morning

---

[27] See, for example, how the word *local* is used in NATO, 'Defence and Related Security Capacity Initiative', 12 July 2018, https://www.nato.int/cps/en/natohq/topics_132756.htm; NATO, 'Trust Funds: Supporting Demilitarization and Defence Transformation Projects', 21 June 2016, https://www.nato.int/cps/en/natolive/topics_50082.htm.

[28] EPI project focus group for youths, Gudele II Hai Battery, South Sudan, 26 October 2013.

[29] John Brewer, *Peace Processes: A Sociological Approach* (Cambridge: Polity, 2010).

[30] Guzel Yusupova, 'Cultural Nationalism and Everyday Resistance in an Illiberal Nationalising State: Ethnic Minority Nationalism in Russia', *Nations and Nationalism* 24, no. 3 (2018): 624–647. See also Ash Amin, 'Ethnicity and the Multicultural City: Living with Diversity', *Environment and Planning A* 34 (2002): 959–980.

may all contribute a specific vernacular identity. This is a peculiarly banal form of banal nationalism whereby everyday actions, routes, turns of phrase, and forms of distraction contribute to the creation of an identity.[31] The newspaper bought, the radio station listened to, and the style of dress may mark an individual out as belonging to a particular culture. The individual may simply be staying abreast of the news, listening to music, and getting dressed to ward off the cold. These constitute mundane everyday acts that very probably merit little mention. To an outsider, however, and particularly to someone from an opposing group in a divided society, all of those acts are potential identity markers and thus are political. The particular newspaper, radio station, or style of dress may be a way of reinforcing an ethnic or national identity and thus can be seen through a political lens.[32]

From the perspective of this book, the everyday provides a lens through which to view pro-social and pro-peace acts and modes of thinking that occur at the ground level. While many of us might view the lives of those in war zones as exceptional, for many inhabitants and combatants the exceptional becomes normalised. Often they have little choice but to become inured to the circumstances of long-term conflict. Within such contexts, an everyday is forged, even if this everyday existence contains privations and violence. Depending on the context, life might contain a mix of what might be considered 'normal' (e.g., getting the kids to school and sleeping in one's own bed) with the 'abnormal' that comes with conflict (e.g., an increased military presence or shortages of goods).[33] The ways in which conflict inflects everyday life might be very subtle, with, for example, algorithms working behind the scenes to analyse whether our purchasing and travel habits constitute a security threat.[34] I come from Northern Ireland and recently hired a car at a Belfast airport. When leaving the hire car back at the airport, I made sure that the car radio was not tuned to a radio station based in the Republic of Ireland lest the employees of the hire car company make a judgement as to my identity and then 'find' damage to the car. Conflict logics, in this case linked with sectarianism, run deep and inhabit the most mundane aspects of life. The lens offered by the everyday allows us to capture the ways in which life is enacted and embodied. It encourages us to see beyond the elite level and view how so-called ordinary people endure conflict but also are—sometimes—empowered by it. As developed in more detail in chapter 2, everyday peace rests on three concepts and types of action that are often deployed as part of everyday life: sociality, reciprocity, and solidarity. In situations of conflict or in deeply divided

---

[31] Michael Billig, *Banal Nationalism* (Thousand Oaks, CA: Sage, 1995).

[32] J. Paul Goode and David R. Stroupe, 'Everyday Nationalism: Constructivism for the Masses', *Social Science Quarterly* 96, no. 3 (2015): 718.

[33] See Stathis N. Kalyvas on the normalisation of brutality, *The Logic of Violence in Civil War* (New Haven, CT: Yale University Press, 2006), 55–58.

[34] Louise Amoore, 'Algorithmic War: Everyday Geographies of the War on Terror', *Antipode* 41, no. 1 (2009): 49–69.

societies, these concepts can operate across groups and thus can play a pacific and pro-social role. Sociality, reciprocity, and solidarity between a Muslim and a Christian in northern Nigeria or in Ambon Province in Nigeria can occur at the everyday level of interactions in the street or marketplace. As chapters 4 and 5 will reveal, humane and pro-social acts can take place in the 'everyday' of the battlefield. The core focus of this book is to explore the nature and motivation of such acts and to investigate their importance. Do individual or apparently isolated pro-social and everyday peace acts have any significance beyond the action itself? This brings us to the issue of scale and whether we can think of everyday peace actions or modes of thinking as contributing to a wider context. The next two sections, on circuitry and scalability, discuss the connectedness of the everyday to other domains and the potential of everyday and grassroots peace to influence other levels.

Circuits and Circuitry

Having established that everyday peace is made up of micro-social practices, our next task is to connect those highly localised everyday practices to wider social, economic, political, and cultural contexts. Is the friendship between Serbian and Albanian work colleagues in an otherwise divided Kosovan town simply an isolated social practice, or does it represent something more significant? Can we think of scaling up localised and everyday peace acts and stances so that they resonate with wider communities and institutions? To answer these questions, we need to consider issues of scale or level of analysis. We are also encouraged to think of the wider significance of everyday peace as a series of actions and modes of thinking. Is the workplace friendship a one-off that is isolated from wider societal and political dynamics, or might it represent something more significant? Could it be that the friendship between two individuals who identify differently across a political divide is a signifier of something more important? Could this friendship be a case of conflict disruption (a concept developed in more detail in chapter 7) that confronts the conventional wisdom on the irresolvable nature of the conflict? Fundamentally, is there a possibility that everyday peace best practice could be scaled up from its highly localised base?

Where there are multiple countercultural actions in a conflict-affected context, and the logic behind such everyday peace is shared among more than a handful of people, then everyday peace has the potential to become something more significant. It becomes scaled out and possibly scaled up and can make violent conflict, and the logics behind it, unsustainable. It can disrupt conflict and create space that other forms of conflict response—namely, conflict management, conflict resolution, and conflict transformation—can exploit. All of this is, of course, highly context-dependent, and everyday peace often takes place opportunistically, on the margins, or in hidden spaces. Yet it has the potential to be disruptive and to upset the apparent logic and path-dependency that often accompanies violent conflict. The simple notion that conflict might change or end is powerful and a challenge to reasoning that sees the continuation of conflict as inevitable.

This book uses the notion of circuitry to understand the links between apparently isolated pro-social acts of everyday peace and the wider levels of the community, the state, the international, the transnational, and all levels in between. In drawing on network and complexity theory,[35] circuitry allows us to envisage how highly localised actions between individuals or small groups of individuals can be situated in much broader systems. Rather than think of a conflict in the singular, it seems more appropriate to think of 'a complex system of conflict processes' and 'a set of interlocking sub-processes of various events that are mutually influencing'.[36] This section will proceed by discussing levels of analysis and the need to embrace a multi-scalar approach that can see all levels of political and social organisation in one gaze. It will then introduce circuitry, first placing it in the context of network and complexity theory and then explicating the benefits of using circuitry as an analytical device and not just a metaphor.

The discipline of international relations has long discussed the appropriate levels of analysis with which to interpret the world.[37] Many classical international relations scholars identified a tripartite distinction between the individual (often traditionally called 'man'),[38] the state or domestic front, and the international system.[39] Despite much critical scholarship adding nuance to this picture, the three-part distinction has been surprisingly enduring.[40] This traditional view

---

[35] A particularly good rendition of the relevance of complexity theory for the study of peace can be found in Cedric de Coning, 'From Peacebuilding to Sustaining Peace: Implications of Complexity for Resilience and Sustainability', *Resilience* 4, no. 3 (2016): 166–181. See also Emillie M. Hafner-Burton, Miles Kahler, and Alexander H. Montgomery, 'Network Analysis for International Relations', *International Organization* 63, no. 3 (2009): 559–592; Emilian Kavalski, 'Waking IR from Its "Deep Newtonian Slumber"', *Millennium* 41, no. 1 (2012): 137–150; Ericka Cudworth and Stephen Hobden, 'Anarchy and Anarchism: Towards a Theory of Complex International Systems', *Millennium* 39, no. 2 (2010): 399–416.

[36] Jeong, *Understanding Conflict*, 105.

[37] Owen Temby, 'What Are Levels of Analysis and What Do They Contribute to International Relations Theory?', *Cambridge Review of International Affairs* 28, no. 4 (2015): 721–722; Laura Sjoberg, 'Scaling International Relations Theory: Geography's Contribution to Where IR Takes Place', *International Studies Review* 10, no. 3 (2008): 472–500.

[38] For critiques that stress our need to gender the levels of analysis debate, see Laura Sjoberg, 'Gender'; Jean Bethke Elshtain, 'Women, the State, and War', *International Relations* 23, no. 2 (2009): 289–303.

[39] Kenneth Waltz, *Man, the State, and War: A Theoretical Analysis* (New York: Columbia University Press, 2001); David J. Singer, 'The Level of Analysis Problem in International Relations', *World Politics* 12, no. 3 (1961): 453–460. See also a discussion of levels of analysis in Robert W. Cox, 'Social Forces, States and World Orders: Beyond IR Theory', *Millennium* 10, no. 2 (1981): 126–155.

[40] See, for example, Steven Spiegel, 'Regional Security and the Levels of Analysis Problem', *Journal of Strategic Studies* 26, no. 3 (2003): 75–98; Anthony C. Lopez and Dominic D. P. Johnson, 'The

often saw a hierarchy that was defined in Hobbesian terms: individuals needed protection from violence and so gave fealty to the state. In turn, states found themselves in a harsh environment of other states and so were either prone to war, invasion, or coercion or had to engage in strategies (such as joining alliances and collectives) to survive.[41] This hierarchical framework saw power as moving upwards from the individual to the state and from the state to more powerful states and a collective security system.

Our aim of situating everyday peace in its wider contexts requires us to transcend the 'Russian doll' model. Instead of seeing a simple three-part model, and placing the individual and everyday as axiomatically subordinate to the national and the international, this book suggests circuitry as a way of capturing the complexity of systems. These systems are transnational as well as international, and rather than containing the individual, the national and the international are co-constituted by the individual (who also shapes and constrains them). Circuits are able to better capture the messy and dynamic nature of the peace and conflict systems. Consider, for example, efforts to address civil rights in the United States in the 1950s and 1960s. These efforts occurred at multiple levels, from individuals and families to some enlightened politicians and legislators at the state and national levels. In between, a multitude of actors were involved—from high school teachers to civil society activists and lawyers. The story is too complex to be told in a coherent and linear way. It involves a mix of the formal and the informal, the national and the local, the top-down and the bottom-up, all coalescing to form a jumble.[42] In keeping with sociological analyses, systems analyses acknowledge the interconnectedness of the different levels of societies and institutions, how they leach into one another and have multiple sites of connection. It is prudent to think in terms of complex adaptive systems that are messy and dynamic and do not easily fit into analytical or conceptual schemes that have neat boundaries.[43] Such systems have pluralities, unintended outcomes, hard-to-see aspects, and very probably aspects that defy easy explanation.[44]

Determinants of War in International Relations', *Journal of Economic Behavior and Organization* 178 (2020): 983–997.

[41] Andrew Linklater, 'Process Sociology in International Relations', *Sociological Review* 59, no. 1 (2011): 48–64. See also Michael Howard, *The Invention of Peace* (Princeton, NJ: Princeton University Press, 2000); Charles Tilly, *Coercion, Capital and European States, AD 990–1992* (London: Wiley-Blackwell, 1992).

[42] The firsthand accounts in the following show how the micro was implicated in the macro and vice versa: Kim Lacy Rogers, *Righteous Lives: Narratives of the New Orleans Civil Rights Movement* (New York: New York University Press, 1995).

[43] De Coning, 'Complexity thinking'.

[44] Dugan, 'A Nested Theory', 15.

Attempts to conceive of a more interconnected and less realist world can be regarded as part of a wider attempt to decolonise international relations[45] and move it towards a purview that is more cognizant of the situated and complex lives that people actually live and the contexts they construct and reconstruct through their daily lives.[46] So, rather than binaries (local and global, traditional and modern, etc.) and simple hierarchies, we need to move our analyses away from Euro-Atlanticist perspectives that are overly respectful of traditional levels of analysis.[47] It is also worth turning a reflexive gaze at ourselves and asking why we engage in the peculiar forms of sense-making that dominate our thinking. These forms of sense-making are often highly gendered, ethnocentric, institutionalist, and incurious about large swathes of the planet. As Pankaj Mishra puts it, Western assumptions 'are no longer a reliable vantage point and may even be dangerously misleading'.[48]

The turn to circuits and circuitry has been influenced by network and complexity theories and their recognition of the need to capture the dynamic and interconnected nature of social relations. It also draws on works by Karl Marx and David Harvey, who respectively sought to capture the circulation of money and people in systems.[49] The task facing this book is to explain how the everyday peace actions of an individual or a small group of individuals contribute to the wider systems they inhabit. Importantly, the individuals do not merely inhabit these systems; they help constitute them. By their pro-social and pacific actions and stances, they have the capacity to change the wider system, perhaps making it more humane and helping to puncture myths of a united in-group. Consider the example, used in the introductory chapter, of the actions of a small group of Sudanese soldiers in April 2019. In the midst of long-running street protests against President Bashir, a small detachment of soldiers intervened to protect the protesters from unknown assailants (probably from the national intelligence agency) who were firing on the crowd.[50] We cannot know the motivations of the soldiers, but it is fair to assume that they were acting humanely in attempting to protect civilian lives. How can we make sense of this apparently isolated action?

---

[45] J. Srivavasta and A. Sharma, 'International Relations Theory and World Order: Binaries, Silences and Alternatives', *South Asian Survey* 21, nos. 1–2 (2014): 20–34; Picq, 'Critics'.

[46] Ann B. Tickner, 'Core, Periphery and (Neo)imperialist International Relations', *European Journal of International Relations* 19, no. 3 (2013): 627–646.

[47] Sabaratnam, 'Avatars'.

[48] Pankaj Mishra, *From the Ruins of Empire: The Revolt against the West and the Remaking of Asia* (London: Allen Lane, 2012), 8.

[49] Karl Marx, *Capital: A Critique of Political Economy*, Vol. I, Book One, *The Processes of Production of Capital* (New York: International Publishers, 1887); David Harvey, 'The Geography of Capital and Accumulation: A Reconstruction of Marxian Theory', *Antipode* 7, no. 2 (1975): 9–21.

[50] 'Sudan Protest: Clashes among Armed Forces at Khartoum Sit-in', *BBC News*, 8 April 2019, https://www.bbc.co.uk/news/world-africa-47850278; 'Sudan Protests: Soldier "Killed while Protecting activists" as Clashes Break Out', *Sky News*, 8 April 2019, https://news.sky.com/story/sudan-protests-soldier-killed-while-protecting-activists-as-clashes-break-out-11687949.

A traditional analysis might stick to an institutionalist explanation and discuss rivalries between different state bodies and the possibility of a schism or coup in the state security apparatus. This explanation may also seek to place Bashir's regime in the strategic context of a sensitive region and discuss the fallout of US sanctions.[51] A sociological explanation, however, has the capacity to go much further and consider the actions and motivations of the soldiers who acted to protect the civilians. This lens is capable of seeing the soldiers not as mere robots of a military organisation but as individuals and members of other collectives such as families and clans. It recalls micro-sociological studies that examined the sociodynamics of street corners or neighbour-to-neighbour relations. As William Foot Whyte noted in his study of an Italian slum in Boston, 'the individual must be put back in his social setting and observed in his daily activities. In order to understand the spectacular event, it is necessary to see it in relation to the everyday pattern of life'.[52] Scholars such as Elliot Liebow 'hung around' in order to access the banal and the everyday.[53] For Mitchell Duneier, ethnographic approaches allow 'those kind of transcendent connections and recognitions of the humanity of others . . . where it is possible to gain access to the humanity of "others" despite the normal barriers that there are'.[54]

Network and complexity theories allow us to see social phenomena as part of assemblages. They stress the interconnected nature of the social world in which the human and non-human interact and constitute a whole. Rather than a strict separation between structure and agency, or between dependent and independent variables, they accommodate the merging and co-constitution of concepts. In this view, no actor exists in a vacuum. Seemingly isolated actions—like those of a small number of troops at a protest in Khartoum—are part of the wider web of connections. These multi-scalar explanations are uncomfortable with the abstractions of grand theories, the overly simplistic nature of single explanations (e.g., as provided by Marxist or realist lenses), and the necessity of capturing in a single frame a dynamic reality.[55] Indeed, the apparently made-up words that populate the literature on networks—holism, assemblage, relationality, intersectionality, interrelatedness—are indicative that traditional frames and diction are unable to adequately capture the dynamism of social categories.

---

[51] See, for example, Mai Hassan and Ahmed Kodouda, 'Sudan's Uprising: The Fall of a Dictator', *Journal of Democracy* 30, no. 4 (2019): 83–103.

[52] William Whyte Foot, *Street Corner Society: The Social Structure of an Italian Slum*, 4th ed. (Chicago: University of Chicago Press, 1993), xvi.

[53] Elliot Liebow, *Tally's Corner: A Study of Negro Street Corner Men* (Boston: Little, Brown, 1967).

[54] Mitchell Duneier and Les Back, 'Voices from the Sidewalk: Ethnography and Writing Race', *Ethnic and Racial Studies* 29, no. 3 (2006): 548–549.

[55] Nick Srnicek, 'Conflict Networks: Collapsing the Global into the Local', *Journal of Critical Globalisation Studies* 2 (2010): 46.

This book argues that circuits provide a useful analytical device with which to understand the messy interconnectedness of the top-down, bottom-up, local, international, everyday, exceptional, and everything in between. The notion of circuitry adopted by this book draws on evolved or biological circuits, like the root networks of plants or the neural networks in our brain, *and* engineered circuits like those in our computers or phones. The reason for using *both* biological and engineered networks is that each brings something to the table. Biological circuitry allows us to think of organically growing and self-repairing circuits, and thus allows us to get beyond the idea that circuits are necessarily the site of path-dependency, repetition, and automatic action and response that might be associated with engineered or electronic circuits. Engineered circuitry encourages us to think about power and particularly the power of those who design, construct, and maintain circuits. If we think of both engineered and biological circuits together—in a biotech assemblage—then we can conceive of a messy but comprehensive picture, a series of circuits that are able to encompass the static and the dynamic, the established and the developing.

In this understanding, numerous circuits operate simultaneously. They will operate on very different scales, some global and regional and others hyperlocal. They overlap, merge, and compete. The circuits might have different purposes. Some will be overwhelmingly concerned with economic matters and others with cultural, family, or security matters. All of this would be contained within a meta-circuit whose fundamental purpose is the continuation of life itself. If we go back to the example of the Sudanese soldiers, then we can see that an individual soldier might be a member of multiple circuits. Not only is he a member of the Sudanese armed forces (one circuit), but he will also be a member of a particular regiment or unit (another circuit). And within that larger unit, he will be in a subunit such as a company (a circuit), and within that, he might have a close group of comrades (another circuit). He may perform a specialised task within his military unit, for example, as a medic or radio operator, which would mean membership of another circuit. Simply within the military, he might be implicated in multiple partially overlapping circuits. Outside the military, the soldier may be a member of, or aligned with, a series of familial, friendship, clan, linguistic, and cultural circuits. He may identify more strongly with some circuits than others. For example, the family circuit is likely to resonate more strongly than that of the boys he went to school with—with the exception of a few close friends. Through marriage, the soldier may connect with other geographical and familial circuits. The soldier may support the English soccer team Arsenal. He has never been to the United Kingdom, and even the cheapest ticket to see a match is likely to swallow a considerable amount of his disposable income.[56]

---

[56] For pay in the Sudanese armed forces, see 'Sudan Approves 22% Pay Raise for Military', *Sudan Tribune*, 9 May 2013, http://www.sudantribune.com/spip.php?article46520. For Arsenal ticket prices, see https://www.arsenal.com/tickets/non-member-ticket-prices.

Yet he identifies with this team and thus is connected—perhaps through online chats—with other Arsenal supporters. As soccer is increasingly globalised, he may come into online contact with transnational networks of supporters.

The picture that emerges is complex and dynamic. In this young man's story (it seems unfair to reduce him to the label 'soldier'), some circuits have more power and resonance than others. The military has powers of discipline, while his immediate family may exercise considerable moral power. Other circuits might be weaker or change over time. He may be an avid soccer fan in his twenties, but that interest might wane with age. Some circuits, such as his interest in soccer, might connect him with people he—ostensibly—has little else in common with. A London hedge-fund manager with a season ticket at Arsenal's ground might watch and retweet a snippet of a match that the young Sudanese has posted online. The connection is fleeting and impersonal, but it shows a commonality that transects a number of cultural boundaries. Taken together, the circuits tell a story about identity and orientation.

The Sudanese soldier may (it is impossible to be certain) have taken action to protect civilian protesters from gunfire from other members of the Sudanese security apparatus. This pro-social and humane act opens a window onto everyday peace or actions and thinking that might disrupt conflict. As will be discussed in chapter 2, everyday peace actions may involve sociality, reciprocity, and solidarity. By offering protection to protesters, the soldier and his comrades might be showing basic solidarity and humanity with other Sudanese citizens. They might also be acting on a worldview that believes in reciprocity, or that pro-social actions will contribute to the greater good of society and should, if possible, be repaid. They might even be acting in a solidaristic way and believe, despite their membership in the Sudanese military, that Bashir should resign and that a series of social and economic issues should be addressed.

Circuits hold a number of advantages as an analytical device and are particularly suited to situating everyday actions (such as those connected with everyday peace) in wider systems that they help to constitute.[57] The first advantage of circuits and circuitry is that they remind us of the need for intellectual humility. Our patchy understanding of neural networks and the functioning of the human brain reminds us that not everything can be understood.[58] The key purpose of the social sciences, and indeed the motive force of the Enlightenment, is the assumption that social phenomena can be captured and explained.[59] The complexity of circuits, their unexpected routes and connections, their material and

---

[57] This section draws on ideas first sketched in Mac Ginty, 'Circuits'.

[58] K. D. Davis, 'The Neural Circuitry of Pain as Explored with Functional MRI', *Neurological Research* 22, no. 3 (2000): 313; T. Warr, 'Circuitry', *Performance Research* 6, no. 3 (2001): 12.

[59] Marinus Ossewaarde, 'Living off Dead Premises: The Persistence of Enlightenment Mentalities in the Making of Social Sciences', *European Quarterly of Political Attitudes and Mentalities* 4, no. 4 (2015): 1–14.

immaterial nature, and their sometimes hidden or unseen nature mean that circuits can be beyond the grasp of our attempts to capture and rationalise them, at least at the moment. Indeed, actors in conflict contexts may deliberately seek to hide everyday pro-social activities lest they contravene conflict norms and invite suspicion. When attempting to understand neural circuitry, we often rely on proxies, experimentation, and representations of phenomena rather than phenomena themselves. As Warr explains, 'These experiences represent, rather than accurately report what is going on in the world'.[60] The key point is that despite the apparent sophistication of the natural and social sciences, there are many areas—neural circuitry being prominent here—that we do not fully understand.

The second advantage of circuits, as an analytical device, is that they represent movement.[61] Circuits facilitate the movement of people, ideas, power, goods, and capital. Indeed, Marx's analysis of global capital referred to the 'restless currency of money' that was 'perpetuum mobile'.[62] They are a transmission device. In some cases, the chief ideas being transmitted will be related to order and discipline. But there may also be room for alternative or counter-hegemonic ideas. For example, and related to the notion of everyday peace, circuits might allow for ideas of dissent to spread. Towards the end of World War I, many German, Russian, and French soldiers mutinied.[63] As Louis Barthas, a French private in World War I, confided in his diary, 'Ah, how extravagant our generals were with the lives of others!'[64] Many soldiers were no longer prepared to follow their political and military leaders. The ideas of dissent that allowed the mutinies to take root relied on networks or circuits to spread information. These circuits had to be beyond the surveillance of superiors, and the sharing of doubts among comrades relied on hidden transcripts. Importantly, a multitude of circuits, some overlapping and others only tangentially connected with larger circuits, allows for the movement of people, ideas, capital, and goods in multiple ways—not just top-down and bottom-up. Movement may trigger responses (or none) and can be direct or indirect. It might be contained within one micro-circuit or have consequences across the wider series of circuits.

A third advantage of using circuitry as an analytical tool is that it entails an infrastructure along which ideas, people, capital, practices, goods, and power can travel. This infrastructure allows for discipline and regularity; think of the

---

[60] Warr, 'Circuitry'.

[61] Nick Gill, Deirdre Conlon, Dominique Moran, et al., 'Carceral Circuitry: New Directions in Carceral Geography', *Progress in Human Geography* 90, no. 2 (2016): 183–204.

[62] Marx, *Capital*, 85.

[63] See, for example, Stephen Kotkin, 'One Hand Clapping: Russian Workers and 1917', *Labor History* 32, no. 4 (1991): 604–620. See also John Horne on the need to go beyond master narratives of war, 'End of a Paradigm? The Cultural History of the Great War', *Past & Present* 242, no. 1 (2019): 155–192.

[64] Louis Barthas, *Poilu: The World War I Notebooks of Corporal Louis Barthas, Barrelmaker 1914–1918* (New Haven, CT: Yale University Press, 2014), 16.

constrained journeys we have through airports or IKEA in which opportunities to deviate are rare and by conforming we reinforce the structure. By following a route, we normalise it and (usually subliminally) accept the authority of those who constructed it. Thus, the ability to build infrastructure and regularise its usage denotes power. This might be the power of capital and the accumulation of material goods and force to build physical infrastructure, but it also refers to the immaterial power that encourages or compels people to use that infrastructure in particular ways. As Logue and Clegg observe, circuits can be 'obligatory passage points . . . that stabilize and destabilize existing fields of power relations'.[65] We can think of infrastructure as being physical and intended to make statements of power, authority, and aspirations. Here, for example, it is worth thinking about the architecture of palaces and parliaments and the messages they were designed to convey.[66] It can also be immaterial, in the form of networks of power and discipline such as regulatory systems that might control the trade of a particular commodity like oil or diamonds. Particularly relevant to everyday peace, however, are forms of infrastructure that are social and informal.[67] Here, for example, we might think of an informal cross-community friendship network in a deeply divided society. This circuit might not have any physical trace in the form of infrastructure, but it might be enduring and regularised.

A final point in relation to the infrastructure of circuitry is that infrastructures can be modified, expanded, updated, and repaired. As we know from physical infrastructure, it is prone to becoming overburdened or damaged through use, or made irrelevant through other developments. Thus, even large circuits that may have symbolised the accumulation and projection of very significant amounts of power can fade in importance over time. There can also be differences between prescribed or normative use of a circuit and actual use, with actors deploying initiative to use circuits in non-prescribed ways.[68] Biological circuits can 'dissolve when they are done', and others can self-repair.[69] The picture that emerges is of a complex and adaptive social infrastructure. Much of the infrastructure might be co-opted and regulated by a state or social movement that is part of a partisan or war system. But, and as will be illustrated throughout this book, there may be space for alternative systems that may be pro-peace and pro-social and have the capacity to disrupt conflict norms.

---

[65] Danielle M. Logue and Stewart R. Clegg, 'Wikileaks and the News of the World: The Political Circuitry of Labelling', *Journal of Management Inquiry* 24, no. 4 (2015): 394–404.

[66] Charles T. Goodsell, 'The Architecture of Parliaments: Legislative Houses and Political Culture', *British Journal of Political Science* 18, no. 3 (1988): 287–302.

[67] On social infrastructure, see Eric Klinenberg, *Palaces for the People: How Social Infrastructure Can Help Fight Inequality, Polarization and the Decline in Civic Life* (New York: Crown, 2018).

[68] Shakini Shankar, 'Metaconsumptive Practices and the Circulation of Objectifications', *Journal of Material Culture* 11, no. 3 (2006): 294.

[69] Elizabeth Pennisi, 'Tracing Life's Circuitry', *Science* 302, no. 5651 (2003): 1649.

A fourth factor recommending circuits as an analytical tool is that circuits remind us of the importance of agency. Through their construction, maintenance, and operation, networks are agential. They are the site of decision-making (for example, whether to control or allow the movement of information), reaction, construction, modification, and energy. In some cases, agency will be autonomous or automatic. Often, the circuit will be designed precisely in order to facilitate this and thus regularise a particular process. In this view, circuits can be viewed as a site of order-making, constraint, and path-dependency. While this is the case in many instances and explains much of the regularity we find in life through state-making, technocracy, and the power of institutions. Yet we can also think of agency in ways that are disruptive, subversive, entrepreneurial, accidental, and non-standard. In this view, agency can disrupt rather than reinforce the circuit. It can help modify existing circuits and build new ones. For example, individuals might subvert official forms of information with their own informal network. While we must be careful in labelling all alternatives as forms of resistance,[70] we can conceive of circuits, in some instances, as being sites of innovation and disruption as well as being path-dependent sites of replication. It is here that we can think of circuits that disrupt the norms of conflict and offer the possibility of contributing to peace. As examples from chapters 4 and 5 will show, there are multiple examples of soldiers in World Wars I and II deviating from mandated warlike behaviour and instead exhibiting pacific behaviours of sociality, reciprocity, and—in some cases—solidarity. To do so, they often had their own micro-circuits of comrades with whom they privately discussed their dissatisfaction with military and political leadership or their feelings on exhortations to see the other side as inhuman. These networks were often marginal and operated outside of surveillance. In the case of the large-scale mutinies towards the end of WWI in France, Germany, and Russia, however, the circuits grew to a considerable size and threatened the orthodox circuits that had been prosecuting the war.[71] The chief point is that circuits are constituted through agency and that, in some cases, this agency can be disruptive, be non-standard, and contribute to notions and practices of everyday peace.

A fifth point in favour of adopting circuitry as an analytical device is that there can be different orders of circuits. By conceiving of circuits within circuits, we can envisage how highly localised circuits might fit within a wider whole. This helps us answer the scalar puzzle that runs through this book: how do we connect the individual and the small group of individuals to the state, the international, the transnational, and all levels in between? Or, to put it another way,

---

[70] Mac Ginty, 'Circuits'.
[71] Leonard V. Smith, *Between Mutiny and Obedience: The Case of the French Fifth Infantry Division during World War I* (Princeton, NJ: Princeton University Press, 1994).

can seemingly isolated or localised events have impact on the wider scale? Some circuits might appear to be hyperlocal and unconnected with wider and apparently 'higher-order' circuits. Indeed, this micro-level might be where most of us spend most of our energies.[72] Yet these apparently highly localised processes are also likely to be a site of connection.[73] The micro-circuit is highly unlikely to be completely self-contained. The sociality of humanity, our economic and cultural interdependence, and the means of organisation of states and other (social) institutions mean that most humans have multiple connections with multiple circuits. As demonstrated by the example of the Sudanese soldier earlier in this chapter, the micro-circuit constituted by his immediate colleagues is contained within broader circuits that operate on multiple spheres (familial, social, tribal, institutional, transnational). Importantly, and as underscored by the next point, micro- and macro-circuits (and all levels in between) combine to produce an assemblage that defies the neat categorisations of horizontal and vertical, or formal and informal.[74]

The sixth point to make recommending circuitry as an analytical tool is that we can conceive of different types of circuits. Not only are they of a different scale and operating at different levels, but they can also have different orientations, functionality, and purposes. A financial circuit that specialises in share trading or currency exchange might be largely automated. Trading will occur in nanoseconds, perhaps a billionth of a second, and have limited human interference.[75] This is a world of advanced technology, specialised argot, and complex regulations. It is very different from a circuit that might be immaterial and based on spirituality and a belief system steeped in religion or superstition. Yet these different systems combine—sometimes tenuously and with the linkages not always obvious—to create complex adaptive systems.[76]

It is useful to think in terms of assemblages of circuits in which the formal and the informal, the complete and the under construction, the well used and the less used, operate alongside one another. Bearing everyday peace and conflict disruption in mind, it is also useful to think of how individuals and groups of individuals may be able to deftly use different circuits in different ways at different times. Thus, for example, the Sudanese soldier may use the formal and institutional circuits of the Sudanese armed forces when appropriate and useful.

---

[72] Carol H. Weiss, 'The Circuitry of Enlightenment: Diffusion of Social Science Research to Policymakers', *Knowledge: Creation, Diffusion, Utilization* 8, no. 2 (1986): 274.

[73] Logue and Clegg, 'Wikileaks', 399.

[74] Richard Grant and Martin Oteng-Ababio, 'Mapping the Invisible and Real "African" Economy: Urban E-Waste Circuitry', *Urban Geography* 33, no. 1 (2012): 11.

[75] On the race to make financial trading faster see Donald Mackenzie, 'Just How Fast?', *London Review of Books* 41, no. 5 (2019): 23–24; Philip Stafford, 'Trading Monitoring Goes into Seconds', *Financial Times*, 24 February 2011, https://www.ft.com/content/ce35dd98-3ffa-11e0-811f-00144feabdc0.

[76] De Coning, 'Complexity Thinking'.

But when he is among a family or friendship network and out of surveillance by the state, he might express his dissatisfaction with the regime. The circuits can sit alongside one another, operating simultaneously and possibly in contradictory ways. Some parts might be more visible than others, and some might only be active opportunistically. We can think of hybrid circuits that bring together different types of circuits. Here, perhaps, it is useful to think of biotechnology that combines biological and engineered circuits, producing new possibilities and sites of invention.[77] Circuitry allows us to conceive of politics and social spaces that are messy, evolutionary, and based on complex forms of interaction.

Figure 1.1 provides a highly simplified version of some of the circuitry found in a conflict-affected country. Most visible are the formal circuits of the state and the military. These actors and institutions attract resources, play a performative role in society, and are able to wield coercive power as well as incentives. An ethnic group might have less clear boundaries of inclusion and exclusion—hence the wavy line. These major circuits would be joined by other major circuits that would attract a substantial following, such as faith-based organisations or political parties. But crucial to the system are the faint messy circuits. These are families, friendship networks, colleagues, and sporting or prayer groups. They add an additional texture. If the figure were completely filled out, the result would be close to indecipherable—a messy collections of lines of different thicknesses and significance. Some of the circuits would interact. Some would have more power than others. Some would be broken, and others would be under repair. Given our interest in everyday peace, most of our attention goes to the faint lines. These are the circuits that give life to peace through enactment and embodiment. Importantly, all of the circuits form a whole, and the circuits in the figure would be contained in other international and transnational circuits.

Scalability

Is there the potential for highly localised everyday peace acts and stances to scale up and thus have greater significance or impact beyond the locale? For example, can the pro-social work of a charismatic individual in a particular neighbourhood be adopted and scaled up city-wide? Or is everyday peace destined to remain localised? Indeed, is there a danger that the organic and valuable qualities of everyday peace may be lost if it is scaled up? In order to investigate the possibilities of scaling up everyday peace, this section conceptualises the notion and practice of scaling up. Again, the most useful literature on this is to be found outside of peace and conflict studies and international relations, and instead

---

[77] Pennisi, 'Tracing', 1646–1649.

46 EVERYDAY PEACE

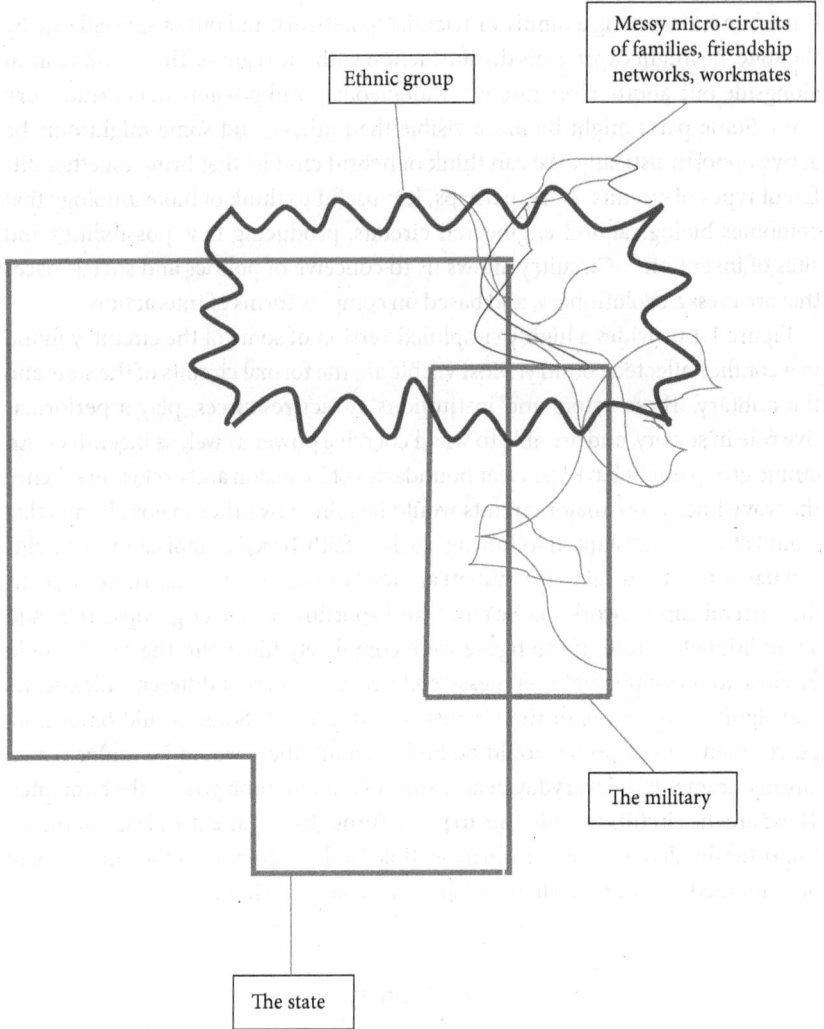

Figure 1.1. Circuitry in a conflict-affected country.

comes from development, agriculture, and ecology. Policymakers, donors, and academics in these fields have been pondering the extent to which localised success stories can be factored up, thus having greater impact on people's lives and delivering greater value for donors. As this section, and indeed a good portion of this book, will show, scaling up is very much concerned with balancing risk and reward. It is also context-dependent and will usually depend on the integration of other conditions.

Before proceeding with a conceptualisation of scalability, it is worth stressing that this volume is mainly concerned with interpersonal civility and actions and stances that occur below the level of organisations and formal institutions. Many everyday peace acts and stances are informal, impromptu, and highly localised and occur 'under the radar'—characteristics that make replication, formalisation, and scaling up difficult. They tend to occur at the level below civil society organisations and peacebuilding projects and programmes. An everyday peace act might involve an older brother encouraging a younger counterpart to steer clear of a gang that engages in sectarian behaviour. This might entail quiet mentoring or subtle acts of guiding the younger sibling towards alternative pursuits. While this could be scaled up, for example, through organised programmes encouraging older siblings to look out for younger ones, such schemes might be very difficult to organise in practice and might seek to formalise and replicate what is happening organically. As will be explored below, scaling up often involves formalisation of procedures and wider territorial reach—thus posing difficulties for localised and personal actions and stances.

Literature on agriculture, ecology, and development has long been convinced of the multiplier benefits of scaling up and out practices that have worked at the local level.[78] Increasingly, the literature has differentiated between scaling up (vertical) and scaling out (horizontal). This distinction is useful to us given this book's recognition that peace and conflict are part of a multi-scalar systems or complex circuits of connections. It is possible to think of scaling up and out as overlapping or constituting part of the same process of complex adaptation. Scaling up might be thought of in terms of the professionalisation and formalisation of localised good practice. A violence-reduction scheme that works in one locality might be spotted by a donor and funded in order to run in other localities. This might involve the professionalisation of staff, the formalisation of processes that had been ad hoc, compliance with a range of norms (for example, on gender inclusion), and linkages to other organisations or networks. The temptation is to replicate and proselytise 'islands of success' in the hope that they will have greater success.[79] As André and Pache note, 'Rationalized systems and formalized processes have to be designed—they have to be introduced into the organizations and be maintained once introduced. They are often accompanied by

---

[78] Kindie Getnet and Charlotte MacAlister, 'Integrated Innovations and Recommendation Domains: Paradigm for Developing, Scaling-Out, and Targeting Rainwater Management Innovations', *Ecological Economics* 76 (2012): 34–41.

[79] Hans P. Binswanger and Swaminathan S. Aiyar, 'Scaling Up Community Driven Development: Theoretical Underpinnings and Programme Design Implications', *World Bank Policy Research Working Paper* 3039 (May 2003): 15.

a division of labor and differentiation'.[80] The advantages of this scaling up would include greater reach and efficiency.

From the point of view of this book, however, and its interest in sub-institutional and informal acts and stances of everyday peace, the concept of scaling out might be more useful. Many of the instances of everyday peace considered in this book are informal, ad hoc, and highly localised and often occur 'under the radar'. The formalisation and bureaucratisation might not sit well with the organic and hyperlocalised nature of many everyday peace activities. Scaling up also suggests intervention by an external actor, perhaps a donor or agency of the UN, who might seek to initiate, organise, and direct the scaling up. Thus, issues of power become germane. Scaling out, on the other hand, suggests a more organic process and sounds more appropriate in relation to everyday peace. This might involve the horizontal spread of a pro-peace or pro-social activity through imitation and word of mouth. Scaling out is about diffusion and spatial spread.[81] It conforms with John Paul Lederach's notion of 'middle out', whereby mid-level leaders can act as bridges between top-level leaders and the grassroots and might have a flexibility that more conspicuous leaders may not have.[82] The WWI trench ceasefires discussed later in this book provide a good example of how scaling out often occurs in practice: tentatively, locally, through word-of-mouth contact, and often out of sight of those in authority. Likewise, in contemporary conflict-affected areas, it might be the case that the pro-social actions of an individual or a small group of individuals are imitated by social entrepreneurs in other neighbourhoods. It could be that initiatives to be scaled out are seemingly irrelevant to those in positions of power given the scale of the conflict. They might include the gradual return to civility in everyday interactions between Serbs and Croats in the marketplace. This 'trend' might initially be restricted to a few individuals, and it might seem too localised to matter when compared with elite or national-level initiatives. Yet local-level practices may scale out organically with others adopting a civicness based on their own observations.

Issues of scalability should be borne in mind throughout this book. The promise of everyday peace is that it is something more than isolated instances of civility. If scaled out, and possibly scaled up, it can become a conflict disrupter that punctures the norms, narratives, and logics of violent conflict. In this view, everyday peace is a game changer through which individuals and communities, through speech acts and stances, change 'the feel' of a locality. In a sense, they

---

[80] Kevin André and Anne-Claire Pache, 'From Caring Entrepreneur to Caring Enterprise: Addressing the Ethical Challenges of Scaling Up Social Enterprises', *Journal of Business Ethics* 133 (2016): 666.

[81] Didi van Doren, Peter PJ Driessen, Hens Runhaar, and Mendel Giezen, 'Scaling-Up Low-Carbon Urban Initiatives: Towards a Better Understanding', *Urban Studies* 55, no. 1 (2018): 175–194.

[82] Lederach, *Building Peace*, 42.

give life to peace through their actions, help pacify communities and localities through everyday interactions. Clearly, such scalability will be dependent on the wider context and the extent to which it might be safe to engage in intergroup civic-ness or other signs of everyday peace. But at the same time, it is worth remembering that the micro-actions of individuals and small groups of individuals can help constitute the wider context. What seems to matter in many contexts is the organic adoption of pro-peace and pro-social behaviour. It is not simply about making new technology or information available; it is about its adoption.[83] This everyday adoption will involve repetition, iteration, and perhaps a growing awareness among participants and observers that pro-peace and pro-social acts are acceptable and can, possibly, be normalised. Much of this depends on the power context—a topic discussed in chapter 2.

Conclusion

The chief aim of this chapter has been to introduce two key concepts that will run through this book: the everyday and circuitry. Both can be regarded as epistemologies as they offer a way of seeing the world. They invite us to think seriously about issues of scale and the vantage point from which we see societies, actors, and structures. In particular, they invite us to move beyond naturalising the state or formal political institutions as the automatic starting points of investigations into how peace might be made and maintained. By looking beyond states, international organisations, INGOs, military actors, and political elites, we can more clearly see a political and social environment that is populated by a wide array of actors that include individuals, groups of individuals, families, friendship and colleague networks, and interest groups. This might be a more complex world than orthodox approaches to international relations and political science may be used to dealing with, but it also is likely to be more accurate in terms of the lives that people actually lead. The notions of the everyday and circuitry allow space for dynamism, innovation, and alternatives. Deviation from norms may occur only rarely, on the margins, or away from surveillance. But it does offer the chance to break away from thinking and practices in which conflict and discrimination against the other are regarded as normal.

Circuitry in particular allows us to think about connectivity and the ways in which seemingly isolated actions and thinking are parts of wider schemes. It allows us to see the everyday as a legitimate frame of reference and not one that

---

[83] Joanne Millar and John Connell, 'Strategies for Scaling Out Impacts from Agricultural Systems Change: The Case of Forages and Livestock Production in Laos', *Agricultural and Human Values* 27 (2010): 14.

must necessarily be seen as subservient to somehow more important frames such as the state or the international. While important in its own right, the everyday can be seen as connected to a series of institutions, practices, and modes of thinking. We can regard everyday peace actions and modes of thinking as parts of assemblages or complex adaptive systems. They might be difficult to see. For example, it might be difficult to situate a daily routine of a mother bringing her child to a cross-community playgroup in Belfast from wider political, economic, and cultural dynamics.[84] Yet circuitry opens the possibility of transnationalising and internationalising seemingly hyperlocal and inconsequential actions, stances, and modes of thinking. It allows us to see webs of implication and complex political and ideational economies that connect actors and actions on very different scales. This is important when thinking about everyday peace and the possibility of the actions of individuals and small groups of individuals to scale up and have more of a micro or immediate significance.

I conclude this chapter with the example of the Sudanese soldier who was among a relatively small group of soldiers who decided to protect civilian protesters from attacks by personnel of the intelligence services.[85] His action could have been a one-off act of humanity aimed at saving the lives of fellow citizens. But possibly it was more than that. A few days later, Bashir, who had been in power for twenty-six years, was deposed by a military coup. The civilian protests continued, and the military leaders were forced into a dialogue with the protesters about a transition to a more inclusive form of rule. While the picture is unclear,[86] it is worth considering whether the leaders of the military coup were unsettled by the actions of the soldier and his comrades. Perhaps they calculated that a mutiny was brewing and that they should partially satiate the demands of the protesters by deposing the president. The key point is that there is a possibility that the spur-of-the-moment actions of the soldier contributed in a pacific way to a wider situation. Thus, a micro-action may have impacted a macro-political situation, a situation that itself must be seen in the light of much wider political dynamics and structures at the international and transnational levels. Through circuitry, we can link the actions of the individual and a small group of individuals to much wider dynamics.

---

[84] Lisa Smyth and Martina McKnight, 'Maternal Situations: Sectarianism and Civility in a Divided City', *Sociological Review* 61, no. 2 (2013): 304–322.
[85] David Pilling, 'Sudan's Army Clashes with Security Forces over Protests', *Irish Times*, 8 April 2019.
[86] Human Rights Watch, 'Sudan, Events of 2019', https://www.hrw.org/world-report/2020/country-chapters/sudan.

2
Sociality, Reciprocity, and Solidarity

Introduction

This chapter seeks to add conceptual certainty to the concept of everyday peace by exploring three socio-material ideas that undergird it: sociality, reciprocity, and solidarity. These concepts help us understand the reasoning and actions that lie behind everyday peace. They also help explain structuration, or how micro and macro processes and structures come together.[1] The concepts of sociality, reciprocity, and solidarity are relatively unexplored in the peace and conflict studies literature and so deserve a detailed treatment. Everyday peace is taken to be the modes of thinking, stances, and actions deployed by individuals and groups to navigate through life in a deeply divided society. Everyday peace in this understanding is opportunistic and context-dependent and operates at the inter- and intragroup levels. The chapter is interested in the thinking and calculations behind pro-social intergroup exchanges across major conflict-related boundaries. Thus, for example, it is interested in the friendship between the Israeli and the Palestinian, or the small act of kindness shown by a Kosovan to a Serb, or the act of commercial solidarity shown by a Muslim to a Christian in Ambon, Indonesia, a city marked by sectarian tension and violence.[2] Tying the three concepts of sociality, reciprocity, and solidarity together, and indeed undergirding the concept of everyday peace, is the relational nature of peace. It requires social skills, emotional intelligence, and a recognition that we live in a world made up of other human beings.[3]

These positive intergroup exchanges are crucial to the story of everyday peace. They are important in any society and indeed make a society a society rather than merely a site of unbounded individualism. Acts of tolerance, kindness, patience, and sociality that cross age, class, gender, and geographic boundaries make life liveable and social. In a society marked by tension and violence, however, such

---

[1] Giddens, *The Constitution*.
[2] Sumanto Al Qurtuby, *Religious Violence and Conciliation in Indonesia: Christians and Muslims in the Moluccas* (London: Routledge, 2011), pp. 168–190.
[3] On relationality and peacebuilding, see Morgan Brigg, 'Relational and Essential: Theorizing Difference for Peacebuilding', *Journal of Intervention and Statebuilding* 12, no. 3 (2018): 352–366; Charles T. Hunt, 'Beyond the Binaries: Towards a Relational Approach to Peacebuilding', *Global Change, Peace and Security* 29, no. 3 (2017): 209–227.

acts have a particular importance. Everyday peace can be regarded as the first and last peace. It can be the last peace in that it may be the factor that prevents a situation from slipping from tension into violence. Sociality, reciprocity, and solidarity may be the social glue that means that community leaders can restrain hotheads. They may be the first steps towards normalisation after violence and may even, with time, lead to forms of reconciliation. Importantly, reconciliation is seen as an ongoing process rather than an end point. The contention of this chapter, in line with the rest of the book, is that the micro-actions and intentions of people on the ground do much to shape peace. They may give the peace its character, pace, and intensity. A peace might (or indeed might not) be declared by political leaders, but it is the everyday actions that embody and enliven it and give it its timbre. This everyday peace takes place on the street, in the grocery store, in the stairwell of the apartment building, on the school run, and in the workplace. It is the amalgam of millions of micro-actions and intentions that aggregate into society. Everyday peace, or the processes whereby societal norms and behaviours even out, takes place in every society but is especially salient in societies marked by tension and violent conflict. In such societies, careless actions and words can be inflammatory and lead to violence.

While this chapter concentrates on the everyday, the local, and the seemingly banal, it is worth noting that everyday peace occurs within, and contributes to, broader contexts. As discussed throughout this work, the notion of circuitry is proposed as a way of understanding how very localised attitudes and behaviours fit into wider political and economic schemes. These circuits, rather like biological, neural, or electronic circuits, illustrate the connectivities and apparent disconnectivities between local acts of everyday peace and wider political economies and movements. The circuits can be localised and appear self-contained, but ultimately they are housed in and made up of wider circuits. Understanding the connectivities—or lack of them—is crucial to the intellectual ambition of this book. There is a tendency to see conflict and violence as occurring 'over there', in faraway places populated by people who do not look or sound like us.[4] Such thinking, a form of conflict orientalism, means that we (if we live in the global north) can regard violent conflict as alien and removed from our way of life and logic. The notion of circuits allows us to see how chains of implication (if not more concrete chains of money, weapons, and conflict goods such as timber or diamonds) stretch from seemingly faraway conflict-affected locations to us—in a classroom or on a main street in Europe, North America, or elsewhere.[5]

---

[4] Tarak Barkawi and Keith Stanski, eds., *Orientalism and War* (London: Hurst, 2012).
[5] Christine Jojarth, *Crime, War and Global Trafficking: Designing International Collaboration* (Cambridge: Cambridge University Press, 2009); Aleksi Ylonen, 'Conflict Diamonds "Alive and Well": Failing Controls and the Changing Landscapes of Global Diamond Landscape', *African Security Review* 21, no. 3 (2012): 62–67.

The chapter proceeds by first reminding the reader of the pervasive nature of tension and conflict in many societies. It makes the point that in many societies, sectarianism, ethnic division, or racism may be so embedded into lifeworlds that it is structural.[6] This point is an important one, as it reminds us of the bravery involved in even micro-acts of everyday peace. Such acts may seem minuscule and insignificant against a backdrop of generalised tension and violence. Yet they may have significance in the sense that they are countercultural and amount to a form of resistance against dominant fissuring forces in society. To be identified as a conflict disrupter (and perhaps called a traitor or a coward) can be lonely, if not dangerous, in a society marked by tension and violence. This section also makes the point that conflict is apparently totalising. The 'apparently' is important. While conflict may seem all-encompassing, this book makes the case that it is very rarely completely totalising. Despite the power of states and others to mobilise populations and resources, it is important that we also acknowledge that space may exist for human agency, 'hidden transcripts',[7] dissent, and conflict disruption and disrupters. Indeed, the concept of everyday peace relies on these spaces—however small and temporary—being carved out and maintained. The refusal to accept that conflict and violence can be completely totalising is also in keeping with this book's belief in intersectionality and a rejection of the notion that domains such as public and private, or militant and civilian, are hermetically sealed and separate. Instead, apparently discrete domains often leach into one another, people are inconsistent in their beliefs and stances, and contexts change. One way of explaining the multiple connectivities between apparently separate domains is to draw on the concept of circuitry, as developed in chapter 1.

In its second substantive section, this chapter sketches the notion of everyday peace as a prelude to unpacking the concepts of sociality, reciprocity, and solidarity. Everyday peace is discussed both as a mode of reasoning and as a repertoire of actions and stances. Sociality, reciprocity, and solidarity are regarded as sometimes interlocking concepts. All depend on calculations of risk and reward, and they require emotional intelligence and the ability to 'read' and understand social contexts.

Third, the chapter unpacks the concept of sociality or the view that humanity is a uniquely cooperative species. Sociality may be readily apparent at the intragroup level. More interesting from our point of view are situations in

---

[6] For sophisticated renderings of the concept of structural violence, see O'Reilly, *Gendered Agency*; Wendy A. Vogt, 'Crossing Mexico: Structural Violence and the Commodification of Undocumented Central American Migrants', *American Ethnologist* 40, no. 4 (2013): 764–780; Katherine Hirschfeld, 'Rethinking "Structural Violence"', *Society* 54, no. 2 (2017): 156–162.

[7] Scott, *Domination*.

which sociality crosses major divisions in society. As will be explained later in the chapter, cross-boundary sociality is more than the particular act and intention behind it. It can also be a signifier of other factors, such as the recognition of out-group members being valid members of society or a statement on the type of society one would like to live in. The fourth section of the chapter examines the concept of reciprocity, or the mutual obligation that often follows actions. Again, the focus will be on reciprocity that crosses boundaries that are regarded as dominant in a context.

In its fifth section, the chapter unpacks the concept of solidarity, or the sense of identification that individuals and groups might have with others. Solidarity and group cohesion are crucial to the mobilisation of populations that may rally around a single national, religious, or racial identity. In short, it is often crucial in wars or nationalistic projects. As Siniša Malešević argues, 'In-group solidarity is not something that just happens. Instead it requires a great deal of long-term institutional work by states or social movements to promote group cohesion'.[8] What is less well explored, particularly in relation to conflict-affected scenarios, is how solidarity might cross boundaries. Such solidarity may be a highly political act, in that individuals and groups may stand with individuals and groups that are, through tradition or community-accepted norms, generally regarded as oppositional or antagonistic. As such, solidaristic acts in times of conflict are rare and risky. They might only take place during extraordinary circumstances. The nascent socialist internationalism before, during, and after World War I comes to mind as an example of when some soldiers and populations found common ground around rights and inequality in face of entrenched nationalism.[9] This form of conflict disruption is explored in greater detail in chapter 7.

In order to illustrate the mainly abstract discussion of sociality, reciprocity, and solidarity, the final substantive section of the chapter shows how these concepts operate in the real world. This illustration draws on thirty-one interviews conducted with adults in Lebanon in the summer of 2013. The focus of the interviews was on intergroup relations, with, for example, a Sunni interviewee being asked about their relations with non-Sunnis. The essential purpose of the chapter is to give intellectual scaffolding to the notion of everyday peace. An in-depth unpacking of its constituent concepts should allow us a clearer understanding

---

[8] Siniša Malešević, *The Sociology of War and Violence* (Cambridge: Cambridge University Press, 2012), 179.

[9] Kevin J. Callahan, 'The International Socialist Peace Movement on the Eve of WWI Revisited: The Campaign of "War against War" and the Basle International Socialist Congress in 1912', *Peace and Change* 29, no. 2 (2004): 147–176.

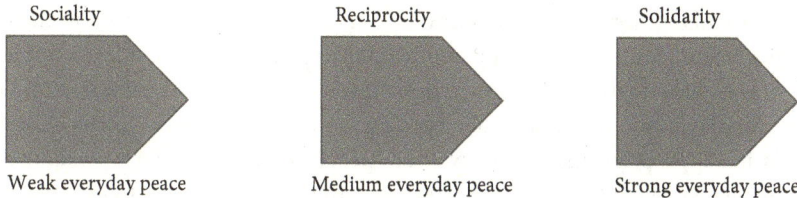

Figure 2.1. Everyday peace continuum.

of the calculations and mindsets required for everyday peace. The chapter also helps illustrate the contingent and context-dependent nature of everyday peace and the extent to which we can conceptualise different intensities of everyday peace. In very broad terms, we can equate sociality with weak everyday peace, reciprocity with medium everyday peace, and solidarity with strong everyday peace (see Figure 2.1).

The Apparently Totalising Nature of Conflict and Violence

I grew up in a small town in Northern Ireland at the height of the 1969–1994 civil war known as 'the Troubles'. Virtually all aspects of life were impacted by the three-sided tension, conflict, and violence between the British state, Catholic-nationalist-republicans, and Protestant-unionist-loyalists. Catholics and Protestants lived on different sides of the town, sent their children to different schools, socialised in different pubs and venues, and tended to shop in mainly Catholic or mainly Protestant shops. The smallest and most mundane aspects of life were shaped by the conflict and politico-religious affiliations. Catholics and Protestants tended to read different newspapers, follow different sports, and prefer different holiday destinations. This bifurcation was so ingrained into everyday life that it was regarded as normal. As the Troubles intensified, relationships and friendships between Catholics and Protestants came under increasing strain and were often difficult to maintain. For many people, especially those growing up in the 1970s and 1980s, it was unusual to have friends or contact with people from outside their in-group.

Before further exploring the notion of everyday peace, it is worth reminding ourselves of the pervasive and apparently all-encompassing nature of conflict and violence in many societies. The case is made in this book that violent conflict can be nearly, but not completely, totalising. These non-totalised spaces are of particular interest to this study as everyday peace can take root in them. While violent conflict can be apparently totalising, this book provides examples of where individuals and groups of individuals can sometimes carve out space for everyday peace. Given their ability to do so in the face of such overwhelming odds, it is appropriate that we see everyday peace as a form of power (as explored in chapter 3). The near-totalising nature of conflict has the ability to infringe on and shape multiple aspects of life. In such contexts, anything that stands counter to the totalising logic of conflict and division can be seen as disruptive, brave, and a form of subversion and hence is a worthy subject of study. It is important to see conflicts not as a series of incidents and episodes[10] but instead as the product of a mix of proximate and structural factors.[11] Certainly, violent conflict is marked by some incidents that have the ability to change the course of the overall conflict. Yet the conflict is more than the sum of the incidents. Instead, conflict, and especially civil conflict and predation and intimidation by armed groups, is best seen as a politico-social-cultural-economic amalgam that has the ability to pervade all aspects of life.[12] Work on conflict systems, that is, conceptualisations that regard conflict as part of interlocking and complex mechanisms, has been particularly good in capturing the extent to which conflict cannot be easily compartmentalised (something that feminist literature on intersectionality also does well).[13]

The following are excerpts from interviews conducted as part of the research project led by me (although the interviews were conducted by my very courageous colleague Zuhair Bashir).[14] The project involved interviewing Darfurians who had fled Darfur to UN-run refugee camps in Chad.[15] The interviews show that violent events had become normalised and that the fear of violence, intimidation, and arrest was ever present:

---

[10] Read and Mac Ginty, 'The Temporal Dimension', 153.

[11] Michael E. Brown, 'The Causes and Implications of International Conflict', in *Ethnic Conflict and International Security*, edited by Michael E. Brown (Princeton, NJ: Princeton University Press, 1993), pp. 3–26.

[12] A number of works have been particularly good in capturing the changing nature of violent conflict and its civil-military aspects, including Mary Kaldor, *New and Old Wars*, 3rd ed. (Cambridge: Polity, 2012); Ashutosh Varshney, *Ethnic Conflict and Civic Life: Hindus and Muslims in India* (New Haven, CT: Yale University Press, 2002); Stuart J. Kaufman, *Modern Hatreds: The Symbolic Politics of Ethnic War* (Ithaca, NY: Cornell University Press, 2001); David Keen, *Complex Emergencies* (Cambridge: Polity, 2008).

[13] See, for example, Harvey Starr and Stanley Dubinsky, *The Israeli Conflict System: Analytic Approaches* (London: Routledge, 2015); Nadine Ansborg, 'How Does Militant Violence Diffuse in Regions? Regional Conflict Systems in International Relations and Peace and Conflict Studies', *International Journal of Conflict and Violence* 5, no. 1 (2011): 174–187.

[14] Making Peacekeeping Data Work for the International Community project 2013–2017, funded by Economic and Social Research Council, ES/L007479/1.

[15] For context, see Marco Boggero, 'Darfur and Chad: A Fragmented Ethnic Mosaic', *Journal of Contemporary African Studies* 27, no. 1 (2009): 21–35.

Rape of women used to take place on [a] daily basis. Beating and killing of men happened repeatedly.[16]

Rape incidents were also very common to the extent that people in the camp stopped making reports about it to the police or to the UNAMID [United Nations African Union Mission in Darfur].[17]

Men were randomly arrested and killed. That is why they stopped moving outside their homes. It was only women [who could] go to the market to bring food or go outside the town to work and collect firewood. Though there was a high risk on women too; when [the] Janjaweed [a pro-government militia] met them they [raped] and beat them too.[18]

There was no security. Arabs were free to do anything, but our group was harassed, their movement was restricted, and they [could] be killed at any time. Even during the day no one was able to go to his or her farm and come back safe. Women were unable to go and collect firewood. During the night people were unable to visit their neighbours' homes. This was because it was too dangerous to move. The Janjaweed were hanging around and could loot anything.[19]

There was suppression and domination. The perpetrators would get into your house without your permission and do whatever they wanted to do: loot, beat and rape your family member in front of your eyes. If you [attempted] to resist, you would be shot dead on the spot. For me the situation was far too humiliating.[20]

The research interviews contain many other statements like the above. They point to the pervasive nature of violent conflict and how it has the potential to inflict multiple aspects of life. Moreover, the impact of conflict will be further increased by the effect of gender, class, and race.[21]

In an extreme case of compartmentalisation, or where conflict is apparently compartmentalised from the rest of life, we may think of the operator of a military drone that is controlled from Creech Air Force Base in Nevada in the United States.[22] The drone operator may work a regular shift pattern, go home in the evenings, have a reasonably normal family life, and remain, at all times, twelve thousand kilometres from the site of operation in Afghanistan. Yet if we scratch

---

[16] Interview with male, Goz Amir refugee camp, 6 May 2015.
[17] Interview with male, Goz Amir refugee camp, 8 May 2015.
[18] Interview with female, Djabal refugee camp, 21 May 2015.
[19] Interview with male, Djabal refugee camp, 23 May 2015.
[20] Interview with male, Djabal refugee camp, 26 May 2015.
[21] Joyce E. Everett, J. Camille Hall, and Johnnie Hamilton-Mason, 'Everyday Conflict and Daily Stressors: Coping Responses of Black Women', *Affilia: Journal of Women and Social Work* 25, no. 1 (2010): 30–42.
[22] M. C. Elish, 'Remote Split: A History of US Drone Operations and the Distributed Labor of War', *Science, Technology and Human Values* 42, no. 6 (2017): 1100–1131.

the surface of this division of labour that allows soldiers to be violence specialists and other members of society to be free from that responsibility, then we see that even professionalised militaries rely on the orientation of society to accept militarism.[23] The notion of circuitry, explored in chapter 1, can help us to conceive of the apparent compartmentalism at play in conflict contexts. The drone operator and his or her colleagues may be thought of as one branch of a circuit connected to the wider circuitry of the US military and associated bodies pursuing the war in Afghanistan. The individual drone operator will be connected to other familial and social circuits—some quite removed from the military and violent conflict. The drone operator, for example, may also be the mother of a young daughter and spend her weekends ferrying her child to ballet, swimming lessons, and birthday parties. These 'mommy circuits' may seem far removed from the business of waging war, but it is worth stressing the intersectionalities of life that are full of connectivities and fuzzy boundaries. In such a context, it is difficult to maintain the notion of an 'ideal type' of compartmentalised military organisation or campaign. Alongside its war-fighting capabilities, the US military (and many other militaries) is also host to a series of societal dysfunctions such as mental health problems among (former) troops, self-medication through drugs and alcohol, and spousal abuse.[24] A conflict such as the war against the Islamic State or the Taliban may seem to be removed from many in the United States, yet it has an impact on the everyday operation of society. Indeed, with a budget of $716 billion in 2019, a figure that amounts to 3.2 percent of gross domestic product, one can understand how defence spending plays a substantial role in the US economy in terms of employment and cultural impact.[25] The key point is that apparently compartmentalised aspects of conflict are actually interlinked with many other factors.

While the example above relates to a professionalised military in an apparently stable country, a major focus of this book is on deeply divided societies whereby potentially hostile populations live side by side or in close proximity to one another. Thus, the focus is on cases like families in Ukraine, some of whom might orientate culturally and politically towards Russia and others who are adamantly Ukrainian; or on villagers in northern Uganda, some of whom may have

---

[23] Kostas Gouliamos and Christos Kassimeris, eds., *The Marketing of War in the Age of Neo-militarism* (London: Routledge, 2012).
[24] Bryan G. Garber, Mark A. Zamorski, and Rahesh Jetly, 'Mental Health of Canadian Forces Members while on Deployment to Afghanistan', *Canadian Journal of Psychiatry* 57, no. 12 (2012): 736–744; Deborah A. Gibbs, Sandra L. Martin, and Ruby E. Johnson, 'Child Maltreatment and Substance Abuse among US Army Soldiers', *Child Maltreatment* 13, no. 3 (2008): 259–268; Erika J. Brooke and Jacinta M. Gau, 'Military Service and Lifetime Arrests: Examining the Effects of the Total Military Experience on Arrests in a Sample of Prison Inmates', *Criminal Justice Policy Review* 29, no. 1 (2015): 24–44.
[25] World Bank, 'Military Spending (% of GDP)', Washington, DC, 2019, https://data.worldbank.org/indicator/MS.MIL.XPND.GD.ZS.

been abducted as children and fought with the Lord's Resistance Army (LRA) and now are settled back among people who might be suspicious of their past deeds;[26] or on Coptic Christians living precariously in Muslim-majority Egypt. In these cases, and many others like them, the complete compartmentalisation of conflict is impossible. Some actors might have specialist roles, for example, as police officers or members of a militia, and the roles that people play will be shaped by class, gender, age, and other factors such as geography. Yet everyone in a conflict-affected society will be impacted to some extent by the tension and conflict. These impacts go far beyond the shocks and disruptions accruing from acts of direct violence. They pervade fundamental aspects of life such as identity, posture towards others, and the very logic that individuals and groups use when thinking about themselves, others, and political and economic problems. The sense-making tools and survival skills that people use to navigate through life in a conflict-affected society constitute a pathology or an all-encompassing means of processing information and acting accordingly.

Sectarianism, racism, and strongly held nationalism are systems of thinking and living.[27] They provide codes of prescriptions and proscriptions, ready-made scripts, and boundaries of acceptable and unacceptable attitudes and behaviours. The phrase 'banal sectarianism'[28] well sums up how exclusion along religious or other identity grounds permeates multiple aspects of life. For Halperin, the totalising nature of life in deeply divided societies means that

> it [the conflict] directly involves them, occupies a central position in public discourse and the public agenda, supplies information and experiences that compel society members to construct an adaptable worldview, is a determinative factor in the selection of lines of behaviors, continuously shapes the lives of the involved societies, and imprints upon every aspect of individual and collective life.[29]

Conflict in such circumstances dominates the lifeworld, even aspects of life that might be considered marginal and ephemeral. While this book concentrates on everyday peace, this peace often occurs within contexts of everyday conflict. Crucially, the conflict logic shapes life in the in-group. Contact with the

---

[26] Pamina Firchow and Roger Mac Ginty, 'Indivisibility as a Way of Life: Transformation in Micro-Processes of Peace in Northern Uganda', in *From Transitional to Transformative Justice*, edited by Paul Gready and Simon Robbins (Cambridge: Cambridge University Press, 2019): 261–280.

[27] This is well captured in Simeon Magliveras, 'The Ontology of Difference: Nationalism, Localism and Ethnicity in a Greek Arvanite Village', PhD diss., Durham University, 2010.

[28] Fanar Haddad, 'Sectarian Relations and Sunni Identity in Post–Civil War Iraq', in *Sectarian Politics in the Persian Gulf*, edited by Lawrence G. Potter (Oxford: Oxford University Press, 2014), 69.

[29] Eran Halperin, 'Emotion, Emotion Regulation, and Conflict Resolution', *Emotion Review* 6, no. 1 (2014): 69.

out-group might be limited, regulated, or non-existent. Meaningful Palestinian–Israeli encounters, for example, are extraordinarily difficult because of the Israeli separation wall designed to police and contain Palestinians, as well as a series of other legislative and security impediments.[30] In very many cases, most of life is lived at the in-group level. It is here that we see the policing and disciplining that encourage in-group homogeneity.[31] Depending on circumstances, to dissent from this homogeneity may be a courageous (even foolhardy) step. Work from social psychology is useful in illustrating the pressure to conform.[32] Dissent may incur costs. At a minimum, these costs might be recognition or being noticed as somehow different from the in-group. More seriously, it may involve being disciplined, sometimes through violence or sanctions, for breaking with the in-group code.

> *I remember, as a child of about six or seven, going to the local swimming pool with my big sister. I played with another boy of a similar age whom I had not met before. He asked me what religion I was, and I told him. We played some more, and then it was time to go home. On the walk, I told my sister about the question I had been asked. "What did you say?" she asked, and appeared cross that I had answered the boy's question. She then told my mother when we got home, and I was left in no doubt that I had broken the rules by answering the question. But I was confused, because I had never been told Northern Ireland's 'whatever you say, say nothing' rule before.*

Of course, the homogeneity of the in-group, and the extent to which the in-group/out-group boundary is policed, will differ according to context.[33] Groups are unlikely to be completely homogeneous. Instead, they are likely to be marked by a spectrum of identity intensity ranging from zealots to those with more malleable viewpoints. The intensity of feeling is likely to change over time according to conflict phase, electoral cycle, or exogenous factors such as pressures from the global economy. Yet the basic fact holds: conflict in deeply divided societies can be near totalising. It can saturate life from the fundamental (the identity we

---

[30] Stéphanie Latte Abdallah and Cédric Parizot, eds., *Israelis and Palestinians in the Shadows of the Wall: Spaces of Separation and Occupation* (Farnham, UK: Ashgate, 2015).

[31] Jojanneke Toorn, Naomi Ellemers, and Bertjan Doosje, 'The Threat of Moral Transgression: The Impact of Group Membership and Moral Opportunity', *European Journal of Social Psychology* 45, no. 5 (2015): 609–622.

[32] See Stephen Benard, 'Cohesion from Conflict: Does Intergroup Conflict Motivate Intragroup Norm Enforcement and Support for Centralized Leadership?' *Social Psychology Quarterly* 75, no. 2 (2012): 107–130; Jolanda Jellen and Matthew J. Hornsey, 'Deviance and Dissent in Groups', *Annual Review of Psychology* 65 (2014): 461–485.

[33] Roger Mac Ginty, 'Everyday Social Practices and Boundary-Making in Deeply Divided Societies', *Civil Wars* 19, no. 1 (2017): 4–25.

profess) to the subtle and seemingly banal (the foods we eat and what we call them).[34] The marginal spaces in which people might dissent, consider, and deviate from the in-group norms are the primary focus of this book. It is in these spaces that everyday peace might take root.

This section has outlined the often pervasive nature of tension and violent conflict in order to set the scene for the three undergirding concepts that contribute to everyday peace: sociality, reciprocity, and solidarity. These three ways of thinking and seeing the social world are disruptive to the norms of conflict. They have the potential to confront what might be taken-for-granted and internalised modes of thinking about the out-group. They represent behind-the-scenes stances and actions that constitute everyday peace. In themselves, they are forms of power. This power is often highly contingent and operates alongside, and sometimes in opposition to, other forms of power, but nevertheless it is a form of power in its own right. As discussed in chapter 3, it can be termed *Everyday Peace Power*.

Sociality

Humans are a social species, relying on social and affective bonds to make life at a minimum liveable but ideally convivial and fulfilling. This sociality occurs in all societies and is often superficial, banal, and a way of managing the co-presence of multiple individuals and groups. It relies on face-to-face encounter but also an implicit side-by-sidedness whereby individuals and groups 'rub along'.[35] Sociality extends to a shared sense that there should be joint goals and is dependent on sophisticated emotional intelligence unique to humans.[36] Key components of sociality include empathy, altruism, reciprocity, fairness, and collaboration—all of which give human life its texture, its ability to innovate and combine forces for public betterment.[37] It means that human populations, despite doomsayers proclaiming that the selfie and social media are a threat to humanity, are not made up of atomized individuals but are rich social constructions that extend beyond individualism.[38]

---

[34] Liora Gvion, *Beyond Hummus and Falafel: Social and Political Aspects of Palestinian Food in Israel* (Berkeley: University of California Press, 2012).

[35] Sophie Watson, 'The Magic of the Marketplace: Sociality in a Neglected Public Space', *Urban Studies* 46, no. 8 (2009): 1580. The notion of 'side by side' is explored in Eric Lepp, 'Division on Ice: Shared Space and Civility in Belfast', *Journal of Peacebuilding & Development* 13, no. 1 (2018): 32–45.

[36] Tim Lewis, 'Between the Social and the Selfish: Learner Autonomy in Online Environments'. *Innovation in Language Learning and Teaching* 7, no. 3 (2013): 201.

[37] Lewis, 'Between the Social and the Selfish', 198.

[38] Theodore R. Schatzki, 'A New Societist Social Ontology', *Philosophy of the Social Sciences* 33, no. 2 (2003): 174.

Focus group transcripts from the EPI project are full of references to family, friends, and community—all of which underline that we are, fundamentally, a social and relational species. Many respondents narrate peace, development, and (in)security in the first person. But alongside these first-person views, there are many that narrate their lives in the plural and see peace as a public and relational good. Youth focus group respondents in Atlantis, a town in South Africa's Western Cape, reflected on peace in the following ways: 'Peace for me is when a community is in peace and harmony', 'Peace for me is communication', 'Peace gives you a sense of belonging'.[39] For participants in a focus group among females in Kanyagoga in northern Uganda, peace existed 'when there is love between us', 'when I have the money to buy things . . . like food and clothes for my family members', and 'if community members are united'.[40] In these examples, and many others like them, peace was social and relational.

Taken together, the 'totality of interaction',[41] acts and attitudes of sociality constitute society. For Studdert, it is

> any and every conversation, every inter-action between people and objects, people and buildings, people and state apparatuses. Every day, everywhere, our lives are composed of social interactions, sociality of different strengths and meanings. It is the smile between two strangers, the groups chatting in the supermarket, or at work, at home or at the school gate. It occurs when fans sing team songs together at football matches. It happens online among the poor, the middle-class and the rich. It occurs when people talk to each other or enter a 12th-century cathedral or speak their mind about their job or give their opinions. It is the smallest of actions occurring infinitely in the largest of arenas; and again in the smallest.[42]

Such an expansive definition obviously creates problems for comprehension. If every speech and act by a human involving another human is—potentially—sociality, then we may struggle to define it or develop ways of using sociality as an analytical tool. To help us with these endeavours, four points are worth making.

The first is that sociality dwells, to a large extent, in the affective realm.[43] As such, it might be difficult to identify and access and will vary enormously from person to person and context to context. Sociality manifests itself differently in

---

[39] EPI project youth focus group, Atlantis, South Africa, 17 September 2013.
[40] EPI project female focus group, Kanyagoga, Uganda, 14 February 2014.
[41] David Studdert, 'Sociality and a Proposed Analytic for Investigating Communal Being-ness', *Sociological Review* 64, no. 4 (2016): 624.
[42] Studdert, 'Sociality'.
[43] For discussion of emotion and politics, see Linda Åhäll, 'Affect as Methodology: Feminism and the Politics of Emotion', *International Political Sociology* 12, no. 1 (2018): 36–52; Linda Åhäll and Thomas Gregory, *Emotions, Politics and War* (London: Routledge, 2015).

different cultures, is dynamic, and is impacted by race, gender, age, and class. Anything connected with the emotional spectrum can be deeply unnerving to social scientists and positivists who might want to, quite literally, get the measure of life through a series of metrics. Understanding sociality means coming to terms with the fact that not all aspects of life are measurable.[44] Instead, the affective aspects of life are about feelings, sentiment, warmth, and understanding, as well as negative and antisocial emotions such as envy and a desire to maintain a distance from others. The essential point is that it does not serve us well to see individuals or groups of individuals through a completely rationalist prism made up of the 'rational, unitary, logocentric subject as agent'.[45] Yes, people will act rationally in many instances, but life, and particularly the social and familial aspects of it, are made up of much more than rational calculation. Instead, sociomoral logics are at play, and the 'selfishness of homo economicus' is tempered by a range of other influences that draw on the affective human repertoire.[46]

A second point is to underscore that human sociality is emergent, evolving, and sometimes experimental. Of course, it might follow patterns, be based on a shared script, and depend on the comfort offered by familiarity. In some circumstances, however, it might generate new forms of intra- and intergroup contact and new spaces of agency.[47] This might involve individuals and groups feeling their way through a social environment and working out what is possible and impossible given social strictures. Thus, for example, would it be possible for a member of Myanmar's Bahar majority to employ a member of the Rohingya minority at a time of heightened tensions between the groups (especially if that tension was fomented by the state)? It may be that individuals and groups who would want to participate in such engagements might have to wait and see, take small exploratory steps, and pick the most propitious moment. Writing on intergroup contact in India, Hoek and Gandhi note how 'the information required to build social aptitude is necessarily partial, fragmentary, evanescent, speculative and conjunctural'.[48] In other words, we often operate on the basis of imperfect information, and information deficits may well be enlarged in contexts of division and conflict. Acting on the basis of imperfect information can involve risks.

---

[44] For discussion of researching hard-to-measure subjects and hard-to-access populations, see Firchow and Mac Ginty, 'Including Hard-to-Access Populations'.
[45] Couze Venn, 'Post-Enlightenment Cosmopolitanism and Transmodern Socialities', *Theory, Culture & Society* 19, no. 1–2 (2002): 65–80.
[46] Dominique Roux and Valérie Guillard, 'Circulation of Objects between Strangers in Public Space: An Analysis of Forms of Sociality among Disposers and Gleaners', *Recherche et Applications en Marketing* 31, no. 4 (2016): 38.
[47] Ivan Arenas, 'Assembling the Multitude: Material Geographies of Social Movements from Oaxaca to Occupy', *Environment and Planning D: Society and Space* 32 (2014): 433–449.
[48] Lotte Hoek and Ajay Gandhi, 'Provisional Relations, Indeterminate Conditions: Non-Sociological Sociality in South Asia', *South Asia: Journal of South Asian Studies* 39, no. 1 (2016): 69.

This leads to the third point in relation to sociality: timing matters. There may be circumstances and times when intergroup sociality is impossible, for example, a period of heightened tension following a violent incident. But at other times, there may be temporary overrides whereby the normal distance between groups can be disrupted. Bissell notes how 'Through the movement of affect, dispositions become fostered and bodies become primed to act in different ways'.[49] Very specific and often localised contexts come into play that may make it possible for individuals and groups to act beyond convention. This will require careful navigation, a feeling of the way to ascertain what is possible and what might incur costs from both the in-group and the out-group. Hoek and Gandhi mention 'temporary toeholds' and say 'Provisionally positioning oneself within a given space or set of relations, such perches are temporary as shifting alliances and changing time-frames require relocation'.[50] This notion of 'perches' is useful, as it suggests the precarity of those engaging in intergroup sociality. The term does not necessarily suggest comfort or necessarily a long-term and secure arrangement. It suggests acting on imperfect knowledge, sometimes taking a risk, and always being alert to possible dangers. It is worth reducing (if this is the correct word) this to the everyday and prosaic levels and how people make calculations in real time. A female focus group respondent in South Africa noted, 'You have to look up and down the street before you leave your house'. Another female respondent in the same focus group gave an insight into how she 'reads' street scenes and evaluates situations: 'You see their body language. People look suspicious. They walk slowly with their hands in their pockets. They dress in a creepy way with a balaclava or big hair or a big coat—a bomber jacket to hide weapons'.[51] The key point is that context, and the ability of individuals and groups of individuals to read context, is crucial.

A final point to make on sociality at this stage is to counsel in favour of caution in relation to literature on social media and sociality. Much of this literature verges on the alarmist regarding how social media and our apparent addiction to technological devices are interrupting and threatening the very existence of more traditional forms of communication.[52] Certainly, social media offers 'a new kind of sociality'—one that is scaled differently and is often more visual.[53] Societies, as with all forms of technology, are finding hybrid and complementary forms

---

[49] David Bissell, 'Passenger Mobilities: Affective Atmospheres and the Sociality of Public Transport', *Environment and Planning D: Society and Space* 28 (2010): 284.
[50] Hoek and Gandhi, 'Provisional Relations', 72.
[51] EPI female focus group, De Doorns, South Africa, 11 December 2016.
[52] Katherine Ormerod, *Why Social Media Is Ruining Your Life* (London: Cassell, 2018).
[53] Janet Borgerson and Daniel Miller, 'Scalable Sociality and "How the World Changed Social Media": Conversation with Daniel Miller', *Consumption Markets & Culture* 19, no. 6 (2016): 532; Maurizio Ghisleni, 'The Sociology of Everyday Life: A Research Program on Contemporary Sociality', *Social Science Information* 56, no. 4 (2017): 536–537.

of sociality and modernity that see an evolving accommodation between existing social practices and social practices enabled by technology.[54] Rather than seeing 'network sociality' as threatening a 'de-socialization' of human relations, it offers blended forms of sociality.[55] Indeed, Richmond notes how digitalisation allows for the 'fundamental amplification' of existing networks that has potentially 'augmented humanity, changed society, altered the nature of the state (and its relevance), influenced global governance, and created new forms of global collaboration and conflict'.[56] Crucially, we must be careful not to underestimate the continued role of emotional intelligence to be deployed by people in their everyday encounters. Notwithstanding the fact that they might be clutching the latest iPhone and organise their lives with the help of multiple apps, sociality still requires human sensibility, an ability to gauge situations, and being able to form and maintain interpersonal relationships. The social is still important in an era of social media.

Reciprocity

The second concept that lies at the heart of everyday peace is reciprocity, or the notion and practice that humans will return the favour. As with sociality and solidarity, reciprocity is formative of social cooperation and order in any society, not necessarily one lumbered by conflict and tension. As Narotzky and Moreno observe, reciprocity 'appears to be linked to the idea of a social contract and seems to underpin the contract itself, transforming a Hobbesian hell full of selfish warring individuals into "a society"'.[57] At its base, in a positive sense, is sociality or a recognition of the other and a belief that sharing will make life better. This basic understanding of the utility of sharing was represented in focus groups in South Africa, with women in one community variously noting, 'We need each other', or 'we must stand together. We must look after each other—share our setbacks'.[58] Reciprocity comes in different forms and intensities. Altruistic reciprocity may see an individual or group giving up resources without expectation of a specific reward. Instead, they may be motivated by a desire to promote a generalised system of reciprocity or by the notion that they can expect an inward transfer at a time of need. They may even be motivated by their own indebtedness in the past

---

[54] Dong-Hoo Lee, 'Smartphones, Mobile Social Space, and New Sociality in Korea', *Mobile Media & Communication* 1, no. 3 (2013): 273.

[55] Andreas Wittel, 'Towards a Network Sociality', *Theory, Culture & Society* 18, no. 6 (2001): 64.

[56] Oliver P. Richmond, 'Peace in Analogue/Digital International Relations', *Global Change, Peace and Security* 32, no. 3 (2020): 9.

[57] Susana Narotzky and Paz Moreno, 'Reciprocity's Dark Side: Negative Reciprocity, Morality and Social Reproduction', *Anthropological Theory* 2, no. 3 (2002): 284.

[58] EPI project female focus group, Atlantis, South Africa, 17 September 2013.

and the desire to make restitution.[59] Strategic reciprocity is guided by an expectation of future rewards, and so it is rational and self-interested. Yet if transformed into a system, this self-interested reciprocity can allow a society to operate with multiple beneficiaries.

Consider, for example, the practice of holding open a door for someone else as you enter a building; it is extremely unlikely that you will meet the beneficiary at precisely the same moment that you exit it. In other words, it is unlikely that you will receive a direct reward. Instead, the calculation is more complex. In the first instance, you may receive performative rewards by being seen to hold open a door for someone else; it is classic virtue signalling. You will be perceived as a 'good person'. But more than this, you are signalling about the type of society you want to live in: one in which people hold open doors and observe manners and courtesy. In a deeply divided society, or one emerging from violent conflict, signals of civicness can be instrumental in lowering identity-related temperatures and normalising intergroup relations.

All reciprocity faces the spectre of free riders, or those who exploit inward transfers but do not reciprocate.[60] Yet what makes reciprocity interesting, and crucial to the story of pro-social dynamics and pacific relations in times of conflict, is that pure economic rationality does not explain many cases of transfer and exchange. Certainly, economic rationality based on observed evidence is important in many instances. Firms in business with one another, for example, may wait for payment before extending more goods or credit to other parties.[61] Economic theory, however, is not always a reliable guide to instances of people acting on sentiment, intuition, guesswork, and 'taking a punt'.[62] A core aspect of reciprocity is how it might shape the wider society. It is not simply a transfer of resources, possibly in the expectation of a return transfer. Instead, the principle and practice of reciprocity set communal norms, signify interdependence, and underscore human ties and sociality. Komter notes the 'morally binding character of reciprocity' and how the informal contracts of such exchanges are 'effective in creating the social cement of society'.[63]

The 'special bonds and obligations between people' arising from reciprocity can help give a society its character.[64] They can be 'system stabilizing' and

---

[59] Anita Manatschal, 'Reciprocity as a Trigger of Social Cooperation in Contemporary Immigration Societies?' *Acta Sociologica* 58, no. 3 (2015): 235.

[60] Andrew Lister, 'Markets, Desert, and Reciprocity', *Politics, Philosophy & Economics* 16, no. 1 (2017): 61.

[61] Anna Swärd, 'Trust, Reciprocity, and Actions: The Development of Trust in Temporary Interorganizational Relations', *Organization Studies* 37, no. 12 (2016): 1841–1860.

[62] Luigino Bruni, 'The Happiness of Sociality. Economics and Eudaimonia: A Necessary Encounter', *Rationality and Society* 22, no. 4 (2010): 383–406.

[63] Aafke Komter, 'Gifts and Social Relations: The Mechanisms of Reciprocity', *International Sociology* 22, no. 1 (2007): 103.

[64] Narotzky and Moreno, 'Reciprocity's Dark Side', 281.

institutionalised in the sense of creating and maintaining a moral order.[65] They will be shaped by culture[66] and the prevailing societal ethical compass that will draw from religiosity and spiritual belief,[67] as well as more prosaic factors such as the immediate geography and the economic context.[68] Given the interest of this book in everyday peace, our particular interest is in cases of intergroup reciprocity in conflict-affected societies. A key issue in many conflicts is the development and maintenance of narratives that paint the other as being untrustworthy and possessing a different, necessarily deficient, moral outlook. To engage in reciprocal behaviour with out-group members might therefore require a leap of faith or a hope that faith in the other will be repaid. It may also require courage to override the prevailing worldview of the in-group who might write the other off as being deceitful. This might especially be the case during and in the aftermath of violent conflict in which atrocities have been committed and intergroup relationships have been strained, if not ruptured.

Initiating contact with the other side, especially if it involves the first move, can be risky. But it can also be the 'starting mechanism' for new forms of social cooperation.[69] This chimes with the view of everyday peace as being 'the first peace'. Reciprocity can disrupt the expected norm of deceitfulness and treachery by the other side. If embedded in the everyday, and taking on banal characteristics, it can help kick-start notions of normalcy and mainstream intergroup exchange.

Solidarity

Solidarity is the third component of everyday peace and may be regarded as the most onerous of the triad of sociality, reciprocity, and solidarity. The concept and practice of solidarity takes sociality to a new level. While sociality can take multiple forms of entanglement, some of them very slight, such as merely recognising the existence of the other, solidarity suggests a much more definite and action-oriented path. Thus, solidarity involves active support for a cause. It is not enough to quietly sympathise with a cause, for example, the Extinction Rebellion. This sympathy must take shape in activism or some material form.

---

[65] Manatschal, 'Reciprocity as a Trigger', 234.
[66] Namrata Goyal and Joan G. Miller, 'The Importance of Timing in Reciprocity: An Investigation of Reciprocity Norms among Indians and Americans', *Journal of Cross-Cultural Psychology* 49, no. 3 (2017): 381–403.
[67] Xiangqun Chang, 'Reciteriety (lishang-wanglai): A Chinese Model of Social Relationships and Reciprocity—State and Villagers' Interaction 1936–2014', *Journal of Sociology* 52, no. 1 (2016): 106.
[68] Narotzky and Moreno, 'Reciprocity's Dark Side', 282
[69] Manatschal, 'Reciprocity as a Trigger', 235.

Solidarity is the stuff of many societies engaged in conflict. Nations, armed groups, resistance movements, authoritarian leaders, and many others rely on a sense of solidarity or of shared communal sentiment.[70] This is a key mobilisation tool that creates and seeks to maintain social capital based on identity claims or shared grievances.[71] Communitarian logic is based on identification with others. In deeply divided societies, however, these forms of identification will often have a negative dimension, with individuals and groups identifying themselves as against or different from the other. EPI project focus groups showed a good deal of what might be termed 'negative solidarity' or exclusive, in-group solidarity that emphasised in-group unity and blamed outgroups for trouble. A December 2016 focus group in a poor community about 140 kilometres from Cape Town, South Africa, heard many cases of outsiders being blamed for crime: 'You can't actually walk [on the streets]—it's not safe. There are refugees from Zimbabwe and Lesotho'; 'Zimbabweans mean South Africans can't get jobs'; 'Most crime is by Zimbabweans'; 'The girl was found dead. The man was from Lesotho'.[72] Our interest, however, goes beyond this intragroup solidarity and seeks to unpack intergroup solidarity in contexts of division and conflict. In such cases, solidarity would involve pro-social acts across the main fissure in society. As such, it may involve bravery on the part of those involved, as they may be vulnerable to censure or worse from their in-group peers.

One example of solidarity has been community members in northern Uganda tolerating, accepting, and even welcoming back people who had been abducted by the LRA. These former community members may well have been perpetrators of atrocities in the very towns and villages in which they grew up. Yet, and as was demonstrated in some of the EPI project focus group transcripts, solidarity was shown to these community members. One male in a focus group in Attiak said, 'these days we live with strangers and even welcome them. But [in] those days you could think that the stranger was a rebel'. A fellow focus group member and a former child soldier remarked, 'While I was still in captivity I felt no peace, but now . . . I can move to any place I want to without fear'. Remarkably, one focus group respondent said, 'We need help for formerly abducted persons. They have returned home, but they have nowhere to start from. If possible, they should be helped to start their lives afresh'.[73]

Like sociality and reciprocity, solidarity is likely to be context-dependent, with some contexts and time periods more favourable than others.[74] In some

---

[70] Toorn, 'The Threat'.

[71] Clarissa I. Cortland et al., 'Solidarity through Shared Disadvantage: Highlighting Shared Experiences of Discrimination Improves Relations between Stigmatized Groups', *Journal of Personality and Social Psychology* 113, no. 4 (2017): 547–567.

[72] EPI project verification focus group, De Doorns, South Africa, 11 December 2016.

[73] EPI project focus group, Attiak, Uganda, 4 October 2013.

[74] James Hawdon and John Ryan, 'Social Relations That Generate and Sustain Solidarity after a Mass Tragedy', *Social Forces* 89, no. 4 (2011): 1363–1384.

cases of conflict, a particular event has sparked intergroup solidarity whereby groups that normally do not associate or show solidarity are prompted to protest together. The kidnap and subsequent murder of a local politician, Miguel Ángel Blanco Garrido, by Basque militants in 1997 provoked mass rallies across Spain including in the Basque Country.[75] Many Basques who were normally supportive of the separatist group Euskadi Ta Askatasuna found themselves—perhaps temporarily—in sympathy with Spaniards who supported a unitary Spain. Similarly, Northern Ireland experienced relatively unprecedented intergroup solidarity following the 1998 Omagh bombing. The bombing, which killed twenty-nine people, came months after the Belfast Agreement peace accord had been reached, and many believed that a corner had been turned. Individuals and groups who ordinarily would not worship or socialise together held joint protests and vigils to remember the dead. Very probably, this did not change participants' outlook on wider political issues. But interdenominational prayer services in remembrance of the dead did continue for decades, suggesting that the solidarity was more than momentary.[76]

For Kolers, solidarity is inherently political: 'The essential condition of solidarity is acting with others, even if one disagrees with the group's chosen ends or means'.[77] It requires a crossing of a significant societal boundary to stand with others. Such solidarity could take multiple forms, such as advocacy on behalf of others, protesting alongside them, or helping out-group members who have been affected by violence. In many instances, it may have a performative and public dimension, thus potentially making those engaged in solidarity with out-group members visible to in-group members. In many conflict contexts, however, that would simply be too dangerous. Concealing Jews in occupied Europe, during World War II, for example, was necessarily a secret activity.

Two issues seem important with regard to solidarity. The first is sustainability: to what extent can acts of solidarity between individuals and groups be sustained over time? While acts of solidarity can be important, they may simply be episodes that disrupt—only temporarily—the meta-politics of the society. The examples above illustrate how specific outrages can prompt cross-communal sentiment. But is it possible to find durable solidarity, especially as most of the conflicts that interest us are long-standing? As the section on

---

[75] 'A Murder Too Far', *Economist*, 17 July 1997, http://www.economist.com/node/151703. For an account of these events, and the general context at the time, see Ludger Mees, 'The Basque Peace Process, Nationalism and Political Violence', in *The Management of Peace Processes*, ed. John Darby and Roger Mac Ginty (Basingstoke, UK: Macmillan, 2000), 154–193.

[76] Hawdon and Ryan, 'Social Relations', 1364; 'Service to Mark 19th Anniversary of Omagh Bomb', *Ulster Herald*, 12 August 2017, http://ulsterherald.com/2017/08/12/service-mark-19th-anniversary-omagh-bomb/.

[77] Avery H. Kolers, 'Dynamics of Solidarity', *Journal of Political Philosophy* 20, no. 4 (2012): 365–383.

remarkable friendships in chapter 7 shows, it is possible to find examples, often at the individual or small-group level, of long-term support for the other. Many anti-Zionist Jews, for example, have a track record of protesting against the nationalism and exclusion that seem part of a Zionist version of Israel. For some, the main issue is the nature of Israel and its internal disposition in relation to secular versus religious matters.[78] For others, the anti-Zionism is concerned with the treatment of Palestinians. One American anti-Zionist Jew noted the 'daily brutality, land occupation, militarism, settlements, and dispossession' suffered by Palestinians but also noted how his anti-Zionist stance incurred significant in-group censure and policing: 'While in Israel this year I lost count of the number of times I was quizzed as to my religious heritage by random Israelis. The question, "Are you a Jew?" was asked of me more in a month than at any other time in my life. Refusing to answer caused some consternation.'[79] The key point is that a stance of solidarity with the out-group may come with costs, and so individual or groups of individuals may feel cautious about sustaining that position.

A second issue in connection with solidarity is the depth of the solidarity or the extent to which it is meaningful. This is difficult to gauge, as solidarity can occur at many different levels. One indicator of the depth of solidarity, however, may be the extent to which an individual or group risks the opprobrium of in-group members by showing solidarity with out-group members. Clearly, this is context-dependent. Standing up to an authoritarian regime to protect members of a persecuted minority requires immense courage. The nascent White Rose movement of German students against Nazism, for example, saw its members arrested and executed.[80] Solidarity that is completely under the radar, out of sight and earshot, for example, an Israeli Jew expressing sympathy to an individual Palestinian in response to Israeli government actions, is of more limited value than forms of solidarity that take material or public form. Yet it may be difficult for Israeli Jews to show such solidarity. The demise of the Israeli peace movement, for example, is instructive of how difficult it is to maintain pacific and solidarist views in a polity increasingly geared towards nationalism and exclusion.[81]

---

[78] Nir Hasson, 'The Last Jewish Community Holding Out against Zionism', *Haaretz*, 18 August 2017, https://www.haaretz.com/israel-news/.premium.MAGAZINE-the-last-jewish-community-holding-out-against-zionism-1.5443981.

[79] Ray Filar, 'Why I'm an Anti-Zionist Jew', *OpenDemocracy*, 16 April 2016, https://www.opendemocracy.net/transformation/ray-filar/why-i-am-antizionist-jew. See also commentary on the Jews for Justice for Palestinians website, https://jfjfp.com/.

[80] Inge Scholl, *The White Rose: Munich 1942–1943* (Middletown, CT: Wesleyan University Press, 1983); Erin Blakemore, 'The Secret Student Group That Stood Up to the Nazis', *Smithsonian Magazine*, 22 February 2017, https://www.smithsonianmag.com/smart-news/the-secret-student-group-stood-up-nazis-180962250/.

[81] Giles Fraser, 'Against the War: The Movement That Dare Not Speak Its Name in Israel', *Guardian*, 7 July 2014.

Sociality, Reciprocity, and Solidarity in Action

Having discussed sociality, reciprocity and solidarity largely as conceptual abstractions, this section now draws particularly on interviews from Lebanon to illustrate these aspects of everyday peace in action. Specifically, it looks at whether we can identify active and meaningful intergroup interactions and exchange in a context in large part defined by conflict and division. Interviewees were seventeen men and fourteen women, ages twenty-two to eighty-five (mean age fifty-one), drawn from the main politico-religious groups in Lebanon. Thirteen interview subjects self-identified as being religiously or culturally Christian (including Orthodox, Maronite, Armenian, and Catholic) (seven female), nine were Sunni (four female), seven were Shia (two female), and two were Druze (neither female). Given that Lebanon has not had a census since 1932,[82] it is impossible to judge how scientifically representative the interview sample was, but I am confident that a good cross-section of society and opinion is contained in the sample.

By way of context, it is worth remembering Lebanon's long history of conflict, division, and sectarianism.[83] The country is a confection of politico-religious identity groups, with strong kinship networks.[84] It is a colonial invention in which postcolonial state-building has had limited success.[85] Indeed, it can be argued that elites in charge of the state have generally shown little interest in state-building in the sense of exerting a maximal version of sovereignty and developing an efficient and comprehensive bureaucracy that has a monopoly of violence.[86] Instead, and in keeping with a pattern in many postcolonial states, we have seen the capture of some state functions and markets by various elites and the promotion of sectarian logics. Lebanon, and the territory that pre-existed the state of Lebanon, has been the site of multiple conflicts, ethnic cleansings and pogroms, and chronic intergroup tension.[87] In the modern era, the 1975–1990 civil war has been a defining event,[88] costing an estimated 70,000 to 150,000

---

[82] Rania Maktabi, 'The Lebanese Census of 1932 Revisited: Who Are the Lebanese?' *British Journal of Middle East Studies* 26, no. 2 (1999): 219–241.

[83] A good insight into the entrenched nature of sectarianism is provided by Melani Cammett, 'Sectarianism and the Ambiguities of Welfare in Lebanon', *Current Anthropology* 56, S11 (2015): S76–S87.

[84] Fawwaz Traboulsi, *A History of Modern Lebanon* (London: Pluto, 2007): 128–183.

[85] Elizabeth Thompson, *Colonial Citizens: Republican Rights, Paternal Privilege and Gender in France, Syria and Lebanon* (New York: Columbia University Press, 2000).

[86] Kristina Tschunkert and Roger Mac Ginty, 'Legitimacy in Lebanon', in *Local Legitimacy and International Peacebuilding*, ed. Oliver P. Richmond and Roger Mac Ginty (Edinburgh: Edinburgh University Press, 2020), 247.

[87] Ussama Samir Makdisi, *The Culture of Sectarianism: Community, History, and Violence in Nineteenth Century Ottoman Lebanon* (Berkeley: University of California Press, 2000).

[88] For a searing account of the civil war, see Robert Fisk, *Pity the Nation: Lebanon at War* (Oxford: Oxford University Press, 1990).

lives, and displacing about 1 million people.[89] Crucial to the story of Lebanon's conflicts and divisions is its location, with Israel being a particularly aggressive neighbour responsible for invasions, occupations, and punitive attacks. Syria acted as a coercive, but partially stabilising, force in the aftermath of the 1989 Ta'if Accord that ended the civil war[90] and, more recently, a destabilising force with its own descent into civil war and the movement of about 1 million Syrian refugees into Lebanon.[91]

As befits a deeply divided society, the interviews contained many references to sectarianism. So, for example, a Christian interviewee mentioned how, as a child, he was not allowed to play outside lest he come into contact with Shias.[92] A Sunni interviewee told of how she had stopped frequenting the nearby Shia-run grocery store because of intensifying sectarianism.[93] A Christian told of how he advocated not selling land in the area to non-Christians,[94] a view shared by a Sunni real estate developer who would not sell residences to Shias for political reasons or to Christians for religious reasons.[95] These views, and many like them, constitute the sectarian lifeworlds that make up a deeply divided society. They illustrate the embedded and subtle ways in which divisions are marbled through multiple aspects of life.

While many accounts of Lebanon's past and present concentrate on violence and sectarian tension, it is worth noting that between, and even during, periods of violence, there has been much accommodation, toleration, and acceptance of the other. This has occurred at the local level of the village, town, and city neighbourhood and involved individuals and very often family groups. It is, in a very real sense, everyday peace. Often, it occurs on the margins and is the exception to an otherwise dominant worldview of exclusion. The remainder of this section draws on the interview material to identify the components of everyday peace already discussed in this chapter: sociality, reciprocity, and solidarity. Sociality was represented in the interviews through empathy and affective connection with out-group members and through a sense of fairness and collaboration with others. Thus, for example, many interviewees were able to make cross-communal identification with out-group members. One eighty-one-year-old female villager reflected:

---

[89] The low estimate is from Taboulsi, 'A History', 238; the high one is from Marie-Joëlle Zahar, 'Peace by Unconventional Means: Lebanon's Ta'if Agreement', in *Ending Civil Wars: The Implementation of Peace Agreements*, ed. Stephen John Stedman, Donald Rothchild, and Elizabeth M. Cousens (Boulder, CO: Lynne Rienner, 2012): 572.
[90] Karam Karam, 'The Ta'if Agreement: New Order, Old Framework', *Accord* 24 (2012): 36–39.
[91] Zahar, 'Peace', 75–76.
[92] Interview with male Christian, Jouniyeh, Lebanon, 10 June 2013.
[93] Interview with female Sunni, Beirut, 6 July 2013.
[94] Interview with male Christian, Deir El Amar, 11 July 2013.
[95] Interview with male Sunni, Beirut, 27 June 2013.

Days here moved quickly, we all grew up, we lost people, some are sick and some people are holding, but throughout our lives we stayed one hand even during the wars. We shared everything here—bad days, good days, wedding, funerals, everything, and we don't have to talk about our differences.[96]

A seventy-nine-year-old from a different village shared the following sentiment:

We share the same village, same land, same history, we just differ in our religious belief and ways of thinking, so that was never a problem. . . . We were one hand against any potential threat from outside the village or what we back then called strangers, whether a Muslim or a Christian. A stranger for us is anyone who doesn't belong to this village.[97]

What is interesting about these quotations is that geographical belonging—to the village—is privileged above sectarian identification. Obviously, this is specific to the socio-geography of place, but it does disrupt the dominant sectarian logic that religious identity supersedes other claims to identity. As one interviewee observed, 'sharing a common religion does not mean that it is enough for someone to base his entire life and build circles of persons and friendships upon only this condition'.[98] This seemingly banal observation is actually significant in a society often characterised in blunt homogenising terms as 'sectarian' or 'divided'.

This claim to an identity that was not primarily sectarian was found in other quotations that mentioned either Lebanon as a single nation or the notion of society as preferable to compartmentalised sectarianism. This is significant in that many Lebanese politicians—even those in government—do not promote the idea of Lebanon. A number of interviewees objected to the conflation of religion and politics, and especially the automaticity whereby religious identity was regarded as a signifier of political preference.[99]

One Shia interviewee emphasised the importance of intergroup sociality thus: 'You [will] see no more social ties if they form different sects. . . . Now you hear voices categorising people: he is Shia, he is Sunni, so I don't deal with Christians, no I don't speak with Shia, and so on. No society can survive like this'.[100]

---

[96] Interview with female Shia, Werdanieh, 2 June 2013.
[97] Interview with female Christian Orthodox, Tal Abbas, 19 June 2013.
[98] Interview with Shia female, Beirut, 30 July 2013.
[99] Interview with male Sunni, Beirut, 24 June 2013; interview with male Sunni, Beirut, 21 June 2013; interview with male Shia, Tyr, 5 July 2013.
[100] Interview with male Shia, 26 June 2013.

This recognition of common bonds with the other was repeated in the interviews, with one interviewee noting, 'we are all the creation of one God',[101] another that 'We are—above all—Lebanese',[102] and another that we are all 'brother[s] in humanity'.[103] In a similar vein, one interviewee decried the logic of separation: 'If we apply this [religious separation] everywhere, then it is better for each religion and sect to have its own compound. Then there won't be a nation—we will become religious states'.[104]

Reciprocity was harder to find in the interview transcripts. One interviewee referred to the mutual social contract that lies at the heart of reciprocity: 'I treat people with respect—the way I would want them to treat me'. Perhaps the paucity of examples reflects the rather limited actual exchanges between people of different sects, rather than declaratory ambitions to have exchanges in the future.

The interview material revealed some stunning cases of solidarity from Lebanon's civil war era at the individual and familial levels. These examples showed that the othering process, whereby out-group members are cast as irredeemable, was incomplete.[105] A Shia interviewee, for example, recounted how Beirut was divided during the civil war: 'So whenever the roads were closed and my Christian colleagues could not make it to west Beirut to collect their salaries, they would authorise me to do it on their behalf and keep them with me. If there was no trust, this wouldn't happen'.[106] A Sunni interviewee recalled how her mother had a Christian hairdresser during the civil war who would attend to the mother in their house: 'We offered him custody during the civil war as he used to live in a Muslim neighbourhood. My dad opened our house for him, and when he decided to leave the city and go to his village, my parents used to call him frequently to check on him'.[107] Another Sunni interviewee recounted how she lived in a Christian neighbourhood of Beirut when the civil war broke out. Her husband was working away in the Gulf. Her Christian neighbours 'didn't only evacuate me but also rented me a house and paid all my expenses until my husband made it back to the country'. The person responsible for her evacuation was a member of the Lebanese Forces, a Christian militia group, but 'we stayed in touch for years during and after the civil war … ties were never cut … our kids ended up in the university so this reinforced the relationship'. She pointed to a graduation

---

[101] Interview with female Sunni, Kefraya, 10 July 2013.
[102] Interview with female Shia, Werdaniyeh, 2 June 2013.
[103] Interview with male Sunni, Beirut, 24 June 2013.
[104] Interview with male Druze, Aley, 31 July 2013.
[105] Gearoid Millar, 'Our Brothers Who Went into the Bush: Post-Identity Conflict and the Experience of Reconciliation in Sierra Leone', *Journal of Peace Research* 49, no. 5 (2012): 721.
[106] Interview with male Shia, Beirut, 26 June 2013.
[107] Interview with female Sunni, Beirut, 6 July 2013.

photograph and asked, 'Can you differentiate us? Can you tell who is a Christian and who is not? Does it make any difference?'[108]

This trope of protection offered by the other side was also reflected by a Shia interviewee whose family lived in the Christian neighbourhood of Beirut during the civil war: 'They protected us during the civil war and supported us many times.... We used to run to their homes to hide or use the phone to check on my father'.[109]

Another expression of solidarity came in the form of solidarity with Lebanon and its people. An Armenian interviewee whose ancestors had fled to Lebanon from the Armenian genocide told how his family was 'paying back' Lebanon 'by standing out neutral and refusing to take sides'. He continued, 'We didn't ever think to leave this country or emigrate while other communities like Muslims and Christians did in leaving the country'.[110] For him, solidarity with the idea of Lebanon as a multi-identity state was a responsible act.

In concluding this section, it is worth noting that many of the interviewees held malleable and contradictory views. For example, interviewees may have supported conciliation and tolerance in some aspects of their lives but were unwavering in other aspects. The notion of intergroup marriage was a red line for many.[111] Interviews also pointed to how people were often inconsistent over time.[112] For example, some interviewees were militarily involved in the Lebanese civil war but were now tolerant and even regretful. Others were fearful for the future and regarded the tensions following the 2005 assassination of former prime minister Rafik Hariri as posing an existential threat to Lebanon.[113] The key point is that there are no iron laws of sociality, reciprocity, and solidarity in deeply divided societies, just as there are no iron laws of everyday peace. Instead, everyday peace is tentative and context-dependent. It may occur in the margins and at opportune moments, and often at the very local level of individual to individual or family group to family group. The concluding section will discuss the possibility of everyday peace or the constituent parts of everyday peace factoring up.

Conclusion

This chapter has further unpacked the notion of everyday peace and provided illustrations of its manifestations in real life. The picture of everyday peace painted

---

[108] Interview with female Sunni, Kefraya, 10 July 2013.
[109] Interview with male Shia, Beirut, 17 July 2013.
[110] Interview with male Armenian Catholic, Anjar, 3 July 2013.
[111] 'Not at Home: Lebanon's Mixed Marriages', *Economist* 392, no. 8647 (5 September 2009): 46.
[112] Mac Ginty, 'Everyday Social Practices'; Reece Jones, 'Categories, Borders and Boundaries', *Progress in Human Geography* 33, no. 2 (2009): 179, 184.
[113] William Harris, 'Investigating Lebanon's Political Murders: International Idealism in the Realist Middle East', *Middle East Journal* 67, no. 1 (2013): 9–27.

thus far prompts the question, do the 'incidents' of everyday peace have implications for the wider society and polity? Can they be scaled up and out? It is certainly possible to make a case that small acts of everyday peace can provide societies with the stability and 'social glue' required to prevent them from deteriorating into more serious conflict. At a minimum, those engaging in intergroup sociality, positive reciprocity, and solidarity are not—at that moment—engaged in stoking tension or contributing to violence. Moreover, they may act as exemplars to others, showing that it is possible to disrupt the dominant conflict logic in which groups are automatically oppositional.[114] In an optimistic scenario, this might allow for the normalisation of non-antagonistic intergroup relations. A point made too rarely in the academic literature is that societies that have been affected by violence *can* undergo forms of intergroup conciliation and healing. Such processes are not without problems, but they do indicate that attitudes and behaviour can change for the positive.

Consider, for example, Northern Ireland. In the early 1990s, virtually no one would have predicted that the militant organisations would call ceasefires or that a viable political peace process could take root.[115] The paths of the peace process, and the peace accord that was reached in 1998, have been fraught, but generally Northern Ireland has experienced significant positive transformation. This can be found at the elite political level, notably with a power-sharing Assembly (albeit one that is often dysfunctional)[116] but also at the grassroots level, where there is much more everyday exchange between Catholic nationalists and Protestant unionists. Intergroup marriages between Catholics and Protestants are still relatively rare, but they are thought to be increasing.

> *My wife and I are from Northern Ireland and are in a Catholic–Protestant marriage. The wedding planning was more fraught than usual. We wanted a Catholic priest and a Protestant minister to officiate at the wedding. It was clear that neither was—at that time—used to dealing with clergy from the 'other side'. The minister in the church where the wedding ceremony was to take place had been in his post for seventeen years but had never been asked to officiate at a Protestant–Catholic wedding. This was despite the fact that his church was located in a very small town in which the population of the surrounding area would have been approximately 35 percent Catholic and 65 percent Protestant.*

---

[114] Watson, 'The Magic', 1582.

[115] For accounts of the Northern Ireland peace process, see Jonathan Powell, *Great Hatred, Little Room: Making Peace in Northern Ireland* (London: Vintage, 2009); Chris Gilligan and Jonathan Tonge, *Peace or War? Understanding the Peace Process in Northern Ireland* (London: Routledge, 2019).

[116] Paul Moss, 'Northern Ireland: A Year without Devolved Government', *BBC News*, 8 January 2018, https://www.bbc.co.uk/news/uk-northern-ireland-politics-42608322.

There are no official statistics on Protestant–Catholic marriages and partnerships, although a 2005 estimate put the figure at between 5 and 12 percent.[117] The Northern Ireland Life and Times survey has been tracking attitudes to mixed marriages for some time, and the picture that emerges is of steadily increasing tolerance of such marriages. For the question 'Would you mind if a close relative were to marry someone of a different religion?' the figure has increased from 71 percent acceptance in 1998 to 78 percent in 2006 and 85 percent in 2018.[118] It should be noted that intergroup marriages and partnerships are still distinctly in the minority and hence that survey attitudes are not an indicator of actual behaviour. Yet the overall point that deeply divided societies can become less divided holds true. Firmer evidence of change comes from Northern Ireland's education sector. The vast majority of Catholic and Protestant schoolchildren are still educated apart. Only 7 percent of children attended 'integrated schools' in 2014–15.[119] Yet that 7 percent represents an increase from one integrated school in the whole of Northern Ireland where Catholics and Protestants were taught side by side in 1981 to more than sixty schools and colleges in 2017.[120]

For the notion of everyday peace to be significant, it relies on the scaling up of entanglements between individuals and small groups so that they will have a broader effect across the community and society. This is difficult to model or predict, as many incidences of sociality, reciprocity, and solidarity might be regarded as minimal, fleeting, fragmentary, and speculative.[121] Yet the potential to interrupt the dominant conflict narrative is there. In an optimistic scenario, intergroup contact would be normalised into a 'banal cosmopolitanism'[122] and an 'unproblematic co-existence'[123] that would pass by unremarked. The sociality between individuals and small groups would contribute to a widely 'shared set of values, virtues and expectations within society as a whole'.[124] The development of a shared set of values will, to some extent, depend on observed evidence from one's own social circle (a key part of reciprocity). An anecdote of how an

---

[117] Katrina Lloyd and Gillian Robinson, 'Intimate Mixing—Bridging the Gap? Catholic–Protestant Relationships in Northern Ireland', *Ethnic and Racial Studies* 34, no. 12 (2011): 2135.
[118] Northern Ireland Life and Times survey, http://www.ark.ac.uk/nilt/1998/Community_Relations/SMARRRLG.html; http://www.ark.ac.uk/nilt/2006/Community_Relations/SMARRRLG.html; https://www.ark.ac.uk/nilt/2018/Community_Relations/SMARRRLG.html.
[119] Department of Education (Northern Ireland), 'Integrated Schools', https://www.education-ni.gov.uk/articles/integrated-schools.
[120] Northern Ireland Council for Integrated Education, *Annual Report 2016-17* (Belfast: NICIE, 2017): 8.
[121] Hoek and Gandhi, 'Provisional Relations', 69.
[122] Greg Noble, 'Cosmopolitan Habits: The Capacities and Habits of Intercultural Convivialities', *Body and Society* 19, nos. 2–3 (2013): 166.
[123] Anita Harris, 'Youthful Socialities in Australia's Urban Multiculture', *Urban Studies* 55, no. 3 (2018): 605–622.
[124] Jacek Tittenbrum, 'Social Capital: Neither Social, nor Capital', *Social Science Information* 53, no. 4 (2014): 454.

out-group member was welcoming or rude is enough to shape wider attitudes to the out-group.[125] In thinking about scaling up and scaling out, it is useful to recall John Paul Lederach's idea of moving beyond the notion of 'critical mass' and instead thinking of 'critical yeast' or the active agents that can change society for the better. In his view, what often mattered was 'getting a small set of the right people involved at the right places'.[126] As explored in more detail in chapter 7, it is often charismatic individuals who are the key influencers and exemplars of everyday peace at the local level.

Three issues are worth highlighting with regard to the possibility of the scaling up and scaling out of everyday peace. The first point is that all societies are fluid and that everyday peace will be highly contingent on the prevailing dynamics within a society. This dynamism may well be connected to the conflict or a peace process, but it may also be a product of changing economic conditions or social change. The second point is to emphasise the importance of scale. Sociality between intergroup neighbours in an apartment block is one thing. A more generalised intergroup sociality is another. Much here depends on the context and the extent to which it is permissible to have friendships and exchanges with out-group members. A good indication of this will be the extent to which such exchanges are visible and part of the public transcript of everyday life. Individuals and groups may feel their intergroup activities will incur costs (mainly from their own group) and therefore be surreptitious in their activities. In other contexts, those engaged in positive intergroup activities might feel enabled and empowered to conduct their activities in a public manner.

Consider, for example, the extent to which gay couples can show affection in public. In Manchester in the United Kingdom, where part of this book was written, it is unremarkable for gay couples to hold hands or kiss in public areas of the city centre. This was not always the case, not least because homosexuality was illegal in the United Kingdom until 1967 but also because it was widely reviled or ridiculed. Over a period of time, public displays of affection between members of gay couples have become more acceptable. In part, this has been due to the changing legislative context. But it is also due to changing public attitudes. There have been multiple, often subtle, drivers of this change. The key point is that societal attitudes changed over a period of time, and at some point a tipping point was reached. This is not to say that homophobia has ceased to exist. It is, however, to highlight the 'blotting paper' nature of social attitudes and how individual attitudinal changes can aggregate into significant societal transformation. There has been positive societalisation whereby stances, practices, and identities that

---

[125] Interview with female Sunni, Beirut, 6 July 2013. See also Goyal and Miller, 'The Importance', 2.
[126] John Paul Lederach, *The Moral Imagination: The Art and Soul of Building Peace* (Oxford: Oxford University Press, 2005): 91.

were once frowned upon by the wider community became more acceptable. This depended on a 'frontlash', or a small number of courageous individuals willing to engage in transgressive behaviour and acts.[127]

Crucial in everyday peace taking root and the possibility of it scaling up and scaling out are the opportunities of members of different communities to meet. In many conflict-affected societies, this is difficult or even dangerous. Conflict actors often work hard to impose physical barriers between communities, whether in Belfast, Israel–Palestine, or Western Sahara. Yonatan Mendel, writing on the proximity of Tel Aviv and the West Bank, notes how the Israeli government has worked hard to separate and tightly control interactions between Israelis and Palestinians. But more than this, he captures how this physical separation helps constitute a profound perceptual separation: 'One side experiences it [the conflict] on a daily basis, suffers its consequences and wants it to end; the other goes about its business—and leisure—at its own pace, in no real hurry for change. One society lives in the thick of it, the other beyond it. For Jewish Israelis the conflict has become so "manageable" that many can imagine it as a thing of the past, bursting out occasionally'.[128]

The final point to make, and one that will be the focus of chapter 3, is the extent to which everyday peace is dependent on power. Certainly, those engaging in sociality, reciprocity, and solidarity must have some power and agency in order to act. Yet they will act in a context over which they do not have complete control. Much depends upon the ability of other actors to impose their power, including the power of surveillance, on others. In contexts in which there is significant societal control exercised by actors who frown upon intergroup contact, exchange, and conciliation, those engaging in intergroup sociality have to make a calculation. They could calculate that it is prudent to avoid any intergroup activity. They could pursue intergroup activity but do so 'under the radar' or at a level less than they would like, or they can go ahead and risk incurring costs. Such calculations require significant emotional intelligence and, depending on the circumstances, bravery.

---

[127] Jeffrey C. Alexander, 'Frontlash/Backlash: The Crisis of Solidarity and the Threat to Civil Institutions', *Contemporary Sociology* 48, no. 1 (2019): 6.

[128] Yonatan Mendel, 'Diary', *London Review of Books*, 15 August 2019.

3
Everyday Peace Power

Introduction

A legitimate reaction to the notion of everyday peace is to ask, how does it work in the context of very powerful and violent actors? In other words, what is the use of everyday peace in a context like Syria, in which the state is prepared to use extreme violence against its own citizens? Or how can it take place in Israel–Palestine, where the opportunities for Israelis and Palestinians to interact are very limited, and the Israeli state seems vastly more powerful than Palestinian actors? Or can there be space for everyday peace in western China, where the Xighur population face immense oppression from the Chinese state? The answer, disappointingly, is that in these contexts, people with guns and repressive legal apparatus have more power than those who do not. The space for everyday peace is limited. Yet in the margins, under the radar, and at opportune moments, individuals and groups can engage in acts of sociality and toleration and even more expansive acts such as forgiveness or reconciliation. In order to understand this, we need to think differently about power and conceive of everyday peace as a form of power. Rather than the coercive power of states and armed groups over people, this is a power that rests on individual initiative and emotional intelligence. It draws on the concepts of sociality, reciprocity, and solidarity that were explored in chapter 2. This Everyday Peace Power (EPP) involves skills that are far removed from the power of states to discipline and incentivise the behaviour of citizens or subjects. Instead of the power of deterrence through guns, riot gear, and legislative apparatus,[1] EPP relies on self-restraint, participation, moral example, and leadership.

Remarkably few books on peace list the word *power* in their indexes. Yet the concept and practice of power seem central to how peace becomes manifest. This chapter puts forward an understanding of power that is very different from orthodox conceptualisations of power that rely on military might, economic accumulation, and the domination of one group or individual over others. Instead, this chapter sees power in relation to the everyday, and especially everyday peace. It develops the notion of EPP, or a sociological understanding of power

---

[1] Michael Emin Salla, 'Integral Peace and Power: A Foucauldian Perspective', *Peace and Change* 23, no. 3 (1998): 312–332.

that is mindful of the concept as human and sometimes humane. It is interested in the power involved in the Bosnian widow forgiving the wider Serbian community that was involved in the murder of her husband, the northern Ugandan village that can accept former LRA soldiers back into its fold, or the Rohingya and Bamar farmers in Myanmar who do business together after intercommunity violence has calmed down. All of these interactions involve assemblages of power. This will include the power of states, institutions, and armed groups that can provide rules, impose norms, and use coercion and threats. These institutions will most likely have material power and will be able to mobilise cultural and symbolic power. But there is also individual and group power that involves brokerage, human capital, emotional intelligence, and opportunism. Our interest in these fluid and often hard-to-see forms of power requires us to take a step back from orthodox understandings of power and to think about how power is accumulated and deployed in everyday life—especially in conflict-affected contexts. While orthodox notions of power remain important, and often provide the meta-context in which other types of power operate, this chapter presents power as a skill set, the projection of norms, the use of emotional intelligence, and brokerage. This is EPP.

The chapter first reviews orthodox understandings of power and, second, contrasts them with an alternative view of power: EPP. Orthodox understandings of power regard power as 'power over', while the alternative ones developed here regard power more optimistically as 'power to', 'power with', and 'power from'. This more positive form of power has been labelled 'integrative power' by Kenneth Boulding and relies on communication, love, respect, and reciprocity.[2] It involves a logic that allows the individual to perceive 'an increase in his or her own welfare when he or she perceives an increase in the welfare in some sense of the surrounding world'.[3] Despite the structure of the chapter, it is worth pointing out that power should not be seen in strict binary terms:[4] on the one hand, an orthodox understanding of power that is reliant on domination and might and, on the other, a more participative and non-hierarchical form of alternative power or EPP. In reality, the picture is complex, with different types of power often engaged in dialectics with one another. They shape and condition each other to produce often jumbled assemblages of power. Here it is worth thinking of overlapping circuits with different types of power coursing around circuits that sometimes overlap. Some of these assemblages are more conducive to everyday peace, tolerance, and coexistence than others. These two sections—on orthodox and alternative readings of power—will refer back to chapter 2, which sketched

---

[2] Kenneth E. Boulding, *Three Faces of Power* (London: Sage, 1990), 9.
[3] Boulding, *Three Faces*, 115.
[4] More complex taxonomies abound. See, for example, John H. Galbraith, *The Anatomy of Power* (Boston: Houghton Mifflin, 1983).

three concepts that shape everyday peace: sociality, reciprocity, and solidarity. All three represent forms of power eked out in their particular contexts. They have the power to be transgressive of the norms of conflict and violence, to indicate alternatives, and to provide different narratives to widely accepted scripts. In its last substantive section, this chapter returns to the notion of circuitry and how it can help us understand power in relation to everyday peace. Circuitry is especially useful when thinking of power as fluid, dispersed, and often hidden.

Before delving into explications of orthodox and alternative views of power, it is worth acknowledging that the academic literature on power is extensive and somewhat unsatisfactory, in that much of it remain trapped in disciplinary silos that do not speak to one another. The literature is best thought of in a plural form—as literatures. Multiple (sub)disciplines have had their own debates on power and have often used different terminology and concepts. While politics and international relations, perhaps reflecting their realist origins, prefer the term *power*, sociology and anthropology often use the term *agency*. Indeed, the power-versus-agency debate has occupied much space in sociological literature, with agency usually linked to individual capacity and power linked to those structural factors that might limit agency.[5] Moreover, the word *power* lends itself to prefixes and meanings that can shape it in various ways. For example, one article consulted in the compilation of this chapter contained thirteen prefixes of power: *local, kin-based, elite, corporate, exclusionary, centralised, political, ritual, instrumental, creative, materialised, dominant,* and *royal*.[6] That article, from an anthropological journal, discusses the term *power* in ways that are different from discussions in sociology, politics and international relations, gender studies, and history. This chapter borrows from multiple disciplines, and from some practitioner work, in the hope of developing a coherent notion of EPP—a notion that resonates throughout the book.

It is also worth emphasising, by way of introduction, that the primary focus of this work is on individuals and small groups and on forms of organisation that are not necessarily formally institutionalised. Thus, the focus is not on peace groups and civil society organisations. Instead, it is on levels of society that operate alongside and below these formal levels. They may be institutionalised but not necessarily in strictly formalised ways. Thus, for example, it might take the form of a charismatic individual who undertakes pro-peace and pro-social

---

[5] A good discussion of this can be found in Pierpaolo Donati and Margaret S. Archer, *The Relational Subject* (Cambridge: Cambridge University Press, 2015), especially chap. 3. See also Clarissa Hayward and Steven Lukes, 'Nobody to Shoot? Power, Structure, and Agency: A Dialogue', *Journal of Power* 1, no. 1 (2008): 5–20.

[6] Cameron J. Monroe, 'Power and Agency in Precolonial African States', *Annual Review of Anthropology* 42 (2013): 17–35.

initiatives rather than a peacebuilding civil society organisation that may do the same thing but in more formalised ways.

Orthodox Understandings of Power

This section investigates the orthodox understanding of power based on domination of an individual, group, or institution over others. It is 'power over' or, as Boulding termed it, 'threat power'.[7] The next section investigates alternative views of power that might be described as 'power to', 'power with', and 'power from'. These are broadly emancipatory views of power and align with notions and practices of EPP. The reason for spending time exploring orthodox understandings of power is that these explain much about contemporary conflict and violence, as well as international peace-support interventions. They also do much to explain how power is rendered and framed in much media and policy documentation. The argument is made in this section that many peace-support interventions actually support forms of domination and authority and thus are limited in how they might be able to promote the meaningful transformation of conflict.[8] By emphasising state-building and other institutionalised responses, they may reinforce the state and formal institutions and not necessarily empower the organic social infrastructure and exchanges required for deep pro-social interactions between individuals from different groups.

Orthodox explanations of power are usually restricted to the notion of domination. In this view, power is wielded over others. It is 'the ability to affect others to obtain the outcomes you want'.[9] Although crude, the 'power over' viewpoint is still a dominant lens used by many states, institutions, and observers.[10] It has a blunt logic that emphasises might and rests on self-belief. A primitive example is encapsulated in this address to a rally by Adolf Hitler: 'And if the British airforce drops three or four thousand kilograms of bombs, then now in one night we shall drop 150,000, 180,000, 230,000, 300,000, 400,000, a million kilograms. If they declare that they will launch large-scale attacks on our cities—we shall obliterate their cities'.[11] For Chinn and Falk-Rafael, 'power-over powers include ... the use

---

[7] Boulding, *Three Faces*, 10.

[8] This is a major trope in the strand of literature that is known as the critique of the liberal peace. See, for example, Oliver P. Richmond, 'The Problem of Peace: Understanding the "Liberal peace"', *Conflict, Security & Development* 6, no. 3 (2006): 291–314; David Chandler, 'The Limits of Peacebuilding: International Regulation and Civil Society Development in Bosnia', *International Peacekeeping* 6, no. 1 (1999): 109–125; Gerald Knaus and Felix Martin, 'Lessons', 60–74.

[9] Joseph S. Nye, 'Public Diplomacy and Soft Power', *Annals of the American Academy of Political Science* 616, no. 1 (2008): 94.

[10] Michael Karlberg, 'The Power of Discourse and the Discourse of Power', *International Journal of Peace Studies* 10, no. 1 (2005): 3.

[11] Cited in Frederick Taylor, *Coventry, Thursday, 14 November 1940* (London: Bloomsbury, 2015): 58.

of rules, hierarchy, command, results (ends justify means) and expediency'.[12] These powers are in tune with capitalist systems in that they tolerate, and often depend on, competition.[13] They are also in tune with authoritarian and Marxist systems and their emphasis on strong leadership, hierarchy, and obedience. At the heart of the realist canon in international relations is the notion that 'states must maximize power'.[14] According to Kay:

> Power has traditionally been measured in terms of military capabilities, economic strength and natural resources, and the capacity to transform these assets into the exertion of interest. In the classic sense, power is the ability to get someone to do something that they otherwise would not do.[15]

In the realist and 'power over' paradigm, power is hierarchical and measurable. Ranking states according to their military might and measuring their material power can tell us much about states' orientation towards peace and war.[16] Many studies of political economy can show how states accumulate, shepherd, and project power and sometimes suffer from overreach.[17] In such a reading, power derives from a negative or Hobbesian view of humanity: people are not to be trusted and should be controlled.[18] Power is hierarchical, with some actors—the powerful—attaining a higher position than others because of their accumulation of coercive, economic, or symbolic power and their ability and willingness to use it.[19] As James C. Scott notes, states and institutions seek to convert their power into authority, that is, authority over subjects.[20] States will usually assemble a legitimating discourse to justify their assumption of top-dog position. In the United Kingdom, for example, these claims to legitimacy are based on the provision of protection, welfare, and the drawing on comforting myths. A July 2018 speech by then-Prime Minister Theresa May referred to the role of the government in 'protecting the integrity of our precious union, supporting growth,

---

[12] Peggy L. Chinn and Adeline Falk-Rafael, 'Peace and Power: A Theory of Emancipatory Group Process', *Journal of Nursing Scholarship* 47, no. 1 (2015): 65.
[13] Chinn and Falk-Rafael, 'Peace and Power'.
[14] Sean Kay, 'Globalization, Power and Security', *Security Dialogue* 35, no. 1 (2004): 11.
[15] Kay, 'Globalization', 14.
[16] Jin Jun Wang, 'Questions and the Exercise of Power', *Discourse and Society* 17, no. 4 (2006): 531.
[17] See, for example, Paul Kennedy, *The Rise and Fall of the Great Powers: Economic Change and Military Conflict from 1500 to 2000* (London: Fontana, 1989); David Egerton, *Britain's War Machine: Weapons, Resources and Experts in the Second World War* (London: Penguin, 2012); Joseph A. Tainter, *The Collapse of Complex Societies* (Cambridge: Cambridge University Press, 2003).
[18] Stephen Zunes, 'Questions of Strategy', in *Understanding Nonviolence*, ed. M. C. Hallward and J. M. Norman (Cambridge: Polity, 2015): 53–54.
[19] Wang, 'Questions', 531.
[20] James C. Scott, *Decoding Subaltern Politics: Ideology, Disguise and Resistance in Agrarian Politics* (London: Routledge, 2013), 18.

maintaining security and safeguarding British jobs'.²¹ These tropes—whether they have a basis in truth or not—combine to provide an overarching story justifying the power wielded by the state over its subjects.

Many states have forms of participation, offer rights to citizens, and have oversight over the political executive. All of these are limited in their extent. Parliaments tend to be conservative institutions and rarely tolerate radical change. In some states, elections, rights, and an independent judiciary are mere theatre. It is clear that the state or sovereign holds absolute power and must be obeyed. Saudi Arabia, for example, has a parliament, a bill of rights, and other protections. Yet it routinely arrests, imprisons, and tortures political dissidents. In 2017, it executed 149 people, mostly for nonviolent drugs offences.²² In 2018, Freedom House listed the state as 'not free', awarding it the worst possible score for political rights and civil liberties.²³ The state was also graded 169th out of 180 states in terms of press freedom.²⁴ The chief point is that states have been extremely successful in exercising power and authority, whether through the blunt use of coercive power or looser versions that involve forms of participation, rights, and judicial oversight. Mutual support from other states means that state sovereignty is rarely threatened.²⁵

Yet the story of state and institutional power is not simply that of states accumulating material and military power over citizens through threat and extraction, as well as enticements. As Rafanell and Gorringe argue, many of us collude in our own powerlessness. They ask: 'Why do many of the oppressed either accept or collude with unjust social conditions?'²⁶ For them, subaltern populations are conscious of their plight and often complicit in it. In this view, power is not something completely external, alien, and top-down. Instead, it is part of a complex assemblage containing multiple (top-down and bottom-up) elements. It involves co-creation and co-dependency. Crucial here is the 'central role that all individuals play in creating regimes of power'.²⁷ Rafanell and Gorringe's argument is a difficult one to accept, especially when we bear in mind the coercive power wielded by states such as Saudi Arabia, China, Israel, or Turkmenistan,

---

[21] Theresa May, 'PM's Speech at Farnborough International Airshow: 16 July 2018', https://www.gov.uk/government/speeches/pms-speech-at-farnborough-international-airshow-16-july-2018.

[22] Human Rights Watch, 'Saudi Arabia', 2018, https://www.hrw.org/middle-east/n-africa/saudi-arabia.

[23] Freedom House, 'Freedom in the World 2018—Saudi Arabia,'' 2018, https://freedomhouse.org/country/saudi-arabia/freedom-world/2018.

[24] Reporters without Borders, 'World Press Freedom Index', https://rsf.org/en/ranking.

[25] While enforced change attracts headlines, it tends to be rare. Indeed, elite political changes often bring little change at non-elite levels. See Hans-Joachim Giessmann and Roger Mac Ginty, eds., *The Elgar Companion to Post-Conflict Transition* (Cheltenham, UK: Edward Elgar, 2018).

[26] Irene Rafanell and Hugo Gorringe, 'Consenting to Domination? Theorising Power, Agency and Embodiment with Reference to Caste', *Sociological Review* 58, no. 4 (2010): 604.

[27] Rafanell and Gorringe, 'Consenting', 605.

where dissent can be deadly. Yet the argument is worth serious consideration. It recognises that these states cannot act without the collusion of millions of servants—many of whom probably know the inhumaneness of the system. Daniel Goldhagen's argument in *Hitler's Willing Executioners* shows how notions of exclusion can become embedded within a culture to the extent that extreme violence is not just tolerated but becomes a mass participation activity.[28] Individuals are individually and collectively knowledgeable of the system, and through their collective practices they normalise it. In an important sense, they empower the regime. This point is not to underestimate the task of those who may want to resist an oppressive regime. It is, instead, to highlight the complexity of power and how it is, as Foucault and many others have argued, systemic and embedded.[29]

Michael Karlberg has been among the most perceptive analysts of the subtle and embedded nature of power.[30] This is especially so in relation to how social hierarchies and activities become normalised; they become embedded in how we think, speak, and organise society. Karlberg notes:

> western liberal societies have structured their political systems as partisan contests, their justice systems as contests of advocacy, their economic systems as contests of material production and consumption, and their educational systems as contests of intellectual achievement (all reinforced by the fact that most recreational activities are structured as contests of physical or mental performances).[31]

Analyses such as this encourage us see power as systemic. It is not simply about one actor having power over another actor. It is about the system of domination that enables and normalises the system. Thus, alongside realist and 'power over' accounts, we need to drill down to the substate level and examine power at a relational level. This is something that feminist scholars have been particularly good at, and it is explored in greater detail in chapter 6. Diana Francis notes how 'the most widespread oppression of all [is] the oppression of women by men'.[32] Others have reinforced the point that power needs to be seen as a suite of strategies deployed in a variety of figurations.[33]

---

[28] Daniel Goldhagen, *Hitler's Willing Executioners* (New York: Knopf, 1996). See also the incredulity of David Render about German citizens living near a concentration camp, claiming they knew nothing of it. David Render (with Stuart Tootal), *Tank Action: An Armoured Troop Commander's War 1944–45* (London: Weidenfeld & Nicolson, 2016).

[29] Cynthia Harding, 'Refugee Determination: Power and Resistance in Systems of Foucauldian Power', *Administration and Society* 35, no. 4 (2003): 462–488.

[30] Karlberg, 'The Power of Discourse', 1–25.

[31] Karlberg, 'The Power of Discourse', 9.

[32] Diana Francis, *People, Peace and Power: Conflict Transformation in Action* (London: Pluto, 2002), 5.

[33] Monroe, 'Power and Agency', 29.

Many international peace-support interventions seek to challenge or ameliorate the problems of power that may have resulted in conflict. One can think of international interventions as ranged along a continuum, with violent regime change at one end and soft power forms of intervention at the other, such as cultural diplomacy, the use of symbolism, or patient and gentle mediation. All of these forms of intervention involve the power of international actors, and many involve the redistribution (or attempted redistribution) of power in the conflict-affected context. The issue of the power (and indeed powerlessness) of international actors involved in peace-support interventions has been well covered by the extensive literature on the liberal peace.[34] It has shown how a number of states from the global north have engaged in hard and soft power interventions under the guise of liberalism.[35] Crucial here has been norm diffusion, or the promotion of the notion that liberal ideas of rights, democracy, and markets should be prioritised.[36] In other words, alongside the obvious deployment of power, whether through military intervention or economic incentives, has been the spread of a set of ideas. This is particularly significant in terms of governance. Good governance interventions, many funded by bilateral donors, have sought to regularise and make more transparent how states operate. In one way, such actions can be seen as the introduction of modern standardised and accountable mechanisms into ministries and municipalities. Yet such interactions can have profound implications for relationships between people, governments, businesses, and civil society. Seemingly innocuous interventions in the name of peace or governance change the very structure and dynamics of society. The introduction of electronic cash registers to societies in which business transactions are usually informal and cash-based provides an excellent example of how a seemingly unimportant action, often introduced at the behest of international actors, can have a significant impact on a series of relationships.[37] Importantly, coercion, or 'power over', often lies at the heart of such changes. The introduction of electronic cash registers was often mandated by the international financial institutions (IFIs) as part of financial regularisation initiatives to encourage

---

[34] See, for example, Mac Ginty, *International Peacebuilding*; Oliver P. Richmond and Roger Mac Ginty, 'Where Now for the Critique of the Liberal Peace', *Cooperation and Conflict* 50, no. 2 (2014): 171–189.

[35] Mac Ginty, *No War*, 46–49.

[36] For a hubristic championing of these ideas, see Michael Mandelbaum, *The Ideas That Conquered the World: Peace, Democracy and Free Markets in the Twenty-first Century* (New York: Public Affairs, 2004). See also Amartya K. Sen, 'Democracy as a Universal Value', *Journal of Democracy* 10, no. 3 (1999): 3–17; and, most famously, Francis Fukuyama, 'The End of History?' *National Interest* 16 (1989): 3–18.

[37] See, for example, Ministry of Finance (Sierra Leone), 'Mathew Dingie Due Diligence Mission to Georgia on the Introduction of Electronic Cash Registers', 13 February 2019, https://mof.gov.sl/2019/02/13/matthew-dingie-due-diligence-mission-to-georgia-on-the-introduction-of-electronic-cash-registers/; Hans Krause Hansen, 'Numerical Operations, Transparency Illusions and the Datafication of Government', *European Journal of Social Theory* 18, no. 2 (2015): 203–220.

transparent accounting and an increase in tax revenue. The introduction programme would very likely be linked with conditions set by the IFIs and thus is a form of coercion. In turn, the national government would introduce legislation requiring businesses to use electronic cash registers or face penalties. The chief point is that the international interventions can come in multiple formats and have impact on power relations in quite profound and diffuse ways. As academic critiques of the liberal peace have shown, liberal peace interventions were rarely unopposed. Conflict-affected states, and groups and individuals within them, used a wide variety of resistance techniques to change, subvert, extend, delay, and increase the costs of intervention.[38]

In terms of attempts by international coalitions to redistribute power in conflict-affected states in the name of peace or security, the most obvious examples are the ousting of the Taliban in Afghanistan (2001), the invasion of Iraq (2003), and the ousting of Muammar Gaddafi in Libya (2011).[39] In all of these cases, Western techno-military power prevailed with relative ease in the initial task of regime change. The governance vacuums and ineptitude that followed, however, showed the limited reach of top-down international interventions.[40] Aside from cases of regime change, international interventions have often been interested in encouraging or supporting the redistribution of power. Most peace accords, for example, usually prescribe some form of public participation in the parliamentary or presidential electoral system that is managed to take account of competing claims.[41] International support for these activities has included technical assistance in the drawing up of electoral rolls, training of electoral officers, and monitoring of elections.[42] A number of peace accords have instituted forms of power-sharing that institutionalise the representation of groups that might be competing for power. The peace accords in Lebanon and Northern Ireland, for example, mandate that the main politico-confessional groups are represented in the government.[43]

A criticism of power-sharing, however, is that it accepts competition based on identity politics and is content to manage rather than confront it. According to

---

[38] Richmond, *Failed Statebuilding*; Mac Ginty, *No War*.

[39] Giessmann and Mac Ginty, *The Elgar Companion*.

[40] Jonathan Marcus, 'An Obituary of the Age of Intervention?' *BBC News*, 17 September 2017, https://www.bbc.co.uk/news/uk-politics-37372597. A particularly revealing account of the ineptitude and incapacity of interveners can be found in Rajiv Chandrasekaran, *Imperial Life in the Emerald City: Inside Baghdad's Green Zone* (London: Bloomsbury, 2007).

[41] Peter Wallensteen, *Understanding Conflict Resolution*, 4th ed., (Los Angeles: Sage, 2015), 135–139.

[42] See, for example, Mathias Koenig-Archibugi, 'International Electoral Assistance', *Peace Review* 9, no. 3 (1997): 357–364; Therese Laanela, 'Crafting Sustainable Electoral Processes in New Democracies', *Representation* 36, no. 4 (1999): 284–293.

[43] A good overview of the promise and pitfalls of power-sharing can be found in Caroline A. Hartzell and Andreas Mehler, eds., *Power Sharing and Power Relations after Civil War* (Boulder, CO: Lynne Rienner, 2019).

the criticism, it does not challenge or seek to transform the basic confrontational and contested nature of identity politics. In Lebanon and Northern Ireland, the identity-based political parties have agreed to differ rather than reconcile, and the power-sharing system allows them to do so.[44] Similar criticisms have been made of the many governance and rights interventions made by international organisations, IFIs, and INGOs. While these organisations have spent billions in multiple locations on good governance and empowerment programmes, rarely have they actually challenged the bases of power. Power is still usually organised according to economic, political, and social systems based on contestation and competition. Rashid notes that well-meaning interventions that stress empowerment and autonomy risk reinforcing the exclusion of the women and minorities they are aimed at. Writing on women's empowerment schemes in Bangladesh, she observes that women participants are often painted as 'vulnerable' and 'mute' and that their own forms of agency are overlooked.[45] Münch and Veit's study of the International Security Assistance Force (ISAF) in Afghanistan found that ISAF was reluctant to change local power structures and 'cemented' existing power figurations.[46] Indeed, international actors became part of the power figuration and reinforced the power of warlords and tribal chiefs: 'By injecting considerable monetary resources and military capabilities into the respective regions, international interveners underwrote the restoration and perpetuation of indirect rule.'[47]

The chief points of this section have been to underline the prominence of orthodox, top-down types of power and to reinforce how populations are often implicated in its operation and dominance. Even apparently peaceful societies rely on a battery of threats and coercion. Failure to comply with regulations on multiple quotidian spheres of life (parking, tax, disposal of rubbish) can result in fines and imprisonment. Much of the coercion exercised by states is socially sanctioned.[48] States are complex assemblages of sanctions but equally adept at engendering loyalty and sacrifice—often through the clever use of mobilisation narratives. Importantly, many people feel part of these narratives. Just as states use top-down power, so too do militant groups and partisan movements. These have their own forms of discipline (exclusion, accusations of being a traitor, etc.) but also can mobilise immense loyalty. To take a stand against such movements

---

[44] Michael Kerr, *Imposing Power-Sharing: Conflict and Coexistence in Northern Ireland and Lebanon* (Dublin: Irish Academic Press, 2016).

[45] Syeda Rozana Rashid, 'Bangladeshi Women's Experiences of Their Men's Migration: Rethinking Power, Agency and Subordination', *Asian Survey* 53, no. 5 (2013): 885.

[46] Philipp Münch and Alex Veit, 'Intermediaries of Intervention: How Local Power Brokers Shape External Peace and State-Building in Afghanistan and Congo', *International Peacekeeping* 25, no. 2 (2018): 279.

[47] Münch and Veit, 'Intermediaries', 285.

[48] Alice Hills, 'What Is Policeness? On Being Police in Somalia', *British Journal of Criminology* 54 (2014): 768.

from within its support-base community is a transgressive act and also constitutes a form of power. It can be a form of conflict disruption and has the potential for multiplier effects. It is much safer to remain within, or compliant with, the main political and cultural circuits. To inhabit or forge new circuits through taking a counter-hegemonic stance is potentially a dangerous act.

Everyday Peace Power

Understanding the types of power that enable everyday peace requires us to move beyond the 'power over' explanations of orthodox approaches to power in order to investigate 'power to', 'power with', and 'power from'. These are more expansive and optimistic forms of power. Understanding these forms of power requires us to think about our own epistemology and positionality and our ability to escape dominant paradigms and discourses.[49] This is not always easily done, as we are often embedded within, and often help constitute and reinforce, systems of thinking. Gramsci feared that we were trapped by 'cultural hegemony', while Marx and Engels believed that many suffered from a 'false consciousness'.[50] More contemporaneously, peace activist and scholar Rick Wallace has noted the need, especially if one comes from an international relations perspective, to decolonise our narratives and to see alternative theorisations of power 'as part of a profound wider contestation of knowledge and repositioning of authority'.[51] An awareness of post-structuralist-, postcolonial-, feminist-, and indigenous-inspired ways of thinking and seeing the world requires us to look beyond orthodox frameworks. Yet power relations and ways of thinking about power are often so normalised that it is difficult to leave them behind.[52] The standard reference points in much thinking about power are states, borders, militant groups, and mass movements and economic and legal sanctions, duties, and inducements. The concept of EPP requires us to think beyond this and consider more sociological and people-centred conceptualisations of power.

Three key elements help us to think through the implications of EPP. The first concerns the level of analysis. Many studies, particularly those from international relations or political science, take the state as the natural unit of analysis and pay close attention to institutions. Even when these disciplines look at the substate level, they struggle to see beyond formal institutions or seek to

---

[49] Stefano Guzzini, 'Max Weber's Power', in *Max Weber and International Relations*, ed. Richard Ned Lebow (Cambridge: Cambridge University Press, 2017), 97–118.
[50] Karlberg, 'The Power of Discourse', 3.
[51] Rick Wallace, *Merging Fires: Grassroots Peacebuilding between Indigenous and Non-indigenous Peoples* (Halifax: Fernwood, 2013), 19. See also Meera Sabaratnam, *Decolonising Intervention: International Statebuilding in Mozambique* (New York: Rowman & Littlefield, 2017).
[52] Francis, *People, Peace and Power*, 10.

impose categories (like 'civil society'). That is, they seek to reorder the social world in ways that are readily understandable but not always accurate. A complex swirl of religious, tribal, and traditional organisations and practices might be shoehorned into the neat phrase 'faith-based organisations'. While a shorthand, it fails to capture the vibrancy and complexity of the situation as lived on the ground. Picq has observed, 'epistemologically speaking, IR remains a confined space'.[53] In order to comprehend EPP, we need to think about power in multi-scalar, transversal, and sociological terms. It is embodied through the everyday lives of people. It is networked through their connections and aspirations. It courses through the social infrastructure of life via religious institutions, cultural and social meeting places, and charitable organisations. This understanding of the circulation of power lies behind this book's use of the concept of circuits to understand the multi-scalar nature of societies. EPP occurs in the microcosms of everyday life such as the stairwell of the apartment block, the elevator in the university library, or the rush-hour crush in the metro system. In order to reach down and capture the everyday sphere of life, we are required to learn from anthropology, ecology, feminism, sociology, and other disciplines that are alert to the lived and everyday aspects of life. In international relations, some of the literature on the everyday[54] and the concept of 'ontological security'[55] can be helpful here. The key point is that we need to be alert to levels of analysis other than the formal and institutional.

A second element in encouraging us to think through the implications of EPP is the need to see it as a skill set and a mode of reasoning.[56] A key part of orthodox approaches to power is their attention to material power, such as the weapons in an armoury, accumulated financial wealth, or natural resources. Indeed, it is remarkable how traditional demonstrations of hard power still play a prominent role in foreign policy arsenals in an era when more sophisticated (and

---

[53] Picq, 'Critics', 446.

[54] David Roberts, 'Beyond the Metropolis: Popular Peace and Postconflict Peacebuilding', *Review of International Studies* 37, no. 5 (2011): 2535–2556; Helen Berents and Siobhan McEvoy-Levy, 'Theorising Youth and Everyday Peace (Building)', *Peacebuilding* 3, no. 2 (2015): 115–125; Audra Mitchell, 'Quality/Control: International Peace Interventions and "the Everyday"', *Review of International Studies* 37, no. 4 (2011): 1623–1645. See also a 2019 special issue of *Cooperation and Conflict* on 'Everyday International Relations'.

[55] Ann Dupuis and David C. Thorns, 'Home, Home Ownership and the Search for Ontological Security', *Sociological Review* 46, no. 1 (1998): 24–47; Catarina Kinnvall, 'Globalisation and Religious Nationalism: Self, Identity and the Search for Ontological Security', *Political Psychology* 25, no. 5 (2004): 741–767; Catarina Kinnvall and Jennifer Mitzen, 'An Introduction to the Special Issue: Ontological Securities in World Politics', *Cooperation and Conflict* 52, no. 1 (2017): 3–11; Stuart Croft, 'Constructing Ontological Insecurity: The Insecuritisation of Britain's Muslims', *Contemporary Security Policy* 33, no. 2 (2012): 219–235.

[56] Peter M. Gardner, 'Respect for All: The Paliyans of South India', in *Keeping the Peace: Conflict Resolution and Peaceful Societies around the World*, ed. Graham Kemp and Douglas P. Fry (New York: Routledge, 2004), 59.

considerably softer) options are available.[57] EPP is less reliant on material assets. Instead, its chief value lies in human skills and emotional intelligence. It requires individuals and groups to have situational awareness, to recognise opportunities, to have the intuition and human intelligence to let an insult pass, or, more positively, to show a sign of friendship to an out-group member. While many of the skills necessary for everyday peace can be taught, they are mostly observed and often draw on personality traits such as outgoingness, skills of observation, or the ability to use humour to defuse a tense situation. For Boulding, these are 'unconscious skills . . . which arise spontaneously out of the nature of the person'.[58] The skills might be deployed opportunistically, selectively, and inconsistently. They will rely on a way of seeing the social world. This may take the form of a maturity of thinking that enables an individual to see past a communitarian or single-identity worldview and, instead, elevate notions of sociality and common humanity. One Northern Ireland Protestant, who had joined a state-backed militia known for its anti-Catholic activities, recalled that some years later, he got a new civilian job where the workforce was both Catholic and Protestant:

> [I]t took me a while to actually get to know people. I remember the first Christmas I was there, everybody was having a party and I was asked to join. The majority of the people were Roman Catholics and I found that a shock. Here's a guy, he's not long here, he's a Protestant, they know nothing about him; but they are quite willing to invite me into their office for a drink and then, come Christmas to the actual dinner itself![59]

The example shows emotional intelligence and a certain degree of trust and risk-taking by the interviewee and his new colleagues. It is—in essence—a mode of thinking that might take the form of a considered judgment or a snap decision on the battlefield (see chapters 4 and 5). The ability to think and act in counter-hegemonic ways, which confound the prevailing sociopolitical order, may be seen as a form of power. It is a positive form of power in that the individual has 'power to'. Through observed evidence, he made a calculation about the sincerity of his new colleagues and decided to transgress established community boundaries that were based on division and wariness of the other.

A third constituent of EPP is the need to see it in terms of an assemblage or a package of factors. It does not operate in isolation. Instead, it is relational,

---

[57] Julian Borger, 'US Deploys Aircraft Carrier and Bombers after "Credible Threat" from Iran', *Guardian*, 6 May 2019, https://www.theguardian.com/world/2019/may/06/us-deploys-aircraft-carrier-and-bombers-after-troubling-indications-from-iran.
[58] Boulding, *Three Faces*, 121.
[59] Nigel Gardiner, cited in Borderlines Project, *Borderlines: Personal Stories and Experiences from the Border Counties* (n.p.: Borderlines, 2006), 55.

networked, and very much contextualised. In this reading, EPP is one type of power in a complex configuration of multiple types of power. EPP may not be the most visible form of power, especially if it occurs in a context dominated by more obvious forms of power such as material or military power. But, as the next section on circuitry will illustrate, it can coexist with other forms of power, often operating in ways and dimensions that are beyond them. It may operate on the margins, in unoccupied spaces, and at opportune moments. It requires us to conceive of power in a plural sense, with different types of powers coexisting. There is a danger that orthodox conceptualisations of power have become so normalised that it is difficult to think of power beyond the mainstream. So, for example, power might be thought of exclusively in terms of military might, material accumulation, or the 'naked power' of political and military leaders. But other types of power need to be taken into account as well, such as consensus or relational power that seeks to get beyond the often pervasive competitive imperative.[60]

EPP can take the form of individual pro-peace or pro-tolerance acts, or it can take the form of social organisation and decision-making. In the former, it often relies on individuals taking a stand (solidarity), repaying goodwill (reciprocity), and reacting to humanity with humanity (sociality). As Diana Francis observed, 'In the midst of so much ugliness—kindness, decency and courage survive. People maintain and recreate their sense of dignity and meaning, they laugh, love each other, care about strangers and hope and even act for better things.'[61] EPP can be seen as an ability and willingness to engage in often small acts of conciliation, tolerance, and friendship that, in totality, can pattern society to be safe, expansive, encouraging, and optimistic. Importantly, this type of power is not necessarily authority.[62] It does not feel the need to transform itself into 'power over'. These acts can be public or private, principled or expedient, individual or collective. They rely on human agency and initiative and are very context-dependent. In societies unaffected by serious conflict and tension, they probably go unnoticed and are regarded as the system of manners and exchange that keeps a society social. In conflict-affected societies, however, EPP can be counter-hegemonic, threatening, unorthodox, and fundamentally disruptive to the norms of conflict. It can take the form of 'small acts of disruption and defiance'.[63] In the optimum case, acts of EPP would be observed by others and imitated, thus having a cumulative and wider impact on a situation or society. In many cases, however, they will be one-off events that were of the moment.

EPP actors may be brokers or informal mediators who act as bridges between communities. They seek to span the gaps in social structures.[64] These are not

---

[60] Karlberg, 'The Power of Discourse', 8.
[61] Francis, *People, Peace and Power*, 5–6.
[62] Zunes, 'Questions of Strategy', 60.
[63] Zunes, 'Questions of Strategy', 82.
[64] Katherine Stovel and Lynette Shaw, 'Brokerage', *Annual Review of Sociology* 38, no. 1 (2012): 141.

brokers in a competitive sense who profit from their unique position of connecting otherwise unconnected parties in a market.[65] Instead, they may be on the periphery of two or more groups and be prepared to take risks to benefit the collective. This is close to what Boulding refers to as 'exchange power' which may be integrative in the sense that it relies on trust and courtesy.[66] It is, formally, *tertius iungens*—or a form of brokerage that 'focuses on the benefits accrued by the collective'.[67] While *tertius gaudens* profits from the gaps between parties and often works hard to maintain the gaps between them (think estate agent or realtor here), *tertius iungens* has an interest beyond the immediate transaction. In the optimistic case, it is about piloting new structures and processes. As Collins-Dogrul notes, 'Iungens brokerage is attuned to the formation, reproduction and sustenance of social networks over time, seeing brokerage as both building and sustaining connection. More than a bridge, brokerage is a catalyst that enables and enhances cooperation'.[68] They may, for example, be the football coach who encourages an ethnic Serb to join a mainly ethnic Albanian football team in Kosovo—and stands up to attempted bullying from teammates. Or they may be the villager in northern Uganda who stands up for returning formerly abducted persons and gives reasons that they must be accepted. They may be the Protestant at a mainly Protestant workplace in Belfast who makes a point of inviting her Catholic colleague for Friday-night drinks. In Lederach's phrase, these people are the 'critical yeast' that can make pro-social links and inspire others. In such guises, the EPP practitioner is not merely a bridge. He or she is also creating new assemblages and showing that alternative configurations and usages of power are possible.[69] These assemblages of social interactions open up new experiences and possibilities. The assemblages might be short-lived or take root. In deeply divided societies and societies affected by violence and tension, such intergroup contact may be a first step on a journey to other contacts and relationships, hence scaling up and scaling out. In addition to creating new assemblages of social relations, these EPP actors may also be forging new norms. Their actions may be experimental and one-off, but they may be exemplars to others. They may be part of a process of socialisation and example whereby, over time, what passes as normal becomes embedded in a society.[70]

---

[65] Matthew A. Peeples and W. Randall Haas Jr., 'Brokerage and Social Capital in the Prehispanic U.S. Southwest,' *American Anthropologist* 115, no. 2 (2013): 234.

[66] Boulding, *Three Faces*, 28.

[67] Elizabeth Long Lingo and Siobhan O'Mahoney, 'Nexus Work: Brokerage on Creative Projects', *Administrative Science Quarterly* 55 (2010): 47.

[68] Julie Collins-Dogrul, 'Tertius Iungens Brokerage and Transnational Intersectoral Cooperation', *Organization Studies* 33, no. 8 (2012): 989–1014.

[69] Yves Van Leynseele, 'White Belonging and Brokerage at a South African Rural Frontier', *Ethnos* 83, no. 5 (2018): 864.

[70] Andres Persson, 'Shaping Discourse and Setting Examples: Normative Power Europe Can Work in the Israeli-Palestinian Conflict', *Journal of Common Market Studies* 55, no. 6 (2017): 1416.

Consider the example of Belfast City Hall on a Saturday afternoon. The City Hall, as the site of municipal power in a divided city, has a long association with politico-sectarian discrimination and controversy.[71] The grounds of the City Hall, adjacent to Belfast's central business district, have become a Saturday-afternoon gathering place for many of the city's youth. In recent years, it has been skater kids who assemble to show off tricks and generally hang around. Some years before that, it was largely goths, then briefly emos, and before that punks.[72] What is remarkable about these gatherings is that the youth (both Catholics and Protestants) associate over a common cultural interest—skateboarding—rather than a politico-sectarian identity. Given that Belfast is a divided city, with high levels of sectarian residential and educational segregation, and regular bouts of inter-communal violence[73], the weekly gathering of skater kids (often many hundreds) is countercultural. What is particularly interesting from the point of view of EPP are the types of power on display. There is a disruptive and defiant power in ignoring, if only temporarily, the dominant narrative of primary identification with the pro–United Kingdom Protestant-unionist-loyalist bloc or the pro–united Ireland Catholic-nationalist-republican bloc. There is the power of initiative in that at some point, there were the first brave kids who started to assemble and agreed to share the territory. And there are multiple powers of emotional intelligence whereby the kids tacitly agree not to mention political topics that might be uncomfortable. All of these powers are very different from the 'power over' narrative that is based on hierarchy, competition, and possibly imposition. Instead, it is 'power with', 'power to', and 'power from'.

EPP is a form of social entrepreneurship. This form of social entrepreneurialism is organic in that it is bottom-up and often dependent on the creativity, independence, and flair of individuals. It is not formal, institutionalised, and corralled into a civil society organisation. It is civil society but not necessarily with an office, a website, and the need to produce an annual report to satisfy donors. The term *social entrepreneur* has been sullied by its dalliance with neoliberalism whereby pro-social activities have been marketised or used as an excuse to cut public funds. Instead, in the context of everyday peace, the social entrepreneur is the individual or group of individuals who takes initiatives that benefit society. Just like commercial entrepreneurialism, this will involve risk-taking and

---

[71] See, for example, Máirtín Ó'Muelleoir, *Belfast's Dome of Delight: City Hall Politics 1981–2000* (Belfast: Beyond the Pale, 2000); Henry McDonald, 'Belfast's City Hall Attacked by Loyalist Demonstrators over Union Flag Vote', *Guardian*, 3 December 2012, https://www.theguardian.com/uk/2012/dec/03/belfast-city-hall-flag-protest.

[72] Madeleine Leonard, *Teens and Territory in 'Post Conflict' Belfast: If Walls Could Talk* (Manchester, UK: Manchester University Press, 2017), 143–145; 'Belfast City Hall Opens Its Doors after "Goth Invasion"', *BBC Newsbeat*, 23 July 2015, http://www.bbc.co.uk/newsbeat/article/33626947/belfast-city-hall-opens-its-doors-after-goth-invasion.

[73] See, for example, Madeleine Leonard, 'Parochial Geographies: Growing Up in Divided Belfast', *Childhood* 17, no. 3 (2010): 329–342; Eric Lepp, "Division," 32–45.

spotting opportune moments. It might involve engaging in activities that are regarded as deviant or norm-breaking for the in-group. It may mean appealing to communities rather than the single community. However, many communities contain these everyday peace leaders who are prepared to take a stand, make or maintain inter-communal friendships or acquaintanceships, and show signs of sociality, reciprocity, and solidarity with the out-group (a theme explored more fully in chapter 7). This peace entrepreneurship is a form of power that relies on personal insight and intuition, strength of personality, and force of character. Indeed, the much-used term *entrepreneurial spirit* is applicable here, as pro-social and pro-peace entrepreneurship requires an energy or power to see things differently, to engage in active steps to turn pro-peace thought into actions, and to withstand criticism from the in-group.

To carry the EPP = social entrepreneurialism analogy a little further, EPP is a form of disruptive entrepreneurialism. The 'market' is a conflict-affected society dominated by the main market players—political parties and militant groups—who all maintain the market in its traditional form. They all buy into the notion that there is a single core market that is characterised by division based on identity, race, sectarianism, or political preference. EPP disrupts this market. It does not accept the premise of the dominant market and its main players. It offers an alternative business model with different measures of what might constitute success. Rather than success being the capture of state institutions, an increase in votes for a mono-ethnic political party, or the further marginalisation of a minority, success in the alternative EPP market rests on different calculations. It may disrupt the hegemonic narrative by refusing to accept that the other side is inherently bad or that hard security measures are necessary. As befits everyday peace, the actions of everyday peace entrepreneurs may happen on the margins, at opportune moments, and when it is safe to engage in what the majority in society may consider to be 'deviant' behaviour. Yet such behaviour can be an important statement that the market is not a complete monopoly of identity- or ethnic-driven politics. Everyday peace activities, even if marginal, constitute a defiance of the norm and a disruption of the dominant market model. The concept of conflict disruption is explored further in chapter 7.

EPP is not just a case of strong individuals (peace entrepreneurs) taking a stand against injustice or having a sense of mutuality with others. It can also take the form of social organisation and decision-making. In some enlightened workplace situations, the practice of 'Peace and Power' has taken root through consensus decision-making, feedback loops, and group learning. According to Chinn and Falk-Rafael, 'Inherent in "Peace and Power" is a constant habit of critique, enacted in regular habits of critical reflection, assuring that the group's knowing-doing is informed by ongoing careful examination of the group's lived experience in light of the patriarchal context that shaped the past, and the hoped-for ideals of peace toward which the group reaches'.[74] This is in sync with some indigenous approaches to power. According to Taiaiake Alfred, a scholar and indigenous advocate from Kahnawake,[75] power in indigenous settings depends on the active participation of individuals; is balanced, dispersed, situational, and non-coercive; and respects diversity.[76]

Indigenous conceptualisations of power chime with notions of conflict transformation, with their emphasis on self-awareness, self-education, and participation.[77] It involves 'ensuring that those who have been the subjects of structures of domination discover and develop the power to participate in what affects them'.[78] We can see EPP in peace and non-violent movements that very consciously campaign for different approaches to social and political problems. Stephen Zunes refers to non-violent action as 'the ultimate asymmetrical warfare',[79] in that it requires states and orthodox power actors to adopt a different calculus. States can be thrown off guard by the incongruity of their heavy-handedness in the face of innovative and non-violent forms of protest and dissent: 'the oppressive apparatus can be mocked in such a way that shows that the subjected population is not only unafraid but willing to expose the absurdity of the restrictions imposed upon them'.[80] As will be discussed further in chapter 7, this is conflict disruption, or the unsettling of the assumptions and norms of conflict.

All situations of power are dependent on context, but they can also be co-constitutive of their context. Certainly, the agency of actors and the proclivity of individuals and small groups to engage in everyday acts of tolerance and coexistence are important. But such agency will be bounded by the conflict context. EPP might be enabled by the context, but it may also have its own power and resourcefulness to withstand some of the pressures of the context. Factors at play in shaping the conflict will include the character of the conflict, the stage of the conflict, and the ability of actors to impose costs on those engaging in acts or processes of everyday peace. The character of the conflict will influence the extent to which zero-sum attitudes may prevail in society with regard to the out-group. In situations of total conflict, there may be very little space for sociality, reciprocity, and solidarity. Individuals and collectives from different groups may not even

---

[74] Chinn and Falk-Rafael, 'Peace and Power', 66.

[75] In an issue that illustrates power (in this case, naming power), indigenous scholar Alfred is from Kahnawake, an indigenous area that predates the modern state of Canada. Yet the legal and normative power that a state like Canada is able to muster, and the sociocultural power of maps, means that it is difficult to refer to this area without reference to Canada.

[76] Taiaiake Alfred, *Peace, Power and Righteousness: An Indigenous Manifesto* (Don Mills, ON: Oxford University Press, 1999), 26–27.

[77] Roger Mac Ginty, 'Indigenous Peacemaking versus the Liberal Peace', *Cooperation and Conflict* 43, no. 2 (2008): 139–163.

[78] Francis, *People, Peace and Power*, 8.

[79] Zunes, 'Questions of Strategy', 81.

[80] Zunes, 'Questions of Strategy', 84.

have the opportunity to physically meet each other, and so only weak versions of everyday peace will be possible. Also important in shaping the context in which EPP might be operationalised is the stage of the conflict. Situations of extreme violence will probably preclude most acts of everyday peace. Situations of tension leading up to peaks in violence and situations in the aftermath of violence may offer better opportunities for the operation of EPP. It is worth noting the micro-level at which everyday peace acts take place and how there may be localised pockets in which acts of civility and pro-peace actions can take place. These actions may take place within a more generalised situation of insecurity, tension, and violence. Media reporting of violent conflict often generalises, giving the impression that all areas of a country or territory are conflict-affected. The nature of many conflicts, however, means that there can be considerable spatial differentiation, with, for example, one town suffering significant intergroup violence but a town a few dozen miles away experiencing much less.[81]

A final contextual factor worth noting is the costs that might be associated with engaging in everyday peace. These might range from being shunned by community members to legal sanction or the wrath of the mob. The context will play a large part in determining three factors: visibility, extent, and issue significance. In terms of visibility, the context will help determine the extent to which individuals or groups will conduct their actions publicly or in the margins. For example, does a Bosnian Muslim warmly greet a Bosnian Serb friend if they meet in the centre of the city? Or do they save the familiarity and warmth for possibly safer and less public territory? The answer will probably depend on the social sanctions associated with public displays that cross identity boundaries. The nature and strength of these sanctions may be linked with the wider political timetable. For example, elections and the language mobilised by politicians during election campaigns may make intergroup contact injudicious for particular time periods. In terms of extent and issue significance, it obviously matters if signs of everyday peace are extensive. The more people who engage in them, the more difficult for the state or community to sanction them. Everyday peace actions are often deliberately restricted to the margins and kept out of sight, lest they attract attention and opprobrium. Communities in a divided society may be prepared to countenance intergroup encounters on an issue that is deemed marginal or unimportant. For example, a mother-and-toddler group in Northern Ireland might be frequented by both Catholics and Protestants. But this intergroup sociality may be quite easily compartmentalised from wider inter-communal dynamics.[82] If such activities were to be scaled out and normalised, then they might pose a threat to the conflict system.

---

[81] Varshney, *Ethnic Conflict*; Moore, *Peacebuilding in Practice*.
[82] Smyth and McKnight, 'Maternal Situations'. See also Mac Ginty, 'Everyday Social Practices', 4–25.

Before moving on to examine how the concept of circuitry can help us understand how we can connect the power of the everyday with more orthodox understandings of power, it is worth stressing that we should be careful not to romanticise EPP. There is a danger that the tone associated with explanations of bottom-up, indigenous, consensual, and participative forms of power might seem somewhat self-righteous.[83] All of these forms of power are subject to capture and control by elements that might be exclusionary or discriminatory. There are no guarantees that forms of power that are labelled as bottom-up do not actually duplicate, or even reinforce, patriarchy or identity-based particularism—a point developed in chapter 6.

Power and Circuitry

A key point in this chapter is that there are different types of power. Some power can be formal and institutionalised through a state. It can rely on material expressions such as a police force or military. Other forms of power may be more social, relational, and informal. They may be 'hidden' or less visible. It is here that the notion of circuitry can be helpful. We can conceive of a large and complex circuit that involves multiple types of power. The formal power of the state may be visible through its governing institutions and coercive apparatus. This main circuit might have tremendous reach with sub-circuits that connect with many levels of society. For example, the state, through its social offerings such as schools and clinics, might be present in many communities. While the state may have the power to sanction its citizens and non-citizens within its reach, it is worth noting that many may support the state and welcome what it has to offer. Yet the complex circuitry constructed and maintained by the state is not the totality of circuitry. Beyond the international, national, and municipal circuits of statehood, there are also informal sets of circuits created and maintained by people. These will take various forms, most obviously of the family and kin groups but also wider political and cultural identity groupings. These social and relational circuits might not wield formal material power in the same way that a police force might, but they may have the power of obligation, social conformity, and cultural assumptions. Clearly, this notion of circuitry takes us beyond ideas of circuits as sites of a mechanical path-dependency. Instead, they are sites of complexity, messiness, emotion, and what might appear—from the outside—as irrationality.

---

[83] See, for example, Kristina Fagan, 'Aboriginal Nationalism in Taiaiake Alfred's *Peace, Power and Righteousness: An Indigenous Manifesto*', *American Indian Quarterly* 28, nos. 1–2 (2004): 12–29.

We can conceive of multilevel circuits and circuits within circuits as different spheres of life overlap with one another to produce a complex assemblage of circuitry. Consider, for example, a policeman who lives in northern Uganda, an area that has been affected by violent conflict. The policeman will be connected with various circuits. Through the police force, he will be connected to the state and will be obligated to perform formal duties. His oath of allegiance, taken upon completion of training, states:

> I, *name*, swear that I will bear true allegiance to the Republic of Uganda and that I will truly and faithfully obey all lawful commands of the Government of the Republic of Uganda as by law established and of any officer set over me, serving in the office for the preservation of peace and prevention of crime and the apprehension of offenders against peace in all respects to the best of my skill and knowledge, discharging all duties of the office according to law.[84]

The policeman is clearly implicated in a formal circuit mandated by the government and codified into law. But the policeman might also be part of multiple other circuits. For example, it could be that he serves in a part of northern Uganda that is far from the reach of the government in Kampala. He and his colleagues might engage in their own informal revenue generation by extracting small bribes from motorists.[85] This is, of course, illegal, but the policeman's colleagues all engage in such behaviour, and their immediate superior is willing to let it occur—for a cut. This de facto police culture constitutes another circuit that overlaps with the formal circuitry provided by the state. The policeman derives his authority from the formal connection with the state and the trappings of a state mandate such as uniform, insignia, and car. Yet he is then able to use these in his informal policing.

The policeman may be involved in another type of informal policing. He may, through his force of personality, the respect he might have among the local population, and his connections with tribal and church networks, have a reputation as a problem-solver. He may be one of a number of 'go-to' individuals (along with the village head man and pastor) in the locality who are often able to solve disputes informally. For the policeman to do this, he must step outside of his formal role as a policeman and use informal sanctions and encouragements. Again, the policeman's entry into this circuit is very

---

[84] Uganda Legal Information Institute, Oaths Act, schedule 1 (1995), https://ulii.org/ug/legislation/consolidated-act/19.

[85] Survey evidence suggests that a high proportion of Ugandans believe that the police force is corrupt. Abdur Rahman Alfa Shaban, 'Ugandans Believe Police Are 75% Corrupt—Report', *AfricaNews.com*, 23 June 2016, http://www.africanews.com/2016/06/23/ugandans-believe-police-are-75-percent-corrupt-survey//.

probably aided by his position as a policeman, but his actions are independent of the formal sanctions offered by the law. His role here might contribute to EPP. For example, there may be tension in the locality among youth—some of whom had been abducted by the LRA but are now semi-settled back in the community. The policeman might work to reduce these tensions through an informal chat here and there. He might encourage individuals to calm down and connect them with role models and figures of authority. He might also, however, suggest that if the informal route of dispute resolution does not work first, then the formal route—through the police and the sanctions they can deploy—is still available.[86]

On top of these semi-overlapping circuits, there are other circuits. For example, the policeman may be a member of a minority tribe from the north—such as the Teso—and will identify with other Teso. He might be more lenient with other Teso while on traffic duty and tend not to extract bribes from them. This circuit of tribal identification will map, to a certain extent, with his extended family and their geographical concentration. The policeman case study shows the interweaving nature of circuitry and how individuals and groups of individuals are capable of maintaining multilevel identities and stances. This involves considerable emotional intelligence and situational awareness. It also involves the deployment of different types of power—formal, material, informal, cultural, and social. The complex circuitry inhabited and maintained by the policeman contains the 'straight lines' of what the state might mandate, but it is also overlaid with messier configurations that are constructed through the policeman's actions and allegiances.[87] He deploys power both individually and as part of a number of collectives (police force, small unit of police colleagues, tribal affiliation).

We are all implicated in multiple circuits. In deeply divided and conflict-affected societies, however, some of these circuits may involve strong obligations (for example, to the identity group) or threaten harsh sanctions if one deviates from the accepted norm. To the extent that they have agency and that circumstances allow, individuals and groups of individuals may be able to navigate around multiple circuits simultaneously. Different circuits may require different skills and different levels of affiliation. One may be lightly implicated in a social circuit but heavily implicated in a familial one.

---

[86] Insights into the organisation of Ugandan society can be found in Sophie King and Sam Hickey, 'Building Democracy from Below: Lessons from Western Uganda', *Journal of Development Studies* 53, no. 10 (2017): 1584–1599; Jennifer M. Larson and Janet I. Lewis, 'Ethnic Networks', *American Journal of Political Science* 61, no. 2 (2017): 350–364.

[87] Good examples of the intersectionality of police officers, this time in France, can be found in Didier Fassin, *Enforcing Order: An Ethnography of Urban Policing* (Cambridge: Polity, 2011).

Conclusion

The chief point of this chapter has been to outline the plural nature of power and to argue that everyday peace is a form of power: EPP. Power can be formal, informal, visible, invisible, material, immaterial, long-standing, and emergent. Power—in its various formats—circulates to form a complex assemblage. Individuals and groups of individuals will be guided through these circuits through a mix of inducements and sanctions. To the extent possible, and depending on the context and need, some individuals and groups might engage in activities that are pro-social and pro-peace. Such activities, for example, in a society emerging from violent conflict, might disrupt the norms and assumptions upon which single-identity worldviews rest. They might take the form of a friendship or business relationship forming between a Sinhalese trader and a Tamil supplier or a romantic relationship between a Northern Ireland Catholic and a Protestant in an interface area of Belfast. It is important to see such actions, and the modes of thinking that underpin them, as a form of power.

Depending on the context, EPP will involve a variety of types and manifestations of power. First, it involves an ability to read a situation and think through the possibilities of action. This may seem a modest skill, but given that many contexts have prescribed ways of thinking of the other and of a conflict, the ability to have independent thought can be significant. Second, EPP can involve the identification of opportune moments in which individuals can act. For example, is it acceptable for a Muslim trader to publicly show friendship, familiarity, or generosity to a Christian customer following an upsurge in violence in northern Nigeria? This decision requires emotional intelligence, a calculation of risks, and often a snap judgement. It is a form of power, especially if it deviates from the in-group norm and disrupts the accepted norms of conflict. Third, EPP may also involve a resilience to ward off criticism from in-group members and to persist with a course of action that is out of the norm. Fourth, it may, again depending on circumstances, require the individual and the group to consider factoring up their actions. While many instances of everyday peace are one-off actions (for example, the snap decision to take a prisoner on the battlefield rather than kill the opponent), some actions are replicable and can be extended to others. The market trader in northern Nigeria may become more open in his friendships and business dealings with Christians. His actions may become an exemplar of intergroup relations and serve as a public rebuke to those who maintain particularistic worldviews. To take such a course of action depends on circumstances and requires courage. It is a form of power.

This chapter and chapters 1 and 2 have outlined the conceptual bases of this book. They have underlined the importance of the everyday and the local and the need to take these domains seriously. At the same time, they have been concerned with how the local and the everyday can be contextualised alongside wider frames of reference such as the municipal, national, international, and transnational. Circuitry has been proposed as an analytical device that can capture the complex and relational nature of agency involved in various forms of peace, conflict, and everything in between. The chapters have also conceptualised everyday peace as made up of sociality, reciprocity, and solidarity and constituting a form of power. Chapters 4 and 5 put the concept of everyday peace to the test. They deliberately focus on the 'difficult cases' of warfare and explore the extent to which it has been disrupted by everyday peace actions and stances. This allows us to raise questions about the extent to which everyday peace is actually a form of peace and to illustrate the intensities of everyday peace along its range of weak to medium to strong.

4
Parley, Truce, and Ceasefire

Introduction

This chapter is best read in conjunction with chapter 5. Together, the chapters examine and illustrate everyday peace in the context of war. A critique of the concept of everyday peace is that it is unable to operate, or is very severely constrained, in contexts in which those with power oppose or forbid it. War, and the organisation for war through militarism, can be considered as a heightened form of power. The task facing this chapter and chapter 5 is to show that everyday peace, or at least some elements of sociality, reciprocity, and sometimes even solidarity, is possible, even in extreme cases such as war. This chapter examines formal mechanisms—such as ceasefires and international humanitarian law—that can inject civility into war. Chapter 5 explores informal 'everyday' interruptions to war or instances in which combatants have been able to carve out spaces of less than warlike activity during warfare. This includes informal and tacit truces, insubordination to military superiors, desertion, or kindness and empathy to enemy prisoners or combatants. While this chapter discusses top-down conflict management, chapter 5 discusses bottom-up conflict disruption. The argument is made that unscripted, bottom-up pro-social and pacific acts constitute a form of Everyday Peace Power (EPP).

The two chapters, particularly chapter 5, are the antithesis of the 'normal' war story in which the enemy is brutal, the home front is united, and there are clear demarcations between combatants and civilians. They draw on a source rarely exploited in the academic study of peace and conflict: soldiers' memoirs and personal diaries. Most of the extracts are from soldiers in the lower ranks—supposed cogs in the military machine whose primary job was to obey orders, even if those orders meant killing and performing roles far removed from their prior civilian lives. The picture that emerges is messy. There are plenty of cases of warlike behaviour—following orders, carnage, and hatred—but there are also hints of humaneness, empathy, and sympathy. The chapters do not attempt to romanticise war. Instances of everyday peace do not, on the whole, change the course of wars at the meta level, but they offer glimpses of resistance to war and the persistence of humanity in the most adverse of conditions. Given that the chapters examine empathy, mercy, and sociality within war, the focus is largely on negative peace. Yet these contexts of everyday peace in extremis are underexplored, hence the extended consideration here.

This book addresses two issues central to everyday peace in particular and peace and conflict studies more generally: power and the connections and disconnections between everyday experiences and systems-level structures (discussed as 'circuitry' in this work). Power runs through accounts of warfare. War, especially 'total war', often involves the mobilisation of populations and national institutions. It also involves a unity of purpose and mass discipline. Individual needs are subjugated to the national interest through conscription, rationing, and the curtailment of freedom of expression. War is perhaps the ultimate case of the harvesting and channelling of state and national power—sometimes (in defensive war) for existential purposes. Yet, as will be demonstrated in chapter 5 in particular, there are cases in which subversive and individual power can be used. Key here, and as discussed in chapter 3, is the need to recognise that there are different *types* of power. While power can be mobilised and exercised at the national and international levels, and while it can be used for massive industrial, strategic, and martial purposes, there are instances in which the individual, family, and small groups can wield alternative types of power based on a sociality with fellow humans and a sense of empathy and humanity. They can organise around domains such as kinship, humour, or legitimacy that the state or military organisations cannot reach. As chapter 6 illustrates, the family is a site of power relations that has been largely overlooked in much peace and conflict and international relations literature. The extracts from the war memoirs and personal diaries will show that these forms of power can happen alongside national and warlike forms of power. For example, loyal soldiers who were fully committed to the war aims espoused by their leaders were also capable of showing mercy to their enemy on the battlefield. In some cases, these subaltern forms of power can be seen as resistance to the dominant warlike spirit of the time. What becomes clear is that war, violent conflict, and sectarianism are rarely completely totalising. As these chapters show, even the world wars had space for dissent and pro-peace activity. Individuals and groups of individuals can forge spaces for dissent and resistance. This conflict disruption is a form of EPP.

The second issue running through this book is the scalar and levels of analysis problem. How do we connect the actions and experiences of the individual and the small group to the events, systems, and structures that occur at the national, international, and transnational levels? How can a soldier who takes part in a localised truce in the trench warfare of World War I be placed in a much broader context that encompasses national politics and a global strategic power play? Is there a possibility of scaling up or scaling out localised everyday peace stances and actions so that they might resonate across a wider context or perhaps inspire others? Here the concept of circuitry is relevant. The seemingly isolated individual or event can be identified as one circuit, or part of a circuit, in a much broader system of circuitry. In other words, there can be a positive societalisation whereby norms, stances, and actions of intergroup civility are internalised by community members and do not rely on top-down intervention. The concept of circuitry allows us to see the connections between actors, ideas, power, and material resources—however complex, convoluted, or tenuous. Circuits within circuits also allow us to explain why the individual, or the ground-level military unit, may feel unconnected to the wider picture. It is useful to think in terms of an assemblage whereby multiple circuits intersect, coalesce, cooperate, compete, and operate side by side to constitute a complex adaptive system.[1]

This chapter has three substantive sections. The first is a methodological note on using personal diaries and memoirs, especially those from wartime, as a source for academic work. While they are a revealing and entirely legitimate source, it is prudent to be aware of their historiographical limitations. The second section reminds us (as if such a reminder were needed) of the brutality of warfare. The purpose of the section is to illustrate just how 'out of character' everyday peace is in the context of war. It requires bravery on the part of individuals and small groups to engage in countercultural, indeed potentially treasonous, behaviour. The section also reminds us that military organisations and nations in warfare rely on discipline and hierarchy. Again, to depart from such 'power over' discipline and respect for hierarchy requires bravery, initiative, and the ability to prioritise human sociality and solidarity over national and military goals. The chapter's last substantive section examines the formal ceasefires, parleys, and humanitarian pauses that can be reached in war. These have been the subject of considerable academic study and are, in some circumstances, motivated by a desire to save lives and relieve suffering. In the optimal case, a ceasefire might be a first step on the journey to a peace process and a peace accord. But in other cases, it may be a tactical pause used to regroup and rearm. The conclusion reconnects with the wider aims of the book and underscores the importance of power and scale in our considerations of everyday peace. Chapter 5 examines bottom-up pacific actions in the midst of war. These might include tacit ceasefires, acts of mercy and empathy to the enemy, and activity that might be described as 'unwarlike'. They constitute EPP and a form of conflict disruption.

The essential purpose of the two chapters is to demonstrate that war is not always totalising. Even within the context of apparently all-out war, there may be spaces for initiative, dissent, resistance, and forms of peace. These spaces are often hidden and unseen. They are unlikely to receive attention in official narratives of war that might prefer to emphasise national unity and a romanticised

---

[1] De Coning, 'Complexity Thinking'.

view of stoicism.² Occasionally, war memoirs hint that on-the-ground loyalty to political and military leaders was less than full.³ Yet even events and actions on the margins of war are useful in illustrating the power and persistence of mercy, empathy, and sociality. They also illustrate the utility of sociological approaches to the study of conflict and the need to look behind official narratives in order to access alternative perspectives that may indicate everyday peace.

War Memoirs and Personal Diaries as a Source

The voices of combatants are—oddly—largely absent from the academic study of peace and conflict.⁴ This chapter draws heavily on war memoirs and personal diaries, especially those from the two world wars.⁵ The vast majority of contemporary peace and conflict studies examines the conflicts of the post–Cold War era. This is for entirely understandable reasons. In order to be useful, much of peace and conflict studies examines contemporary conflicts and conflict responses. As a result, it has been accused of ahistoricism or a lack of interest in history and an often misplaced assumption of the novelty of the contemporary era.⁶ These chapters can be read as a counter to that accusation. They can also be read as a corrective to the widespread exclusion of the world wars in most of the peace and conflict studies literature. The overwhelming focus of contemporary studies is on intra-state wars—a legitimate research focus given their prevalence.⁷ Yet to overlook perhaps the most significant martial mobilisations in human history is to overlook an important evidential trail.

It is also worth noting that despite significant changes in the technologies of war, many of the basics of warfare remain the same. Whether a soldier is

---

² A compilation of tales of 'Blitz spirit' during the World War II aerial bombing of the United Kingdom can be found in Jacqueline Mitchell, *Blitz Spirit* (Oxford: Osprey, 2010). Discussion of the manufacture of national memory can be found in David Clampin, *Advertising and Propaganda in WWII: Cultural Identity and the Blitz Spirit* (London: I.B. Tauris, 2014). A rare questioning of the blitz spirit is evident in Render, *Tank Action*, 30.

³ Robert Boscawen, *Armoured Guardsmen: A War Diary June 1944–April 1945* (Barnsley, UK: Leo Cooper, 2001), 48.

⁴ A new, and excellent, addition to the literature of military sociology draws on UK war memoirs published from 1980 onwards: Rachel Woodward and Neil Jenkins, *Bringing War to Book: Writing and Producing the Military Memoir* (Basingstoke, UK: Palgrave, 2018). A very impressive exercise in the systematic use of such sources for political science is Kalyvas, *The Logic of Violence*.

⁵ I am grateful to Tom Rodwell for his advice to use the term *personal diaries* rather than *war diaries*, as the latter are often official accounts of a campaign by a particular regiment or military unit. I am grateful to him more generally for his advice on the methodology of using personal diaries and war memoirs as a source.

⁶ Suthaharan Nadarajah and David Rampton, 'The Limits of Hybridity and the Crisis of the Liberal Peace'. *Review of International Studies* 41, no. 1 (2015): 49–72.

⁷ Peter Wallensteen and Margareta Sollenberg, 'An End to International War? Armed Conflict, 1989–1995', *Journal of Peace Research* 33, no. 3 (1996): 353–370.

crouching in fear in a ditch in WWII or civilians are being displaced by aerial bombardment in twenty-first-century Yemen, many of the actions, stances, and emotions remain the same. The bias towards the modern that is evident in much peace and conflict studies and international relations literature seems like a dereliction of responsibility to review available evidence and make reasoned judgements.

War diaries and memoirs are a rich source of firsthand material by those who were at the sharp end of warfare: fighting, killing, ethnic cleansing, atrocity, and being taken prisoner. One veteran soldier wrote, 'No words, however set together, can convey even a minute concept of the searing mental and physical impact of the shambles of infantry action unless one has personally experienced it'.[8] These chapters make extensive use of war memoirs and diaries and—at times— use quite lengthy extracts from them. Predominantly, the memoirs used here are by 'ordinary' soldiers and relatively low-ranking officers rather than military commanders. There are plenty of diaries and memoirs by senior military figures who, in novelist Evelyn Waugh's phrase, retired to their country estates to write their memoirs.[9] Many of these figures were removed from the battlefield action, and their works often seek to convey the bigger picture of strategy, politics, and logistics (and to secure their reputation in history).[10] While there are collections and edited volumes of first-person accounts of wartime experience,[11] most of the works consulted for these chapters are single-author books. The advantages of these are that one can often access the war history of an individual (rather than just an excerpt) and get a fuller autobiographical and contextual picture. The soldierly works used in these chapters are often unpolished from an academic point of view and are usually the sole literary output of the author.[12] Yet the rawness of many of the memoirs (and it should be said that some are extremely well written) is to be celebrated. There is a danger of the writing over non-academic sources with academic claptrap. This risks sanitising or over-theorising what are often visceral, human, and even humane accounts of war. Academic attempts to connect such accounts with finessed theories and concepts risk sophistry and conceit.

---

[8] Peter White, *With the Jocks: A Soldier's Struggle for Europe 1944–45* (Stroud, UK: Sutton, 2004), xx.

[9] Quoted in Charles Lamb, *War in a Stringbag* (London: Cassell, 2001), 322.

[10] See, for example, Gary Sheffield and John Bourne, eds., *Douglas Haig: War Diaries and Letters 1914–1918* (London: Weidenfeld & Nicolson, 2005); Alex Danchev and Daniel Todman, eds., *War Diaries 1939–1945: Field Marshal Lord Alanbrooke* (London: Phoenix, 2002).

[11] See, for example, Studs Terkel, *The Good War: An Oral History of World War Two* (London: Penguin, 1985); Walter Kempowski, *Swansong 1945: A Collective Diary of the Last Days of the Third Reich* (New York: Norton, 2015).

[12] There are some cases in which the authors of the war memoirs used in these chapters went on to become accomplished literary figures: Ernst Jünger, George MacDonald Fraser, and Patrick MacGill.

Some war memoirs and diaries reproduce hegemonic martial narratives,[13] and certainly, many seem unreflective about the politics and inequalities behind war. Yet, here and there, a number of memoirs do show some signs of dissent from dominant national narrative and offer glimpses of unwarlike thinking and behaviour. It is this evidence of transgressive behaviour that forms much of the basis of this chapter and the next. Importantly, memoirs and diaries bring the level of analysis down to the individual and his or her immediate surroundings, experiences, families, and comrades. They are useful for this book's ambition of looking at the lowest level of society, that is, the level below organised civil society: the individual, the group of individuals, the family, the network of friends, or comrades. The fact that memoirs and diaries are used so rarely in international relations and in peace and conflict studies tells us something about the usual frames of reference and units of analysis.[14]

While valuing the rawness and the firsthand nature of many accounts of war, we do need to be prudent in using such sources for academic purposes. Five points of methodological concern are worth raising. The first is that published war diaries and memoirs are overwhelmingly written by males about males. We know that war is gendered and affects men and women in different ways.[15] Most published war memoirs and diaries, however, are written by (former) soldiers and so tend to relate a strikingly male version of war. Females were not conscripted into combatant roles in the United States, the United Kingdom, and Germany, and there are very few, if any, female accounts of traditional frontline combat from the world wars. The closest are often from female medical professionals in combat zones.[16] Yet, in both world wars, the frontline extended far beyond the battlefield, especially in WWII, with area bombing, the rounding up and murder of Jews and dissidents, and mass displacement of entire populations.

---

[13] Bina D'Costa, 'Once Were Warriors: The Militarized State in Narrating the Past', *South Asian History and Culture* 5, no. 4 (2014): 457–474.

[14] For a discussion of the role of biography and bibliography in international relations, see Oliver P. Richmond, 'The Green and the Cool: Hybridity, Relationality and Ethnographic Biographical Responses to Intervention', *Mediterranean Politics* 23, no. 4 (2018): 479–500.

[15] Examples of this very rich literature include Fionnuala Ní Aoláin, Dina Francesca Haynes, and Naomi Cahn, *On the Frontlines: Gender, War and the Post-Conflict Process* (Oxford: Oxford University Press, 2011); Joshua S. Goldstein, *War and Gender: How Gender Shapes the War System and Vice Versa* (Cambridge: Cambridge University Press, 2004). There are also important issues concerning how we are able to see and adequately research the extent to which violent conflict is gendered. See, for example, Jelke Boesten and Marsha Henry, 'Between Fatigue and Silence: The Challenge of Conducting Research on Sexual Violence in Conflict', *Social Politics: International Studies in Gender, State and Society* 25, no. 4 (2018): 586–588; Elisabeth Jean Wood, 'The Ethical Challenges of Field Research in Conflict Zones', *Qualitative Sociology* 29, no. 3 (2006): 373–386.

[16] For an account of a medical professional, see, for example, Vera Brittain, *Testament of Youth: An Autobiographical Study of the Years 1900–1925* (London: Fontana, 1979); Alan Bishop and Mark Bostridge, eds., *Letters from a Lost Generation: First World War Letters of Vera Brittain and Four Friends* (London: Little, Brown, 1998). For an account of someone who worked in espionage, see Hermoine Ranfurly, *To War with Whitaker: The Wartime Diaries of the Countess of Ranfurly* (London: Bello, 2014).

This is captured by many firsthand accounts by females.[17] The focus of this chapter and the next, however, is on frontline experiences, and so male voices dominate. Chapter 6, with its focus on gender and everyday peace, goes some way towards addressing this imbalance.

A second methodological concern regarding the use of war memoirs and personal diaries relates to temporality. Many were written considerably after the event, sometimes decades later,[18] and so questions can be raised about the accuracy of memory and the possibility that the events of the author's youth are refracted through modern-day sensibilities. Indeed, war memoirs probably contain a good deal of self-censorship.[19] This may be particularly true of those on the losing side of conflict, lest victor's justice or a war crimes prosecution catch up with them. Some authors are alert to the frailty-of-memory issue, however. George MacDonald Fraser, who later found fame as the novelist behind the Flashman series, reflected on his experiences as a WWII British conscript who was sent to Burma:

> Looking back over sixty-odd years, life is like a piece of string with knots in it, the knots being those moments that live in the mind forever, and the intervals being hazy, half-recalled times when I have a fair idea of what was happening, in a general way, but cannot be sure of dates or places or even the exact order in which events took place.[20]

David Render, a British tank commander during WWII, has similar concerns about his powers of recall:

> I kept no diary; few of us had any time or inclination for that. Consequently my recall is less than complete. The distance of time has no doubt taken its toll and while some recollections are retained in vivid Technicolor detail, as if they happened only yesterday, others are masked by obscurity and I have only a vague sense of the time and space in which they occurred.... I can still remember the satisfying feel of my beautifully balanced black-blue Luger pistol in my hand,

---

[17] Myrna Goldenberg, 'Lessons Learned from Gentle Heroism: Women's Holocaust Narratives', *Annals of the American Academy of Political and Social Science* 548, no. 1 (1996): 78–93; Karen Tei Yamashita, *Letters to Memory* (Minneapolis: Coffee House, 2017).

[18] See, for example, Bill Bellamy, *Troop Leader: A Tank Commander's Story* (Stroud, UK: Sutton, 2005), xi.

[19] L. H. E. Kleinreesink and Joseph M. M. L. Soeters, 'Truth and (Self) Censorship in Military Memoirs', *Current Sociology* 64, no. 3 (2016): 373–391. See also Norman Hampson, *Not Really What You'd Call a War* (Caithness, UK: Whittles, 2001), ix; Stuart Hills, *By Tank into Normandy: A Memoir of the Campaign in North-West Europe from D-Day to VE Day* (London: Cassell, 2003), 15; George Coppard, *With a Machine Gun to Cambrai: A Story of the First World War* (London: Cassel, 1999), xv.

[20] George MacDonald Fraser, *Quartered Safe Out Here: A Recollection of the War in Burma* (London: HarperCollins, 2000), xiv.

with its wonderfully smooth action. But for the life of me, I can remember nothing of the German I took it from or where and when he was captured.[21]

In some cases, memoirs and diaries have been edited by family members[22] and friends, and, again, there is the risk that later generations sanitise, distort, and write over firsthand accounts. One memoirist, a former member of the Waffen-SS, pleaded with readers 'for fairness in that those who judge me do not do so from under that banner of "political correctness" which prevails in the current epoch'.[23]

Just as there are concerns about accounts written or edited decades after an event, we should also be concerned about diary accounts written in the heat of battle. Frontline warfare is unlikely to be conducive to diary writing, given the frequency of movement, the risk of losing a diary, and the rules against keeping diaries lest information fall into the hands of the enemy.[24] Frontline diaries also often have gaps in the chronology—a result of frontline 'busyness', fatigue, injury, or leave—or a combination of the list.[25] Some historians have been dismissive of 'instant history' or contemporaneous journalistic accounts of warfare that are devoid of context and do not offer the ability to go back and check facts.[26] At least one author, Robert Kee, was glad not to have the opportunity to polish his account of being a prisoner of war. His memoir, written just after WWII, was 'an immediate distillation of personal experience without the advantage or disadvantage of . . . hindsight, maturity or sophistication'.[27] Another, with the benefit of hindsight, recognised that his diaries 'made cruel, superficial (not infrequently) inaccurate initial judgements which now rather disgust me'.[28] Similarly, some war diaries may be criticised for being focused too heavily on the present moment and unable to see the larger picture. Again, Fraser was alert to the tendency of the ground-level soldier to see the immediate and tactical rather than the strategic and contextual:

---

[21] Render, *Tank Action*, xxiv–xxv.
[22] See, for example, Andreas Hartinger, *Until the Eyes Shut: Memories of a Machine Gunner on the Eastern Front, 1943–45* (Zurich: Andreas Hartinger, 2019).
[23] Herbert Maeger, *Lost Honour, Betrayed Loyalty: The Memoir of a Waffen-SS Soldier on the Eastern Front* (London: Frontline, 2019), xiii–xiv.
[24] Alan J. M. Miller, *Over the Horizon, 1939–1945* (Finavon, UK: Finavon Print & Design, 1999), v; White, *With the Jocks*, xix.
[25] See, for example, Jack Swaab, *Field of Fire: Diary of a Gunnery Officer* (Stroud, UK: Sutton, 2007).
[26] Kevin Williams, 'War Correspondents as Sources for History', *Media History* 18, nos. 3–4 (2012): 343. For an example of a book with virtually no personal or political context, see Wilhelm Johnen, *Duel under the Stars: The Memoir of a Luftwaffe Night Pilot in World War II* (Barnsley, UK: Greenhill, 2018).
[27] Robert Kee, *A Crowd Is Not Company* (London: Phoenix, 2000), 7.
[28] Swaab, *Field of Fire*, xviii.

With all military histories it is necessary to remember that war is not a matter of maps with red and blue arrows and oblongs, but of weary, thirsty men with sore feet and aching shoulders wondering where they are, and when the historian writes: '17th Division closed in on Pyawbwe from all directions' that this involved the advance of long green lines of bush-hatted men ... little Nixon making his usual philosophic remark that we'd all git killed and he didn't want to die Tojo's way, and someone falling down a well and having to be pulled out, and it ended with a hectic charge to a wrecked railway line, and we caught them in the open on the other side....

Eleven hundred Japanese died in that battle; the official history records the fact, but doesn't tell you how.[29]

From the perspective of this book, the ground-level accounts are highly valued. They tend to be contextualised not in terms of geo-strategy but in terms of an immediate circle of comrades, the circumstances of a battle or billet, and a host of prosaic issues such as food, sanitation, and comfort. These accounts are particularly useful in illustrating everyday peace, as it was often infantry soldiers who encountered civilians and enemy troops and had opportunities to show sociality, reciprocity, and solidarity.

A third methodological issue is the phenomenon of the fake war memoir. The falsification of war memoirs is not widespread, but it does exist. Misha Defonseca's best-selling Holocaust memoir[30] 'described how she set out alone, at age 7, to find her Jewish parents who had been deported by the Nazis. Walking 1,900 miles across Europe, over the course of five years, she spent time in the Warsaw Ghetto, lived with wolves and killed a German soldier in self-defense'.[31] It was later discovered that the author was Catholic and had been attending school in Brussels during the war. Similarly, Slavomir Rawicz's 'true story of a trek to freedom' from WWII Soviet Russia is fictitious—or contains very substantial fictional additions—despite the book's success in spawning a Hollywood movie.[32] The authenticity of most war memoirs is relatively easy to verify, however, in that the authors signal multiple points of identification (for example, a regiment or ship) and mention the names of comrades and commanding officers and places where the regiment or ship might have been on particular dates.

---

[29] Fraser, *Quartered Safe*, xii–xiii.
[30] Misha Defonseca, *Misha: A Memoire of the Holocaust Years* (Boston: Mount Ivy, 1997).
[31] Lyn Garrity, 'Five Fake Memoirs That Fooled the Literary World', *Smithsonian Magazine*, 20 December 2010, https://www.smithsonianmag.com/arts-culture/five-fake-memoirs-that-fooled-the-literary-world-77092955/.
[32] Slavomir Rawicz, *Long Walk: The True Story of a Trek to Freedom* (New York: Lyons, 2010). See also Hugh Levinson, 'How the Long Walk Became the Way Back', *BBC News*, 4 December 2010, http://www.bbc.co.uk/news/world-11900920.

A fourth methodological point is to note the omissions in many war memoirs. While many firsthand accounts are searing in their honesty and many are self-deprecating and downplay individual acts of bravery, very few admit to egregious acts of violence against non-combatants. While theft and looting were part and parcel of warfare, few memoirs contain admissions of theft.[33] Of particular concern is the almost complete ignorance of the Holocaust in German WWII memoirs.[34] Even troops who invaded eastern and central Europe and Russia, spent considerable time there, and presumably witnessed the actions of the Einsatzgruppen and other anti-Jewish operatives express ignorance of the Holocaust in their memoirs.[35] What makes this ignorance difficult to believe is that secret recordings of German prisoners of war contain multiple references to the mass murder of Jews.[36] There are a few exceptions to the professed ignorance in the memoirs. SS soldier Herbert Maeger recalled a fellow patient in a military hospital telling him he participated in a massacre of more than three thousand Jews in Odessa in November 1941.[37]

A final point to note with regard to historiography is that most 'bottom-up' published accounts of war originate from those who served in militaries from the global north. The world wars were reasonably global, with extensive theatres of operation and conscription. The British, for example, used very substantial numbers of soldiers and ancillary workers recruited from their empire.[38] As Barkawi notes, 'Around 1.27 million men passed through the Indian army's ranks in the first world war, with nearly 50,000 Indian soldiers among the 947,000 British and imperial war dead'.[39] Accounts from colonial personnel do exist, especially in the form of letters and oral histories, but they are rare in comparison with those from soldiers from the global north.[40] The dominance of Atlanticist views of the

[33] The taking of 'trophies' is quite common, such as Miller taking binoculars from a German U-boat captain (*Over the Horizon*). Taking food and drink also seemed to be 'fair game'. See, for example, Richard Freiherr von Rosen, *Panzer Ace: The Memoirs of an Iron Cross Panzer Commander: From Barbarossa to Normandy* (Barnsley, UK: Greenhill, 2018), 57. Swaab is explicit in his mentions of 'loot' and 'booty' (*Field of Fire*, 346, 351).

[34] See, for example, Arnim Böttger, *To the Gate of Hell: The Memoir of a Panzer Crewman* (Barnsley, UK: Frontline, 2012), chap. 17; Rosen, *Panzer Ace*, 386.

[35] An exception can be found in the journals of Hans Roth. See Christine Alexander and Mason Kunz, eds., *Eastern Inferno: The Journals of a German Panzerjager on the Eastern Front 1941–1943* (Philadelphia: Casemate, 2010), journal 1, 26 September 1942.

[36] Sönke Neitzel and Harald Welzer, *Soldaten: On Fighting, Dying and Killing: The Secret Second World War Tapes of German POWs* (London: Simon & Schuster, 2012). The book contains multiple excerpts referring to the mass murder of Jews (pp. 99–135) as well as many other privations and human rights abuses.

[37] Maeger, *Lost Honour*, 361.

[38] D'Costa, 'Once Were Warriors'.

[39] Tarak Barkawi, 'Culture and Combat in the Colonies: The Indian Army in the Second World War', *Journal of Contemporary History* 41, no. 2 (2006): 329.

[40] See, for example, Adrienne Israel, 'Measuring the War Experience: Ghanaian Soldiers in WWII', *Journal of Modern African Studies* 25, no. 1 (1987): 159–168; Laura Rice, 'African Conscripts/European Conflicts: Race, Memory and the Lessons of War', *Culture Critique* 45 (2000): 109–149; Christian Koller, 'Representing Otherness: African, Indian and European Soldiers' Letters and

world wars defies the historical evidence that these were extremely complex and geographically widespread events.[41] While they did involve large numbers of uniformed men from Germany, France, the United Kingdom, Russia/the Soviet Union, and the United States fighting in clearly defined battles in Europe, the wars also impacted a series of more localised conflicts, many of them beyond the European core. Thus, for example, the Japanese attempted to fan anti-colonial resentment in India, Burma, and elsewhere during WWII.[42] Nationalist groups were co-opted by various militaries to act as partisans and guerrillas.[43] Much of this messy history of shifting subnational alliances and localised nationalisms has been subsumed into overly neat accounts of the wars.

Methodological and historiographical concerns notwithstanding, the vividness and immediacy of firsthand accounts are irreplaceable. One of the remarkable features of many war memoirs and personal diaries is their inconsistency. In one passage, the author might express empathy for the plight of the enemy, especially if that enemy is wounded. In another passage, he might make assertions about the beastliness of the enemy. This inconsistency is useful in helping our thinking on everyday peace. Indeed, one WWII British gunnery officer captures well the mixed emotions when his regiment crossed into Germany in early 1945:

> The Germans here—so few have remained—are servile and distracted. It is difficult to be as hard-hearted as one would like at the sight of these wretched old men and women and children watching even the ruins of their houses burned by their own shelling. But plenty of old and young have wept because of the Germans during the last few years—it is good that they should taste now, for the first time, the bitter medicine they have forced down the throat of Europe for the past five and a half years.[44]

In many cases, everyday peace is episodic and opportunistic. It does not define the person permanently in all his or her actions and thinking. Instead, individuals and groups might deploy sociality and solidarity with the out-group when they can—perhaps when outside the surveillance of others. This point illustrates the utility of our focus on power and circuitry. Acts of everyday peace by

---

Memoirs', in *Empire and First World War Writing*, ed. S. Das (Cambridge: Cambridge University Press, 2011), 127–142; David Omissi, ed., *Indian Voices of the Great War: Soldiers' Letters 1914–1918* (Basingstoke, UK: Macmillan, 1999).

[41] Gary Sheffield, *Forgotten Victory: The First World War: Myths and Realities* (London: Headline Review, 2002), 324–331.
[42] T. R. Sareen, 'Subhas Chandra Bose, Japan and British Imperialism', *European Journal of East Asian Studies* 3, no. 1 (2004): 69–97. See also Joachim Oesterheld, 'The Last Chapter of the Indian Legion', *South Asian Chronicle* 5 (2015): 120–143.
[43] See, for example, Fitzroy Maclean, *Eastern Approaches* (London: Penguin, 2009).
[44] Swaab, *Field of Fire*, 344.

individuals and small groups denote an exercise of power. But this power might be constrained by the actions and power of other actors, notably power mobilised through a state for warfare and the extreme hierarchical power found in military organisations. Acts of everyday peace, mercy, and empathy occurring outside the surveillance of others, especially powerful others, are a reminder of the usefulness of circuitry as an analytical device. Individuals and small groups may be thought of as circuits within circuits. Ultimately, they inhabit a series of wider systems such as a company, regiment, national military, and a system of alliances. But they can feel removed from these large circuits and sometimes operate with minimal surveillance.

The war memoirs and personal diaries also help us think about scale. These sources often see grand historical schemes, like the world wars or campaigns within them, through highly personalised and localised frames. Thus, a battle to capture a particular town or city is rendered into an account involving the soldier and his comrades and the immediate battlescape of foxholes, bridges, hedgerows, and routes. The immediacy and smallness of scale allow us to envisage the interpersonal and intimate scale on which everyday peace takes place. The decision of whether to shoot the prone figure in front of you or take him prisoner ultimately is a snap decision made by the individual or a small group of individuals. Military commanders and political leaders can control the wider context, but the individual must make decisions or follow orders from immediate superiors, often in chaotic or fast-moving circumstances. It may be that individuals are able to show sociality, reciprocity, and even solidarity towards the enemy in spaces that they can—circumstances permitting—carve out. Making this space, even if momentarily, is a form of power. It has the potential to disrupt the dominant narrative and mode of societal organisation.

The Apparently Totalising Nature of War

Before examining formal truces, ceasefires, and attempts to inject civility into war, it is worth noting the apparently totalising and brutalising nature of warfare. The reason for this approach is to remind us of the courage and bravery required by those prepared to dissent from, and resist, official narratives of the war. In the context of war, everyday peace, or the showing of empathy and solidarity with 'the enemy', is exceptional and, as will be discussed further in chapter 7, has the potential to disrupt conflict and the logic that underpins it. Importantly, the emphasis in this section is on the *apparently* totalising impact of war and conflict. Everyday peace operates on the premise that individuals and groups can create space in which to disrupt the norms of war. Nevertheless, violent conflicts can seem totalising, with little space for anything other than total mobilisation and loyalty to the in-group. This section paints a more complex and nuanced picture in which there may be space for actions and stances that can constitute everyday peace

Both intra- and inter-state wars can be apparently totalising in the sense that they compel the extraordinary mobilisation of people and resources for the cause. Conscription, rationing, and the direction of people and material towards a single aim require an extraordinary justificatory narrative, often couched in terms of an existential threat or the need to address a grievance. Playing a key role in this is the elevation of the military to an exalted role in society. As one Soviet schoolgirl noted in her diary in the midst of the Siege of Leningrad (September 1941–January 1944), 'Every one of our soldiers is a hero of the Motherland'.[45] Sustained and total war leads to the normalisation of militarism, where valour and virtue are associated with the life of the soldier. In this extraordinary extract, future British prime minister Winston Churchill comes close to onanism with this ecstatic riff from the frontlines of the Second Boer War (October 1899–May 1902):

> Those who live under the conditions of the civilised city . . . gain luxury at the expense of joy. But the soldier wakes in an elation of body and spirit without an effort and with scarcely a yawn. There is no more moment delicious in the day than this, when we light the fire . . . knowing that there is another whole day begun . . . free from all cares. All care—for who can be worried about little matters of humdrum life when he may be dead before night? . . . Here life itself, life at its best and healthiest, awaits the caprice of a bullet.[46]

A key organising principle of military life is the subjugation of the individual to the organisation and a rigid respect for rules and hierarchy.[47] As one former British soldier of WWII reflected, 'One thing I had learned during my army training was the importance of keeping my mouth shut . . . anything but blind obedience would be counter-productive'.[48] In a sense, the military is an extreme version of Weberianism. On joining the military, the individual is given a number, a uniform, and a regulation haircut; sleeps in a dormitory; eats regulation food at set times; and has his or her day set out for them. It is a process that strips autonomy from the individual so that he or she follow orders and

---

[45] Lena Mukhina, *The Diary of Lina Mukhina: A Girl's Life in the Siege of Leningrad* (Basingstoke, UK: Macmillan, 2012), 67.

[46] Cited in W. J. Reader, *At Duty's Call: A Study in Obsolete Patriotism* (Manchester, UK: Manchester University Press, 1998), 32.

[47] Alexander Cooley, *Logics of Hierarchy: The Organization of Empires, States and Military Occupations* (Ithaca, NY: Cornell University Press, 2005); Mark J. Osiel, *Obeying Orders: Atrocity, Military Discipline and the Law of War* (Piscataway, NJ: Transaction, 2001).

[48] Render, *Tank Action*, 27, 31.

use violence when directed to do so. Military training regimes are a form of 'institutionalised programming' that compels soldiers to conform and adopt the 'cultural grammar' of the organisation.[49] Although military organisations in wartime were principally orientated towards violence against other militaries (and 'hostile' civilians), it is also clear that militaries are also sites of considerable in-group coercion and bullying.[50] Whether through initiation ceremonies, the inclusion and exclusion of bonding, or the very obvious hierarchies of rank, there are multiple accounts of violence *within* militaries. This was often directed against those who were regarded as different, difficult, or nonconformist. Militarism, in a sense, is an extreme exercise in social control and the numbing of dissent and individualism. It is, in the language of peace studies, a form of indirect violence.

Hierarchy is important in militaries, with the flow of orders unidirectional except in the most exceptional of circumstances.[51] To a large extent in the United Kingdom, France, and Germany, the class system was superimposed on military structures, with the landed and titled classes assuming leadership roles.[52] One British soldier recalled of his Officer Selection Board, 'How you held your knife and fork and asked someone to pass the salt, without using an expletive, was deemed to be important'.[53] A German officer recounted how, during his pre-WWII training, 'Social affairs were arranged so we could practice our social graces and be evaluated. We often had dances to which daughters of older officers were invited. Anyone who had not learned how to dance properly had to learn now'.[54] During WWII, German officers in particular seemed zealous in demanding respect from the lower ranks. One German soldier remembers hearing a wounded officer, on a hospital train leaving the eastern front, protesting, 'I am an officer and demand a hospital compartment for officers'.[55]

The military emphasis on hierarchy and the institution of penalties for not obeying hierarchy meant that military organisations were able to compel

---

[49] Christopher Coker, *The Warrior Ethos: Military Culture and the War on Terror* (London: Routledge, 2007), 92. Indeed, the military ethos can contain lessons for the business world. See, for example, Leslie E. Sekerka and Roxanne Zolin, 'Professional Courage in the Military: Regulation Fit and Establishing Moral Intent', *Business and Professional Ethics Journal* 24, no. 4 (2005): 27–50.

[50] See the quite shocking stories of bullying in Arkady Babchenko, *One Soldier's War in Chechnya* (London: Portobello, 2008). See also Brian Sewell's account of being raped during his military service in *Outsider: Always Almost, Never Quite: An Autobiography*. (London: Quartet, 2012).

[51] Hew Strachan, 'Introductory Essay: The Changing Character of War', in *Conceptualising Modern War*, edited by Karl Erik Haug and Ole Jørgen Maaø (New York: Columbia University Press, 2011), 5. For an exception to the hierarchical rule, see George Orwell's description of revolutionary forces in the Spanish Civil War in *Homage to Catalonia* (London: Penguin, 1989), 8.

[52] Reader, *At Duty's Call*, 96.

[53] Render, *Tank Action*, 33.

[54] Siegfried Knappe and Ted Brusaw, *Soldat: Reflections of a German Soldier 1936–1949* (New York: Orion, 1992), 107–108.

[55] Böttger, *To the Gate of Hell*, 20. See also White, *With the Jocks*, 324, 513.

individuals and groups of individuals to engage in activities that—ordinarily— would be regarded as exceptional. One WWII German veteran of the eastern front recalled, 'The simple infantryman never had a choice. It was simply a matter of fight, or die. We were soldiers, and we did our duty, and that was all there was to it'.[56] Ashworth notes that the 'norm of offensiveness' was inculcated into soldiers: 'The exemplary soldier . . . was the soldier who, on his own initiative, instigated action likely to cause the enemy deprivation. The object of war was to eliminate the enemy both physically and morally'.[57] Yet the norm of offensiveness was not the condition that many men were used to—especially those coming from the relatively settled Europe of the early twentieth century who would soon find themselves in WWI. One Australian infantryman serving in the trenches of northern Europe in WWI opined, 'Probably we are becoming callous, but wouldn't you be, living among the things we experience?'[58] A German soldier recalled in the first days of the WWII invasion of France, 'The first dead soldiers I saw were French Moroccans. . . . The experience was impossible to forget'. A few days later, he noted, 'How quickly the definition of "normal" can change in just a few short days'.[59] As a US WWII soldier noted, 'one becomes incredibly hardened'.[60] He later reflected, 'I know that I hate my work in this war, that the war itself is slowly attempting to destroy all that I hold jealously as my own'.[61] Soldiers new to combat were 'blooded' or encouraged to engage in offensive activity. A British tank commander who did not machine-gun fleeing Germans during WWII on the grounds that it would be 'unsporting' was left in no doubt by his superior of the need to develop a 'killer instinct'.[62]

Certainly, the experiences of warfare inure men and women towards the toughness and insensitivity that were required to keep going. Militaries, states, and their propaganda organs work hard to condition publics and soldiers to killing. In a very prosaic example, the executioners at the Butovo shooting range, the execution site outside Moscow where more than 21,000 people were shot in the Stalinist 'Great Terror', were provided with buckets of vodka to make their task more palatable.[63] But more sophisticated methods, especially propaganda, were utilised. A WWII German paratrooper confided in his diary his reaction to a speech by Nazi propaganda minister Joseph Goebbels in the aftermath of the

---

[56] Albrecht Wacker, *Sniper on the Eastern Front: The Memoirs of Sepp Allerberger, Knights Cross* (Barnsley, UK: Pen and Sword, 2008), chap. 12.
[57] A. E. Ashworth, 'The Sociology of Trench Warfare 1914–18', *British Journal of Sociology* 19, no. 4 (1968): 409.
[58] E. P. F. Lynch, *Somme Mud: The Experiences of an Infantryman in France, 1916–1919* (London: Bantam, 2008), 57.
[59] Knappe and Brusaw, *Soldat*, 149, 152.
[60] J. Glenn Gray, *The Warriors: Reflections of Men in Battle* (Lincoln, NE: Bison, 1998), 9.
[61] Gray, *The Warriors*, 163.
[62] Render, *Tank Action*, 162.
[63] Karl Schlögel, *Moscow 1937* (Cambridge: Polity, 2012), 472, 484.

German defeat at Stalingrad: 'I can't get the Goebbels speech calling for total war out of my mind. The speech was so tremendous.... Everyone was carried away by his words, all of us were under his spell. He spoke to us from the heart. Total War at last—yes of course, but why not earlier?'[64] Hugo Slim's *Killing Civilians* notes the multiple ways in which regimes condition populations so that killing can be normalised: dehumanising the enemy; coercive forms of authority, obedience, and conformity; euphemistic distancing from killing; entry into an altered state; mobilising grievances; acceptance of traditions of violence; blooding; repeating and normalising killing; and social bonds around killing.[65] This chimes with the discussion of power in chapter 3 and the extent to which we might be complicit in actions that are injurious to us and to society more generally. Ashworth sets out how WWI soldiers were conditioned to hate the enemy:

> During the socialization process the state and military organizations had equipped the soldier with an image of the enemy which . . . provided a surrogate motive for violence. Thus the enemy was defined as a sub-human thing capable of all conceivable crimes, from the crucifixion of prisoners to the killing and raping of women and children. The organisation image was designed, in short, to maximize the difference between the soldier and his foe.[66]

Memoirs by unreformed Nazis often reveal just how complete the process of dehumanisation of the other had been. Hans Ulrich Rudel, a celebrated Stuka pilot and post-war unrepentant Nazi, referred to Soviet soldiers as 'oriental hordes'.[67] Fellow Nazi Hans Roth recalled after a battle with Soviet troops, 'How wonderful it is that we are able to exterminate these murderous beasts. How good it is that we have pre-empted them; for in the coming weeks these bloodhounds might have been standing on German soil'.[68] Another German soldier serving on the eastern front noted that, 'Within me at least, they [Soviet soldiers] had sowed a seed of hatred for them all without exception, and I vowed that I would never spare a single one of them if I had the chance to shoot'.[69] This viewpoint was reciprocated by Soviet soldiers. One female Soviet soldier recounted:

> We took prisoners, brought them to the detachment. . . . We didn't shoot them, that was too easy a death for them; we stuck them with ramrods like pigs, we cut them to pieces. I went to look at it. . . . I waited! I waited a long time for the

---

[64] Martin Pöppel, *Heaven and Hell: The War Diary of a German Paratrooper* (Staplehurst, UK: Spellmount, 2000), 101.
[65] Hugo Slim, *Killing Civilians: Method, Madness and Morality in War* (London: Hurst, 2007), 217.
[66] Ashworth, 'The Sociology of Trench Warfare', 420–421.
[67] Hans Ulrich Rudel, *Stuka Pilot* (London: Black House, 2011), 4.
[68] Alexander and Kunz, *Eastern Inferno*, journal 1, 22 June 1942.
[69] Wacker, *Sniper*, location 727.

moment when their eyes would begin to burst from pain.... The pupils.... They burned my mother and little sisters on a bonfire in the middle of our village.[70]

Mobilising all of these factors requires resources and effort, yet it can produce the desired result. In a remarkable autobiography, Andy Balaam, a special forces soldier in the Rhodesian military in the late 1970s and early 1980s and later a mercenary for various African regimes, tells of his mental detachment from killing. After an ambush on pro-independence fighters, he recalled:

> I stared at the bodies twenty metres in front of me. I felt absolutely nothing. No sorrow at having killed another human being, no pride or happiness in having killed an enemy of my country, nothing, just emptiness. . . . There was also the occasional young girl—civilians, unarmed and caught in a terrorist camp, they never stood a chance. Innocent civilians caught in the crossfire? Innocent? You decide . . . they blended in. . . . In the heat of battle, it would be impossible to distinguish between civilians and terrorists.[71]

Later he recounts the start of an attack on a suspected rebel base inside Mozambique:

> [We] headed to the closest of several stores, our task being to kill any enemy therein and burn them to the ground. We were like two kids on a picnic, smiling and chatting, AK-47s in one hand, petrol bombs in the other.[72]

The key point is that war is brutalising and dehumanising and places individuals and groups in contexts in which they engage in extraordinarily harmful activities. Some soldiers may have an inclination for killing. A British officer of WWII remembered one of his sergeants as 'a ruthless personality who appeared to relish killing and had personally accounted for many of our enemies'.[73] Another recalled a British sergeant of 'unbelievable ferocity'.[74] Yet many other soldiers were probably socialised and conditioned into a position where killing was acceptable and justified through revenge.[75] One WWII soldier referred to 'blunting and mental brutalization',[76] while studies of veterans in more recent wars have

---

[70] Unnamed Soviet soldier quoted in Svetlana Alexievich, *The Unwomanly Face of War* (London: Penguin, 2017), xxxii.
[71] A. J. Balaam, *Bush War Operator: Memoirs of the Rhodesian Light Infantry, Selous Scouts and Beyond* (Solihull, UK: Helion, 2014), 56–57.
[72] Balaam, *Bush War Operator*, 106–107.
[73] Robert Woollcombe, *Lion Rampant: The Memoirs of an Infantry Officer from D-Day to the Rhineland*, Kindle ed. (Edinburgh: Black and White, 2014), 12.
[74] Swaab, *Field of Fire*, xvii.
[75] Wacker, *Sniper*, location 727.
[76] Hans Heinz Rehfeldt, *Mortar Gunner on the Eastern Front*, Vol. 1, *From the Moscow Winter Offensive to Operation Zitadelle* (Barnsley, UK: Greenhill, 2019), iv.

identified the concept of 'moral injury' or the long-lasting impact of involvement in war on outlook and decision-making.[77] Murdering prisoners and firing on stretcher-bearers and medics were routine in both world wars, despite international conventions prohibiting such actions.[78] The phrase 'no prisoners were taken' is reasonably common in war memoirs,[79] and one can surmise that there are very many cases in which prisoners were murdered but no records were kept. Charles B. MacDonald, a US officer in WWII, recounts how a subordinate whom he told to escort a German prisoner to the rear reported to him in Normandy in 1944:

> 'To tell you the truth, cap'n, we didn't get to A company. The sonofabitch [a German prisoner] tried to make a run for it. Know what I mean?'
> 'Oh, I see', I said slowly, nodding my head. 'I see'.[80]

Referring to another incident of prisoner murder, MacDonald recorded, 'Company C today committed a war crime. They are going to win the war, however, so I don't suppose it really matters'.[81] A British naval lieutenant commander recounts how the Polish commander of a destroyer responded, 'Prisoners—what prisoners?' when asked about the fate of German sailors who had been picked up from the Mediterranean following an Allied–Axis encounter in WWII.[82]

The experiences of war, along with the deliberate conditioning of soldiers to dehumanise the enemy, created contexts in which prisoner murder was acceptable. Here a Welsh soldier serving in WWI recounts:

> I met a man of one of our companies with six German prisoners whom he told me he had to take back to a place called Clapham Junction, where he would hand them over... he said 'Look here, Dick. About an hour ago I lost the best pal I ever had, and he was worth all of these six Jerries [Germans] put together.

---

[77] Joseph M. Currier, Jason M. Holland, and Jesse Malott, 'Moral Injury, Meaning Making and Mental Health in Returning Victims', *Journal of Clinical Psychology* 71, no. 3 (2014): 229–246; Tine Moledijk, 'Moral Injury in Relation to Public Debates: The Role of Societal Misrecognition in Moral Conflict-Colored Trauma among Soldiers', *Social Science and Medicine* 211 (2018): 314–320.

[78] Heather Jones, *Violence against Prisoners of War in the First World War: Britain, France and Germany, 1914–1920* (Cambridge: Cambridge University Press, 2013). See also Ernst Jünger's revelation on the routinisation of killing Russian prisoners of war in *A German Officer in Occupied Paris: The War Journals, 1941–1945* (New York: Columbia University Press, 2018), 29. See also Maeger, *Lost Honour*, p. 141. A rather surprising exception to most accounts of Japanese brutality to Allied prisoners can be found in R. P. W. Havers, *Reassessing the Japanese Prisoner of War Experience: The Changi POW Camp, Singapore, 1942–5* (London: RoutledgeCurzon, 2012).

[79] Herbert W. McBride, *A Rifleman Went to War*, Kindle ed. (London: Endeavour Compass, 2015), location 2692; Wacker, *Sniper*, location 2692.

[80] Charles B. MacDonald, *Company Commander: The Classic Infantry Memoir of WWII* (London: Endeavour, 2015), 44.

[81] MacDonald, *Company Commander*, 47.

[82] Miller, *Over the Horizon*, 113.

I'm not going to take them far before I put them out of mess'. Some little time later I saw him coming back and I knew it was impossible for him to have reached Clapham Junction and return in time. . . . As he passed me again he said, 'I done them in'. I had often heard some of our chaps say they had done their prisoners in whilst taking them back.[83]

In some cases, war created a logic in which the murder of prisoners was routine. Nazi Hans Roth, serving on the eastern front, confided in his diary, 'We have taken our first prisoners—snipers and deserters receive their just reward'.[84] Four days later, he records, 'A few comrades have pulled the remaining Rotamisten [Red Army soldiers] and Jews from their hiding places. A solo gun performance echoed across the square and with that . . . we move on'.[85] WWII German soldiers on the eastern front were required to obey the Commissar Order whereby 'Commissars and other political personnel taken prisoner were to be shot dead on the battlefield. I never saw it done during my four years in the East, but certainly many Commissars were liquidated in this way'.[86]

When prisoners were taken, their treatment was often appalling: unsanitary, degrading, and with much insensitivity as to whether they lived or not.[87] In some cases, prisoners were beaten to death.[88] Theft from prisoners was commonplace; indeed, theft of watches from prisoners seems to be mentioned in just about every memoir of those captured.[89] WWII German Luger pistols were also much prized by Allied troops.[90] At times, the thefts could be brutal. Ray Ellis, a British sergeant captured by Rommel's Afrika Korps in northern Africa, recounted:

> Here the Germans were collecting together all the prisoners taken in the vicinity. Amongst them was a [British] officer, still carrying his field glasses on a leather strap over his shoulders. A German officer walked up to him and demanded that he should hand over the glasses. The officer refused, whereupon, without further ado, the German drew his revolver and shot him point-blank in

---

[83] Frank Richards, *Old Soldiers Never Die* (Cardigan, UK: Parthian, 2016), 20.
[84] Alexander and Kunz, *Eastern Inferno*, journal 1, 22 June 1942, location 257.
[85] Alexander and Kunz, *Eastern Inferno*, journal 1, 26 June 1942, location 329.
[86] Rehfeldt, *Mortar Gunner*, iv.
[87] See, for example, Otto Carius, *Tigers in the Mud: The Combat Career of German Panzer Commander Otto Carius*, Kindle ed. (Mechanicsburg, VA: Stackpole, 2003), location 4208; Gray, *The Warriors*, 149–150. Charles Lamb, a naval pilot in WWII who was captured by the Vichy French, was particularly exercised by the poor sanitation provided for prisoners; *War in a Stringbag*, 231, 254, 259.
[88] Ellis, *Once a Hussar*, location 3009.
[89] See, for example, Ray Davey, *The War Diaries: From Prisoner of War to Peacemaker* (Belfast: Brehon, 2015), 125; Hein Severloh, *WN62: A German Soldier's Memories of the Defense of Omaha Beach, Normandy, June 6, 1944* (Garbsen, Germany: HEK Creativ, 2007), 84; Ellis, *Once a Hussar*, location 2781; Pöppel, *Heaven and Hell*, 237; Hartinger, *Until the Eyes Shut*, 151.
[90] White, *With the Jocks*, 501; Render, *Tank Action*, xxiv–xxv.

the chest. The stricken man staggered back and fell to the ground, and as he lay there kicking out his life, the German coolly stooped down, took the glasses and swaggered away without so much as a backward glance.[91]

The demonization of the other side reached such an extent that soldiers expected to be killed upon capture—an incentive not to be captured alive and to show little mercy to captives. An American soldier captured by the Germans on D-Day 'asked what would become of them, since they had been told during training in the USA that if they were taken prisoner by the Germans, they would be shot at once'.[92]

In some cases, in the midst of battle, adversaries were reported to have brandished white flags in order to lure soldiers—expecting a surrender—to their deaths.[93] A British officer said of the Germans in 1945:

> Their trick was to shout 'wounded' and wave a white flag, pretending to surrender, so that their comrades from a flank could ambush any of our men who went to bring them in, and as soon as we were wise to this the usual sanctity of a white flag was rudely depreciated.[94]

Just as the white flag was disrespected, the war memoirs include multiple cases in which medical orderlies were targeted, despite conventions outlawing this.[95] One British soldier serving during WWI in what is now Iraq recounted how 'stretcher bearing parties have gone out to collect [the] wounded but the Turks opened fire on them and they are forced to retire'.[96] Later the same soldier, Edward Roe— an 'old contemptible', or regular rather than conscripted soldier in the British Army—noted that respect for medical personnel had completely eroded:

> The laws of the Hague Convention (re) stretcher-bearers are a complete farce as they are grossly ignored. My stretcher-bearers and I wear the brassard of mercy and aid to wounded, friend and foe alike. We are not supposed to be armed; yet we are fully equipped. An extra two bandoliers of ammo is worn around the neck as an extra adornment. We also carry two bombs. I brought this point

---

[91] Ellis, *Once a Hussar*, location 2732.
[92] Severloh, *WN62*, 78.
[93] Fernand Kaiser, *We Will Not Go to Tuapse: From the Donets to the Order with the Legion Wallonie and the 5th SS Volunteer Assault Brigade 'Wallonien' 1942–45* (Solihull, UK: Helion, 2016), 115.
[94] Woollcombe, *Lion Rampant*, 31.
[95] McBride, *A Rifleman*, location 1134; W. H. Downing, *To the Last Ridge: The World War One Experiences of W H Downing* (London: Grub Street, 2005), 63.
[96] Peter Downham and Edward Roe, *Diary of an Old Contemptible: From Mons to Baghdad 1914–1919*, Kindle ed. (Barnsley, UK: Pen and Sword, 2015), location 4236.

before the medical officer and he simply replied, 'You're in a hostile country and it's an order'.[97]

A near-constant trope in WWII German war memoirs is the racist differentiation between the eastern and western fronts. On the eastern front, there seemed to be a widely held view that the Russians were subhuman and bestial, whereas foes on the western front were more amenable to reason:

> The Russian is a different opponent than the Belgian and French. At that time, we fought against men who, as soldiers, applied intelligence, endurance, and experience; the enemy here [on the eastern front] resembles a dull, indifferent, soulless machine of destruction and death . . . the French would have learned from experience and attempted to avoid unnecessary casualties. These guys here fight like mad and until nothing moves. They never surrender.[98]

This differentiation between an allowance for mercy on the western front and no mercy on the eastern front is noticeable in the following vignette from the western front told by a German veteran of the east. Following a German–US skirmish during the 1944 Battle of the Bulge, he noted:

> Their action hadn't ended yet when they [the Americans] sent their medics and an ambulance right into the battlefield to rescue their wounded. I couldn't believe my eyes. What kind of war was this? Nothing like this would have happened at the Eastern front, but here, some of the rules of war seemed still to be in place, valid for both sides. . . . This first encounter seemed to support our general feeling that these Amis [Americans] couldn't be regarded as mortal enemies.[99]

So it was not just antipathy to the enemy that endangered stretcher-bearers but the policy of militaries to militarise humanitarian roles.[100]

Sexual and gender-based violence (SGBV) played a very significant role in both world wars, especially WWII, yet its coverage in many memoirs is patchy.[101] While it is common to mention SGBV by the enemy,[102] there are virtually no admissions that one's own side might be guilty. An exception to this is Soviet dissident Lev Kopelev's memoir of the Russian drive west at the end of WWII. The

---

[97] Downham and Roe, *Diary*, location 5452.
[98] Roth, cited in Alexander and Munz, *Eastern Inferno*, journal 1, 18 July 1942, location 778.
[99] Johann Voss, *Black Edelweiss: A Memoir of Combat and Conscience by a Soldier of the Waffen SS*, Kindle ed. (n.p.: Aberjona, 2013), chap. 23, location 3452.
[100] Lynch, *Somme Mud*, 111.
[101] SGBV is discussed in chapter 6.
[102] For example, Hartinger, *Until the Eyes Shut*, 105.

following two quotations give an idea of the mass rapes and largely uncontrolled sexual assaults conducted by Russian troops in that phase of the war:

> It was evening when we drove into Neidenburg, a small town with tree-lined streets. The place was in flames. Again, the work of our own men. On a side street, by a garden fence, lay a dead old woman. Her dress ripped; a telephone receiver reposed between her scrawny thighs. They apparently tried to ram it into her vagina.[103]
>
> The street in front of the post office is broad, flanked by a neat line of trees. A woman, clutching a bag and bundle, is walking down the middle of the pavement, holding a girl by the hand. The woman's head is bandaged with a bloodied kerchief. The girl has blond pigtails, a tear-stained face and blood on her stockings. They walk hurriedly, ignoring the catcalls of the soldiers on the sidewalk, but look back and stop now and then.[104]

Many memoirs begin with pre-war accounts of an unremarkable childhood, often in stable family situations, in which there is naivete about relations with the opposite sex. Yet the privations of war, the unnaturalness of all-male contexts, and a generalised normalisation of violence seem to have become manifest in many circumstances. Just as the enemy was othered in many of the memoirs, so, too, were women.

The key point of this section has been to underline the brutal and brutalising nature of war and therefore to highlight how conflict disruption amounts to a significant transgression of the norms of war. War normalises killing on a large scale and a range of other harmful activities such as the displacement of people and the theft and destruction of property. In many cases, individuals and groups of individuals who had no experience of warfare were radicalised into becoming killers through conscription, training, and propaganda. Deviation from the 'norm' of offensiveness risked being seen as cowardice or treason. As chapter 5 illustrates, unwarlike activity during war often took place on the margins, after battle, or outside the surveillance of authority. It required the use of subterranean types of power that often connected with the individual's conscience or a sense of sociality. Yet individuals and groups of individuals were able, in some circumstances, to carve out space in which sociality, reciprocity, and even solidarity could be displayed. To do so involved utilising power—EPP. While the main circuitry of society might be mobilised and shaped by the war effort, individuals and groups of individuals were able to create their own micro-circuits. Some of these circuits were transgressive to the main war-oriented circuits and

---

[103] Lev Kopelev, *No Jail for Thought* (London: Secker & Warburg, 1975), 539.
[104] Kopelev, *No Jail*, 54.

allowed space for speech, actions, and stances that allowed for pro-social and pro-peace initiatives.

Before examining informal attempts at everyday peace in the context of war, the next section will examine formal or top-down attempts to limit war. These largely took the form of conflict management or the regulation of conflict and violence within certain parameters.[105] It was not necessarily disruptive to the overall conflict, and the power deployed was often top-down.

Formal Ceasefires and Truces

This section turns to breaks in and from war. It examines the formal truces and ceasefires that are ordered by those in command. These are top-down, authorised windows of pacificity in a wider context of conflict and violence. As they are top-down, we cannot regard them as examples of everyday peace, yet they can provide a context in which everyday peace can be forged at the ground level. This section is followed by the chapter conclusion, which relates back to two constant themes in this book: power and the analytical value of circuitry capture the multi-scalar nature of conflict and violence. Chapter 5 will examine the informal and tacit truces, and acts of empathy and kindness, that might be described as spontaneous, bottom-up, and going against wartime policies of continuous offensiveness. These acts might be described as everyday peace in extremis.

The terms *ceasefire*, *truce*, and *armistice* are often used interchangeably and indeed do mean the same thing or have marginal differences between them. We should not fuss too much about the precise meanings, as all of the terms generally fit under the rubric of negative peace. They are, in most cases, about staunching and regulating violence rather than anything more ambitious such as conflict transformation. A ceasefire, in a literal sense, is simply a cessation of violent hostilities. This might possibly be for strategic purposes such as negotiating a broader peace or shifting the balance of power between combatants through re-armament. A truce and an armistice can be regarded as similar to the ceasefire—a suspension of hostilities. In many cases, the term *truce* is used in relation to localised ceasefires, perhaps on the battlefield, and again may be thought of as a pause rather than a definitive cessation of conflict. Two additional terms to throw into the mix are *parley* and *humanitarian pause*. The term *parley* has gone out of fashion but was commonly used in medieval times to mean 'conversations between belligerents, carried out under a flag of truce either while the assembled orders of battle rested their arms before battle was joined, or at intervals in the

---

[105] Oliver Ramsbotham, Tom Woodhouse, and Hugh Miall, *Contemporary Conflict Resolution*, 3rd ed. (Cambridge: Polity, 2012), 31.

fighting, in conditions of temporary armistice, when neither side was clearly winning.[106] The more modern term *humanitarian pause* refers to temporary pauses in hostilities to allow humanitarian assistance—such as food or inoculations—to reach at-risk populations. Examples include Operation Lifeline Sudan which ran between 1989 and 1995, the N'Djamena Humanitarian Ceasefire Agreement in 2004 in Darfur, and the humanitarian pause declared for the eastern Ghouta suburb of Damascus in early 2018.[107] All of these were contentious and raised the thorny issue of humanitarian organisations having to cooperate with regimes and armed groups that had appalling human rights records.[108]

If we were to put together a general theory of ceasefires based on an optimistic reading of their potential, then we could say that the theory rests on three assumptions. The first of these is that a ceasefire or truce is regarded as step towards something more significant.[109] A ceasefire is, after all, simply a cessation of direct violence and sometimes referred to as a 'mere truce'.[110] The conflict resolution literature regards a ceasefire as a halt of direct violence that then allows for negotiations leading to a settlement. It is a lowering of tensions and the creation of a space that allows confidence-building measures to take effect and more expansive peace accords to be negotiated. The assumption is that the ceasefire is part of a linear conflict model and creates momentum that allows other pro-peace actions to take place.[111] A second assumption is that actors act rationally.[112] In other words, actors in violent conflict will make a rational calculation based on what is best for them. In our optimistic scenario, actors calculate that a ceasefire is a first step to something more substantial and therefore to be investigated in good faith. The ceasefire represents a credible commitment on behalf of the armed group. The third assumption is that hierarchies among combatant groups

---

[106] D. C. Watt, 'Summits and Summitry Reconsidered', *International Relations* 2, no. 8 (1963): 495. See also Laurence W. Marvin, 'War in the South: A First Look at Siege Warfare in the Albigensian Crusade, 1209–1218', *War in History* 8, no. 4 (2001): 384.

[107] S. D. Taylor-Robinson, 'Operation Lifeline Sudan', *Journal of Medical Ethics* 28 (2002): 49–51; Seth Appiah-Mensah, 'The African Mission in Sudan: Darfur Dilemmas', *African Security Studies* 15, no. 1 (2006): 1–19; Martin Chulov and Kareem Shaheen, 'Fighting Resumes in Eastern Ghouta despite "humanitarian pause"'. *Guardian*, 27 February 2018, https://www.theguardian.com/world/2018/feb/27/russia-humanitarian-pause-eastern-ghouta-syria-enclave.

[108] A particularly insightful work on this is Claire Magone, Michael Neuman, and Fabrice Weissman, eds., *Humanitarian Negotiations Revealed: The MSF Experience* (London: Hurst, 2011).

[109] Kristine Höglund and Marcus Wennerström, 'When the Going Gets Tough . . . Monitoring Missions and a Changing Conflict Environment in Sri Lanka, 2002–2008', *Small Wars & Insurgencies* 26, no. 5 (2015): 836–860. The view of a truce leading to something more significant can also be found in the psychiatry literature: Carlos E. Sluzki, 'The Pathway between Conflict and Reconciliation: Coexistence as an Evolutionary Process', *Transcultural Psychiatry* 47, no. 1 (2010): 55–69.

[110] Nir Eisikovits, *A Theory of Truces* (Houndmills, UK: Palgrave, 2016), 5.

[111] Ramsbotham, Woodhouse, and Miall, *Contemporary Conflict Resolution*, 14.

[112] David Stevenson, '1918 Revisited', *Journal of Strategic Studies* 28, no. 1 (2005): 107–139.

are intact and respected. Under such circumstances, once a ceasefire is declared, it would be respected without dissent from spoiler groups.

The assumptions on which the general theory of ceasefires rests are deserving of scrutiny. The first assumption, that a ceasefire leads to something more pacifically substantive, can be true. Many successful peace processes began with a ceasefire. The ceasefire was a first tangible step that resulted in the permanent end to violent conflict, a peace accord, and—crucially—a betterment in the life experiences and chances of people living in the conflict-affected areas.[113] Despite the success stories, many ceasefires and truces do not lead to anything significant.[114] It may be that one or all of the parties to the conflict conclude, having scoped out the possibilities through subterranean negotiations, that the circumstances are not propitious for a meaningful peace process.[115] But it may also be that the parties were not serious in their pacific intentions. Instead, ceasefires can be used as an opportunity to regroup and rearm.[116] Both Myanmar and India have seen the extensive use of ceasefires in anti-government insurgencies. In both cases, the signing of a ceasefire agreement has not resulted in a wider peace accord. Instead, the governments have used the ceasefires to buy time, to focus their military energies on particular insurgencies, and to give the impression that 'something is being done'. The insurgents have used the ceasefires to deflect pressure from government forces and to diversify into economic (much of it criminal) activities.[117] These ceasefires have taken the form of signed agreements, setting ground rules for behaviour during extended ceasefires, and the establishment of monitoring groups. Writing on Myanmar, David Brenner observed:

> For more than two decades the country's army sought to pacify many of these insurrections by negotiating separate ceasefire agreements with individual armed groups. While these armistices did not lead to substantial political

---

[113] See, for example, John Darby and Roger Mac Ginty, eds., *Contemporary Peacemaking: Conflict, Violence and Peace Processes* (Basingstoke, UK: Palgrave, 2003).
Roger Mac Ginty & John Darby, *Guns and Government: The management of the Northern Ireland peace process* (Basingstoke: Palgrave, 2002); John Darby & Roger Mac Ginty eds., 2000. *The Management of Peace Processes*. Basingstoke: Macmillan.

[114] Joseph M. Cox, 'Negotiating Justice: Ceasefires, Peace Agreements, and Post-Conflict Justice', *Journal of Peace Research* 57, no. 3 (2020): 466–481.

[115] This was the case with peace process collapses involving the Kurdistan Workers Party (PKK) and Turkey in 2013 and the Liberation Tigers of Tamil Eelam (LTTE) and Sri Lanka in 2008. See Kumru F. Toktamis, 'A Peace That Wasn't: Friends, Foes and Contentious Re-entrenchment of Kurdish Politics in Turkey', *Turkish Studies* 19, no. 5 (2018): 697–722; Malin Åkebo, *The Politics of Ceasefires: On Ceasefire Agreements and Peace Processes in Aceh and Sri Lanka* (Umeå, Sweden: Umeå University Department of Political Science, 2013).

[116] Dogukan Cansin Karakus and Isak Svensson, 'Between the Bombs: Exploring Partial Ceasefires in the Syrian Civil War, 2011–2017', *Terrorism and Political Violence* 32, no. 4 (2020): 696.

[117] Gurinder Singh, 'A Decade of Ceasefire in Nagaland', *Strategic Analysis* 31, no. 5 (2007): 815–832; Samrat Sinha, 'The Strategic Use of Peace: Non-State Armed Groups and Subnational Peacebuilding Mechanisms in Northeastern India', *Democracy and Security* 13, no. 4 (2017): 273–303.

dialogue, they allowed insurgents to retain their arms and govern pockets of territory. Moreover, these pacts encouraged armed group involvement in what has been referred to as the country's 'ceasefire capitalism' . . . the co-optation of rebels by way of economic incentives . . . produced remarkably stable settlements for many years.[118]

So the assumption that ceasefires lead to something more substantive needs to be tempered by a recognition that parties to a conflict can have 'devious objectives'[119] and regard a ceasefire as a stratagem to advance their cause.

A second assumption associated with ceasefires is that actors will act rationally in their own best interests. What constitutes 'rationality' and 'best interests' will, of course, be open to interpretation. Here it is worth noting that the outside observer's view of what is rational in a conflict situation may differ substantially from the views of those closer to the conflict. The observer furthermore may have the benefit of hindsight, full information, and the absence of an emotional and identity-related investment in the conflict. Moreover, outsiders may regard a conflict as simply not worth it and prioritise the saving of lives above the saving of face. Yet those involved in a conflict are engaged in the conflict in real time, without the benefit of hindsight. They very probably have imperfect knowledge on which to make decisions regarding a ceasefire or other ways to lower the costs of conflict.[120] They may be emotionally invested in the conflict, and indeed many have no choice about their involvement in the conflict. Residents of Gaza, for example, are likely to have been born into an enclave from which it is very difficult to escape. Parties to a conflict may act on the basis of principle, ideology, identity, and perceived righteousness. None of this may be viewed as 'rational' to outside observers, and the course of events may prove such actions to be imprudent. Yet parties to a conflict might be committed to pursuing an ideological objective and seeking revenge and regard alternatives as defeat or betrayal. Put simply, conflict has a considerable emotional dimension, and so rational choice models are of limited value.[121]

A third assumption on which a theory of ceasefires might be said to rest is that each of the parties to a conflict and ceasefire may be said to be unitary and disciplined. While the leadership of an armed group might agree to a ceasefire,

---

[118] David Brenner, 'Ashes of Co-optation: From Armed Group Fragmentation to the Rebuilding of Popular Insurgency in Myanmar', *Conflict, Security & Development* 15, no. 4 (2015): 338.

[119] Oliver P. Richmond, 'Devious Objectives and the Disputants' View of International Mediation: A Theoretical Framework', *Journal of Peace Research* 35, no. 6 (1998): 707–722.

[120] George H. Quester, 'Wars Prolonged by Misunderstood Signals', *Annals of the American Academy of Political and Social Sciences* 392, no. 1 (1970): 30.

[121] Eran Halperin and James J. Gross, 'Emotion Regulation in Violent Conflict: Reappraisal, Hope and Support for Humanitarian Aid to the Opponent in Wartime', *Cognition and Emotion* 25, no. 7 (2011): 1228–1236.

the organisation will require discipline and a respect for hierarchy in order for a cessation of hostilities to take effect. In a number of conflicts, the possibility of a peace process and a peace accord, and therefore the possibility of compromise and a failure to achieve the group's ultimate goal, has fuelled the emergence of splinter and spoiler groups.[122] In these cases, the armed actor (state or non-state) will have lost its monopoly position to speak and act on behalf of a community or constituency.

Ceasefires may be a step on the road to a peace process, a peace accord, and a more pacific society, but in many cases, they are about buying time for combatants who are manoeuvring for advantage.[123] In other words, they are a strategy of conflict and should not axiomatically be regarded as pacific. In most cases, it is appropriate to view ceasefires as within the realm of negative peace. While they might lower the costs of violent conflict, by themselves they do not address the basis of the conflict. In Hartzell's view, 'Negotiated truces focus on the process and modalities of ending violence in the short term rather than addressing questions of how power is to be exercised in the post-war state and by whom'.[124] In this perspective, nationalist groups in conflict with one another do not cease to be nationalists because a ceasefire has been declared. Multiple other steps from the positive peace and conflict transformation toolkits are required if negative peace is to become something more conciliatory and emancipatory.

Counter-intuitive as it may sound, pro-peace arguments can be made against ceasefires. A ceasefire may prolong a conflict and thus, in the long run, lead to greater human suffering. As Metz notes, 'truces are not always ethically appropriate, most clearly when they would inhibit a lasting and just peace, enabling an aggressive or otherwise unjust party to consolidate or make further large gains'.[125] Lest this sound ungenerous towards ceasefires, it is worth noting that in some circumstances, a ceasefire is all that can be achieved. Emotions may be too raw, and circumstances too unpropitious, to allow for anything more ambitious. As will be developed later in the book, the same argument (that this is all that can be achieved) can be applied to everyday peace.

By and large, formal truces and ceasefires are part of negative peace and so can be viewed as in keeping with the jus in bello tradition[126] that seeks to regulate

---

[122] For empirical work on the impact of spoilers and factionalism on peace processes, see Peter Rudloff and Michael G. Findlay, 'The Downstream Effects of Fragmentation on Civil War Reoccurrence', *Journal of Peace Research* 53, no. 1 (2016): 19–32; Hanne Fjelde and Desirée Nilsson, 'The Rise of Rebel Contenders: Barriers to Entry and Fragmentation in Civil Wars', *Journal of Peace Research* 55, no. 5 (2018): 551–565.

[123] Eisikovits, *A Theory of Truces*, 20.

[124] Caroline A. Hartzell, 'Settling Civil Wars: Armed Opponents' Fates and the Duration of the Peace', *Conflict Management and Peace Science* 26, no. 4 (2009): 363.

[125] Thaddeus Metz, 'Jus Interruptus Bellum: The Ethics of Truce-Making', *Journal of Global Ethics* 13, no. 1 (2017): 8.

[126] David Douncher, 'The Just War Tradition and Its Modern Legacy: Jus as Bellum and Jus in Bello', *European Journal of Political Theory* 11, no. 2 (2012): 92–111.

how war is fought without necessarily ending the war or addressing its causes. Attempts to regulate when war can be fought, and how it is fought, have a long history. The Olympic truce dates back almost three thousand years and was designed to give safety to competitors for the duration of the games.[127] Medieval and early modern wars were also subject to rules. The eleventh-century Truce of God, for example, sought to restrict fighting to four days per week across Europe.[128] Important in the regulation of medieval wars was the notion of chivalry, or a code of ethics on acceptable and unacceptable behaviour in battle and among nobility in general.[129] This pan-European princely code of ethics attached valour to combat but also emphasised honour.[130] Indeed, histories of the period make clear that peacemaking was a sophisticated business that involved issues of legitimacy, public perception, perceptions of hierarchy, and—in the European case—narratives of godliness.[131] In the early modern and modern eras, the regulation of warfare was aided by the formation of states that could raise and, crucially, have discipline over militaries.[132] The formation of states allowed for the codification of rules between states, and within this framework, a body of international humanitarian law (IHL) was able to develop.

Crucial to the development of IHL was the Lieber Code, a set of rules for the conduct of war developed during the American Civil War. The jurist Francis Lieber had a peculiar interest in attempting to make war more humane: two of his sons were fighting for the Union side and one for the Confederate side.[133] Lieber's code of conduct was adopted by the Union military and included the provision that prisoners be treated with humanity and that martial law be controlled.[134] Prominent among many other developments of a corpus, or suggested protocols, to humanise war were the 1864 Declaration of St. Petersburg, the 1868 Geneva Convention and establishment of the International Committee of the Red Cross, and the 1899 and 1907 Hague Conventions.[135] Taken together,

---

[127] Cindy Burleson, 'The Ancient Olympic Truce in Modern Day Peacekeeping: Revisiting Ekecheiria', *Sport in Society* 15, no. 6 (2012): 798–813. See also Eisikovits, *A Theory of Truces*, 45.

[128] Eisikovits, *A Theory of Truces*, 9.

[129] E. Amanda McVitty, 'False Knights and True Men: Contesting Chivalric Masculinity in English Treason Trials, 1388–1415', *Journal of Medieval History* 40, no. 4 (2014): 476.

[130] Katie Stevenson, 'Contesting Chivalry: James II and the Control of Chivalric Culture in the 1450s', *Journal of Medieval History* 33, no. 2 (2007): 203; Natasha Hodgson, 'Honour, Shame and the Fourth Crusade', *Journal of Medieval History* 39, no. 2 (2007): 220; Marlen Ferrer, 'State Formation and Courtly Culture in the Scandinavian Kingdoms in the High Middle Ages', *Scandinavian Journal of History* 37, no. 1 (2012): 1–22.

[131] Jenny Bentham, *Peacemaking in the Middle Ages: Principles and Practice* (Manchester, UK: Manchester University Press, 2011).

[132] Howard, *The Invention of Peace*, 12; Tilly, *Coercion*.

[133] David M. Crowe, 'War Crimes and Genocide in History, and the Evolution of Responsive International Law', *Nationalities Papers* 37, no. 6 (2009): 767.

[134] Jeff Roquen, 'International Law and "Humanity" in the Making and Unmaking of European Solidarity, 1830–1915', *European Review of History: Revue Européenne d'Histoire* 24, no. 6 (2017): 808.

[135] Shirley E. Freeman and Helen Ormiston Smith, 'War and International Humanitarian Law', *Medicine, Conflict and Survival* 13, no. 2 (1997): 117–118.

they formed a body of law and protocols designed to regulate war by, for example, banning certain weapons (such as exploding bullets), differentiating between combatants and non-combatants, and making it the responsibility of combatants to afford rights and protections to civilians, the wounded, and prisoners.

As many of the extracts from war memoirs in the previous section made clear, IHL was often ignored or deliberately flouted. Yet, over a century and a half, we have seen the formalisation of the rules of war, their recognition (if not adoption) by states, and the development of systems of global governance with the potential to further codify and police the rules of war. Key here has been the United Nations. Perhaps the most stunning point about the UN is that it still exists. Despite its shortcomings, and despite the continuing dominance and jealousy of national sovereignty, the UN remains the world's primary international security organisation. It has played a significant role in the limiting of types of violence (for example, through policing the manufacture of chemical weapons) and, from an early stage in its existence, has devoted significant energy to monitoring ceasefires.[136] This latter task has been particularly difficult in highly internationalised civil wars with multiple combatant groups. While some parties might agree to limit or cease violence, others might not. In April 2012, for example, following UN brokerage, the Syrian government agreed to:

(i) prohibit armed troops entering towns;
(ii) prohibit the use of heavy weapons within these populated centres; and
(iii) begin the withdrawal of troops currently stationed in and around the towns.

Rebel groups failed to come on board the ceasefire, a fact exploited by the Syrian regime and its external backers.[137]

The problems with ceasefires and the limitation of violence are rarely technical. It is not the case that lawyers need more time or resources to perfect 'Responsibility to Protect' or the finer details of the rules of engagement in an era of technological warfare. The issue instead is one of the political and military will of those involved in violent conflict. In some cases, conflicts are regarded as existential, and combatant parties cannot desist from conflict or cannot be seen to desist. In other cases, a calculation is made that there would be little advantage in limiting

---

[136] For example, the UN Truce Supervision Organisation (UNTSO), 1948–present and the UN Disengagement Observer Force (UNDOF), 1974–present.

[137] Gabriele Lombardo, 'The Responsibility to Protect and the Lack of Intervention in Syria between the Protection of Human Rights and Geopolitical Strategies', *International Journal of Human Rights* 19, no. 8 (2015): 1193.

or ceasing violence. From the point of view of this chapter, the essential point is that ceasefires and other conflict regulation mechanisms are an established part of warfare. They have the capacity to save and improve lives, and despite their often limited ambition, they must be regarded as a positive. They tend to be top-down and directed rather than bottom-up organic processes.

Conclusion

The aim of this chapter has been, first, to outline the brutal and brutalising nature of warfare and thus make clear that transgressive acts of everyday peace may be truly extraordinary in contradicting the norms of violence and conflict. Everyday peace actions and stances during war require considerable bravery and often occur outside of surveillance. The second aim of the chapter has been to provide a brief overview of top-down and authorised breaks in conflict. The point has been to illustrate that these forms of conflict management are often formulaic and scripted. They occur within the wider trope of conflict and formal attempts to limit and civilise war. The chapter deliberately chose examples from the 'hard cases' of the world wars in order to illustrate the exceptional nature of everyday peace in the context of war. The illustration of the brutality of war and militarism and the discussion of formal truces and attempts to 'civilise' war connect with two themes that run through this book: power and circuitry. The notion and practice of everyday peace face a considerable obstacle in the form of actors with the power to forbid, marginalise, or oppose everyday peace. States, governments, militaries, armed groups, and many others have the power to direct individuals and groups of individuals and to censure their behaviour. As we have seen in this chapter, war allows actors to accumulate and mobilise power for extraordinary purposes. Warfare usually involves a declaration of a state of emergency, the suspension of many citizen rights, and the extension of state rights into spheres previously not under the ambit of the state. Yet, and as will become clearer in chapter 5, individuals and groups of individuals can—in some circumstances—have the power and agency to resist, and dissent from, the mobilisations of states and other large-scale armed actors.

This subaltern power reminds us that different types of power, including EPP, exist. The power mobilised and wielded by states and armed actors may be quite different from the power exercised by individuals and groups of individuals. The types of power differ in obvious ways, such as their scale of operation (national, local, family level, etc.) and the amount of material resources they can mobilise. Another less easy-to-grasp difference between the types of power relates to resonance and legitimacy. Power can operate in the affective realm and connect with cultural expectations and what is regarded as legitimate and right.

Norman Lewis, a British military intelligence officer stationed in Italy following the collapse of the Mussolini regime, was particularly perceptive regarding the affective and culturally specific nature of many forms of power:

> The fact is that we have upset the balance of nature here. I personally have been rigid when I should have been flexible. Here the police—corrupt and tyrannical as they are—and the civil population play a game together, but the rules are complex and I do not understand them, and through this lack of understanding, I lose respect. Every single person who comes to the office to ask me for a travel pass puts a one-hundred-lire note down on the desk, and I push it away. What I cannot and must not in my position accept, is that these people are not offering what we think of as a bribe, but making a routine gesture of courtesy. This is an African tribal system in which every well-bred person expects to give and receive dashes. My predecessor, who was more flexible than I, handed out dashes in accordance with the list he left me. This I have not done, and by failing to do so I am probably dismissed as ill-mannered and avaricious.[138]

The point he makes in the quotation, and more generally through his memoir, is that individuals and communities are capable of engaging in sophisticated multilevel 'games' in which they might express fealty to multiple sources of power. They can engage in shape-shifting feats of ingenuity to please different actors, at different times, and on different issues. One of these forms of power is the ability to dissent from the dominant and official power during time of war. Such agency has to be exercised with caution and is often manifest on the margins or in realms considered 'safe' places to exercise it. The existence of such agency allows us to question the totalising nature of war and see that despite its pervasive aspects, there may be opportunities for individuals and groups to exercise EPP.

The second issue running through this book is the utility of circuitry as an analytical device with which to understand the multi-scalar nature of peace and conflict in general and everyday peace in particular. The essence of circuitry is connectivity, and the discussion of the brutalising nature of war and militarism makes clear how militaries are—or try very hard to be—hierarchical and dominating circuits. The individual soldier and the small military unit can be regarded as a circuit within a series of circuits that add up to a complex piece of circuitry with multiple elements. Power in these militarised circuits is largely top-down, and the power of individuals and groups is to be mobilised and directed from the top down. As examples in chapter 5 will illustrate,

---

[138] Norman Lewis, *Naples '44* (New York: Carroll and Graf, 2005), 168.

individuals and collectives can, in certain circumstances, create spaces in which acts of everyday peace, such as mercy and empathy, can be performed. These acts often occur in micro-circuits or in circuits that operate within circuits. In a sense, individuals and groups of individuals can disrupt the war circuit. Through stances and speech acts, they can illustrate that alternatives are possible and war need not be totalising.

5
Everyday Peace on the Battlefield

Introduction

This chapter examines informal truces and acts of humanity and reciprocity during violent conflict. Like chapter 4, it is interested in the 'hard cases' of all-out warfare and draws on World War I and World War II personal diaries and memoirs. Although overlooked in the contemporary peace and conflict studies literature, these sources have much to tell us about human conduct in extremis. The chapter demonstrates that in some circumstances, everyday peace—or at least everyday tolerance and civility—has been possible during warfare. It contains multiple examples of 'ordinary' combatants showing humanity, compassion, and generosity to their supposed opponents. These cases are particularly interesting from the point of view of this book as they often occurred 'under the radar' or outside the surveillance of the state and others. Indeed, in many cases, they were expressly forbidden by military organisations and were contrary to the prevailing national mood of antagonism towards the enemy. They show individual and group initiative, as well as resistance to a national or wider group. This may have been time-limited and context-specific, but it does show that apparently monolithic and powerful forces, such as states and militaries, may not be as powerful as generally thought. As many of the examples show, there may be space for Everyday Peace Power (EPP) in the midst of violence and conflict. While the formal truces of chapter 4 can be regarded as conflict interruption, the acts of humanity covered in this chapter can be regarded as conflict disruption. That is, they contradict—even in minor ways—the norms of conflict. Of course, we must be careful not to claim too much on behalf of everyday peace or civility. The cases described in this chapter might be more accurately described as compassion or shared humanity, yet they fit within the broad category of everyday peace.

In terms of organisation, the chapter has three substantive sections that draw on an imagined continuum of weak, medium, and strong everyday peace. As this is a continuum, it is prudent to think of these categories as leaching into one another. Their primary function is to assist us in conceptual scoping, or thinking through the dimensions and gradations of everyday peace. The continuum maps onto the constituent parts of everyday peace that were discussed in chapter 2: sociality (weak), reciprocity (medium), and solidarity (strong) (see figure 2.1). This overlap is not precise, but it helps us comprehend how everyday peace manifests itself and evolves. In broad-brush terms, solidarity conforms to strong everyday peace. Cases of solidarity with the other are found rarely in warfare, as this is a political act that involves standing with the enemy. For obvious reasons, this can be dangerous. And it often proved difficult for alternative narratives to 'outgun' the mobilisation potential of nationalism and group identity. Cases of reciprocity conform to medium everyday peace. At the heart of reciprocity lies a self-interest, albeit a mutual self-interest. It is found, for example, in the multiple cases of 'live and let live' localised truces in WWI. Soldiers looked the other way or managed their offensiveness in order to enhance their own chances of survival. Weak everyday peace correlates with sociality. Here we might see the exercise of compassion for fellow humanity. This is often very context-specific and time-limited. Yet such cases humanise war and leaven its ruthlessness, and they can be seen as micro instances of resistance to the top-down exhortations for warlike behaviour.

It is worth reminding ourselves, as illustrated in chapter 4, that the norm in warfare is one of violent antipathy. The apparently all-consuming nature of total warfare stretches from the battlefield to the organisation of politics, society, culture, and economics. Many wars relied on the mass mobilisation of the population and the orientation of just about every aspect of life towards the war effort. Whether it was encouraging adults to procreate to produce children who would grow up to be soldiers or workers or propagandising the school curriculum, war impinged on multiple domains of life.[1] Given such near-totalising contexts, any type of everyday peace is extraordinary and constitutes conflict disruption. It involves individuals and groups of individuals acting against the mores of the state or military organisation. As we will see, such acts were able to inhabit and develop micro-circuits that are outwith the surveillance of the state or other authorities and can provide space for pro-peace and pro-social stances and speech acts. Although often very context-specific and reliant on opportunism, these acts of compassion, respect, and humanity entail bravery and the risk of censure and discipline from authorities and the in-group. While we must be careful not to overstate the significance of everyday peace, it is worth exploring the failure of war to become completely totalising. Acts of everyday peace, humanity, and compassion illustrate that national and militaristic injunctions to conform and show antipathy towards the out-group are not always completely successful.

---

[1] P. K. Whelpton, 'Why the Large Rise in the German Birth-Rate?' *American Journal of Sociology* 41, no. 3 (1935): 299–313. John E. Wade, writing on US high schools during WWII, noted that 'the war has given an immediate and practical application to almost every subject in the curriculum' and went on to describe how mathematics and physics would be useful to pilots and navigators; 'The Wartime Curriculum', *Journal of Educational Sociology* 16, no. 7 (1943): 404.

There are 'limits of hate'.[2] This indicates that feelings—the affective dimension—deserve to be taken seriously in our considerations of peace and conflict. They also suggest (in a very tentative way) hope for what might come after war—that there are people with the foresight and emotional intelligence to look beyond the immediate animus and be ready to engage in intergroup contact.

Running through this chapter, and indeed this book, is the issue of power. To what extent did the various actors depicted in this chapter have power over their own actions and destiny, and over others? War reduces and constrains the power of many. They might be conscripted, directed in their economic behaviour, their food intake, dress, travel habits, and cultural consumption. For others, power might increase. Being armed and joining the military might give some new leverage and privileges. Military memoirs frequently contain stories of theft of goods—often food—from civilians.[3] The thefts are carried out by young men who, in civilian life, would probably not dare steal anything. Yet the circumstances of war may empower them (or leave them desperate enough) to engage in theft and looting.[4] War also gives explicit permission to combatants to engage in violence, often shocking types of violence. Within this exceptional context, there may be room for combatants to engage in everyday peace and actions that draw on a sense of humanity and compassion. This is a form of power and conflict disruption. It is different from the forms of power usually associated with warfare: the material power of weaponry and the mobilisation of people and resources. The power of everyday peace and civility often operates on the margins, at the individual and small-group level, and outside the purview of the state and other forms of authority. It is a form of power that may operate at the affective level, and it may be episodic and inconsistent. Yet it constitutes a disruption, rather than interruption, of war and therefore deserves scrutiny.

A final introductory point is to remind ourselves of the caveats from chapter 4. This entails the importance of circumspection when utilising war memoirs and personal diaries as a source. It also involves recognising the Euro-Atlanticist bias in these memoirs. The voices of many combatants, especially from non-Western theatres of operation, are under-represented in memoirs. Important, too, is the maleness of this chapter. As it draws heavily on memoirs from those who served in conventional armies, the examples used are often male.[5] It is important to note that the male experience of war is not universal. War and peace impact on males and females in different ways (as discussed in chapter 6), and we should be

---

[2] Michael Sturma, 'The Limits of Hate: Japanese Prisoners on Board US Submarines during the Second World War', *Journal of Contemporary History* 51, no. 4 (2016): 738–759.

[3] WWII tank commander David Render recalled that 'by the end of the campaign seeing an Allied soldier wearing several [stolen] watches on his wrist was not an uncommon sight'; *Tank Action*, 138.

[4] Seth A. Givens, 'Liberating the Germans: The US Army and Looting during the Second World War', *War in History* 21, no. 1 (2014): 33–54.

[5] A wonderful exception to this is Alexievich, *The Unwomanly Face of War*.

mindful that this chapter presents a less-than-full picture of war and everyday peace within it. Nevertheless, the challenge facing the concept of everyday peace is to prove that it does not work only in the 'easy cases'. The world wars are 'hard cases' of near-total warfare, and so it is legitimate that we look for evidence of everyday peace within them.

Weak Everyday Peace: Sociality

Sociality is based on a sense of connectedness to other humans. Wars, and the political programmes that underpin them, emphasise connectedness with other humans (for example, through shared nationality) but also disconnectedness from others. Sociality cuts across this and, often drawing on the affective realm, allows humans to express compassion, mercy, remorse, and a sense of fellowship with others. The war memoirs and personal diaries consulted for this chapter contain multiple examples of sociality, some of it surprising. All of the examples are highly contextualised and are often specific to a particular time and place. One account, mentioned in the introduction to the book, comes from a WWII battle and tells of ferocious hand-to-hand fighting momentarily disrupted by a split-second decision by a German machine-gunner in a tank to spare the life of a British infantryman.[6] The machine-gunner, one assumes, calculated that the infantryman was no threat and—with his position overrun—would soon be a prisoner. One further assumes that shortly afterwards the machine-gunner continued in his warlike ways but had made a momentary decision based on notions of mercy. The result was that a young man survived, was transported to Italy as a prisoner of war, escaped, and lived with a family in an Italian mountain range until almost the end of the war. The soldier was then repatriated to the United Kingdom at the end of the war and lived a very full life. Sociality is not necessarily reciprocal; it can be magnanimous and one-sided. It can be termed a weak notion of everyday peace, as it is far removed from expansive versions of positive peace. Yet the micro-actions of individuals and small groups of individuals can have profound consequences, not least in allowing others to live. It can add a modicum of civilisation and humanity to a battlefield.

It is noticeable that some of the examples in this section come from the WWII eastern front—a site, as noted in chapter 4, usually associated with unremitting barbarity. Yet beyond the official narratives and stances, and the myths that develop about the brutish other, there were occasional instances of sociality based on shared humanity. One female Russian medic in WWII recalled a nurse coming to her to ask how some German SS officers were to be

---

[6] Ellis, *Once a Hussar*, location 2691.

bandaged. 'Normally', she responded. 'They're wounded'.[7] Indeed, even accounts of WWII Allied-versus-Japanese encounters—often marked by brutality and not taking prisoners[8]—contain occasional glimpses of a shared humanity. Sergeant Mitsuru Ishida recalled a British sergeant who attempted to negotiate a battlefield truce: 'We admired his dignified attitude. . . . It was an indescribably heartwarming moment on the bloody battlefield'.[9]

A key issue in relation to sociality and war is power and specifically the extent to which actors are empowered to act in social and pacific ways. WWI American soldier Herbert McBride referred to 'the ability to control one's nerves and passions'.[10] As discussed in chapter 4, military training is often about removing autonomy from the individual and directing the unit in martial ways. The ability of everyday or bottom-up peace to manifest itself, even in slight ways, often rested on the extent to which individuals could be the author of their own nerves or destiny, as often these had been subjugated to a higher military authority. As will be seen from the examples in this chapter, sociality was often conducted in a surreptitious way, outside the surveillance of the commanders. It was the unofficial act of individuals and small groups and thus firmly in the informal sphere. These informal spaces were micro-circuits that were outside of the main pro-war circuits. Everyday peace acts were often a spur-of-the-moment act of compassion or mercy that did not mean that those engaging in sociality were in any way less dedicated to their military objectives. In a sense, these were pop-up circuits. The temporary nature of some types of everyday peace is summed up well by WWI German soldier Ernst Jünger:

> Throughout the war, it was always my endeavour to view my opponent without animus, and to form an opinion of him as a man on the basis of the courage he showed. I would always try and seek him out in combat and kill him, and I expected nothing else from him. But never did I entertain mean thoughts of him. When prisoners fell into my hands, later on, I felt responsible for their safety, and would always do everything in my power for them.[11]

---

[7] Cited in Alexievich, *The Unwomanly Face of War*, location 2329.

[8] The history of the Fifth Indian Division tells how, during the 'Battle of the Admin Box' (or Ngakyedauk), a Japanese force entered a hospital: 'Every doctor they could find was murdered. The British patients lying in the darkness in the long tents were butchered. . . . Japanese and Jif [Indians recruited to fight alongside the Japanese] prodded them with bayonets, robbed them of cigarettes, and stabbed some to death, before turning upon the next tent to continue their looting and killing'. Antony Brett-James, 'Ball of Fire: The Fifth Indian Division in the Second World War', Wikia.org, 1951, https://military.wikia.org/wiki/Battle_of_the_Admin_Box.

[9] Mitsuru Ishida, cited in Kazuo Tamayama and John Nunneley, *Tales by Japanese Soldiers* (London: Cassell, 2001), 79.

[10] McBride, *A Rifleman*, location 170.

[11] Ernst Jünger, *Storm of Steel* (London: Penguin, 2004), 58.

This sense of respect for the other side, on the basis of a shared humanity, was reasonably common. As one soldier in the British Army observed in WWII, 'we have no particular hatred of the men across the way'.[12] This was manifest in expressions of compassion, remorse, and humanity in the midst of war.

Cases of compassion for the wounded run through the memoirs and personal diaries. A German soldier in 1944 recalls not firing on an American who was helping to load a wounded comrade into a tank: 'Those of us witnessing the scene, whether nearby or more distant, instinctively felt that there was no honor to be won by firing on this death-defying act of comradeship'.[13] There are many other cases from both world wars of the wounded being able to walk back to their lines, of recognising their victim status, and of treating their wounds.[14] A number of the memoirs record protecting prisoners of war from civilian mobs.[15] Other memoirs record instances of civilian generosity to prisoners. One captured British Red Cross worker remembered Italian civilians giving his column of prisoners 'figs, tomatoes and anything they had and were very friendly and ready to help in any way they could'.[16] While there are plenty of accounts of dreadful behaviour by captors towards their prisoners,[17] there are accounts of civility and decency.[18] One German described his Russian post-war guard as 'good natured and kind ... polite, almost comradely'.[19] Svetlana Alexievich's remarkable collection of firsthand accounts from women who served in the Red Army contains several glimpses of civility and compassion that run counter to the norms of warfare. Natalya Ivanovna Sergeeva, a nurse's aide, is quoted thus:

> And so ... you never know your own heart. In winter some captive German soldiers were led past our unit. They walked along all frozen, with torn blankets on their heads, holes burnt in their overcoats. It was so cold that birds dropped in flight. The birds froze. A soldier marching in that column ... a young boy ... There were tears frozen on his face ... And I was taking bread to the mess in a wheelbarrow. He couldn't take his eyes off that wheelbarrow; he didn't see me, only the wheelbarrow. Bread ... Bread ... I broke a piece off that

---

[12] Patrick MacGill, *The Great Push: An Episode of the Great War* (London: Caliban, 1984), 229.
[13] Voss, *Black Edelweiss*, chap. 23, location 3545.
[14] See, for example, George C. Blackburn, *The Guns of War* (London: Robinson, 2000), 388–390; Lynch, *Somme Mud*, 110; Downham and Roe, *Diary*, location 2015.
[15] Ralph G. A. Hamilton, *The War Diary of the Master of Belhaven 1914-1918* (London: Endeavour, 2016), 123; Frank Broome, *Dead before Dawn: A Heavy Bomber Tail-Gunner in World War II*, Kindle ed. (Barnsley, UK: Pen and Sword, 2012), locations 6506, 6513.
[16] Davey, *The War Diaries*, 138.
[17] See, for example, the privations suffered by Ellis at the hands of his Italian captors in *Once a Hussar*.
[18] Barthas, *Poilu*, 116. Also see Hartinger, *Until the Eyes Shut*, 156–158, on good and bad treatment of prisoners.
[19] Armin Schiederbauer, *Adventures in My Youth: A German Soldier on the Eastern Front 1941-45* (Solihull, UK: Helion, 2013), 178.

loaf and gave it to him. He took it . . . Took it and didn't believe it . . . He didn't believe it!

I was happy . . . I was happy that I wasn't able to hate. I was astonished at myself then.[20]

Feelings of remorse were apparent in even the most unexpected quarters.

Amidst the carnage and obvious antipathy of the eastern front in WWII, one German soldier reflected on a Russian soldier—'a beginner or he was drunk'—who was shot while cycling towards the German lines: 'So a life was finished, to save others. A poor Russian, like most of his fellow countrymen, harmless and kind when not incited to war by despots'.[21]

There was also remorse and compassion for troops on one's own side who were unable to cope with the war. A WWI British commanding officer reflected, years after the war, on one of his charges, rifleman James Crozier, who had been executed for desertion:

> He was no rotter deserving to die like that. He was merely fragile. He had volunteered to fight for his country . . . at the dictates of his young heart. He failed. And for that failure he was condemned to die—and he did at the hands of his friends, his brothers, with the approval of his church. . . . To us, he was what? He was poor [Crozier]. And we never made up our minds for whom we were sorrier—him, or ourselves. Such is war.[22]

There was also a recognition of what has become known as shell shock or post-traumatic stress disorder.[23] Charles Lamb, a WWII British naval aviator, recalled, 'nobody in the squadron, myself included, was behaving normally . . . there are some people who are unable to crack when the strain becomes too great, but instead are driven by some irresistible internal urge to invite danger by venturing where others do not dare, to the ultimate point where death must win'.[24]

Some of the remorse was highly personalised and showed the failure of national projects to fully demonise the other side. One WWI German soldier reflected on a British soldier he had shot:

---

[20] Cited in Alexievich, *The Unwomanly Face of War*, location 1502.

[21] Thorolf Hillbladed, *Twilight of the Gods: A Swedish Waffen-SS Volunteer's Experiences with the 11th SS-Panzergrenader Division 'Nordland', Eastern Front 1944–45*, Kindle ed. (Warwick, UK: Helion, 2004), location 1708.

[22] C. Corns and John Hughes-Wilson, *Blindfold and Alone: British Military Executions in the Great War* (London: Orion, 2015), 44.

[23] See, for example, Carol Mather, *When the Grass Stops Growing: A War Memoir* (Barnsley, UK: Pen and Sword, 1997), 295.

[24] Lamb, *War in a Stringbag*, 196.

> Outside ... lay my British soldier, little more than a boy, who had been shot in the temple. He lay there, looking quite relaxed. I forced myself to look closely at him. It wasn't a case of 'you or me' anymore. I often thought back on him; and more with the passing of the years. The state, which relieves us of our responsibility, cannot take away our remorse; and we must exercise it. Sorrow, regret, pursued me deep into my dreams.[25]

Roland Leighton, a WWI British junior officer, wrote to his fiancée, Vera Brittain:

> Let him who thinks that War is a glorious thing, who loves to roll forth stirring words of exhortation, invoking Honour and Praise and Valour and Love of Country.... Look at a little sodden pile of grey rags that half cover a skull or shin bone and what might have been its ribs, or at this skeleton lying on its side, half crouching as it fell, supported by one arm, perfect but that it is headless and with tattered clothing still draped round it.[26]

Leighton himself was dead within three months.[27]

An Australian soldier reflected on a colleague who had shot a German soldier on a quiet stretch of the western front. The German had been walking away from his own trench towards the rear, possibly to start a period of leave:

> Snow is queerly affected by having shot the man. ... Now and again we peep over the top ... hoping the man has recovered and been carried out wounded after all. No, there he lies still.... There he lies, laid low by a bullet of a boy with whom he had no quarrel and who would now give all to undo the effects of that shot. We think it over—the killer and the killed who probably had never been nearer each other than half a mile of mud.[28]

There was remorse at the resumption of hostilities after the 1914 Christmas truce on the western front, especially from the source of the resumption:

> About 9:30AM a shot was fired from the direction of our Company Headquarters and a German falls. That started the war again. We found out who fired the shot. It was a young fellow, about sixteen or seventeen years of age.... We did not like the idea of being the first to break the mutual agreement. The honor of the British Army was at stake, and we lost it.[29]

---

[25] Jünger, *Storm of Steel*, 241.
[26] Cited in Bishop and Bostridge, *Letters*, 165.
[27] Brittain, *Testament of Youth*, 236.
[28] E. P. F Lynch, *Somme Mud: The War Experiences of an Australian Infantryman in France 1916-1919* (London: Bantham, 2008), 60.
[29] Downham and Roe, *Diary*, location 2209.

This section has demonstrated the persistence of a basic sociality even in the midst of the most extreme circumstances. The examples in this section do not refer to strategic events that might change the course of a war or a battle. But they may be life-changing at the level of the group or small group of individuals. They constitute EPP in that individuals were able to exercise or eke out a form of power in the midst of contexts that were often highly hierarchical. The examples in this section also constitute a form of conflict disruption in that they disrupted the momentum and purpose of warfare—albeit only usually temporarily or on a small scale. Nonetheless, the everyday peace actions and thoughts described in this section are transgressive acts that question the apparently hegemonic logics and narratives of war and conflict. They show how individuals and groups have been able to create space for countercultural thinking and actions through civility and humane emotional intelligence. They also show micro-circuits at work, or how small groups of individuals might act in ways that evade the strictures of the main martial circuit.

Medium Everyday Peace: Reciprocity

As discussed in chapter 2, reciprocity is a form of social cooperation based on mutual benefit.[30] More than this, it can be seen as system strengthening and in optimal circumstances factoring up and out. The notion and practice of war emphasise maximising benefits for one side and harm for the other. Positive mutuality is the antithesis of war. Yet war memoirs do contain multiple accounts of mutuality, or actions conducted in the knowledge that they will be reciprocated or in the hope that they would be reciprocated if the need arose. This often took the form, particularly during the trench warfare of WWI, of a 'live and let live' policy. Ashworth defines the 'live and let live' principle as 'an informal and collective agreement between front-line soldiers of opposing armies to inhibit offensive activity to a level mutually defined as tolerable. This understanding was tacit and covert; expressed in activity or non-activity rather than in verbal terms'.[31] As one British soldier in WWI observed, 'I sincerely hope that if it is ever the lot of any of my comrades or I to fall into the hands of the Turks, wounded or unwounded, that we will be treated with the same respect, consideration and chivalry as the British Tommies treated them'.[32]

---

[30] The truce was not repeated in subsequent years, mainly because of warnings from senior officers of the consequences of fraternisation. WWI British sapper Jack Martin did note on Christmas 1917 that 'Our guns have fired a few rounds but the Italians and the Australians have religiously abstained from any act of warfare'. Richard van Emden, ed., *Sapper Marin: The Secret Great War Diary of Jack Martin* (London: Bloomsbury, 2009), 156.
[31] Ashworth, 'The Sociology of Trench Warfare', 411.
[32] Downham and Roe, *Diary*, location 4817.

Perhaps the most famous case of WWI reciprocity was the 1914 western front Christmas truce. Although the Christmas truce has been much mythologised, it is estimated that there were various levels of fraternization along about two-thirds of the British-held trenches on the western front.[33] One participant, who gave a tin of raspberry jam to 'a stodgy and bespectacled Saxon', noted, 'At midnight firing ceased as if by mutual consent. . . . The awful slaughter had been unable to check the spirit of Christmas. . . . Goodwill appeared on the battlefield'.[34] It was not all football matches and the swapping of schnapps. Many of the truces were to facilitate the burial of the dead.[35] The Christmas truce was a good example of the reciprocal but highly delicate and localised nature of informal truces. Another British account suggests that officers on both sides knew that fraternization was in contravention of orders and thus tried to stop it, without a return to all-out war: 'When Fritz rolled over two barrels of beer Captain Stockwell went and spoke to two German officers; it was agreed to recall all men to the trenches and have no more fraternizing. But there was no more shooting'.[36]

Captain Stockwell went on to note, 'He [the German captain] played the game, not a shot all night. . . . Then hostilities begin on an agreed signal'.[37]

Accounts of the Christmas truce show how, in one sector at least, there was an attempt at regularisation:

> At 5:00AM word has passed down the trench that the Hampshires and the Germans were fraternising in no-man's land . . . sure enough, British and German warriors [were] in no-man's land, unarmed, talking to each other and exchanging souvenirs. There is a Christ after all. . . .
>
> We made an unofficial truce with the Germans. Conditions:
> 1. Any action taken by the Artillery of either Army did not break our truce as we had no control over Artillery.
> 2. If either side received an order to fire, they would fire the first three rounds high in the air to give the other side time to get under cover.
> 3. If either side fired a shot with the intent to kill, the truce was declared off.[38]

The issue of power, and powerlessness, runs through this example. Local-level commanders and troops were able to carve out space in which to make a truce. They were a minor circuit in a complex system of circuitry, with micro-circuits below them. One German WWI soldier observed 'the near absolute authority

---

[33] Iain Adams, 'A Game for Christmas? The Argylls, Saxons and Football on the Western Front, December 1914', *International Journal of the History of Sport* 32, nos. 11–12 (2015): 1403.
[34] Downham and Roe, *Diary*, locations 2158, 2163.
[35] Anne Williamson, *Henry Williamson and the First World War* (Stroud, UK: Sutton, 2004), 48.
[36] J. C. Dunn, *The War the Infantry Knew 1914–1919* (London: Abacus, 2003), 101.
[37] Cited in Dunn, *The War*, 102–103.
[38] Downham and Roe, *Diary*, locations 2163, 2183.

these local bosses exercised over their subordinates and the local populations'.[39] But that space or circuit was delicate. It breached the norms of war as ordained by one's own side and made one a target for the other side. It is difficult not to think of the bravery of those who made the first move and exposed themselves to the danger of being shot by the enemy, or court-martialled and then possibly shot. The nervousness of both sides is apparent in this extract from a letter from private Henry Williamson to his mother:

> On Xmas eve both armies sang carols and cheered & there was very little firing. The Germans (in some places 80 yds away) called to our men to come & fetch a cigar and our men told them to come to us. This went on for some time, neither side fully trusting the other, until, after much promising to 'play the game' a bold Tommy crept out & stood between the trenches, & immediately a Saxon came to meet him. They shook hands & laughed & then 16 Germans came out. Thus the ice was broken.[40]

This was a literal case of putting your head above the parapet. Those making the first move showed extraordinary faith that their goodwill would be reciprocated by the other side. They also had to be sure (or as sure as they could be) that their comrades would not accuse them of traitorous behaviour. This speaks of an understanding among comrades that was outside the surveillance of commanding officers.

It is worth stressing that the Christmas truce did not extend across all parts of the western front. This German soldier's account shows how the death of a comrade, perhaps keenly felt within a tight-knit military unit, prevented the Germans in his sector from reciprocating a British invitation to respect Christmas:

> We spent Christmas Eve in the line, and, standing in the mud, sang hymns, to which the British responded with machine gun fire. On Christmas Day, we lost one man to a ricochet in the head. Immediately afterwards, the British attempted a friendly gesture by hauling a Christmas tree up on their traverse, but our angry troops quickly shot it down again, to which Tommy replied with rifle grenades. It was all in all a less than merry Christmas.[41]

Aside from the Christmas example, there are plentiful examples of local-level truces to enable the collection of the wounded and the dead. Important in these examples is the presence or expectation of reciprocity. A WWII British soldier on

---

[39] Jünger, *Storm of Steel*, 255.
[40] Williamson, *Henry Williamson*, 47–48.
[41] Jünger, *Storm of Steel*, 58–59.

the western front noted an 'example of chivalry between the opposing sides ... a German emissary came forward under a white flag to ask if they might evacuate casualties and bury the dead, as had been granted to us. An hour's local truce was arranged'.[42] There were obvious suspicions that such truces might be a ruse to gain intelligence or to trick the other side to lower their guard. So sometimes safeguards were introduced. An American soldier recounts a 1945 two-hour truce 'to allow the removal of the dead'. The US officer in charge 'stipulated that the [German] medics ... would be taken prisoner and repatriated later through the Geneva Red Cross'.[43] Officers regularly discouraged soldiers from humane acts that put themselves at risk. One Australian soldier recalled the bravery of a colleague in going to the aid of a wounded German and how the brave soldier was then threatened with a court martial if he repeated his actions.[44]

The notion of offering respect to troops (living or dead) of the other side on the tacit understanding that such respect would be afforded in return was widespread. A WWI British soldier noted, 'Paddy and I visited a German cemetery which had been beautifully kept. There were a number of British soldiers buried in it and their graves had been equally as well cared for as for their own men'.[45] In the WWII Burma campaign, two Japanese officers—Fukunaga and Miyazaki— went looking for the body of a colleague, Lieutenant Ban:

> They discovered that Indian paratroopers had accorded Ban what respect they could for a fearless enemy. His sword was not looted, and he was buried with it neatly rolled in a blanket in a shallow grave.... In response Colonel Fukunaga ordered that the wounded paratroopers be cared for and that POWs from 50th Brigade were not to be harmed. Miyazaki later released many of the Brigade's POWs in their underpants near Kohima.[46]

The nature of trench warfare—extended time in a single location—facilitated numerous tacit truces among soldiers. These were actively discouraged by commanding officers who favoured the aggressive prosecution of war. Yet 'the physical structure of the trench ensured that the activities of the ordinary soldier, for some part at least, were not visible to their officers'.[47] A stretch of trench and the close-knit comradeship of a small group of troops constituted a microcircuit that was contained within a much larger assemblage of circuitry. Tacit truces were surprisingly common and were a rational response by those who

---

[42] Woollcombe, *Lion Rampant*, location 2316.
[43] MacDonald, *Company Commander*, 85.
[44] Lynch, *Somme Mud*, 65–67.
[45] Richards, *Old Soldiers*, 101.
[46] Tarak Barkawi, *Soldiers of Empire: Indian and British Armies in World War Two* (Cambridge: Cambridge University Press, 2017), 224.
[47] Ashworth, 'The Sociology of Trench Warfare', 408.

were, literally, on the firing line. Such informal truces took many forms: not firing at ration or working parties, pretending not to see enemy patrols, artillery aiming high or modulating fire in a mutually beneficial way, or agreements among troops in a particular sector to 'keep things quiet'. One witness to the WWI Macedonian-Bulgarian frontline described a situation of conflict regulation. The actions described fit within the conflict management rubric.[48] The participants accept the existence of conflict and recognise that the conflict will not change at the structural level, but they seek to lower the costs of the conflict through regulation:

> The batteries' gun positions were dug in on the skyline and directed on targets far below in the bottom of the valley. The Bulgars on the hills on the opposite side of the valley were similarly situated... whenever one of our batteries dropped some shells that fell too close for the Bulgars' comfort, they would promptly respond with a salvo of their own shells, which would fall uncomfortably near to the British battery just to let us know that they had no intention of putting up with that kind of thing. Here, as on the Struma, the Bulgars had demonstrated their willingness to pursue a Live and Let Live policy; but if we preferred to be unpleasant then they could be unpleasant too.[49]

One WWI combatant noted that the 'Saxons... were the quietest, and wouldn't go out of their way to foment strafing'.[50] Local ceasefire or 'low-fire' arrangements were context-dependent, highly localised, and mutual. They were able to take place because of the relatively stable and static nature of trench warfare. It is noticeable how many diaries and memoirs from WWI use terms such as *quiet* and *calm* to describe the frontlines in periods that could not be described as battle. J. C. Dunn, a British medical officer in WWI, noted that 'ordinary activity by both sides consisted of sniping, patrolling and the occasional "hate"'.[51] A 'hate' was a non-strategic upsurge in fighting, often ordered by commanders to keep their men alert and the enemy on edge. Yet the routinized nature of WWI did allow for some pacific regularity. Chiu notes, 'Such ritualized aggression still looked like a battle from outside, and reports could be sent to high command about the times and duration of the battles and how much ammunition was spent'.[52] This 'live and let live' quietness contravened the norm of offensiveness

---

[48] The distinctions between conflict management, conflict resolution, and conflict transformation are explained in chapter 7.
[49] Cited in Ashworth, 'The Sociology of Trench Warfare', 412.
[50] Coppard, *With a Machine Gun*, 53.
[51] Dunn, *The War*, 116.
[52] Yvonne Chiu, 'Conspiring with the Enemy and Cooperating in Warfare: "Live and Let Live" as a Representative Element of War', Institute for Advanced Study, 2014, https://www.ias.edu/ideas/2014/chiu-war.

that guides warfare. In some circumstances, a period of calm was sanctioned by military commanders—perhaps a particular sector was being rested or rearmed. The general mode of warfare is, however, towards offensiveness, and the informal truces were in contravention of the militaristic norm. Louis Barthas, a corporal in the French Army who unwillingly served for the duration of WWI, is worth quoting at length as he describes a scene from Franco-German trenches that were a mere six metres apart in the summer of 1916. This was the same summer during which the Battle of the Somme raged:

> the French and German sentries [were] seated tranquilly on their parapets, smoking pipes and exchanging bits of conversation from time to time, like good neighbors taking some fresh air on their doorsteps. From relief to relief, we passed along the habits and customs of these outposts. The Germans did the same.... Sometimes there were exchanges of gifts, like packets of tobacco from the Régie Français which went to fill the big German pipes, or delicious German cigarettes which came over to the French side. We also exchanged lighters, buttons, newspapers, bread.
>
> Here was a crazy business of commerce and intelligence with the enemy which would have stirred up the indignation of the patriots and super-patriots....
>
> You can be sure that this gesture of fraternity occurred in more than one place, in fact wherever the proximity of outposts allowed it. And our big bosses, our leaders, had no illusions about it. If the trenches had been closer together, if they hadn't been separated by prickly barbed wire, hands would have reached out everywhere.[53]

One WWI British Army soldier noted: 'At night when out on working parties I saw figures moving out by the enemy trenches, mere shadows that came into view when an ephemeral constellation of star shells held the heavens. We never fired at these shadows, and they never fired at us; it is unwise to break the truces of the trenches'.[54] Another noted, 'Even with the naked eye the Germans could be seen working on their trench'.[55] A German officer observed, 'When friend and foe alike go to fetch straw from the same rick to protect them from the cold and rain and to have some sort of bedding to lie on—and never a shot is fired'.[56] Barthas recorded his heavy work assignment pushing enormous coils of barbed wire towards the front lines: 'it rolled noisily down into a ravine, on the other side of which were the Germans who certainly heard all the racket.

---

[53] Barthas, *Poilu*, 243–244.
[54] MacGill, *The Great Push*, 87.
[55] Dunn, *The War*, 113.
[56] Rudolph Binding, cited in Adams, 'A Game', 1397.

But they never fired a shot. This was reciprocal; we rarely fired on each other's work details'.[57] Even in WWII, at certain times as the western front stabilised, there were tacit agreements of 'leaving the ration supplies of the other side alone'.[58] A British officer noted, 'As we sat in the stillness we could hear with great distinctness the sound of transport on the Radinghem road bringing up the German rations, in the same way as they must have heard the wheels of our wagons rumbling through the streets of Houplines and down the dog-leg road. But there seems to have been some unwritten law of "live and let live", for the ration parties of either side were never strafed'.[59] Another form of pacific reciprocity came was artillery agreeing—probably tacitly—to limit their actions: 'Nieppe was not shelled by the "Jerries" in my time, as our gunners and the Germans came to some kind of agreement it seemed. If you do not shell Warneton (a big town on our front beyond the river Lys and in "Jerry" lines) we will not shell you'.[60] Such actions could only be informal, as they contravened the spirit of war and the exhortations from senior military commanders to display aggressiveness towards the enemy.

The 'live and let live' stance of many soldiers, and the tacit ceasefires they reached and observed, speak of micro- or highly localised circuits that are beyond the surveillance and control of major circuits. The major circuits of military and popular support for the war continued largely unaffected by the actions of individuals and small groups of individuals who formed micro-circuits through their stances and actions. In some situations, as we will see, the actions of the micro-circuits did affect the wider circuit, and there were opportunities for scaling up and out.

Also fitting into the reciprocity category were spur-of-the-moment actions that reflected the ridiculous circumstances often resulting from warfare. Barthas records a case from 1915:

> The next day, December 10, at many places along the front line, the soldiers had to come out of their trenches so as not to drown. The Germans had to do the same. We therefore had the singular spectacle of two enemy armies facing each other without firing a shot.
>
> Our common suffering brought our hearts together, melted the hatreds, nurtured sympathy between strangers and adversaries. Those who ignore it are denying human psychology.[61]

---

[57] Barthas, *Poilu*, 137.
[58] White, *With the Jocks*, 38–39.
[59] Lieutenant Hutchinson of 2/Argylls, cited in Adams, 'A Game', 1397.
[60] Downham and Roe, *Diary*, location 2357.
[61] Barthas, *Poilu*, 143–144.

A German account from the same period of heavy rain reads: 'The occupants of both trenches had emerged from the morass of their trenches onto the top, and already a lively exchange of schnapps, cigarettes, uniform buttons and other items commenced between the two barbed-wire lines'. The mood changed, though, when a German was shot and hurried negotiations took place: 'For clarity's sake, we gave a solemn mutual declaration of war to commence three minutes after the end of our talks, and following a "Good night!" on his part, and an "Au revoir!" on mine, to the regret of my men I fired off a shot'.[62] Perhaps an even more ridiculous picture came from the eastern front:

> A bunch of Russians are running directly towards us, as if they are chased by the very devil. As they're running they're flapping their arms all about, as if trying to fly.... I'm already behind my machine gun and keeping a careful watch....
> The oberleutnant, who has been keeping them under observation through his field glasses, lays his hand gently on my shoulder.
> 'Don't shoot! They're unarmed!'
> 'What the devil's going on?' I hear our chief calling.
> Then someone replies 'Bees! A great swarm of mad bees!'[63]

The Russians were taken prisoner instead of being shot.

Perhaps the most interesting aspect of the temporary truces was their tacit nature and how they often relied on non-verbal communication. In some cases, verbal communication was possible. Barthas recalls a Private Gontron who regularly visited the German trench opposite and 'had gotten to know the German captain, a good family man who always asked about his own children and gave him a few cigarettes. Whenever Gontron stayed too long, the captain pushed him out of the German trench saying, "Let's go, on your way." '[64] Such cases were, however, clearly not the norm. While a white flag could be used, in many other cases, the chief means of intergroup communication was an affective understanding—an implied or implicit sense that a particular course of action was to be taken and should be reciprocated. The understanding to leave ration parties alone or for artillery to avoid particular targets relied on a complex mix of faith and past evidence. It relied on human (and humane) judgement and the privileging of civility (however temporary or scant) over military authority. It constituted a mode of thinking that was contrary to the established norms or the imposed norm. The thinking and actions behind the reciprocity were a form of power in that individuals and groups of individuals were able to carve out space

---

[62] Jünger, *Storm of Steel*, 57.
[63] Günter K. Koschorrek, *Blood Red Snow: The Memoirs of a German Soldier on the Eastern Front*, Kindle ed. (Barnsley, UK: Frontline, 2011), location 3660.
[64] Barthas, *Poilu*, 144.

to deviate from top-down forms of power. Like sociality, reciprocity and these medium forms of everyday peace and civility were not a threat to the war system in its totality, but they did show that alternatives were possible.

Strong Everyday Peace: Solidarity

There are few cases of solidarity with the other side in warfare. As discussed in chapter 2, solidarity is not merely showing passing support of or sympathy with the other side. It requires identification with them and meaningful action in support of them or their cause. Thus, to be truly solidarist in the context of war can be regarded as traitorous and carries danger. Suspected sympathisers with the enemy were rounded up. In WWII, for example, tens of thousands of people of German, Italian, and Japanese descent were interned in the United Kingdom and the United States.[65] Many of them posed no threat whatsoever.

Those few in the United Kingdom or the United States who publicly identified with the political aims of the Nazi regime were branded traitors and imprisoned or executed.[66] Even those who were suspected of showing slight sympathy with the enemy were treated harshly. A good example of this was the humourist and author P. G. Wodehouse. He was living in France when Germany invaded in 1940. During his long internment by the Nazis, he was persuaded to write and broadcast some humorous material. As a result, he was regarded in the British press as a traitor. Wodehouse was an other-worldly figure, best described as naive.[67] Yet in the 'us versus them' narrative of war, there seemed to be little space for those who did not fit in. Or consider the case of Christabel Bielenberg, an Anglo-Irish woman who married a German in 1934. She and her husband were anti-Nazis, but because of prevailing attitudes in Germany and Nazi intrusion into many aspects of life as WWII progressed, they had to be extremely guarded in what they said. Here she recalls conversations with new neighbours in Berlin:

> The conversation would at first be guarded and non-committal. We knew that we were none of us Nazis, but were all of us, drunk or sober, also discreet? Had we other mutual friends? . . . I would find it hard to describe the wary approach, the half-finished sentence, the guarded reference which led at the time to a mutual confidence. . . . The procedure was a delicate one, one that had to be

---

[65] Richard Reeves, *Infamy: The Shocking Story of the Japanese-American Internment in WWII* (New York: Henry Holt, 2015); Mary Matsuda Gruenewald, *Looking Like the Enemy: My Story of Imprisonment in Japanese-American Internment Camps* (Troutdale, OR: NewSage, 2005).

[66] Colin Holmes, *Searching for Lord Haw-Haw: The Political Lives of William Joyce* (London: Routledge, 2016).

[67] Richard Norton-Taylor, 'I Was Not a Nazi Collaborator, PG Wodehouse Told MI5', *Guardian*, 26 August 2011). See also Robert McCrum, *Wodehouse: A Life* (New York: Norton, 2004).

carefully learned if we valued our lives, and would trust our fellows sufficiently to put our lives in their hands.[68]

As the case demonstrates, transforming thoughts of solidarity into actions of solidarity requires a careful cost-benefit analysis. In many cases, the in-group social control associated with war—whether this is among fellow citizens on the home front or within the military—makes this impossible.

At various times, combatant countries or blocs have used the language of solidarity and attempted to recruit soldiers or civilians from the other side, but these tended to be shallow attempts to undermine enemy morale and fighting ability. As Strachan notes, 'War tries to foment revolution on the other side'.[69] German support for Irish independence during WWI can hardly be attributed to the kaiser's heartfelt concern for the plight of the Irish. Japan established a Greater East Asia Co-Prosperity Sphere in 1940 and branded it as a counterweight to Western colonialism that would allow Asian and Pacific populations to come together for mutual cooperation. In actual fact, it was 'enforced regionalism' and primarily a vehicle for Japanese imperialism.[70] Attempts to promote pan-Asianism were subjugated to the Japanese war effort.[71] Japanese attempts to foment anti-British sentiment in India were largely about trying to oust the British from India (or parts of it) rather than provide genuine emancipation for Indians. Similarly, German collaboration with various nationalist or anti-Soviet groups in the Soviet Union during WWII was not about finding a genuine solidarity between peoples.[72] The Nazi invasion of eastern Europe was, after all 'racially-motivated aggression'.[73]

Only a few of the war memoirs consulted for this book contained reference to an overarching ideology that might counter rival nationalisms.[74] Barthas, the pacifist socialist French conscript, recounts one experience from WWI. It is worth quoting in detail, as it highlights the difficulty of a unifying narrative (such

---

[68] Christabel Bielenberg, *The Past Is My Life* (London: Chatto and Windus, 1968), 90.
[69] Strachan, 'Introductory Essay', 17.
[70] Mark Beeson, 'Geopolitics and the Making of Regions: The Fall and Rise of East Asia', *Political Studies* 57, no. 3 (2009): 503.
[71] Mishra, *From the Ruins*.
[72] Anton Wiess-Wendt, *Eradicating Differences: The Treatment of Minorities in Nazi-Dominated Europe* (Cambridge: Cambridge Scholars, 2010).
[73] Peter J. Lyth, 'Traitor or Patriot? Andrey Vlasov and the Russian Liberation Movement 1942-45', *Journal of Strategic Studies* 12, no. 2 (1989): 230.
[74] Germans who mentioned a common anti-communism or anti-Bolshevism in their memoirs tended to be first and foremost unreformed Nazis. The idea of a common German-British anti-communism also featured on propaganda leaflets distributed over British lines in France/Belgium in 1944. One such leaflet noted 'our common heritage and with it all those values—moral, spiritual, cultural and material which we have, all of us Englishman and German alike—recognised, cherished and striven to maintain'. Reproduced in Render, *Tank Action*, 165. For the wider context, see Olga Baranova, 'Nationalism, Anti-Bolshevism or the Will to Survive: Collaboration in Belarus under the Nazi Occupation of 1941-1944', *European Review of History* 15, no. 2 (2008): 113–128.

as socialism or another form of solidarity) trumping militaristic nationalism. It also shows the willingness of governments to use violence to threaten their own subjects:

> One day, a huge devil of a German stood up on a mound and gave a speech which only the Germans could understand word for word, but everyone knew what it meant, because he smashed his rifle on a tree stump, breaking it in two with a gesture of anger.
> Applause broke out on two sides, and the 'Internationale' was sung. Well, if only you had been there, mad kings, bloody generals, fanatical ministers, jingoistic journalists, rear-echelon patriots, to contemplate this sublime spectacle!
> But it wasn't enough that the soldiers refuse to fight one another. What was needed was for them to turn their back on the monsters who were pushing them, one against the other, and to cut them down like wild beasts. For not having done so, how much longer would the killing go on? Meanwhile, our big-shot leaders were in a furor. What in the Lord's name would happen if the soldiers refused to kill each other? Our artillerymen received orders to fire on any assemblies of men which were pointed out to them, and to mow down indiscriminately both Frenchmen and Germans, just like when in the ancient circuses they slaughtered wild beasts who were too intelligent to tear each other's throats out and devour each other. Furthermore, once the front line was established again, for better or worse, it was forbidden under the penalty of death to leave the trench. Any act of familiarity with the Germans had to cease.[75]

In another case of attempted solidarity involving a British soldier and his Turkish prisoner, the British soldier is sceptical:

> He is an out and out socialist and hates war and states that capitalists make war to enrich themselves. He made a solemn agreement that if we ever met in an attack we would not fire on each other. Well, I would not like to trust you just the same Mr Noureddin. I think I would try and get the first one in.[76]

If allowed to manifest itself, strong everyday peace would take the form of situations in which individuals and groups of individuals are unconvinced of the causes or means of all sides in a conflict and refuse to participate. This might involve conscientious objection or the establishment of zones of

---

[75] Louis Barthas, *Poilu: The World War I Nottebooks of Louis Barthas, Barrelmaker 1914–1918* (New Haven CT: Yale University Press 2014), pp. 143–144.
[76] Downham and Roe, *Diary*, location 4819.

peace.[77] Conscientious objection may involve a refusal to be conscripted on the grounds that the individual's religious or ethical worldview finds war, militarism, or a particular political project objectionable. A core part of states' claim to a monopoly of violence is the ability to mobilise citizenry for military (defensive or offensive) purposes. For a citizen to excuse himself, especially in times of war and if there is an existential threat to the state, is a significant step.[78] States are peculiarly effective in mounting a mobilising narrative. In the United States, the hegemonic narrative regards WWII as a 'good war' in which US servicemen had unimpeachable qualities of 'patriotism, tenacity, hard work and sacrifice'.[79] Of the 34 million US citizens who were registered for the draft in WWII, only 0.3 percent are believed to have objected on the grounds of conscience. In such circumstances of near-hegemonic social unity, conscientious objectors can quite easily be branded as deviant and often classed as cowards or traitors.

The account of Archibald Baxter, a doughty New Zealand conscientious objector, makes clear, however, that considerable bravery was involved in taking the stance of objecting to war.[80] Baxter endured the most dreadful privations in WWI. After being imprisoned in New Zealand, he was shipped to England and then to the frontline in France. He was forced to wear a military uniform, endured torture, and was starved. He survived the war but suffered harassment and difficulties when he returned to New Zealand.[81] Baxter was given repeated opportunities to conform but refused to do so, betraying a remarkable strength of character.

While there were cases of mutiny in WWI, and very occasionally in WWII, these were not attempts to side with the enemy and so do not fall into the category of solidarity. Instead, they usually revolved around dissatisfaction with circumstances: food, pay, leadership, and a sense that their commanders were inept and uncaring.[82] Mutiny was reasonably common in the French, German, and Austro-Hungarian armies in WWI, with at least 25,000 French troops mutinying.[83] As it became clear that Germany was losing WWI, mutiny among German troops and sailors increased—some in the name of socialism.[84] It was

---

[77] Landon E. Hancock, 'Agency and Peacebuilding: The Promise of Local Zones of Peace', *Peacebuilding* 5, no. 3 (2017): 255–269; Raymon Lopez-Reyes, 'Establishing Salvadorian Zones of Peace', *Peace Review* 9, no. 2 (1997): 225–231.

[78] Colin Mellors and John McKean, 'Confronting the State: Conscientious Objection in Western Europe', *Bulletin of Peace Proposals* 13, no. 3 (1982): 227.

[79] Leah Rogne, 'The Greatest Generation Revisited: Conscientious Objectors and the Great War', *Humanity and Society* 34, no. 1 (2010): 4.

[80] Archibald Baxter, *We Will Not Cease* (Christchurch, New Zealand: Caxton, 1968).

[81] Rod Edmond, '"It's Your Submission We Want Baxter!" We Will Not Cease: The Autobiography of a Conscientious Objector', *Journal of New Zealand Literature* 33, no. 2 (2015): 142–159.

[82] Rachel Duffett, 'A Taste of Army Life', *Cultural and Social History* 9, no. 2 (2012): 259.

[83] Cathryn Corns and John Hughes-Wilson, *Blindfold and Alone: British Military Executions in the Great War* (London: Cassell, 2005), 379. See also Smith, *Between Mutiny and Obedience*.

[84] W. S. Hewison, *This Great Harbour: Scapa Flow* (Stromness, UK: Orkney, 1985), 128.

much less common in the British military.[85] As Corns and Hughes-Wilson note, 'Given the sheer scale of the killing in the period 1914–18 it is therefore astonishing just how little mutiny figures in the British Army during the First World War'.[86] A key reason for the low mutiny figures is that the sanction was death.[87]

It is true that many combatants were not persuaded by the propaganda from their own side.[88] One WWI soldier, who had witnessed a good deal of carnage in the trenches, remembered, 'None of the men want to attack—despite what military correspondents and Generals say'.[89] Barthas, the French barrelmaker who spent four years in the trenches, reflected after a speech in which his colonel sought to rouse the troops before an offensive, 'This patriotic nonsense didn't arouse the slightest enthusiasm. We hadn't forgotten the horrors of the last offensive'.[90] A German veteran of the WWII eastern front remembered:

After you have spent some time at the front, like I have, you no longer fight for *Führer, Volk* and *Vaterland*. These ideals have long gone. And no one talks about National Socialism or similar political matters. From all our conversations, it's quite obvious that the primary reason we fight is to stay alive and help our front-line comrades to do the same.[91]

These examples, and there are many more like them in the diaries and memoirs, suggest the importance of the micro-circuit of a small number of comrades. Through living, training, and fighting together over extended periods, they would become intimate confidants. The small group—perhaps a tank crew or the inhabitants of a dugout—would have been a space for multiple conversations. These micro-circuits were spaces in which comrades would work out how much dissent from the main circuit was possible or acceptable.

A chilling example of solidarity comes from the memoir of Waffen-SS soldier Herbert Maeger. At one stage in WWII, he was being trained as a medic and was being lectured by an SS officer on the Nazi 'world view' and 'racial hygiene'. The lecturer noted how 'seriously mentally handicapped persons will, after the most thorough medical investigation, be passed on for euthanasia, the procedure will

---

[85] Britain's most significant military mutiny in the modern era occurred in 1931 in reaction to very poor pay and conditions. Alan Ereira, *The Invergordon Mutiny* (London: Routledge & Kegan Paul, 1981).
[86] Corns and Hughes-Wilson, *Blindfold and Alone*, 380.
[87] Douglas Gill and Gloden Dallas, 'Mutiny at Etaples Base in 1917', *Past & Present* 69, no. 1 (1975): 88–112.
[88] Carius, *Tigers*, location 2041.
[89] MacGill, *The Great Push*, 224.
[90] Barthas, *Poilu*, 107.
[91] Koschorrek, *Blood Red Snow*, location 3719.

naturally be carried through with scrupulous attention to humanitarian principles'.[92] Maeger continues:

> There was a rhetorical pause for this to sink in and the air in the room suddenly became icy. Then an SS Junker [student] in the row to the left of me stood up and said in a calm, clear voice: 'I protest formally against this disregard of medical ethics and the Hippocratic oath, to which I feel myself bound as a student of medicine'. Two other young men rose with him. One said, 'I associate myself with the words of my comrade!, the other only, 'I also. What you are propagating is a crime!'
>
> ... For long seconds there was an almost intolerable, breathless hush, The SS-1st Lieutenant lecturer, his face a pallid mask and struggling to compose himself, clutched the edges of his desk. Finally, after a pause, which seemed to be eternal, he took a dep breath and ordered, 'Follow me at once to the office'. He marched off with stiff strides followed by his three crazy opponents, never to be spoken of again.[93]

As this story reveals, solidarity that stands against an authoritarian regime can be very costly. A more typical response comes from this German soldier: 'Even if one knew what was happening to the Jews, it would have been impossible to contest this without risking one's life and few individuals are blessed with such courage'.[94] Yet it is clear from accounts of those who assisted Jews in Germany and occupied Europe during WWII that thousands of people were prepared to show solidarity. This solidarity had to be secretive for obvious security reasons. Jørgen Kieler, a member of the Danish Resistance Movement during the German occupation, reflected that 'two in our group had been shot in action, two had committed suicide, two were executed after torture, and two died in a concentration camp. Four survived deportation and others survived underground in Denmark or as refugees in Sweden'.[95] John Weidner was one of a number of people who organised a network that smuggled an estimated eight hundred Jews from France to Switzerland during WWII. On being interviewed about his motivation, he mentioned 'hav[ing] a heart open to the suffering of others' (sociality), but, importantly, he turned that sociality into action (solidarity): 'you can have all kinds of theories and all kinds of creeds but if you do not have love in action, those theories and creeds do not mean anything at all'.[96] Weidner escaped

---

[92] Maeger, *Lost Honour*, 192.
[93] Maeger, *Lost Honour*, 193.
[94] Erwin Bartmann, *Für Volk and Führer: The Memoir of a Veteran of the 1st SS Panzer Division Leibstand SS Adolf Hitler* (Solihull, UK: Helion, 2013), 264.
[95] Jørgen Kieler, cited in Carol Rittner and Sondra Myers, *The Courage to Care: Rescuers of Jews during the Holocaust* (New York: New York University Press, 1986), 89.
[96] John Weidner, cited in Rittner and Myers, *The Courage to Care*, 64.

Gestapo custody before his execution, but many in his network, including his sister, were murdered.

Conclusion

Most of the examples deployed in this chapter date from World Wars I and II. It is legitimate to ask if such historical examples carry much weight in the contemporary era. After all, the technologies of war have changed, especially with the introduction of digital and remotely operated technologies that place physical distance between combatants. It is worth noting that close-proximity warfare is still with us (indeed, there have been prominent examples of urban warfare and city sieges in recent years), thus giving opportunities for mercy, humanity, and reciprocity. So, although many of the examples in this chapter date from more than seventy years ago, they still retain relevance. This leads into another issue—the ahistorical nature of much of peace and conflict studies. An overwhelming number of publications in peace and conflict studies examine contemporary and ongoing conflicts. This is for understandable reasons. Less understandable is a discipline-wide reticence in adopting historical lenses to shed light on contemporary problems. Much of this book concentrates on re-evaluating peace so that we can take notions and stances of everyday peace properly into account. To help us in this task, it is worth evaluating time as well. Along with formal political time that operates according to the clock and is linear, we should also be aware of more sociological explanations of time. These would take into account family milestones and culturally shaped ways of seeing the world. It is important that peace and conflict studies can accommodate a plurality of timescapes and is not necessarily beholden to a single paradigm that sees time as standardised and linear. Thus, one modest contribution of this book is to draw attention to the utility of using historical and firsthand accounts in building concepts and theories about peace and conflict.

Running through this chapter has been the issue of power, or the ability of individuals and (usually small) groups of individuals to exercise their pacific will during armed conflict. The chapter has deliberately restricted itself to the difficult cases of near-total warfare, with the aim of addressing a significant challenge facing the notion and practice of everyday peace: how it deals with power. How can everyday peace be exercised in contexts in which militarism, aggressiveness, and exclusion are the norm? The answer is that everyday peace is exceedingly difficult in such circumstances. Yet the examples in the chapter show the occasional and slight ways in which everyday peace can become manifest. Individuals are able, in McBride's phrase, to control their nerves and passion, and are able to direct them for humane purposes. This is EPP in which the everyday is the battlefield or a military campaign, and the peace takes the form of conflict disruption rather than a more profound peace. Yet the disruption can puncture a number of the assumptions upon which warfare rests. The most important of these is the assumption that individuals from different identity groups are axiomatically oppositional to one another and are united in their support for demands of their own leadership or military organisation. As the examples in this chapter have been able to show, sometimes individuals are able to carve out pockets of power and disrupt the conflict norm.

The tripartite distinction of weak, medium, and strong everyday peace that maps onto sociality, reciprocity, and solidarity has been useful in helping us think through the gradations of everyday peace. It is especially useful in illustrating its context-dependent nature and how the space in which everyday peace (or everyday compassion and humanity) is constrained in times of war. It is worth thinking about the various layers of power deployed to constrain actors from engaging in pacific acts. These range from overt forms of power backed by military sanction (the court martial) to the anxiety of not being seen as betraying the in-group. The types and strength of power facing everyday peace, compassion, and remorse mean that those who wish to deviate from the norms of warlike behaviour often have to be ingenious. A wide repertoire of social skills may be required. This is especially the case in terms of being able to 'read' a situation and make an assessment of what is, and what is not, possible. Here, as seen in the chapter, considerable bravery may be involved.

A final point is to return to the notion of circuits as a way of understanding how individuals and groups engaging in everyday peace might fit within wider military organisations and societies. Militaries are hierarchical circuits, with power very clearly exercised by those at the upper levels; individuality is to be subjugated to the wishes of the leadership. But individuals and small groups of individuals, perhaps the occupants of a tank or a small stretch of trench, constitute a circuit within a circuit. Not all of their activities might be visible elsewhere and in other circuits. They might be able to engage in hidden transcripts and other discreet activities. Their everyday peace activities of reciprocity or sociality with 'the enemy' may not threaten the wider circuit, but they are a disruption to the smooth running and conflict logic upon which it is based. Crucially, they illustrate that the 'war circuit' is not complete or closed. Instead, alternatives and transgressive behaviour are possible. These alternatives may humanise war, allow lives to be saved and improved, and break the notion that warlike behaviour is shared by everyone in a conflict context.

While scaling up of everyday peace on the battlefield may be impossible, scaling out may be a possibility. It could be that informal norms of taking prisoners and treating them with respect take root among a small group within a larger unit but then spread among the unit. This is similar to Lederach's 'middle-out' idea whereby mid-range personnel and leaders can act as brokers, connectors, and risk-takers. Many of the personal war diaries and memoirs note the role of charismatic leaders, often sergeants and other non-commissioned officers, who led by example. The scaling out of basic humanity in a military unit (and it is worth remembering that inhumanity is also scaled out) may not alter the course of the war at the strategic level, but it does have the capacity to do so at an individual, and indeed fundamental, level. Crucially, lives saved on the battlefield or prisoners protected from the worst of privations do matter at the level of the individual and their families. Snap decisions on the battlefield have an afterlife in terms of the productive lives that former POWs might go on to lead. They contribute to a social memory that not all Germans[97] were—in a phrase used in WWI—beastly. These snap decisions, which might seem inconsequential or highly localised, help disrupt the notion of total war.

---

[97] Or British, French, Russians, Americans, etc.

6
Gender and Everyday Peace

Introduction

Everyday peace is gendered. It is situated in a series of power relationships that constrain it and give it possibilities. This chapter recognises that many aspects of peace, particularly formal peace processes, are dominated by male elites. As befits a focus on everyday peace, however, we will look beyond elite-level peace and concentrate on the often banal aspects of life that constitute society. Here the focus is on the neighbourhood, the workplace, and spaces of public interaction such as the queue in the post office or bakery. The chapter focuses on one aspect of life that is deeply gendered: the family. Families can be incubators of civility and everyday peace, and they constitute circuits. The chapter is particularly interested in 'the authority of mothers, grandmothers and aunts'[1] (but also fathers, grandfathers, and uncles) in helping to tamp down violence and tension and in steering those in their ambit towards civility, sociality, and tolerance. It is worth noting that women are often the driving force in family networks, particularly in terms of rituals and services such as eating, worship, socialisation, visiting, and caring. There is no intention to romanticise the family as an always benign environment. Families might also be the site of a negative pedagogy that reinforces and normalises conflict and exclusion. The focus on the family is consistent with the level of analysis throughout this book: the informal and highly localised. Families are, of course, institutions, but they occupy an area partly removed from state surveillance and are rarely the focus of international relations or of peace and conflict studies.

As will be explained later in more detail, the focus on the family and gender should not be interpreted as equating all things female with the private sphere. Nor should it be interpreted as suggesting that females are without power and agency in other spheres. Instead, the chapter regards gender as being not solely about women—the concept applies to all aspects of society and encourages us to think about the fundamental bases upon which societies are organised.[2] The

---

[1] Mary H. Moran, 'Gender, Militarism and Peace-Building: Projects of the Postconflict Moment', *Annual Review of Anthropology* 39 (2010): 267.

[2] Elin Bjarnegård and Erik Melander, 'Disentangling Gender, Peace and Democratization: The Negative Effects of Militarized Masculinity', *Journal of Gender Studies* 20, no. 2 (2011): 144; Moran, 'Gender', 261.

chapter also emphasises the connectedness or intersectionality of the multiple aspects of peace and conflict. While many accounts of conflict might focus on the kinetic end of violence, such events need to be situated in wider processes and political economies that involve localities, homes, and families—all of which are gendered. In keeping with the rest of the book, the chapter regards circuitry as a useful tool for illustrating the connectedness of ostensibly separate—but actually connected—domains. The focus on the family is justified in that this domain is often left out of considerations of peace and conflict. In many accounts, peace and conflict are public and performative and enacted in the public political sphere. This chapter takes a different view; it challenges discrete notions of public and private and interprets everyday peace as enacted and embodied through everyday life. The focus on everyday peace means that our gaze looks away from peace accord signing ceremonies and other 'big peace' initiatives. Instead, the focus is on how peace becomes manifest on a daily basis in the micro-encounters that constitute everyday life in deeply divided and conflict-affected societies. The everyday domain is a site of (gendered) power, and the Everyday Peace Power (EPP) discussed in this chapter, and throughout this book, is subject to gendered dynamics.

Following a brief note on methodology, the chapter begins with a discussion that underscores the gendered nature of formal, top-down approaches to peace and how these are often dominated by male military and political elites. The second substantive section then explores the meanings and significance of gender in relation to everyday peace. The third section identifies everyday peace actions and processes, many of which are related to the family. The essential aim of the chapter is to illustrate how everyday peace is gendered and how apparently innocuous and banal processes and aspects of family life can have significant implications for the pacific orientation of society. Thus, the chapter looks at the quiet mentorship from a grandmother that steers younger members of the family away from extremism or at the restraint of word or deed that discourages siblings from becoming caught up in militarised political movements. Such actions can be foundational for everyday peace, yet they might be hidden and naturalised into family behaviours and roles. So, while being banal at the individual and familial level, they can be crucial in terms of the impact on the wider society. Here it is worth reminding ourselves of discussions (mainly in chapter 2) about the possibility of scaling up and scaling out everyday peace. It is the accretion of minor acts across populations that matters. A dozen mothers in a valley in Afghanistan preventing their sons from joining a militant organisation—whether the Taliban or a warlord's militia—can have a real impact on peace and conflict in an extended locality. Similarly, one or two big brothers treating out-group members with civility in a small town may have a demonstration and multiplier effect if younger brothers follow their example.

John Paul Lederach uses the phrase 'critical yeast' rather than 'critical mass' to move beyond counting the numbers involved in social movements: 'It seems to me that the key to changing this thing is getting a small set of the right people involved at the right places. What's missing is not the critical mass. The missing ingredient is the critical yeast'.[3] Since many everyday peace acts take the form of events that were prevented and did not happen, it is difficult to capture them. That does not mean, however, that they are unimportant.

As with the other chapters in this book, it is worth questioning here whether what is termed 'everyday peace' is actually peace. Many of the actions, stances, and processes discussed in this chapter are firmly in the negative peace category. They involve, for example, restraining family members from becoming involved in extremist violence. Such preventive processes are clearly socially valuable and potentially save lives and prevent the further inflammation of violent conflict. Yet can we call them pacific? Do they actively promote tolerance and reconciliation? It is the argument of this chapter and the book that these actions and processes do deserve the label 'everyday peace'. In many cases, the three conceptual foundations of everyday peace—sociality, reciprocity, and solidarity—are present. Their presence in the intimacy of the family and other highly localised spaces, however, means that they are often unnoticed or not remarked on. Many of the actions and processes considered in this chapter might be termed 'small peace', or minimal pro-peace activities. If we consider the contexts in which many of these activities take place, however, then we can see that, potentially, they can have a significant impact. As will be discussed later in the chapter, however, many actions of restraint within the family or the immediate vicinity of the home may be considered as reinforcing the status quo. They might mean that discriminatory forms of power go unchallenged, but to overtly challenge patriarchy, despotism, authoritarianism, or majoritarianism might be inadvisable. A final point to make by way of introduction is that the chapter does not focus on gender-based social movements, civil society organisations, or pro-peace groups (already the subject of a very good literature).[4] Instead, the focus is on the level below that: families, individuals, and groups of individuals who are not formally organised for peace but may, if the circumstances allow it, engage in everyday pro-peace thinking and actions.

---

[3] Lederach, *The Moral Imagination*, 91.

[4] See, for example, Gila Svirsky, 'Local Coalitions, Global Partners: The Women's Peace Movement in Israel and Beyond', *Signs* 29, no. 2 (2004): 543–550; Joyati Bhattacharya, 'Gender, Peacemaking and the Case of Northeast India', *Indian Journal of Political Science* 71, no. 1 (2010): 233–239; Peace A. Medie, 'Fighting Gender-Based Violence: The Women's Movement and the Enforcement of Rape Law in Liberia', *African Affairs* 112, no. 448 (2013): 377–397.

A Note on Methodology

The decision to focus on the family as a way of explaining the gendered nature of everyday peace presents a methodological problem. The home and the family are often beyond the gaze of much research. Family life often takes place, literally, behind closed doors. Moreover, much of family life is unremarkable—a series of small acts (many involving drudgery) that constitute a whole. Many aspects of family life are unspoken—gestures, inferences, and assumptions that constitute the stuff of family life but might be difficult for the outsider to observe or understand. Other aspects of family life may be deemed sensitive, and family members may—justifiably—value privacy. While anthropological and sociological studies have dissected family life in many different contexts, international relations and peace and conflict studies have largely ignored the topic (with the prominent exception of feminist approaches to both).[5] The sources that are available to this author—diaries, memoirs, life histories, and interview transcripts—all suffer potential deficiencies. As outlined in chapters 4 and 5 in relation to the diaries and memoirs of soldiers, civilian diaries and memoirs may suffer from a number of potential deficiencies, including self-censorship and cultural biases. For example, many cultures might privilege an oral tradition rather than the written word. It is also worth noting that this chapter is interested in processes and actions that are often regarded as so normal and innocuous that they are not recorded. The moral authority projected by parents over their children and the near-constant nudging or nagging of parenting (Flora, put on your shoes!) may be plain for all to see but may not be the subject of documentary evidence.

Another methodological challenge comes from the fact that certain individuals might have charisma or a particular sway over the family or the local community, but this is something that is difficult to measure or compare.[6] Such powers will be culturally specific, might be time-limited, and will be exercised in non-verbal and non-written ways. Individuals might be able to project and maintain a sense of authority, without this authority being mandated in any formal way. There is probably no rule book on being a big sister, and different individuals will perform the role in different ways.

It is also worth noting that this chapter, in keeping with the rest of the book, encourages us to think through level-of-analysis issues. The chapter should be

---

[5] Christopher Poulos, *Accidental Ethnography: An Inquiry into Family Secrecy* (Walnut Creek, CA: Left Coast, 2009); Lisa M. Tillmann, 'Coming Out and Going Home: A Family Ethnography', *Qualitative Enquiry* 16, no. 2 (2010): 116–129; Reed W. Larson and David M. Almeida, 'Emotional Transmission in the Daily Lives of Families: A New Paradigm for Studying Family Process', *Journal of Marriage and Family* 61, no. 1 (1999): 5–20.

[6] Kenneth J. Levine, Robert A. Muenchen, and Abby M. Brooks, 'Measuring Transformational and Charismatic Leadership: Why Isn't Charisma Measured?' *Communication Monographs* 77, no. 4 (2010): 576–591.

read as a critique of attempts to view societies and systems as compartmentalised. This book emphasises circuitry as an analytical tool to capture connectedness or intersectionality and rejects the notion of discrete public and private spheres and discrete political and non-political domains. The chapter emphasises the interstices between domains. Consider, for example, a US drone strike on suspected Taliban members travelling in a 4x4 vehicle in Afghanistan.[7] We might focus on the kinetic aspects of the incident—a missile attack in a specific place against a specific target and perpetrated by a group of techno-empowered soldiers in a military base in the United States. Yet, in order to have a fuller picture of the incident, it is worth thinking about the multiple systems in which all of the actors are involved. These are highly contextualised systems that stretch far beyond masculine military organisations towards the political economies of drone and 4x4 manufacture, the social construction of notions of defence and patriotism, and the family support systems that enable or compel the soldiers and militants to play particular roles.[8] The phrase 'the attack begins in the factory'[9] gives some idea of the supply chain of industrialised warfare, but actually the attack also begins at the breakfast table that enables the workers to undertake a day's labour. In other words, soldiers and militants are not just soldiers and militants, stand-alone and de-contextualized entities. They are, instead, the product of an immense set of social, economic, cultural, and political interactions.[10] This chapter recognises the complex interactionism that lies behind war and peace and all of the stages in between. In particular, it recognises the role played by family in this, and how family—like other societal domains—is gendered.

The Gendered Nature of Top-Down Peace

Academic and policy work over the past few decades has done much to expose the highly gendered nature of violence, conflict, tension, and discrimination. It has covered both direct and indirect violence and the modes of thinking and

---

[7] On the "backstory" of a drone strike, see, for example, Abigail Fielding-Smith, Payenda Sargand, and Jack Serle, 'The Anatomy of an American Airstrike', *Newsweek*, 18 February 2016, https://www.newsweek.com/anatomy-american-air-strike-afghanistan-drones-united-nations-nato-427918; Brian Glyn Jones, 'The Slaughter of a Wedding Party in Yemen: Anatomy of a Bad Drone Strike', *HuffPost*, 14 January 2014, https://www.huffingtonpost.com/brian-glyn-williams/the-slaughter-of-a-weddin_b_4595274.html?guccounter=1.

[8] For an excellent discussion of how warlike relations can pervade all aspects of life, see Alison Howell, 'Forget "Militarization": Race, Disability and the "Martial Politics" of the Police and of the University', *International Feminist Journal of Politics* 20, no. 2 (2018): 117–136.

[9] Corinna Peniston-Bird, 'War and Peace in the Cloakroom: The Controversy over the Memorial to the Women of World War II', in *Representations of Peace and Conflict*, ed. Stephen Gibson and Simon Mollan (Basingstoke, UK: Palgrave, 2012), 275.

[10] Patricia Hill Collins and Sirma Bilge, *Intersectionality* (Cambridge: Polity, 2016).

political economies that explain violence and its impact. Work on direct violence has highlighted how sexual and gender-based violence (SGBV) is often an integral part of military campaigns and how non-traditional and asymmetrical forms of warfare can impact men, women, and children in different ways.[11] My research on the conflict in Darfur and the UN response to that conflict revealed the extent to which SGBV had become normalised and ingrained into ways of living and persisting. As the following quotations show, conflict impacted men and women in different ways:[12]

> There were violent incidents against women such as kidnapping of women and rape. There was robbery and hijacking. . . . These incidents took place repeatedly on [a] weekly and daily basis.[13]

> The most common incidents were [the] killing of people and lack of freedom of movement, in a sense that men cannot go to their farms. If women go to collect firewood they face sexual abuse and rape, if we see Arabs we run back quickly to the village. In Mugan women were beaten and harassed a lot, however in Gambar we heard about women [who] went missing. They were kidnapped and never came back.[14]

> They started with harassing women at farms or when they go to collect firewood. If they see women they beat them, loot their belongings, and send them back home. Then the harassment developed to sexual abuse and abduction. They raped many women and many others went missing. For more than 10–12 years women [who were] abducted and went missing have not been brought back and nobody knows [their] whereabouts.[15]

> The most common incidents were the arresting and detaining of men at the check points between Kalma camp and Nayla. Also rape of women was very common. For example in April 2008 a woman and her daughter from centre 2 went to collect firewood, when they were attacked by armed men wearing

---

[11] Temitope B. Oriola, '"Unwilling Cocoons": Boko Haram's War against Women', *Studies in Conflict and Terrorism* 40, no. 2 (2017): 99–121; Maria Eriksson Baaz and Maria Stern, *The Complexity of Violence: A Critical Analysis of Sexual Violence in the Democratic Republic of Congo (DRC)* (Stockholm: SIDA Working Paper, 2010). See also the excellent interview material in Roddy Brett, *The Origins and Dynamics of Genocide: Political Violence in Guatemala* (Basingstoke, UK: Palgrave Macmillan, 2016), 188, 199, 205.

[12] The interviews were conducted by Dr. Zuhair Bashar as part of a research project I led: UK Research and Innovation, 'Making Peacekeeping Data Work for the International Community', funded by the Economic and Social Research Council, ES/L007479/1. The interviews were held with Darfarian residents of UN-administered refugee camps in Chad, situated by the border with Sudan. All the interviews were conducted according to an ethics and data management plan set out by the University of Manchester.

[13] Interview with male, Goz Amir Refugee Camp, Chad, 8 May 2015.

[14] Interview with female, Goz Amir Refugee Camp, Chad, 10 May 2015.

[15] Interview with female, Djabal Refugee Camp, Chad, 27 May 2015.

military uniform and riding horses. The attackers raped the girl and the mother managed to escape. After they raped the daughter they buried her up to her head. Luckily a passer-by heard the girl crying and managed to rescue her. He brought her to the camp where she was treated at the MSF [Médecins Sans Frontières] clinic. . . . The incidents of rape were happening repeatedly every week.[16]

Men were randomly arrested and killed; that is why they stopped moving outside their homes. It was only women [who could] go to the market to bring food or go outside the town to work and collect firewood. Though there was high risk on women too; when [the] Janjaweed [a pro-government militia] met them they [raped] and beat them too. . . . Every week incidents were happening.[17]

What comes across from these interview excerpts, and the project gathered extensive testimony similar to this, was the all-pervading and chronic nature of the conflict. Certainly, there were incidents and spikes in violence, but the picture that is conveyed is one of a permanent system of insecurity, degradation, and incivility. This had an impact on multiple aspects of life, such as livelihood, travel patterns, and how people were able to go about their daily business. Indeed, more than impacting lives, it constituted the daily lifeworld. In many respects, lives were the antithesis of everyday peace.

Scholarly work has been particularly good at exploring the gendered nature of indirect violence. This work has examined the political economies, worldviews, and structures that mean that men and women are often affected by, and implicated in, violent processes in different ways. Work on militarism,[18] the microeconomies of military bases,[19] the embodied nature of conflict,[20] humanitarian and peacebuilding practices and spaces,[21], and international structures and processes[22] has all enhanced our understanding of the gendered nature of conflict and violence. Also important has been work that has shown how women

---

[16] Interview with female, Djabal Refugee Camp, Chad, 22 May 2015.
[17] Interview with female, Djabal Refugee Camp, Chad, 21 May 2015.
[18] Laura Sjoberg and Sandra Via, eds., *Gender, War and Militarism: Feminist Perspectives* (Santa Barbara, CA: Praeger, 2010).
[19] Cynthia Enloe, *Bananas, Beaches and Bases: Making Feminist Sense of International Politics* (Berkeley: University of California Press, 1990); Kathleen M. Jennings and Morten Bøås, 'Transactions and Interactions: Everyday Life in the Peacekeeping Economy', *Journal of Intervention and Statebuilding* 9, no. 3 (2015): 281–295.
[20] Jennifer L. Fluri and Amy Piedalue, 'Embodying Violence: Critical Geographies of Gender, Race, and Culture', *Gender, Place & Culture* 24, no. 4 (2017): 534–544; Cristina Masters, 'Bodies of Technology: Cyborg Soldiers and Militarised Masculinities', *International Feminist Journal of Politics* 7, no. 1 (2005): 112–132.
[21] Laura J. Shepherd, *Gender, Peacebuilding and the Politics of Space: Locating Legitimacy* (Oxford: Oxford University Press, 2017); Lisa Smirl, *Spaces of Aid: How Cars, Compounds and Hotels Shape Humanitarianism* (London: Zed, 2015); Autesserre, *Peaceland*.
[22] Laura J. Shepherd, 'Power and Authority in the Production of United Nations Security Council 1325', *International Studies Quarterly* 52, no. 2 (2008): 383–404.

have been consigned specific roles in the narratives of conflict and that these roles often render complexity and difference into formulaic and 'appropriate' roles.[23] What has been less well studied, until comparatively recently, has been the gendered nature of formal peacemaking. The peace of peace processes and internationally supported peacebuilding has been dominated by male elites. This has profound implications for the nature of the peace that is agreed on in top-down peace processes. As Antonia Potter observes, 'the process and substance of peace negotiations and agreements would be richer, subtler, stronger, and more firmly rooted in the societies whose problems they aim to solve with increased participation of women and the issues which are important to them'.[24] This is not only intuitively true, but there is empirical evidence to back it up. One statistical analysis 'demonstrates a robust correlation between peace agreements signed by female delegates and durable peace . . . [and] that agreements signed by women show a significantly higher number of peace agreement provisions aimed at political reform, and higher implementation rates for provisions'.[25]

Four points are worth making with regard to the elite male domination of peace processes and accords. The first is that processes and peace accords tend to be the preserve of institutions. These institutions—primarily governments, political parties, militaries, and non-state armed actors—are often 'male-only enclaves'.[26] Quite simply, in many cases, women are not at the negotiating table, and thus, many of the issues they might raise, and the perspectives they might take, are unheard. As Cynthia Cockburn pointed out, 'Peace negotiations . . . characteristically overlook women and their transversalist insights'.[27] Research by the US Council on Foreign Relations found that nine out of thirty-four post–Cold War peace processes had zero percent female negotiators.[28] A further eight peace process had less than 10 percent female negotiators. The peace processes in which women were most represented at the negotiating table (Colombia at 33 percent and the Philippines at 35 percent) were still male-dominated. Mere presence at the negotiating table may be an empty signifier, however. In one case where a female was included in the top negotiating team (Hanan Ashrawi of the Palestinian delegation during the Oslo process), 'she was side-lined and relegated

---

[23] Nayanika Mookherjee, 'Gendered Embodiments: Mapping the Body-Politic of the Raped Women and the Nation in Bangladesh', *Feminist Review* 88 (2008): 36–53.

[24] Antonia Potter, 'Women, Gender and Peacemaking in Civil Wars', in *Contemporary Peacemaking: Conflict, Peace Processes and Post-war Reconstruction*, 2nd ed., ed. John Darby and Roger Mac Ginty (Basingstoke, UK: Palgrave Macmillan, 2008), 105.

[25] Jana Krause, Werner Krause, and Piia Bränfors, 'Women's Participation in Peace Negotiations and the Durability of Peace', *International Interactions*, 44, no. 6 (2018): 985–1016.

[26] Moran, 'Gender', 265.

[27] Cynthia Cockburn, 'When Is Peace? Women's Post-Accord Experiences in Three Countries', *Soundings* 53 (2013): 157.

[28] Council on Foreign Relations, 'Women's Participation in Peace Processes', 31 July 2018, https://www.cfr.org/interactive/womens-participation-in-peace-processes/explore-the-data.

to a "soft" role in liaising with the media'.[29] In a nod to the importance of recognising that gender involves both men and women, it is also worth highlighting that many males are also excluded from decision-making roles in peace processes. Peace is something that is 'done' to them in much the same manner as it is 'done' to women. While some peace processes are 'democratised' in the form of a referendum on the peace accord, it is worth noting that this takes the form of responding to a yes/no question on a fait accompli.[30]

A second point is that many peace accords do not pay particular attention to gender. This is noteworthy since, as explained earlier in this chapter, conflict and violence impact men and women in different ways. As Maria O'Reilly notes, peace accords provide 'an opportunity for democracy, citizenship and peace to be "re-imagined" in gender-just ways'.[31] Yet in most peace accords, male perspectives are universalised, and the opportunity to reimagine the constitution in genuinely emancipatory ways and wider societal power relations is not taken. A 2015 study by Christine Bell found that only 18 percent of peace accords in the 1 January 1990–1 January 2015 period referenced women, although there was an uptick in the figure after UN Security Council Resolution 1325 was reached in 2000.[32] The 2016 Colombian peace accord is regarded as the most gender-inclusive accord to date, although much depends on its implementation and the extent to which gender issues are mainstreamed rather than compartmentalised.[33]

A third point is that post-peace-accord political dispensations tend to reflect a male bias. Moran observes that 'post-war governmental positions went largely to the well-connected.' Needless to say, the 'well connected' in many societies were males. Table 6.1 shows the percentage of female representatives in the lower chamber of a number of post-peace-accord societies at five-year intervals.[34] With the exception of Rwanda, a peace accord has not been a gateway to a recalibration of gender relations in the polity. It is worth noting, of course, that female parliamentary representation per se is not an indicator of gender relations in the wider society. The figures do suggest that many post-peace-accord polities are a 'cold house' for female politicians.[35] It is not unreasonable to surmise that political

---

[29] Antonia Potter, *Contemporary Peacemaking*, 110.
[30] SungYong Lee and Roger Mac Ginty, 'Context and Postconflict Referendums', *Nationalism and Ethnic Politics* 18, no. 1 (2012): 43–64.
[31] Maria O'Reilly, *Gendered Agency in War and Peace: Gender Justice and Women' Sactivism in Post-conflict Bosnia-Herzegovina* (London: Palgrave Macmillan, 2018) 40.
[32] Christine Bell, 'Text and Context: Evaluating Peace Agreements for Their "Gender Perspective",' " UN Women, 2015, http://www.unwomen.org/-/media/headquarters/attachments/sections/library/publications/2017/textandcontext-evaluating-peace-agreements-en.pdf?la=en&vs=2652.
[33] Roxanne Krystalli and Kimberly Theidon, 'Here's How Attention to Gender Affected Colombia's Peace Process', *Washington Post*, 9 October 2016, https://www.washingtonpost.com/news/monkey-cage/wp/2016/10/09/heres-how-attention-to-gender-affected-colombias-peace-process/?noredirect=on&utm_term=.b5185d1a80bf.
[34] Table compiled using data from Inter-Parliamentary Union, "Women in National Parliaments," 2018, http://archive.ipu.org/wmn-e/classif-arc.htm.
[35] Bjarnegård and Melander, 'Disentangling', 144.

Table 6.1. Percentage of female representation in post-peace-accord lower chambers at five-year intervals.

Country and year of peace accord	September 2003	September 2008	September 2013	September 2018
Bosnia and Herzegovina 1995	16.7	11.9	21.4	21.4
Burundi 2000	18.4	30.5	30.5	11.0
Cambodia 1992	No data	16.3	No data	15.2
Côte d'Ivoire 2007	8.5	8.9	10.4	10.6
El Salvador 1992	10.7	16.7	22.6	31.0
Guatemala 1996	8.8	12.0	13.3	12.7
Lebanon 1989	2.3	4.7	3.1	4.7
Liberia 2003	7.8	12.5	11.0	9.9
Nepal 2006	5.9	33.2	33.2	32.7
Rwanda 1993	48.8	56.3	56.3	61.3

patriarchy extends to other domains of society. In Bosnia and Herzegovina, for example, where only one in five parliamentarians is female, female workers were reported in 2016 to earn only 54 percent of their male counterparts' earnings.[36]

In some post-conflict societies, it may be the case that men's wartime sacrifice is validated and the role of females is subordinated. Men's wartime roles may award them enhanced citizenship, a status that many women cannot reach.[37] Wartime

---

[36] Tea Hadziristic, 'Is Bosnia the Worst Place in Europe to Be a Woman?' *OpenDemocracy*, 2016, https://www.opendemocracy.net/can-europe-make-it/tea-hadziristic/women-in-bosnia.

[37] Moran, 'Gender', 263. See also Stephen Gibson, 'Supporting the Troops, Serving the Country: Rhetorical Commonplaces in the Representation of Military Service', in *Representations of Peace and Conflict*, ed. Stephen Gibson and Simon Mollen (Basingstoke, UK: Palgrave Macmillan, 2012), 143–159.

gendered hierarchies often persist after the war, with the construction of 'appropriate' gender roles. Corinna Peniston-Bird, writing on post-WWII commemorations in Australia, noted that 'repertoires of commemoration' favoured the military over the civilian and thus the male over the female.[38] Indeed, grief after war—a phenomenon that is acutely gendered—has been largely overlooked in narratives of war which often concentrate on male and battlefield experience.[39] Also writing on the Australian context, Joy Damousi notes that 'the distinctiveness of the mother's loss was increasingly being erased, where women generally were marginalised in public commemoration and where the notion of sacrifice was reworked to mean the sacrifice of men alone'.[40]

A fourth point in relation to top-down peacemaking is that peacekeeping and peacebuilding are gendered. The militarised nature of peacekeeping means that personnel in peacekeeping missions are overwhelmingly male.[41] As of 31 August 2018, a total of 91,249 military and police personnel were serving across fourteen UN peacekeeping missions. Just under 5 percent of those personnel were female.[42] The research on Darfur mentioned earlier in this chapter revealed an institutional orientation that downgraded the importance of attacks on women. For example, the way the United Nations African Union Mission in Darfur (UNAMID) reported security incidents tended to record sexual assaults and attacks on women as 'assaults' rather than 'sexual assaults', 'rape', or an obvious signifier of SGBV. The UNAMID Joint Mission Analysis Centre recorded more than five thousand violent incidents in the January 2008–April 2010 period, yet women were virtually written out of this database. This was important, as the database constitutes part of the UN's formal narrative of the conflict, and resourcing and policy decisions are based on it.[43] The interviews with Darfurian refugees in Chad contain many statements like the following:

---

[38] Peniston-Bird, 'War and Peace'.

[39] Vinícius Santiago and Marta Fernández, 'From the Backstage of War: The Struggle of Mothers in the Favelas of Rio de Janeiro', *Contexto Internacional* 39, no. 1 (2017): 40. See also Luc Capdevila and Daniele Voldman, *War Dead: Western Societies and the Casualties of War* (Edinburgh: Edinburgh University Press, 2006), especially 46–52; Juliet Nicolson, *The Great Silence 1918–1920: Living in the Shadow of the Great War* (London: John Murray, 2009). On the upsurge of seances and the use of mystics to contact the dead after WWI (often mothers attempting to reach their dead sons), see Malcolm Gaskill, 'Plot 6, Row C, Grave 15', *London Review of Books* 40, no. 21, 18 November 2018, https://www.lrb.co.uk/the-paper/v40/n21/malcolm-gaskill/plot-6-row-c-grave-15.

[40] Joy Damousi, 'Private Loss, Public Mourning: Motherhood, Memory and Grief in Australia during the Inter-War Years', *Women's History Review* 8, no. 2 (1999): 366.

[41] Autesserre, *Peaceland*, 62. See also Helena Carreiras, 'Gendered Culture in Peacekeeping Operations', *International Peacekeeping* 17, no. 4 (2010): 471–485.

[42] Calculated from United Nations Peacekeeping, 'Summary of Troop Contributions to UN Peacekeeping Operations by Mission, Post and Gender', 2018, https://peacekeeping.un.org/sites/default/files/7_gender_report_5.pdf.

[43] I am indebted to Alex de Waale for access to the database.

These incidents were repeated every day, especially incidents of women's harassment and rape.... No party intervened at all. The Africans [UNAMID] were moving around, but they never provided protection for anyone. It looked as if they were scared [of the] Janjaweed.[44]

I can say the average of rape incidents in the area where I worked was about 2–3 incidents a month.... There was no response of any kind to these incidents. People made complaints and reported these issues to the police and to the UNAMID, but no action has been made [either] by the police [or] by UNAMID.[45]

Peacekeeping missions have been beset by a number of sexual abuse scandals,[46] and the behaviour and orientation of missions in relation to gender have been under increased scrutiny. UN Women, the UN agency tasked with working on women, peace, and security,[47] has played a more prominent role in peacekeeping missions and is backed by a growing number of international commitments to women's rights.[48] The key issue, however, is the extent to which declarations on rights are turned into meaningful action. There is no doubting the energy behind the 'Women, Peace and Security' agenda,[49] and there have been multiple initiatives designed to improve inclusive and due attention to gender issues from UN Security Council Resolution 1325 onwards. According to some commentaries, however, attempts to mainstream gender often do the reverse—they encourage the compartmentalisation of the issue into silos or enclaves removed from the core business of peacekeeping.[50]

Peacebuilding has been more sensitive to issues of gender than peacekeeping has been. It can be more community- and development-focused and thus provides—in theory, at least—greater opportunities to interact with a

---

[44] Interview with female, Djabal Refugee Camp, Chad, 27 May 2015.
[45] Interview with female, Goz Beida Refugee Camp, Chad, 19 May 2015.
[46] Paula Donovan, 'JISB Interview: Immunity, Sexual Scandals and Peacekeeping', *Journal of Intervention and Statebuilding* 9, no. 3 (2015): 408–417; Bonnie Kovatch, 'Sexual Exploitation and Abuse in UN Peacekeeping Missions: A Case Study of MONUC and MONUSCO', *Journal of the Middle East and Africa* 7, no. 2 (2016): 157–174; Olivera Simić, 'Does the Presence of Women Really Matter? Towards Combating Male Sexual Violence in Peacekeeping Operations', *International Peacekeeping* 17, no. 2 (2010): 188–199; Kathleen M. Jennings, 'Unintended Consequences of Intimacy: Political Economies of Peacekeeping and Sex Tourism', *International Peacekeeping* 17, no. 2 (2010): 229–243.
[47] See UN Women, 'Peace and Security', 2018, http://www.unwomen.org/en/what-we-do/peace-and-security.
[48] In particular, the landmark UN Security Council Resolution 1325 from 2000 and seven subsequent supporting declarations. It is also worth acknowledging precursors to 1325 in the form of the 1979 Convention on the Elimination of All Forms of Discrimination against Women and the 1995 Beijing Platform for Action.
[49] Susan Harris Rimmer, 'Barriers to Operationalising the "Women, Peace and Security" Doctrine in United Nations Peacekeeping', *Journal of International Peacekeeping* 20, nos. 1–2 (2016): 49–68.
[50] Tina Wallace, Fenella Porter, and Mark Ralph-Bowman, eds., *Aid, NGOs, and the Realities of Women's Lives: A Perfect Storm* (Rugby, UK: Practical Action, 2013).

cross-section of the population. Moreover, many formal peacebuilding initiatives and agendas place deliberate emphasis on inclusion and gender, with gender programming and women's peace movements playing a significant role in a number of societies moving out of conflict and authoritarianism. Autesserre notes, however, that in some cases, peacebuilding programmes and projects have been 'gamed' and instrumentalised to exploit the funding streams linked with gender issues.[51] This is undoubtedly true, but it is worth noting the pro-social and pro-peace value of work by the UN and others to encourage gender inclusion in peace processes and peacebuilding. This would not have happened without very significant campaigning and behind-the-scenes work by gender activists.[52]

The Family and Everyday Peace

It is worth reiterating that this is not a chapter about women. Gender concerns the power relations in society, and so it is a chapter about women *and* men and how societies, polities, and economies are organised. Differentiated gender roles are a fundamental organising principle behind all human societies, and it is worth considering why this is the case and what assumptions and worldviews lie behind this. In many contexts, gender relations are so normalised that they are 'hidden in plain sight'; they sit unquestioned at the heart of society. As the previous section demonstrated, top-down forms of peace that are organised around institutions, programmes, and projects are gendered. In short, these forms of peace often sideline women. It is worth asking, however, how everyday peace is gendered. How is the banal peace that we find on the streets and in the public spaces of deeply divided societies gendered? How might sociality, reciprocity, solidarity, and EPP reflect gender relations? These questions can be answered by focusing on a fundamental component of society: the family.

The family is a site in which everyday peace can be forged. Given our focus on the bottom-up domain, it is entirely appropriate that we focus on the family, as this is often rooted in communities and localities. Moreover, families are networks, whether the small network of the nuclear family or the extended kinship network of larger families and clans.[53] This fits with the conceptual innovation of this book—the use of circuitry as an analytical device to help us

---

[51] Autesserre, *Peaceland*, 140.

[52] Background can be found in Krause, Krause, and Bränfors, 'Women's Participation'; Thania Paffenholz et al., *Making Women Count—Not Just Counting Women: Assessing Women's Inclusion and Influence on Peace Negotiations* (New York: UN Women, 2016).

[53] There is interesting literature on atomisation and neoliberalism: Pierre Bourdieu, 'The Essence of Neoliberalism', *Le Monde Diplomatique*, December 1998, https://mondediplo.com/1998/12/08bourdieu; Peter Beattie, 'The Road to Psychopathy: Neoliberalism and the Human Mind', *Journal of Social Issues* 75, no. 1 (2019): 89–112.

understand the linkages between the hyperlocal, the local, the subnational, the national, the international, the transnational, and all levels in between. Families can be regarded as circuits in themselves that are contained in wider circuits of communities, localities, and, depending on circumstances, nations and diasporas. Some families, for example, a prominent family in Lebanon, will be extensively networked. Other families will be more self-contained. But all will be contextualised in wider networks of circuitry. These circuits will transmit information, resources, and power to and from the family unit. Families constitute a social ecology. The 'multiple interlocking spheres of family, community, society, nation and state' mean that family 'cannot be considered or studied in isolation'.[54] Although the chapter is careful not to simplistically equate the family with women,[55] it is important to point out that it is often women who are a driving force in family life through everyday socialisation activities and rituals surrounding eating, washing, visiting, schooling, and caring. These activities may offer spaces for the guidance and mentoring that are crucial to the quiet diplomacy of everyday peace. The subtle warning from a big sister or fear of disappointing a grandmother may be a crucial factor in dissuading a youth from joining a radical organisation.

Importantly, there is much heterogeneity in how families are organised (or indeed disorganised), making context all-important. In South Africa, for example, 2014 data recorded that only 35 percent of children lived with both parents.[56] This was largely because of the need for one or both parents to migrate for work. Family structure and composition are also dependent on law and prevailing social attitudes. Same-sex partnership, marriage, and adoption are legal in an increasing number of countries but illegal in others.[57] Some countries, such as Yemen, have no legal minimum age for marriage.[58] Demographics in India and China show a sex ratio imbalance as a result of 'daughter killing' or sex-selective abortion.[59] The key point is that family composition, size, and orientation are

---

[54] Myriam Denov and Atim Angela Lakor, 'When War Is Better Than Peace: The Post-Conflict Realities of Children Born of Wartime Rape in Northern Uganda', *Child Abuse & Neglect* 65 (2017): 258.

[55] Linda Åhäll, 'Confusion, Fear, Disgust: Emotional Communication in Representations of Female Agency in Political Violence', in *Gender, Agency and Political Violence*, ed. Linda Åhäll and Laura J. Shepherd (Basingstoke: Palgrave, 2012), 169, 171–172.

[56] Shahrashoub Razavi, 'Families Can Drive Gender Equality, but Only if We Help Them Evolve', *Conversation*, 15 May 2017, https://theconversation.com/families-can-drive-gender-equality-but-only-if-we-help-them-evolve-77546.

[57] See the interactive map produced by International Family Equality Day, 2018, https://internationalfamilyequalityday.org/same-sex-adoption-worldwide/.

[58] Kaltham A. Al-Ghanim and Abdallah M. Badahdah, 'Gender Roles in the Arab World: Development and Psychometric Properties of the Arab Adolescents Gender Roles Attitude Scale', *Sex Roles* 77 (2017): 170.

[59] Lisa Eklund and Navtej Purewal, 'The Bio-Politics of Population Control and Sex-Selective Abortion in China and India', *Feminism & Psychology* 27, no. 1 (2017): 34–55.

highly contingent on context, and thus, generalisations and ethnocentric assumptions are difficult to sustain.

The study of family is well established in sociology, anthropology, and psychology but largely absent from international relations and from peace and conflict studies. A focus on everyday peace, however, demands that we look at the lowest and most organic form of social organisation. It requires that we look behind the front door and the 'face' that we may choose (or feel compelled to choose) to project to the world.[60] In many cases, the family is likely to be a formative (and sometimes continuing) source of education and moral and spiritual outlook.[61] It may be a source of restraint and common sense but also of incitement or indoctrination. It is a site of sense-making, whereby family members interpret, discuss, and seek to understand the social world.[62] Since what happens in the family may well influence how we act in public, it is worth dismissing a strict public/private dichotomy. Each is co-constitutive of the other. While we may metaphorically 'shut the front door' and seek to maintain a barrier between what happens inside and outside the home, 'external' contexts will infiltrate and shape what happens in the home and in the family. Moreover, aspects of home and family life are likely to pattern how we interact with the public world. Thus, this chapter can be read as a consideration of what feminist scholars call 'intersectionality', or the impossibility of examining separately the various components of society. The focus on the family can also be seen as a critique of orthodox approaches to international relations and their concentration on formal institutions. The family may be regarded as an informal institution[63]—sometimes recognised in law but operating, for the most part, in a self-regulating way.

Our focus on everyday peace means that it is legitimate to concentrate on the family—a basic unit of society. In particular, this chapter looks at the restraint that family contexts might impose on individuals and how that restraint might be gendered. Depending on context, an individual might be at risk of radicalisation. Family members may provide the restraint, mentorship, example, and monitoring to prevent that. The next section will explore these techniques in more detail. It should be noted, however, that many family contexts do not provide the restraint or example that would lead to everyday peace. Many of the memoirs and war diaries referenced in chapters 4 and 5 begin by describing how

---

[60] Erving Goffman, *The Presentation of the Self in Everyday Life* (London: Penguin, 1990).

[61] Carmen R. Valdez, Tom Chavez, and Julie Woulfe, 'Emerging Adults' Lived Experience of Formative Family Stress: The Family's Lasting Influence', *Qualitative Health Research* 23, no. 8 (2013): 1090.

[62] Lisa M. Dorner, 'The Life Course and Sense-Making: Immigrant Families' Journeys toward Understanding Educational Policies and Choosing Bilingual Programs', *American Educational Research Journal* 49, no. 3 (2012): 461.

[63] Bjarnegård and Melander, 'Disentangling', 144.

proud parents were of their son's choice of regiment or militaristic endeavours. Erwin Bartmann, who fought in an SS Panzer division, shows how in the 1930s, his entire family became indoctrinated by the Nazis.[64] Derek Niemann's family memoir records that his grandfather, Karl Niemann, was an SS officer responsible for supplying slave labour in concentration camps.[65] Belief in Nazi Party ideals was normalised within the family. In many conflict settings, the family—and particularly mothers—are regarded as a linchpin of patriotism and warlike endeavour. Fatma Fulya Tepe noted that the Turkish state encouraged the notion of the 'mother citizen', whose role was 'protecting their families as well as the Turkish republic'.[66] This was echoed by Emine Rezzan Karaman, who argued that the Turkish state and public discourse reified 'appropriate mothers' whose role was to 'produce "proper Turkish subjects" who willingly sacrifice themselves for their country'.[67]

Violent conflict can put many families under pressure, not least in terms of family displacement and break-up.[68] Mukasa notes that one of the main impacts of the war in northern Uganda was the wearing down of family support networks through violence, abduction, and displacement.[69] The result was the development of ad hoc family systems—perhaps relying on the extended family, with grandparents and other relatives taking on caring roles. Conflict has often upset the traditional patriarchal balance of families, with many households becoming female-headed.[70] In some cases, this was liberating. One British woman regarded her WWII experience, running a canteen in England, with nostalgia: 'I always felt so worthwhile'.[71] Others have been more sceptical, seeing any such 'liberation' as temporary until the return of men[72] or not empowering in the first place.[73] As a result, we must take care if tempted to axiomatically see female-headed households as a form of empowerment. In many cases, there simply was

---

[64] Bartmann, *Für Volk*, locations 135–297.

[65] Derek Niemann, *A Nazi in the Family: The Hidden Story of an SS Family in Wartime Germany* (London: Short, 2015).

[66] Fatma Fulya Tepe, 'Turkish Mother Citizens and Their Homefront Duties: The Cold War Discourse of the *Türk Kadını* Magazine', *Feminist Formations* 29, no. 1 (2017): 25–52.

[67] Emine Rezzan Karaman, 'Remember, S/He Was Here Once: Mothers Call for Justice and Peace in Turkey', *Journal of Middle East Women's Studies* 12, no. 3 (2016): 399, 389. See also, on the complex issue of 'political motherhood', Mookherjee, 'Gendered Embodiments'.

[68] Uyo Salifu and Irene Ndung'u, 'Preventing Violent Extremism in Kenya: Why Women's Needs Matter', Institute for Security Studies East Africa Report 13, May 2017.

[69] Norman Mukasa, 'War-Child Mothers in Northern Uganda: The Civil War Forgotten Legacy', *Development in Practice* 27, no. 3 (2017): 362.

[70] Cheryl Lee Robertson and Laura Duckett, 'Mothering during War and Postwar in Bosnia', *Journal of Family Nursing* 13, no. 4 (2007): 461–483. For an example, see Carius, *Tigers*, location 120.

[71] Nella Last, *Nella Last's War: A Mother's Diary 1939–45* (London: Sphere, 1983), 292.

[72] Irina Carlota Silber, 'Mothers/Fighters/Citizens: Violence and Disillusionment in Post-War El Salvador', *Gender & History* 16, no. 3 (2004): 567.

[73] Helle Rydstrøm, 'Gendered Corporeality and Bare Lives: Local Sacrifices and Sufferings during the Vietnam War', *Signs* 37, no. 2 (2012): 277.

no other option but for mothers, grandmothers, and big sisters to get on with things.

It is also worth noting that the family might be a site of violence. This might involve the indirect violence of the imposition of gendered hierarchies (often a consequence of capitalist production) but also domestic violence. Indeed, focus groups run as part of the EPI project revealed the extent to which violence in the home can become normalised in contexts of political violence or authoritarianism.[74] One man in a focus group in northern Uganda stated, in a matter-of-fact way, 'If I go home to rest and my wife disturbs me, I may beat her'.[75] A female respondent in the same locality noted, 'Sometimes women are not safe in their homes, especially if they can't bear any children for their husbands'. Referring to another context, Swati Parashar noted the 'continuities between conflict-related sexual abuse and violence and that which occurs daily in our homes, backyards and in the public spaces we inhabit'.[76]

Crucial in all of this is the need to see the family as a political space. There is a sense in some commentary that the family can be compartmentalised as non-political, a space for emotion, privacy, and after-work activities. Instead, it must be seen as very much connected with other domains. It is a site of multiple forms of political thinking, actions, and embodiment. Thus, for example, the family might be a space in which particular kin and identity groups are reified (or demonised), a political economy that dictates how resources are shared and what gender roles are maintained and performed.

In many cases, the family is a source of conservatism and the perpetuation of patriarchy and established social mores. The family may instil restraint, complicity, respect for rules, and order. Depending on circumstances, this might be entirely prudent. To put one's head above the parapet and question or contradict authority might be foolhardy and risk unwelcome attention from the state or members of the in-group or out-group.[77] The first nine months of 2018 saw the murder of at least 190 community leaders in Colombia, and newspaper reporting revealed cases in which family members tried to rein in relatives who

---

[74] There is a significant literature pointing to links between military service, experience of conflict, and spousal violence. See, for example, Bradley J. Schaffer, 'Homeless Military Veterans and the Intersection of Partner Violence', *Journal of Human Behavior in the Social Environment* 22, no. 8 (2012): 1003–1013; Melissa E. Dichter and Steven C. Marcus, 'Intimate Partner Violence Victimization among Women Veterans: Health, Health Care Service Use, and Opportunities for Intervention', *Military Behavioral Health* 1, no. 2 (2013): 107–113; Lene Bull Christiansen, 'Versions of Violence: Zimbabwe's Domestic Violence Law and Symbolic Politics of Protection', *Review of African Political Economy* 37, no. 126 (2010): 421–435.

[75] EPI male focus group, Atiak, Uganda, 4 October 2013.

[76] Swati Parashar, 'This Is a War on Women," *Indian Express*, 3 December 2019, https://indianexpress.com/article/opinion/columns/this-is-a-war-on-women-rape-sexual-violence-6148420/.

[77] From the war memoirs, see, for example, Schiederbauer, *Adventures*, 178; Voss, *Black Edelweiss*, location 422.

risked drawing attention to their activism.[78] Thus, influential members of the family might encourage younger family members to toe the line, keep quiet, and exercise restraint. They might inculcate in younger family members the necessity of using the 'hidden transcript',[79] or the need to have one vocabulary and stance for inside the house and another for outside of it. This might be pacific in that it does not contribute to an escalation of violence. It might prevent a family member from becoming involved in extremism or potentially violent activity. It might allow family members to get on with their everyday lives, to persist, and to avoid unwelcome surveillance and attention. Yet is this 'peace'? It might be termed a 'negative peace' in that it does not promote actively positive processes of peace or reconciliation in a specific context. The 'negative' label may be deserved, as this form of 'peace' may not in any way threaten the prevailing system in an overt way. We must not be too critical of this type of peace, however. It could be that circumstances allow for little else, and a decision not to actively support an odious regime or a violent group may have potential significance—especially if that stance is held by others.

Everyday Peace Actions and Processes in the Family

This section examines three types of action that can occur within families in conflict-affected settings and can help moderate and avoid conflict. The actions are positive parenting and mentoring, restraint, and what might be called proxy avoidance. They conform to the transactions that Veena Das holds to be important in the transmission of conflict and violence.[80] In this view, all three fit within the everyday peace paradigm in that they are pacific or—at least—non-inflammatory. They also depend on emotional intelligence and an ability to 'read' a context and act accordingly. Crucial to these actions is the family setting. It is somewhat tautological to note that families are about relationships (and thus put us in mind of circuits). These relationships will have developed over years. In some cases, this will depend on tradition and the influence of gender and seniority that awards power to elders, matriarchs, patriarchs, and older siblings. In other cases, it will depend on observed evidence and force of personality that might mark out some family members as being influential, well connected, sensible, or canny. The forms of familial everyday peace discussed in this chapter reflect—at a micro-level—the three themes of everyday peace outlined in chapter 2. Sociality, reciprocity, and solidarity operate at the intragroup

---

[78] Nicholas Casey, 'Peacetime Spells Death for Colombia's Activists', *New York Times*, 13 October 2018.
[79] Scott, *Domination*.
[80] Veena Das, ed., *Violence and Subjectivity* (Berkeley: University of California Press, 2000).

level within the family. They are often unspoken, rest on a series of assumptions, and mainly function in the affective domain. Functioning families are social and solidarist. They constitute support networks usually based on biological relationships, a shared sense of kin, common experiences, and often a shared locality. They are incubators and reinforcers of a shared identity. Reciprocity and the sharing of tasks and responsibilities are also standard operating procedures in most families. At the most basic, childcare by a parent may be reciprocated by eldercare by that child once he or she matures and the parents reach old age. Some forms of everyday peace forged and validated in a family setting might then be projected into a wider societal setting, but it is worth remembering that their origin often lies within the confines of the family—hence the focus of this chapter. Crucially, and as demonstrated below, the roles and performances in the family are gendered.

These gendered roles and performances notwithstanding, this chapter is careful not to follow an essentialist path that axiomatically associates females with mothering. This essentialist view is surprisingly common in the countering extremist policy literature (which is voluminous and not always nuanced and aware of context).[81] Thus, for example, we find lines such as 'Given their nurturing and intuitive qualities, the unique strengths and capabilities of women used to preserve the family institution should be fully utilised to Counter Violent Extremism (CVE) efforts'.[82] Or the Quilliam organisation (which defines itself as a counter-extremism organisation) makes an automatic link between women and families thus: 'Families and hence women are the best placed to counter violent extremism'.[83] It is worth challenging such elisions and interrogating the actual roles and contexts that men and women operate in.[84] It is also worth bearing in mind, when reading the countering violent extremism (CVE) literature, that it seeks to instrumentalise families as bulwarks against extremism. Thus, we see a sometimes technical language (for example, 'resilience', 'enabling environment',[85] and 'operational effectiveness'[86]) applied—in a jarring way—to

---

[81] See, for example, the following bizarrely de-contextualised report: Kim Cragin et al., 'What Factors Cause Youth to Reject Violent Extremism? Results of an Exploratory Analysis in the West Bank' (Washington, DC: RAND, 2015), https://www.rand.org/pubs/research_reports/RR1118.html.

[82] Mohamed Bin Ali and Sabariah Mohamed Hussin, 'Countering Violent Extremism: Role of Women and Family', *RSIS Commentary* 179 28 September 2017.

[83] Haras Rafiq, 'Testimony before Terrorism, Non-Proliferation, and Trade Subcommittee', Committee on Foreign Affairs, United States House of Representatives, 27 February 2018.

[84] See, for example, Iffat Idris with Ayat Abdelaziz, 'Women and Countering Violent Extremism', *GSDRC Helpdesk Report*, 4 May 2017; or Fionnuala Ní Aoláin, 'Counter-Terrorism Committee: Addressing the Role of Women in Countering Terrorism and Violent Extremism', *Just Security*, New York University School of Law, 2015, https://www.justsecurity.org/25983/counter-terrorism-committee-addressing-role-women-countering- terrorism-violent-extremism/.

[85] Ivo Veenkamp and Sara Zeigler, *Countering Violent Extremism: Program and Policy Approaches to Youth through Education, Families and Communities* (Amsterdam: IOS, n.d.), 2, 8.

[86] Emily Myers, 'Gender and Countering Violent Extremism', Alliance for Peacebuilding, Washington DC, 2018, 2.

family life. At the heart of much CVE work involving families is the notion that positive roles can be modelled and converted into interventions, projects, and programmes.[87] This may be possible, but it is worth remembering that families are organic institutions and are difficult to 'game'. Three—more organic and naturally occurring—in-family everyday peace actions are discussed below.

Positive Parenting and Mentoring

Positive parenting and mentoring take the form of a family member, usually a parent, grandparent, or older sibling, engaging in monitoring, supervision, counselling, correction, and positive reinforcement that will enhance safety and lead to pacific outcomes.[88] The evidence from social psychology is that parental support is crucial for positive development into adolescence and adulthood.[89] Depending on circumstances, positive parenting may take the form of a family support network that prevents a family member from joining a gang or militant group.[90] Close, functional, and protective relationships, according to the literature, encourage children to internalise what constitutes social and positive behaviour. It is worth stressing that this chapter does not share pejorative views on the optimum family type, nor does it indulge in moralistic or stigmatising notions of the 'good mother'.[91] Families are complex, often more so during conflict, and usually strive to make the best of a situation. Families are pedagogic spaces, and a mix of constructed gender roles and the exigencies of conflict in which men and women must often perform pre-assigned roles means that parenting and mentoring can play formative roles in steering children and youth towards pacific or non-pacific paths. Of course, in cases of conscription or abduction, there may be little agency involved in whether one takes part in violent conflict or not, but even conscripts can display different levels of enthusiasm for martial tasks.

Research I have undertaken in Lebanon shows multiple examples of positive parenting and mentoring. The primary purpose of this activity was to protect the individual concerned from harm and to protect the family and its reputation.

---

[87] 'Women and Preventing Violent Extremism: The US and UK Experiences', CHR & GJ Briefing Paper, New York University School of Law, 6.

[88] Salifu and Ndung'u, 'Preventing Violent Extremism', 5.

[89] See, for example, Rachel Dekel and Dan Solomon, 'The Contribution of Maternal Care and Control to Adolescents' Adjustment following War', *Journal of Early Adolescence* 36, no. 2 (2016): 198–221; Tara E. Sutton, 'The Lives of Female Gang Members: A Review of the Literature', *Aggression and Violent Behaviour* 37 (2017): 142–154.

[90] Rebecca Gutierrez Keeton, 'Sueños y Valor: Dreams and Courage', in *Roads Taken: Women in Student Affairs at Mid-Career*, ed. Kristen A. Renn and Carole Hughes (Sterling, VA: Stylus, 2004), 24.

[91] Joanne Baker, 'Young Mothers in Late Modernity: Sacrifice, Respectability and the Transformative Neo-liberal Subject', *Journal of Youth Studies* 12, no. 3 (2009): 275, 278.

But it had a collateral and pro-social effect: these individual and collective acts contributed to societal stability. In a sense, rather than thinking of 'collateral damage', we can think of 'collateral peace' or the (sometimes) unintended consequences of small acts of peace within the family. As discussed in chapter 7, some of these acts can disrupt conflict. One Druze interviewee was a witness to the Lebanese civil war and reflected that his wartime experiences had impacted how he was rearing his children: 'What is important for me is to raise them to be tolerant, activists, eager for change. I know that's not easy since we are still living in a divided country and since sectarianism is increasing unfortunately, but [we] will do our best not letting them live through the ugliness of another civil war'.[92] Another interviewee noted that her parents had 'taught us that we don't speak about religion outside of the house. Even if we disagree with them regarding religious practices we shouldn't say our opinion in public, especially in front of any neighbour or friend from the other community'. This quotation shows the importance of restraint (discussed in more detail below) and illustrates how the home and the family are often the site of a hidden transcript. A different transcript might be deployed in public.

Nobel Prize winner Seamus Heaney's 1975 poem 'Whatever You Say, Say Nothing' captures well the need for delicate diplomacy in everyday interactions in a deeply divided society. Heaney was writing at a time when Northern Ireland's Troubles were at their worst, with a death toll of several hundred per year.[93] Communities that had lived side by side in an uneasy manner for decades now found themselves in a context of a small-scale but bitter civil war and insurgency. Everyday intergroup interactions required extreme care, and conversations often stayed on uncontentious territory—rather than politics or religion. Hence the poem title and phrases such as 'Expertly civil-tongued neighbours', 'sanctioned, old retorts', and 'the tight gag of place'.[94] In Lebanon, a Druze interviewee reflected on how he taught his children to 'stop talking about differences, stop bringing out bad memories and [creating] political tensions.... We don't need to discuss religious and political differences with people from different religions or communities. Avoid as much as you can similar conversations'.[95]

Many of the Lebanese interviews reveal a strategic thinking in terms of where people choose to live. For example, one Christian Orthodox interviewee noted that her parents who lived in the centre of Beirut were renovating their house

---

[92] Interview with Druze male, Bshamoun, 11 June 2013.
[93] The following place the poem in its context: Desmond Fennell, *Whatever You Say, Say Nothing: Why Seamus Heaney Is No. 1* (Dublin: ELO, 1991); Patrick Crotty, 'The Context of Heaney's Reception', in *The Cambridge Companion to Seamus Heaney*, ed. Bernard O'Donoghue (Cambridge: Cambridge University Press, 2009), 37–55.
[94] Seamus Heaney, 'Whatever You Say, Say Nothing', 1975, https://www.blueridgejournal.com/poems/sh-what.htm.
[95] Interview with Druze male, Aley, 13 July 2013.

in the mountains as a 'backup' in case of another civil war.[96] Another Christian interviewee with young children noted that on becoming a widow, she felt 'I should move to a Christian community. . . . I will only have my community to support me and protect me'.[97] But among the many cases of residential segregation along sectarian lines was the case of a Protestant interviewee who grew up in the mixed Hamra district of Beirut and was convinced of the social benefit that his own children would gain from a similar upbringing: 'It means a lot to grow up as a kid in a mixed community, where you buy your mom's groceries from "Abu Mohammed's shop" and your hairdresser is your Druze neighbour'.[98]

Restraint

Restraint involves the self-restraint of the individual and the restraining of others by those in positions of influence, for example, parents or elders within the family. Restraint has been formally defined as 'tendencies across the life span to inhibit self-focused desires in the interests of promoting long-term goals and positive relations with others'.[99] It involves a mix of impulse control, suppression of aggression, consideration for others, and responsibility.[100] In some circumstances, these will overlap with, or draw on, sociality, reciprocity, and solidarity. In contexts affected by violence or tension, restraint may take the form of avoiding actions or speech that might agitate a situation and encouraging those within one's sphere of influence to show similar restraint. This might involve using a wide repertoire of skills and emotional intelligence to 'read' situations and engage in self-regulation. One Sunni interviewee characterised the sectarian context of Lebanon as 'crazy' and 'unhealthy'. For him, a response was to engage in dissembling when interacting with people he did not know and who might be from different faith backgrounds. He recognised that this meant 'lies' and 'hiding one's thoughts just to avoid a clash between people'.[101] It was a negative form of peace that did not confront the dominant fissure in Lebanese society: sectarianism. Small acts of restraint, however, did enable the transactions and interactions that constitute everyday life. They simultaneously reinforced division and signalled that some form of normality was possible.

---

[96] Interview with Christian Orthodox female, Beirut, 17 August 2013.
[97] Interview with Christian Maronite female, 5 August 2013.
[98] Interview with Protestant male, Beirut, 21 August 2013.
[99] S. Shirley Feldman and Daniel A. Weinberger, 'Restraint as a Mediator of Family Influences on Boys' Delinquent Behaviour: A Longitudinal Study', *Child Development* 65, no. 1 (1994): 195–211.
[100] Feldman and Weinberger, 'Restraint'. For a critique of Feldman and Weinberger's four-part model, see Sindy Resita Sumter, Caroline L. Bokhurst, and P. Michiel Westenberg, 'The Robustness of the Factor Structure of the Self-Restraint Scale: What Does Self-Restraint Encompass?' *Journal of Research in Personality* 42 (2008): 1082–1087.
[101] Interview with Sunni male, Beirut, 21 June 2013.

Some of the 'home-front' accounts of WWII show a restraint in terms of thought. One Briton, in the midst of the London Blitz, confided in her diary that she was attempting to refrain from hating the Germans.[102] Another recorded, just as Germany was defeated, feelings of understanding and empathy that showed remarkable restraint. Nella Last's diary entry for 5 May 1945, less than a week after Hitler had committed suicide, reflects on 'the horror that is Germany, millions of homeless ones adrift in the very essence of the word, no homes, no work, sanitation, water, light or cooking facilities, untold dead to bury, sick and mad people to care for'.[103] The absence of desire for revenge is astonishing, as are the suppression of immediate responses and their replacement by more considered thinking. Like much else in this book, the deployment of restraint (and the suppression of revenge) might be linked to power. In some contexts, self-restraint and restraining family members might be judicious. Unrestrained activity, for example, participating in demonstrations or wearing symbols that the out-group might find offensive, might invite surveillance and responses from security forces or opposing groups. What makes the case of Last interesting is that with Nazi Germany on the cusp of total defeat, she was magnanimous and did not seek to exploit the weakness of others. This issue of power (the power to deploy restraint) is particularly relevant to gender. Emily Myers notes in relation to CVE that women may hold sway within family settings, but the wider environment may not give them the power or ability to make change.[104] For example, in a society prone to violent intergroup tension, a mother may counsel her son to stay away from extremists and hotheads. This counsel, however, must compete with other wider societal and cultural pressures. As a result, the more perceptive CVE literature points out that the best way to tackle extremism is to deal with gender inequality.

Avoidance by Proxy

While some parents have pride in their sons' and daughters' patriotism, others might seek ways to insulate their children from the conflict. In some cases, this might mean acting as a filter to 'edit' the information that might reach the children.[105] For example, do parents narrate ongoing conflict and violence in ways

---

[102] Olivia Cockett, *Love and War in London* (Stroud, UK: History Press, 2008), 170.
[103] Last, *Nella's Last War*, 274.
[104] Myers, 'Gender', 1. See also Belquis Ahmadi and Sadaf Lakhani, 'Afghan Women and Violent Extremism: Colluding, Perpetrating, or Preventing?' USIP Special Report 396, Washington, DC, 2016, 6.
[105] Mukasa, 'War-Child Mothers', 364.

that will downplay violence and tension or ways that might reinforce pejorative understandings of the out-group?

> I remember, as a four-year-old growing up in Northern Ireland, being woken by a bomb explosion in the centre of the town where we lived. Even though my parents were desperately worried about relatives and their business near the site of the explosion, they were careful not to transmit this fear to me. When I asked what the loud bang had been, they simply said, 'Bad men let off a bomb, but everything is all right'. There was no attempt to cause alarm or construct a political explanation. My parents glossed over a complex and highly political backstory, but who can blame them?

A number of the WWII memoirs consulted for chapters 4 and 5 begin by noting that the authors' fathers served in WWI but rarely spoke of their experiences. In some cases, this may have been related to the culturally valued stoicism of the time, but it may also have been related to a desire to protect children from the horrors of war and to take care not to socialise them towards vengeance. The family is the site of the re-narration of conflict and violence, and in some cases, families choose not to escalate conflict or inculcate discriminatory views among children. There is no guarantee, of course, that silence in the family is pacific and necessarily peacemaking. That space might be filled by other narratives. In other cases, for example, the former Yugoslavia, mothers took deliberate steps to keep their children out of harm's way: 'some hid their sons to save their lives. Others sent their sons abroad into uncertain situations and did not see them for years'.[106] One Lebanese interviewee noted that his father made him leave the country to prevent him from becoming radicalised. 'Thanks to my father who kindly obliged me after graduating to leave the country and get a job abroad so [as] not to get involved in this division. . . . I believe if I [had] stayed more in the country I would have become more and more sectarian as many young Lebanese are becoming now'.[107] It is worth wondering if the father would have acted in a similar way in relation to a daughter. Aksana Ismailbekova, writing on Kyrgyzstan, notes that there are often cultural expectations for young males to defend the family, especially its female members. Lest this lead to trouble from the authorities, Uzbek families often 'export' their male youth: 'Young men sometimes start to engage in conflict immediately when their daughters, sisters, or mothers are assaulted. Sending young males belonging to Uzbek communities far away is one of the most commonly deployed strategies for protecting them'.[108]

---

[106] Vesna Nikolić-Ristanović, 'War, Nationalism and Mothers', *Peace Review* 8, no. 3 (1996): 360.
[107] Interview with Shia male, Beirut, 5 July 2013.
[108] Aksana Ismailbekova, 'Coping Strategies: Public Avoidance, Migration, and Marriage in the Aftermath of the Osh Conflict, Fergana Valley', *Nationalities Papers* 41, no. 1 (2013): 117.

Despite all of the examples above, it is worth reiterating that the family is not always a source of pacific counsel and harmony. Families can be a site of tension and conflict. One Sunni female interviewee in Lebanon reported that her Shia husband was adamant that their two children should be brought up as Shia: 'I really don't want my kids to be involved or get into this at this stage ... but I have to be smart because otherwise it will ruin my family and will end up with big clashes'.[109]

A thread running through positive parenting and mentoring, restraint, and avoidance by proxy is the need for emotional intelligence and the ability to quickly read social situations and react accordingly. This reveals that everyday peace is more than an action or series of actions. In addition to these, it is a way of thinking and a stance or attitude. The following extended excerpt from the letter of the mother of a two-year-old boy who lived in Guernsey during its occupation by the Germans in WWII reveals the extent to which individuals have to use the full repertoire of emotional skills. Moreover, the incident described is doubtless gendered, as it involves a male German officer (very probably armed) and a vulnerable female:

One day last week when I was rambling in these parts with junior, we looked up from picking wild flowers to behold a German soldier standing a few paces away. Peter, always ready for a new thrill, eagerly rushed into his outstretched arms as though he were a long lost uncle. Imagine my dilemma with or without the possible raised eyebrows in the upper windows along our lane! There was our little renegade fingering the epaulettes and hat displaying the eagle of the Third Reich. . . . The German, with his broad smile revealing gold filled teeth, looked for all the world as though ready to include me in his fond embrace.

. . . With, I thought, an admirable mixture of good nature, firmness and aplomb, I said to Peter John: 'Say Good-Afternoon', which he did. I then said: 'Now say Goodbye', which he also did, somewhat reluctantly. This done, the German took the hint, put him gently down and, clicking his heels, Heiled Hitler and departed, seemingly unoffended and quite unabashed.

The slightest sign of encouragement and the German would have accompanied us back home and probably become a frequent visitor: we would then have certainly been branded as fraternizers, if not actual collaborators, which we decidedly are not. Needless to say, like a dutiful wife, I told my husband of this encounter. His only comment was: 'The poor devil—he is probably missing his own youngsters'.[110]

---

[109] Interview with Sunni female, Beirut, 16 July 2013.
[110] K. M. Bachmann, *The Prey of an Eagle: A Personal Record of Family Life Written throughout the German Occupation of Guernsey 1940–45* (St. Peter Port, UK: Guernsey Press, 1972).

The example is interesting for the multiple roles that the author must take: mother, wife, and non-threatening civilian who at the same time is anxious not to be seen as collaborating with the Germans. It also shows the importance of micro-incidents and encounters and how seemingly inconsequential acts can have wider significance. The life of the individual or family is blended within a broader context that is complex and dynamic and relies on power relations. This puts us in mind of the highly complex circuitry found in conflict-affected contexts, whereby individuals and groups of individuals find themselves implicated in conflict systems. In many ways, they co-constitute the system, perhaps consciously through support or unconsciously through compliance or silence. While states and militaries have major formalised circuits that require many resources, individuals and families have their own circuits. These circuits are personal, economic, social, cultural, and political as well. Some of them may be beyond the reach of the state or other formal actors who demand loyalty. It is here that everyday peace and dissent from a top-down narrative may emerge.

Conclusion

The key messages from this chapter are very much in keeping with the overall themes and arguments of this book. The chapter encourages us to think about scale (the hyperlocal), domain (public or private), structure (informal institutions, particularly the family), and power. In terms of scale, the chapter focused on a unit of analysis often neglected in international Relations: the family. This unit of analysis is far removed from the much larger units that often dominate studies of peace and conflict, such as states, international organisations, and social movements. While there is no typical family, and while families are context-dependent, the lens provided by the family encourages us to look at an often intimate and locally rooted unit. Many family interactions occur at the affective level and thus present particular challenges to the researcher.

A focus on the family may initially suggest that we explore the private domain. Much family activity occurs behind closed doors, and families might have their own vernaculars and traditions. Yet, on closer examination, the distinction between the public and the private is difficult to maintain. A more worthwhile approach is one based on intersectionality that is aware of the interconnectedness between the different levels and aspects of the society, economy, and polity. What might initially seem like the 'private sphere' is, in fact, nested within a series of other spheres that co-constitute a whole. It is here in particular that the notion of circuitry provides useful analytical purchase. We can conceive of families as being networks in themselves. The extensiveness of the network will depend on cultural context and circumstance. These family networks are then nested within, and contribute to, larger networks of identity groups, diasporas, and a series of political economies and formal and informal structures that shape national, international, and transnational polities and societies. The circuits, or networks, allow the movement of people, information, and material. The notion of circuitry also helps us think about power and how it is wielded, displayed or hidden, and vested. Within the circuits, there may be room for resistance, subversion, and alternative narratives.

The focus on the family in a work on peace and conflict reminds us of the societal and relational nature of peace. It also requires us to think about the structures and institutions that constitute everyday peace. It has been argued in this chapter that the family is a key instrument of everyday peace. This in itself is a critical manoeuvre, as orthodox approaches to peace and conflict studies often prioritise formal structures and institutions such as municipalities, national governments and their ministries, military organisations, and international organisations. Such an approach has many merits but suffers from a path-dependency. An institutionalist gaze will reflect a world made of formal institutions. Ostensibly, this is a world worthy of our attention, as it is a domain of power, policymaking, law, and intervention. Our focus on everyday peace takes notice of this domain—it has a real impact on how people live their lives, the narratives they deploy, and their material conditions. The world of formal institutions declares war, mobilises populations, enacts laws, and directs material resources such as public goods. But in addition to this world, and because of our focus on everyday peace, the world of informal institutions and dynamics demands attention. These institutions, principally the family, are worthy of the title 'institution' given their resilience, hierarchies, and power. They operate in conjunction and parallel with formal institutions. Indeed, in some contexts, the family is reified as part of a national narrative: it is regarded as part of the 'natural' order and a force for stability. It should be said, however, that in most societies, the family is taken for granted; it is simply the way society is organised. As such, there is a danger that the family is ignored in analyses, or, in the case of multiple reports on CVE, it is instrumentalised as a counter-insurgency or counter-'terrorism' tool. The family deserves a more nuanced approach.

The argument is made in this chapter that the family is a site of everyday peace (and indeed tension). This will occur primarily within the family and often takes the form of non-dramatic conditioning behaviour of parents towards children or siblings towards one another. This parenting, role-modelling, and correctional behaviour is the stuff of family life. It is worth remembering, however, that this apparently private domain does not operate in isolation. What happens in the family home also has a bearing on the society. This will be especially noticeable in a deeply divided society in which intergroup tensions pattern the society with indirect violence and escalate into direct violence. Some families might be resolutely nationalistic and are firmly rooted in an in-group mentality. A pro–United Kingdom family in Northern Ireland, for example, might reflect this single-identity orientation in multiple ways. They might have a tradition of joining the British armed forces and exclusively Protestant-unionist cultural organisations. Within the home, they might routinely use language (the 'hidden transcript') that is pejorative towards the out-group. Sectarian language and behaviour by the children might go uncorrected by the parents. The children would, in all likelihood, go to a school for Protestant children, and their friendship network would likely only include co-religionists. Yet other families from the same community might be more open to intergroup encounters. Within these families, sectarian language or behaviour might be discouraged by parents or charismatic siblings. The wider family network might include marriages, relationships, and friendships with Catholics who might hold different cultural, political, and identity-related worldviews. Through their everyday interactions, this family might counter sectarianism. This might be enacted through everyday life in terms of where the children go to school and whom they are allowed to play with, the cultural activities the parents pursue, and the media they consume. This family might not engage in purposeful and public displays of anti-sectarianism through joining social movements or engaging in demonstrations. Their behaviour, however, might be no less demonstrative in a deeply divided society where the norm is to conform to in-group expectations. The activity and stance of this family can reasonably be labelled as everyday peace, as they will have a wider societal impact. At the very minimum, this family will not contribute to violence or inflame a tense situation. In a more maximalist scenario, however, the non-sectarianism of some family members may influence others in the wider familial and friendship networks. Those with a sectarian outlook may moderate their language and behaviour in the company of those they know to be non- (or less) sectarian. If we factor this up, this may then have a societal impact and can help explain a lessening of tensions or the staving off of disorder.

The chapter bears out the sociality, reciprocity, and solidarity conceptualisation of everyday peace. Functioning families depend on sociality, reciprocity, and solidarity. Everyday peace operates within family settings and can also contribute to the calming and non-escalation of societies. In an ideal scenario, this involves the scaling out of civility and tolerance that might originate in a family.

The final key message of this chapter concerns power, particularly the gendered nature of power. Gendered power relations operate in all spheres of society, including the family. Families might be patriarchal and help reinforce prescribed roles for boys and girls. In some contexts, the matriarch figure, although holding some degree of power, might actually reinforce a patriarchal order. As Ismailbekova argues, 'women in Kyrgyzstan achieve culturally accepted authority and negotiate their power over the course of their lives by becoming morally accepted wives, credible daughters-in-law, and respected grandmothers, which contributes to maintaining patriarchy'.[111] In other contexts, females may wield significant power. It is worth stressing again that this chapter does not subscribe to an axiomatic equivalence of female with the family and the home. The so-called domestic sphere is shaped by complex power relations. Within this sphere, however, the memoirs and accounts consulted for this chapter do provide evidence of everyday peace whereby men and women often play different roles. Certainly, in all societies, there are expectations that men and women perform different roles. Families can be the site of EPP. Importantly, power exercised within families, and in the apparently 'private sphere', can also project outwards and have a community-wide impact. The apparently minimalist and highly localised peace may have an exemplar effect—a factor considered in chapter 7.

---

[111] Aksana Ismailbekova, 'Constructing the Authority of Women through Custom: Bulak Village, Kyrgyzstan', *Nationalities Papers* 44, no. 2 (2016): 269.

7
Conflict Disruption

Introduction

This chapter examines conflict disrupters, or individuals and groups who disrupt the main dynamic, logic, or narrative of a conflict. The space created by conflict disruption can, if circumstances allow, become something more significant. It can scale up and out to threaten the normalisation of exclusion and violent conflict. The chapter concentrates on a number of examples of remarkable intergroup friendships and initiatives that have been counter-hegemonic in that they contradict the dominant societal trends of prejudice towards the out-group. The chapter brings together a number of themes that have been running through this book, such as the need to see everyday peace as a form of reasoning and as a form of power (albeit an alternative form of power). The core constituents of everyday peace (sociality, reciprocity, and solidarity) are represented in the chapter, and it is clear that people draw on these modes of thinking and acting as they navigate their way through life in divided and conflict-affected contexts. The chapter also makes clear the importance of circuitry and how it can help us contextualise a single relationship or set of relationships within much broader systems.

By concentrating on friendships and local-level initiatives, the chapter invites us to think about scale. What do individual acts of atonement or the survival of an intergroup friendship despite violent conflict tell us about the wider conflict? Can we envisage scaling up and scaling out relationships and incidents that might be one-off or geographically isolated? As the examples covered in the chapter will show, some of the intergroup friendships have been inspirational for others in a particular community and have been emblematic of the failure of violent conflict to become totalising. It should be stressed that the examples contained in the chapter show enormous bravery on the part of some of those involved in everyday peace. Often it has required personal journeys that have involved immense hardship. The everyday that they have crafted will be personal to them and therefore not an 'everyday' in the sense that it is available to others. Yet it can be an inspiration and a guiding point.

The chapter has two sections. The first gives examples of three remarkable and reasonably high-profile intergroup friendships and explores the wider lessons that can be derived from them: their context-dependency, how they followed trauma, and how they often came after a certain level of maturity had been reached. This section concentrates on what Marc Gopin refers to as 'unusual pairs', or friendships that cross the main fissure in society.[1] The second section sets out the concept of conflict disruption. While the concepts of conflict management, conflict resolution, and conflict transformation are well known in the peace and conflict studies literature, the argument is made that we need to take seriously a precursor step: conflict disruption. The logic, narratives, and normalcy of violent conflict can be disrupted by everyday actions and stances. This disruption might create space in which something more significant—such as conflict management, conflict resolution, or conflict transformation—may take root. Community conflict disrupters are often charismatic community members who adopt (informal) leadership positions through initiatives aimed at staunching crime. Important here is the fact that such initiatives often do not begin as funded projects or programmes. Instead, they are often personal or community initiatives that might, if they show potential, be factored up or adopted by others. A key aspect of the story of community activists and social entrepreneurs is their personality—often energetic, charismatic, articulate, dogged, brave enough to withstand criticisms and threats, and with enough emotional intelligence to know when to speak or act and when to keep quiet.

This focus on individuals and groups of individuals is very much in keeping with the level of analysis favoured throughout this book. The primary focus has been on the level below civil society and formally organised peace initiatives. As researchers, we need to break through this 'concrete floor' in order to see the hyperlocal and actions and stances that might be considered mundane, unremarkable, and yet hard to access.

Remarkable Friendships

This section examines three intergroup friendships that contradicted the dominant narrative in their own societies in which the other was demonised. They involve individuals taking the hard option of making and maintaining intergroup friendships against a backdrop of in-group incomprehension and hostility. They show the extent to which bravery was required to engage in this type of everyday peace. Conciliation with out-group members almost guaranteed criticism from within the in-group. As Gopin noted, 'peace partners sometimes find themselves deserted by their closest friends, family members, and neighbours as a price for their association with a peace partner'.[2] A concentration on interpersonal friendships allows us to examine the extent to which these relationships can be scaled

---

[1] Gopin, *Bridges*, 4.
[2] Gopin, *Bridges*, 4.

up and out. That is, to what extent does small-scale intergroup friendship give permission to others who might wish to investigate similar intergroup friendships? Two of the friendships discussed here (between Ian Paisley and Martin McGuinness in Northern Ireland and between Raymonda Tawil and Ruth Dayan in Israel–Palestine) involved political elites who were able to transcend their political personas and develop friendships.

The first of these friendships comes from Northern Ireland and was so countercultural that it stretched the credulity of many observers.[3] It was between Martin McGuinness, who was widely believed to have been a leading figure in the pro–united Ireland Irish Republican Army (IRA), and Ian Paisley, the leader of the Democratic Unionist Party (DUP), a party with a history of vitriolic opposition to the IRA. From May 2007 to May 2008, Paisley and McGuinness served, respectively, as first minister and deputy first minister of the Northern Ireland Assembly, an institution that had been set up as part of the 1998 Good Friday Agreement. They developed not only a close working relationship but also a friendship. Indeed, they were photographed laughing together so often that they were labelled 'the chuckle brothers'.[4] To understand the significance of the friendship, it is worth briefly outlining their respective histories. Both were significant and long-term players in the Northern Ireland conflict and were demonised by the other side. For many in the Protestant-unionist-loyalist community, McGuinness was a 'terrorist' with blood on his hands and had a long record of attempting to overthrow the state and institutions they held dear.[5] For many in the Catholic-nationalist-republican community, Paisley was a sectarian agitator whose inflammatory words had mobilised others to engage in anti-Catholic violence and whose political stance was one of intransigence. Indeed, Paisley was regularly called 'Dr No' because of his relentless opposition to many peace initiatives.[6]

McGuinness was born in 1950 in Derry, a small city in the northwest of Northern Ireland.[7] Derry, like the rest of Northern Ireland, was deeply patterned by sectarianism. Majoritarian politics meant that state institutions were controlled by the Protestant-unionist majority, with the result that there was

---

[3] Lesley Lelourec, 'The Bad and the Ugly: Good Guys after All: Representations of Martin McGuinness and Ian Paisley in the English Press', *Estudios Irlandes* 4, no. 4 (2009): 32–44.

[4] Liam Clarke, 'Moderates Playing Hardball to Stop Chuckle Brothers' Fun', *Sunday Times*, 9 December 2007, 17; David Sharrock, 'One Final Show for the "Chuckle Brothers"', *Times*, 9 May 2008, 27.

[5] A fairly typical representation of McGuinness as irredeemable can be found in Ruth Dudley Edwards, 'Martin McGuinness', *Spectator* 278, no. 8807 (1997): 22.

[6] Henry McDonald, 'Ian Paisley, the Dr No of Ulster Politics, Dies Aged 88', *Guardian*, 12 September 2014, https://www.theguardian.com/politics/2014/sep/12/ian-paisley-dies-aged-88-northern-ireland.

[7] Liam Clarke and Kathryn Johnston, *Martin McGuinness: From Guns to Government* (Edinburgh: Mainstream, 2001).

extreme discrimination against Catholics in the distribution of public goods such as housing and education.[8] In the late 1960s, inspired by civil rights movements in the United States and elsewhere, Catholics and some liberal Protestants began agitating for greater rights and access to public services.[9] This civil rights movement was met with state repression and pushback from many Protestant unionists who felt that Catholic gains would mean Protestant losses.[10] What began as a civil rights movement morphed, over a number of years, into a sectarianized conflict of pro–united Ireland Catholic nationalists versus pro–United Kingdom Protestant unionists.[11] A tri-cornered conflict involving the British state, pro–united Ireland militants, and pro–United Kingdom militants developed during the 1970s and lasted until ceasefires and the beginning of a peace process in 1994.[12] All the while, Northern Ireland was in a state of permanent political and constitutional crisis.

McGuinness was a key figure during all of this period. Effectively rendered a second-class citizen by the state, he agitated for the extension of rights for Catholics.[13] For McGuinness, however, the route for Catholic emancipation lay in ridding Ireland of British rule, and he was amongst the most effective mobilisers within militant Irish republicanism. He rose quickly in the ranks of the IRA, becoming its commander in Derry[14] and one of its representatives in failed ceasefire talks with the British government in 1975. The IRA campaign had a sectarian quality in that many of its targets in the Northern Ireland security apparatus were Protestant. As his profile increased, a process linked with the rise of the IRA's political party Sinn Féin, McGuinness became a hated figure among many Protestant unionists who regarded him as someone who not only directed 'terrorism' but was directly involved in murders.

Paisley was a Protestant-unionist preacher whose political career, like that of McGuinness, spanned the length of the Northern Ireland Troubles and much of the peace process.[15] Through powerful oratory and charisma, Paisley was

---

[8] Michael Farrell, *Northern Ireland: The Orange State* (London: Pluto, 1976).

[9] On inspiration and comparison with elsewhere, see Gianluca de Fazio, 'Civil Rights Mobilisation and Repression in Northern Ireland: A Comparison with the US Deep South', *The Sixties* 2, no. 2 (2009): 163–185.

[10] Simon Prince, *Northern Ireland's '68: Civil Rights, Global Revolt and the Origins of the Troubles* (Dublin: Irish Academic Press, 2007); Lorenzo Bosi, 'Explaining the Emergence Process of the Civil Rights Protest in Northern Ireland (1945–1968): Insights from a Relational Social Movement Approach 1', *Journal of Historical Sociology* 21, nos. 2–3 (2008): 242–271.

[11] Niall O Dochartaigh, *From Civil Rights to Armalites: Derry and the Birth of the Irish Troubles*, 2nd ed. (Basingstoke, UK: Palgrave Macmillan, 2005).

[12] Primers on Northern Ireland include Richard Rose, *Northern Ireland: A Time of Choice* (Basingstoke, UK: Macmillan, 1973); John Whyte, *Interpreting Northern Ireland* (Oxford: Clarendon, 1990).

[13] 'Obituary: Martin McGuinness Died on March 21st', *Economist*, 23 March 2016, https://www.economist.com/obituary/2017/03/25/obituary-martin-mcguinness-died-on-march-21st.

[14] Eamonn McCann, *War in an Irish Town* (London: Pluto, 1980).

[15] 'No Surrender: Ian Paisley (Obituary)', *Economist* 412, no. 8905 (20 September 2014): 86.

successful in framing the Northern Ireland conflict as a politico-religious endeavour. He emphasised Protestant righteousness and was able to play on the sense of insecurity many Protestant unionists felt in the face of the IRA insurgency.[16] Paisley founded his own political party—the DUP—and was elected a member of the Westminster Parliament and a member of the European Parliament (a body he felt deserved deep suspicion). While he was revered among many Protestants as a staunch defender of the union with Great Britain, many Catholics regarded him as a bigot who, while watching safely on the sidelines, would whip up sectarian feelings and reap a political dividend from violence.[17]

McGuinness was a central figure in the development of Northern Ireland's peace process from the early 1990s onward. He was crucial to Sinn Féin and the IRA's investigation of the possibility of a negotiated way out of the conflict. His profile grew substantially in this period as he became the public face of the militant Irish republicanism and a key negotiator. Many Protestant unionists were deeply suspicious of the peace process, regarding it as giving in to 'terrorists' and threatening Northern Ireland's place within the United Kingdom. Paisley was amongst the most prominent of the peace process opponents calling it 'a surrender process'.[18] When multiparty talks began in 1996–1967, Paisley's DUP boycotted them, stressing that to negotiate with 'terrorists' was an insult to members of the security forces who had died at the hands of the IRA. His party campaigned for a no vote in the referendum on the 1998 Good Friday Agreement. The DUP did take its seats in the power-sharing Assembly and Executive created as a result of the peace accord but maintained an implacable opposition to Sinn Féin. While the Good Friday Agreement paved the way for the end of most political violence in Northern Ireland, many unionists experienced 'buyer's remorse' and regarded the peace process and the peace accord as a threat. Paisley's DUP profited from this electorally and became Northern Ireland's largest political party.[19]

After a number of stumbles, a partial renegotiation of the Good Friday Agreement, and the decommissioning of IRA weapons, Paisley and McGuinness became, respectively, the first minister and the deputy first minister of Northern Ireland's power-sharing Assembly in May 2007.[20] They quickly developed a good

---

[16] Roy Wallis, Steve Bruce, and David Taylor, 'Ethnicity and Evangelism: Ian Paisley and Protestant Politics in Ulster', *Comparative Studies in Society and History* 29, no. 2 (1987): 292–313; Steve Bruce, *Paisley: Religion and Politics in Northern Ireland* (Oxford: Oxford University Press, 2007).

[17] See the comments of one jailed loyalist militant in Ed Maloney and Andy Pollak, *Paisley* (Dublin: Poolbeg, 1986), 389.

[18] Ian Paisley, Text of a Speech by Ian Paisley, Leader of the Democratic Unionist Party, to the DUP Annual Conference, 1995, http://cain.ulst.ac.uk/issues/politics/docs/dup/ip_1995.htm.

[19] Jonathan Tonge, *The Democratic Unionist Party: From Protest to Power* (Oxford: Oxford University Press, 2014), 220–227.

[20] David A. Graham, 'The Strange Friendship of Martin McGuinness and Ian Paisley', *Atlantic*, 21 March 2017.

working relationship that developed into a friendship continued after Paisley retired from his position as first minister and from active politics. The two men even prayed together, and McGuinness attended Paisley's funeral in 2014 and was welcomed by the Paisley family. In turn, when McGuinness became ill, he received support and good wishes from Paisley's family. The friendship embodied sociality, reciprocity, and solidarity. What is remarkable about it is the context and history. Decades of animosity, much of it linked with pain and loss, morphed into a genuine friendship. This did not change Northern Ireland overnight. Yet it was a powerful signal of conflict disruption. Many traditional DUP members and supporters simply did not understand it.[21] It was truly disruptive to their way of thinking. It signalled that there was another way, that there was no axiomatic path-dependency towards intergroup hostility. The Paisley–McGuinness friendship also, to some extent, helped create a 'mood music' in Northern Ireland in which intergroup interaction was less remarkable and more permissible. This did not change the overall Northern Ireland situation in which identity groups struggled to recognise each other's legitimacy. McGuinness's relationship with Paisley's successor, Peter Robinson, was not warm, yet the 'chuckle brothers' imagery stuck in Northern Ireland's popular culture.

A second example of a remarkable friendship comes in the form of the relationship that developed—many years after World War II—between a British former prisoner of war and his Japanese former torturer. Eric Lomax, a junior British officer, was captured by the Japanese in Singapore in 1942[22] and suffered the dreadful privations inflicted by the Japanese on their captives.[23] During Lomax's captivity in Thailand, the Japanese discovered a map and a radio receiver hidden by prisoners and interrogated him to discover more details. The torture involved severe beating and keeping him on a point of death for several weeks. Some of Lomax's comrades did not survive the interrogation. In this extract from his autobiography, Lomax described how he was waterboarded following a sustained beating:

Water poured down my windpipe and throat and filled my lungs and stomach. This is the sensation of drowning, on dry land, on a hot dry afternoon. Your

---

[21] Martina Purdy, 'Ian Paisley Says DUP Told Him to Quit as Leader', *BBC News*, 20 January 2014, https://www.bbc.co.uk/news/uk-northern-ireland-25801295.

[22] For context, see Frank Owen, *The Fall of Singapore* (London: Joseph, 1960); Colin Smith, *Singapore Burning: Heroism and Surrender in WWII* (London: Penguin, 2006). A fictionalised but historically accurate account of the unanticipated and chaotic nature of the fall of Singapore can be found in J. G. Farrell, *The Singapore Grip* (London: Weidenfeld & Nicolson, 1978).

[23] There is an immense literature on the experiences of Allied POWs and civilian internees at the hands of the Japanese military during WWII. A good overview can be found in Charles G. Roland, 'Allied POWs, Japanese Captors and the Geneva Convention', *War & Society* 9, no. 2 (1991): 83–101; Peter Li, 'The Asian Pacific War, 1931–1945: Japanese Atrocities and the Quest for Reconciliation', *East Asia* 17, no. 1 (1999): 108–137.

humanity bursts from within you as you gag and choke. I tried very hard to will unconsciousness, but no relief came. He [a Japanese non-commissioned officer who was the principal torturer] was too skilful to risk losing me altogether. When I was choking uncontrollably, the NCO took the hose away. The flat, urgent voice of the interpreter resumed above my head, speaking into my ear; the other man hit me with the branch on the shoulders and stomach a few more times. I had nothing to say; I was beyond intervention. So they turned the tap on again, and again there was that nausea of rising water from inside my bodily cavity, a flood welling up and choking me.[24]

Lomax survived the war and returned to civilian life in the United Kingdom, but he was damaged by his wartime experiences. His first marriage failed, and he suffered from what would now be diagnosed as post-traumatic stress disorder.[25] As one commentator noted:

For Far East POW veterans, there was no Pomp and Circumstance. Shipped back after the V-J Day bunting had been binned, they arrived in a Britain neither conversant with the horrors of internment nor willing to let ignominious defeats such as the fall of Singapore (of which Lomax had been part) skew the triumphal narrative. In the days before post-traumatic stress disorder was a recognised medical condition, they were expected to suffer in silence; to step out of living hells and back into sedate old lives; to bottle it up and 'get on with it'.[26]

According to Lomax's daughter from his first marriage, the torture and wartime experience patterned family life: 'He was there physically but emotionally he was 100 per cent absent'.[27] Many years after the war, Lomax's second wife, Patti, heard of a former Japanese soldier intent on making a spiritual journey towards reconciliation with former slave labourers who had been forced to work on the 'death railways', or the railways that Japan built during WWII at a huge cost to captive labour.[28] This former soldier turned out to be Nagase Takashi, the interpreter

---

[24] Eric Lomax, *The Railway Man* (London: Vintage, 2014), 163.

[25] 'Eric Lomax: Tortured PoW Who Confronted His Japanese Nemesis—but Chose Reconciliation over Retribution', *Daily Telegraph*, 10 October 2012. See also Lance S. Rintamaki et al., 'Persistence of Traumatic Memories in WWII Prisoners of War', *Journal of the American Geriatrics Society* 57, no. 12 (2009): 2257–2262.

[26] Jeff Dawson, 'Builder of Bridges: The Moving True Story of a British POW on the Death Railway Who Forgave His Torturer Is Now a Film', *Sunday Times*, 22 December 2013, 14.

[27] Charmaine Lomax, quoted in Joanna Moorhead, 'The Railway Man's Secret Daughter on How the Movie Has Helped Her Find Peace', *Sunday Mail*, 5 January 2012, 20.

[28] Kelly E. Crager, *Hell under the Rising Sun: Texan POWs and the Building of the Burma-Thailand Railway* (College Station: Texas A&M University Press, 2008); Peter Brune, *Descent into Hell: The Fall of Singapore—Pudu and Changi—the Thai-Burma Railway* (London: Allen & Unwin, 2014).

and an active participant in the torture sessions. Lomax's wife got in touch with Takashi, and this led to a correspondence between Lomax and Takashi and, eventually, a meeting in Thailand. Lomax recalled the moment of meeting:

> He looked up at me; he was trembling, in tears, saying over and over, 'I am very, very sorry...' I somehow took command, led him out of the terrible heat to a bench in the shade; I was comforting him, for he was really overcome.... It was as though I was protecting him from the force of the emotions shaking his frail-seeming body.[29]

The two men—although late in their lives—began a remarkable friendship. Lomax reflected that 'remembering is not enough, if it simply hardens hate.... Sometime the hating has to stop'.[30] In other words, conflict has to be disrupted. The story is remarkable, not least for the more than three decades between the event and the forgiveness. In this case, the forgiveness and the friendship that developed from it were very much a process that relied on both parties working through their emotions.[31]

A third remarkable friendship comes in the form of a long-standing relationship between Raymonda Tawil, the mother-in-law of the late Palestinian leader Yasser Arafat, and Ruth Dayan, the wife of the late Moshe Dayan, one of the founders of the State of Israel.[32] Moshe Dayan and Yasser Arafat can be seen as among the seminal characters of the modern Israeli–Palestinian conflict. Dayan (1915–1981) was a foundational figure in the creation of the State of Israel. He was particularly associated with Israeli militarism, serving as chief of staff of the Israeli military and later as minister of defence.[33] His reputation among Palestinians and neighbouring Arab states was as a ruthless hard-liner, while for many Israelis, he was a hero. Arafat (1929–2004) was the leader of the Palestinian Liberation Organisation (PLO) and was long associated with resistance to Israeli treatment of Palestinians.[34] He played a significant role in the Oslo peace process and the establishment of the Palestinian Territories, although he spent his

---

[29] Lomax, *The Railway Man*, 304.

[30] Lomax, *The Railway Man*, 319.

[31] Gordon Leah, 'Forgiveness, Pardon and Justice: Critical Reflections on Eric Lomax's *The Railway Man*', *Theology* 121, no. 5 (2018): 345.

[32] Anthony David, *An Improbable Friendship: The Remarkable Lives of Israeli Ruth Dayan and Palestinian Raymonda Tawil and Their Forty-Year Peace Mission* (New York: Arcade, 2015).

[33] Moshe Dayan, *Story of My Life* (London: Weidenfeld & Nicolson, 1976); Yechiam Weitz, 'The Founding Father and the General: David Ben-Gurion and Moshe Dayan', *Middle Eastern Studies* 47, no. 6 (2011): 845–861.

[34] David Downing, *Leading Lives: Yasser Arafat* (London: Heinemann, 2002); Alan Hart, *Arafat: A Political Biography* (New York: Wiley, 1989). For critical accounts of Arafat and the Oslo process, see Jonathan Schanzer, *State of Failure: Yasser Arafat, Mahmoud Abbas, and the Unmaking of the Palestinian State* (New York: Palgrave Macmillan, 2013); Edward Said, *The End of the Peace Process* (London: Granta, 2000).

last years in virtual imprisonment in his compound.[35] For many Palestinians, he was a shrewd and indefatigable leader.[36] For many Israelis and others around the world, however, he was an unreformed 'terrorist' responsible for many deaths. This context makes the friendship between Raymonda Tawil and Ruth Dayan all the more remarkable.

While Israeli–Palestinian friendships are not unknown, they are difficult. The forces mobilised against such friendships are enormous. They come in the structural sense of narratives and group-identity dynamics that set up 'the other' in oppositional ways. They also come in the proximate sense of regular upsurges in violence, a hostile security environment (particularly for Palestinians), and zoning, settlement, and security policies that have effectively minimised the opportunities for Palestinians and Israelis to come into contact with one another. As Yonatan Mendel observed:

> Jewish-Israelis born after 1990 . . . are actually unlikely to have met a Palestinian living in the West Bank or Gaza—unless they are in the army as the occupying force—and . . . their own association with the Palestinian people is likely to have been shaped by the media, and stories of previous years and the Second Intifada told to them by their elder siblings and parents. Indeed, one of the most worrying developments of recent years—and has to be regarded as one of the main post-Oslo failures—has been the complete disconnection between different parts of Israel/Palestine.[37]

Dayan and Tawil were children of elites who went on to live lives of relative privilege, and so their friendship did have some advantages. The two had a frosty first meeting when Dayan was engaged in a humanitarian visit to Palestinian children injured by Israeli violence. But a friendship did develop and endured for many decades.[38] They even planted a peace forest together in central Israel.[39] At the time of this writing, both are advanced in years; and as Tawil resides in Malta and Dayan in Tel Aviv, they Skype on Tuesdays. Raymonda says, 'I really love Ruth. She's very humane and educated. Every time I get angry at something happening in Israel, whether it has to do with Moshe Dayan or (Ariel) Sharon, I scream at her and she replies: "I'm not Moshe! I'm not Sharon!" '[40] Dayan rationalises, 'The

---

[35] Igal Sarna, 'The Prisoner President', *Financial Times*, 21 February 2004, 16.

[36] Schanzer, *State of Failure*.

[37] Yonatan Mendel, 'A New Nationalistic Political Grammar', in *From the River to the Sea: Palestine and Israel in the Shadow of 'Peace'*, ed. Mandy Turner (Lanham, MD: Lexington, 2019), 70.

[38] Kevin Connolly, 'The Friendship That Grew out of War', *BBC News*, 27 September 2015, https://www.bbc.co.uk/news/magazine-34346621.

[39] Ellen Jaffe-Gill, 'Sisterhood across High Barriers', *Jewish News*, 6 November 2015, http://www.jewishnewsva.org/sisterhood-across-high-barriers/.

[40] Cited in Nechama Duek, 'Dayan's Widow, Arafat's Mother-in-Law Talk Peace', *Ynetnews*, 22 October 2017, https://www.ynetnews.com/articles/0,7340,L-5032028,00.html.

point is to talk to each other. It's so easy. We look alike. There are very big similarities between Israelis and Palestinians'.[41]

The key point to arise from these friendships, and others like them, is that they involve individuals stepping outside of the confines of the in-group and exposing themselves to criticism from the in-group and hostility from the out-group. Such friendships involve bravery and the types of self-criticism and awareness associated with ongoing processes of conflict transformation. This involves moving beyond the reciting of grievances to explore something more positive.[42] To relate the phenomenon of remarkable friendships to two prominent themes in this book—power and circuitry—we can see these friendships as a form of Everyday Peace Power (EPP). The individuals concerned make conscious choices to contravene the social norms of the in-group. They have used power—emotional intelligence,[43] a calculation of consequences, a thickness of skin to withstand criticism—to create a space in which a friendship can be created and maintained. These forms of power conform to the 'power with' or 'power to' models, rather than the 'power over' model. Top-down or trickle-down peace usually depends on material, legislative, and institutional power to incentivise and coerce populations into accepting it. EPP, operating at ground level, draws on a repertoire of emotional intelligence, charisma, and strength of character. Importantly, it involves initiative from individuals and groups of individuals. In the top-down peace model, the power of initiative lies with states, institutions, and elites. These friendships can be called a form of power, given their ability to take form in a hostile environment dominated by conflict and the othering of the out-group. The power is manifest in two significant ways. First, it disrupts the hegemonic narrative that the out-group is incorrigible by proving that (some) out-group members are social, reciprocal, and solidaristic. This can be an especially subversive act, as group narratives are often policed, with, for example, pejorative language being routinely employed to describe the out-group. Second, it is a form of power in that it can act as an exemplar. Friendships between individuals, especially non-prominent friendships at the local level, not only stand as a corrective to the dominant narrative, but they can act as an example to others. In the optimal cases, they may be scaled up and out and give permission to others to be imitative.

It is also possible to draw on the notion of circuits to think through the significance that these intergroup friendships have for wider conflict systems.

---

[41] Ralph Gardner Jr. 'A Long Friendship amid an Old Conflict', *Wall Street Journal*, 4 October 2015, https://www.wsj.com/articles/a-long-friendship-amid-an-old-conflict-1444005954.
[42] This is well articulated in Kerri Malloy, 'In Plain Sight: Healing in Northwestern California', paper presented at Building Sustainable Peace conference, Kroc Institute, University of Notre Dame, 7–10 November 2019.
[43] Everett, Hall, and Hamilton-Mason, 'Everyday Conflict', 36.

Circuits allow for unconventional and non-obvious connections. Circuits need not be thought of as routes of path-dependency, certainty, and conformity. Here biological circuits, such as root systems, are useful in reminding us that circuits can mutate, branch out, heal, and develop in unexpected ways. Circuits can have room for innovation, change, and the unconventional. Circuitry may be thought of as a routeway that awards opportunities for unlikely connections. These circuits may not be particularly prominent, but they can survive in unpropitious conditions. They can operate alongside other circuits that conform to the hegemonic narrative and stance of division and othering of the out-group. The intergroup friendships described in this chapter are circuits within wider (conflict) circuits. They are counter-hegemonic circuits that go against the flow. They show that war, division, and othering are not completely all-encompassing and systemic. Instead, space can be carved out for alternative ways of thinking and operation.

Take the example of Megan Phelps-Roper, who grew up as a member of the Christian fundamentalist Westboro Baptist Church in the United States. The church gained notoriety because of the practice of church members to picket the funerals of dead US soldiers with placards reading 'God hates fags' and 'Pray for more dead soldiers'.[44] The church was cultish, with most members coming from the same extended family. The family constituted a reasonably closed circuit; Megan had no school friends outside of the family and ended up working for the church. Eventually, Megan escaped from the church, becoming an advocate for deradicalisation. The story of her own deradicalisation is one of a growing number of circuits—of developing friendships and support networks from people she previously had regarded as ungodly and damned. These circuits involved encouragement, generosity, compassion, empathy, and hope.[45] The development of these circuits was often spontaneous, organic, and informal.

While the friendships showcased above involved some sort of public profile (the Lomax–Takashi and Paisley–McGuinness stories have been turned into movies), such intergroup friendships are possible, and have been observed, at the local level in many contexts. As the interview material from Lebanon shows below, some individuals are able to show sociality, reciprocity, and solidarity across identity boundaries. Political and social psychology has shown that pro-social intergroup contact can, in some cases, be stimulated by violence and shock or revulsion that follows it.[46] Clearly, such a reaction may not be the norm and may come with costs. Yet positive out-group relations can persist even in the

---

[44] Megan Phelps-Roper, *Unfollow: A Journey from Hatred to Hope, Leaving the Westboro Baptist Church* (London: Riverrun, 2019), 182.

[45] Phelps-Roper, *Unfollow*, 254.

[46] Steve Reicher et al., 'Saving Bulgaria's Jews: An Analysis of Social Identity and the Mobilisation of Social Solidarity', *European Journal of Social Psychology* 36 (2006): 49–72.

midst of violence. Many accounts of conflict-affected contexts emphasise division and the intractable nature of the conflict parties. Yet the interviews I conducted in Lebanon show that intergroup boundaries—despite the rhetoric from political leaders—can be malleable and that people, in certain circumstances, can see beyond the politics of division.[47] Othering is complex,[48] and the categories and boundaries 'shift, fold, harden and soften over space/time'.[49]

It was quite common for the Lebanese interviewees to reflect that as children, they played with children from other identity groups and were unconcerned with sectarian division. One Orthodox Christian interviewee remembered that as a child, he 'believed that everyone on this earth is Christian by default' and was therefore surprised when his friend announced that he was Muslim: 'I didn't think to ask him back then why he had hidden this fact'.[50] A Sunni interviewee reflected that his father's best friend was Christian, and upon the death of his father, this friend (known as 'uncle' to the family) stepped up to support the family: 'He was the one who went with the family when I went to propose to my current wife. . . . He was always there for us, all of us including my mom, my sisters and brothers, and never left us for a moment'.[51] A Sunni female interviewee recalled that her mother had a Christian hairdresser when the civil war broke out: 'We offered him custody during the civil war as he used to live in a Muslim neighbourhood. My dad opened our house for him, and when he decided to leave the city and go to his village, my parents used to call him frequently to check on him'.[52] A female Sunni was able to distinguish between the out-group and their political representatives: 'I am not going to judge the Shias in general based on Hezbollah's actions on the ground, [I] will never do that'.[53]

It is worth emphasising that none of the above should be taken as romanticising everyday peace or overemphasising its potential. Intergroup relationships break down at both the elite and non-elite levels, and often violence can be a mass participation affair. Yet it is worth noting, as this section on remarkable friendships has done, the potential of intergroup friendship to disrupt conflict or oppositional norms. The cases illustrate how everyday peace is not about grand declarations of peace. Instead, it is about peace that is enacted and embodied through everyday actions and friendships that doubtless developed tentatively. Often there was a recognition of shared loss and a strength of character to move beyond 'understandable revenge'.[54] This requires a particular sort of personality,

[47] Mac Ginty, 'Everyday Social Practices'.
[48] Millar, 'Our Brothers', 722.
[49] Jones, 'Categories', 184.
[50] Author interview, Orthodox Christian male, Beirut, 3 June 2013. Memoirs of childhood intergroup playing were also evident in an interview with a Shia male, Beirut, 26 June 2013.
[51] Author interview, Sunni male, Beirut, 24 June 2013.
[52] Interview, female Sunni, Beirut, 6 July 2013.
[53] Interview, female Sunni, Saida, 19 August 2013.
[54] Gopin, *Bridges*, 11.

perhaps one that is mature and capable of self-examination (a key part of the conflict transformation playbook), and also involves 'patience, suspension of judgement, observation and constant vigilance with oneself'.[55] There is a sense of growing personal development, with reconciliation being understood as a process rather than an event. While the friendships discussed in this section were high-profile, it is possible to think of cross-community friendships and networks developing in towns, villages, workplaces, and so on. Gopin reflects on the possibility that 'the love between enemies' might create in miniature the community of the future.[56] In this view, these unusual friendships have the capacity to scale out and be imitated. These friendships might be between charismatic individuals who are able to withstand criticism and to inspire others. As will be developed in the next section, many of the individuals are self-starting social entrepreneurs and may be thought of as nodes in a social network: change makers, sources of inspiration, iconoclasts, initiators, and experimenters.

Conflict Disruption

The peace and conflict literature is familiar with the terms *conflict management*, *conflict resolution*, and *conflict transformation*.[57] This book puts forward the notion of conflict disruption as a prior step that may, in favourable circumstances, be able to pave the way for more expansive forms of conflict response. To summarise them briefly, conflict management, resolution, and transformation may be thought of as occupying a continuum, with conflict management being the least ambitious and conflict transformation the most ambitious. Conflict management accepts the existence of conflict but seeks to manage it, perhaps by lowering its costs. Many peace processes between governments and insurgents may be thought of as an exercise of conflict management.[58] They seek to manage the conflict but do not seek to completely extinguish it. Conflict resolution is regarded as more ambitious and seeks to examine the bases of the conflict. It usually accepts the legitimacy of conflict actors and does not question the foundational factors that have led them towards antagonism. While conflict management and conflict resolution are usually top-down endeavours that are restricted to elites and rely on trickle-down peace, conflict transformation is

---

[55] Gopin, *Bridges*, 186.
[56] Gopin, *Bridges*, 29.
[57] An excellent explanation of the genesis of conflict management, conflict resolution, and conflict transformation can be found in Ramsbotham, Woodhouse, and Miall, *Contemporary Conflict Resolution*, 38–67.
[58] Gearoid Millar, 'For Whom Do Local Peace Processes Function? Maintaining Control through Conflict Management', *Cooperation and Conflict* 52, no. 5 (2017): 293–308.

more participative and expansive.[59] It seeks to transform the conflict, especially the deep bases of the conflict, towards more positive dynamics. It involves the parties to the conflict examining their own identity and the factors that make them enjoin in conflict. Conflict transformation encourages bottom-up thinking and actions and is a responsive and reflexive approach to conflict. Clearly, all of these approaches to conflict must operate in the political and material realms. As a result, conflict management is quite common, as it does not involve deep-level reflexivity.

This book argues that everyday peace can be seen as a form of conflict disruption. This disruption can work in three ways, all of which are directed towards the same outcome of puncturing the normalisation of conflict and violence. First, conflict narratives can be disrupted—often through on-the-ground everyday peace actions that contradict official narratives. Elite political actors often invest significant energy in framing the conflict and the other.[60] These conflict narratives usually emphasise the perfidious nature of the other and the heroism and righteousness of the in-group. The narratives often draw on cultural repertoires and are normalised. Much of the Israeli and Palestinian media, for example, denigrate the other so routinely that it is entirely normal to refer to Palestinians as 'terrorists' and Israelis as 'occupiers'. Small acts of everyday peace, for example, a Palestinian referring to Israelis with civility or at least recognising that not all Israelis should be termed 'occupiers', disrupt the dominant narrative. They show that the dominant narrative has competition and that there are alternative ways to frame the other or the conflict.

A second way that conflict disruption can operate is through actions that contradict the norm. Here we can think of transgressive acts that are a challenge to the established norms of the conflict. An example comes in the form of the small number of Israeli citizens who refuse to be conscripted into the military on the basis that they object to the treatment of Palestinians.[61] Their actions often involve significant personal cost such as social ostracism and impact on employability.[62] They are plainly in the solidarity playbook, as they involve action that

---

[59] Conflict transformation is most closely associated with John Paul Lederach, *The Little Book of Conflict Transformation* (Intercourse, PA: Good Books, 2003); John Paul Lederach, *Preparing for Peace: Conflict Transformation across Cultures* (Syracuse, NY: Syracuse University Press, 1995).

[60] See, for example, Andreas R. T. Schuck et al., 'Who's Afraid of Conflict? The Mobilising Effect of Conflict Framing in Campaign News', *British Journal of Political Science* 46, no. 1 (2016): 177–194; Matt Evans and Selcan M. Kaynak, 'Media Framing in Religious and Secular Conflict in Turkey and Israel', *International Political Science Review* 36, no. 2 (2015): 139–152.

[61] See, for example, Erica Weiss, 'Beyond Mystification: Hegemony, Resistance, and Ethical Responsibility in Israel', *Anthropological Quarterly* 88, no. 2 (2015): 417–443; Adi Livny, 'Conscientious Objection and the State', *Armed Forces and Society* 44, no. 4 (2018): 666–687.

[62] Alasdair Soussi, 'Life after the Army: Israel's Conscientious Objectors', *Al Jazeera*, 12 February 2018, https://www.aljazeera.com/news/2018/02/life-army-israel-conscientious-objectors-180211121020314.html.

goes beyond speech and stance. Refusing to be conscripted is not merely verbal dissent, it is a specific act with legal consequences. These actions constitute a powerful statement that not all Israeli citizens are united behind the securitised state-building project. As such, they are a rebuke to the dominant conflict machinery that has sought to normalise military service and the link between defence of the nation and full citizenship.[63]

A third way that conflict disruption operates, and one that is linked to the disruption of narratives of actions, is to challenge the conflict mentality. Many violent conflicts and situations of ingrained intergroup hostility can be characterised by an apparent path-dependency. The righteousness of the in-group and its grievances and the perfidy of the out-group may be normalised as a mode of thinking. Significant material and political power may be directed at maintaining such a position. To puncture this way of thinking and suggest that alternatives might be possible, that the out-group might not be incorrigible, or that the conflict should not be all-consuming is a brave and transgressive act. Northern Ireland's punk music scene in the 1970s and early 1980s, for example, constituted an affront to the established norm that the conflict was 'the only game in town'.[64] As the conflict intensified, it reinforced societal divisions, made the notion of political compromise seem remote, and had direct impacts on the way people lived. In an attempt to minimise risks, many people modified their routes to and from work and how they behaved in public. The streetscape became securitised and militarised, with frequent checkpoints and military patrols. In the midst of this small-scale but intense civil war, a punk music scene developed (mainly in Belfast). It was incongruous when viewed alongside the dominant narrative in the two main communities and constituted a mentality of conflict disruption. Indeed, to many people, it seemed incomprehensible: why would some young people shave their heads and follow dreadful music bands when there were communities to be defended? Those engaged in the music scene made a conscious decision to reject the dominant conflict-related modes of thinking and, instead, follow a different set of passions.

The notion of disruption, sometimes 'rupture', has gained prominence in the social sciences, mainly in economics and business management.[65] It was

---

[63] David Zonsheine, 'The Conscientious Objectors Threatening the Israeli System', *Haartez*, 18 March 2018, https://www.haaretz.com/opinion/.premium-the-conscientious-objectors-threatening-the-system-1.5449772.

[64] Timothy A. Heron, '"Alternative Ulster": The First Wave of Punk in Northern Ireland (1976–1983)', *Études Anglaises* 71, no. 1 (2018): 67–84; Martin Mcloone, 'Punk Music in Northern Ireland: The Political Power of "What Might Have Been"', *Irish Studies Review* 12, no. 1 (2004): 29–38; Robert Martinez, 'Punk Rock, Thatcher and the Elsewhere of Northern Ireland: Rethinking the Politics of Pop Music', *Journal of the Midwest Language Association* 48, no. 1 (2015): 193–219.

[65] Alessio Cozzolino, Gianmario Verona, and Frank T. Rothaermel, 'Unpacking the Disruption Process: New Technology, Business Models, and Incumbent Adaptation', *Journal of Management Studies* 55, no. 7 (2018): 1166–1202.

originally conceived by Austrian economist Joseph Schumpeter as 'the perennial gale of destruction' in which 'many firms will perish' but other forms will innovate and thrive.[66] More recently, Schumpeter's rather Darwinian notion of creative disruption was seized upon by Silicon Valley tech entrepreneurs:

> Broadly speaking, disruption talk among tech entrepreneurs and speculative venture capitalists champions innovation driven destabilization as a positive force. More specifically, disruption is seen as necessary to the outsize return on supposedly radically experimental, high risk start ups that both groups eternally seek. It portrays older industries as staid, outdated, and ripe for enforced irrelevance by bold young technological challengers.[67]

In this view, disruption is recast as a positive force that allows companies to abandon or destabilise established business models and steal a march on the competition. Standard operating practices and other norms that are taken for granted are abandoned. In the contemporary era, no-frills airlines, Uber, and Airbnb can be thought of as market disrupters and innovators whose actions have left established business models looking staid. They have been particularly aided by technology and long-term business plans with an emphasis on growth.[68] In all cases, of course, there have been serious questions asked about the ethics of these business models, especially in terms of consumer and employee rights.[69]

While we must be prudent in adopting concepts and language from one discipline to another, the notion of 'disruption' is useful and resonates with everyday peace. Three conceptual points are worth making in relation to disruption. The first is that the concept developed here is conflict disruption rather than interruption. Interruption suggests creating a space or a break in conflict and is less forceful than disruption. Everyday peace can interrupt conflict, but this book suggests that it has the potential to do more. It is a form of power, a mode of thinking, and inherently critical to the established conflict order. To the extent that an everyday peace stance is visible, it is a rebuke to the myth of the totalising nature of conflict and associated hegemonic narratives. So, rather than mere interruption or a pause, conflict disruption is a disturbance of the equilibrium

---

[66] Joseph A. Schumpeter, *Capitalism, Socialism and Democracy* (London: Taylor & Francis, 2003), 90. See also 'Disrupting Mr Disrupter', *Economist*, 26 November 2015, https://www.economist.com/business/2015/11/26/disrupting-mr-disrupter.

[67] Sarah Knuth, 'Green Devaluation: Disruption, Divestment and Decommodification for a Green Economy', *Capitalism, Nature, Socialism* 28, no. 1 (2016): 100.

[68] Innovation Enterprise, *Positive Disruption in Company Strategy: Disruptive Innovation in the Enterprise* (Bristol, UK: Innovation Enterprise, 2013), 1.

[69] Judd Cramer and Alan B. Krueger, 'Disruptive Change in the Taxi Business: The Case of Uber', *American Economic Review* 106, no. 5 (2016): 177–182.

or trajectory that normalises conflict and thus has the capacity to lead to something else.

A second conceptual point is that disruptive business innovation usually starts at the bottom end of the market and works it way up.[70] Many start-up businesses begin by aiming at a lower price point but, once established, develop more sophisticated (and expensive) products. This resonates with bottom-up peacemaking. Everyday peace operates at the 'bottom end of the market' in the sense that it is a non-elite endeavour. That might involve mundane intergroup interaction in the queue for the bakery or on public transport. It takes the form of rubbing along to get along and can be found among co-workers and those who share the same micro-neighbourhood. There is no guarantee that highly localised conflict disruption will factor up and have any impact on the meta-conflict and its outcomes. The individual acts of battlefield compassion that we saw in chapter 5 humanised war and had an often existential impact on those involved—especially the recipients of the compassion. But they did not change the ultimate outcome of the conflicts. In a similar way, the small acts of peace that constitute everyday peace may not change the ultimate course of the conflict, but they may make it more liveable and play a subversive role in making clear that alternatives, however localised, are possible. In some cases, however, it is possible to think of how localised conflict disruption can resonate politically and with the public. In 2018, for example, Afghan forces and the Taliban observed a short ceasefire for Eid.[71] The ceasefire was reciprocal and widely respected, and it involved many cases of Afghan security forces and Taliban members embracing each other in public.[72] Photographs of such embraces spread quickly. Hostilities resumed shortly afterwards, but the conflict was 'disrupted' in the public mind, and the hundreds (possibly thousands) of instances of intergroup contact may well have an impact on public pressure for an elite-level peace process. It is worth noting that the ceasefire took place against elite-level contacts between the United States and the Taliban and between the Taliban and the Afghan government.[73]

---

[70] John R. Kimberley, 'Disruption on Steroids: Sea Change in the Worlds of Higher Education in General and Business Education in Particular', *Journal of Leadership & Organizational Studies* 23, no. 1 (2016): 10; Roger Smith, 'Technology Disruption in the Simulation Industry', *Journal of Defense Modelling and Simulation* 3, no. 1 (2006): 8.

[71] 'Afghanistan's Ghani Declares Eid Ceasefire with Taliban', *Al Jezeera*, 19 August 2018, https://www.aljazeera.com/news/2018/08/afghanistan-ghani-declares-eid-ceasefire-taliban-180819143135061.html.

[72] Ruchi Kumar, 'Selfies with the Taliban: Afghan Women Buoyed by Ceasefire Snaps', *Guardian*, 6 July 2018, www.theguardian.com/global-development/2018/jul/06/selfies-with-the-taliban-afghan-women-buoyed-eid-ceasefire-photos-viral.

[73] Memphis Barker and Sami Yousafzai, 'Isis Claims Deadly Suicide Bombings as Afghans Celebrate Taliban Ceasefire', *Guardian*, 16 June 2018, https://www.theguardian.com/world/2018/jun/16/isis-claims-deadly-suicide-bombing-as-afghans-celebrate-taliban-ceasefire.

The third conceptual point in relation to conflict disruption is that it is in keeping with the notion of circuitry. Circuits can break and malfunction. Sometimes these circuits may be non-critical. They may be subsidiary circuits that are not vital to the overall functioning of the system. Depending on its extent and complexity, it may be possible to find ways around a broken circuit. On some occasions, the disruption to the circuit may be systemic and threaten the viability of the circuit. Some theoretical modelling suggests that if 60 percent of the links in a network are broken, then the network will collapse.[74] As an example, it is worth thinking of the massive solidarity and public disaffection that attended the end of the WWI. Mass-scale mutinies in the Russian, German, and French militaries made the war increasingly unsustainable.[75] These were by no means the only factors contributing to the end of the war—there were strategic factors at play, too. But it is worth thinking of the mutinies in terms of circuitry: small acts of insubordination can be thought of as occurring in isolated circuits, but these acts multiplied and became mutinies and thus systemic. Disaffection with the war was not restricted to the military—publics had also become worn down by the length and privations of the war.[76] It is possible to think of a complex system of publics, militaries, workers, elites, non-elites, and many others in constant movement and varying degrees of competition and collaboration.[77] The system was made up of many circuits, some critical and others not. Some circuits were subterranean in the sense of being hidden or less obvious. At particular moments, such as workers' strikes or mutinies, the highly localised circuits became more prominent and disrupted the overarching conflict.

On looking across a range of contemporary cases, it is clear that charismatic individuals often play a significant role in conflict disruption. These may be formal community leaders such as a mayor or religious practitioner, or they may be a de facto community leader who, through force of personality or family prominence, is the effective leader of a community in a valley, village, or city neighbourhood. This identification of the importance of community leaders in conflict disruption is in keeping with research on peace zones and on civilian agency in conflict-affected settings.[78] Jana Krause's work on 'resilient communities' in Indonesia, for example, shows how iconoclastic individuals can take a

[74] 'Resilient Cities, Networks and Disruptions', *Environment and Planning B: Planning and Design* 40 (2013): 572.
[75] William A. Pelz, *A People's History of Modern Europe* (London: Pluto, 2016), 103–114.
[76] Matthias Blum, 'War, Food Rationing, and Socioeconomic Inequality in Germany during the First World War', *Economic History Review* 66, no. 4 (2013): 1063–1083.
[77] Bent Dalum, Christian Ø. R. Pedersen, and Gert Villumsen, 'Technological Life-Cycles: Lessons from Cluster Facing Disruption', *European Urban and Regional Studies* 12, no. 3 (2005): 229–246.
[78] Christopher Mitchell and Susan Allen Nan, 'Local Peace Zones as Institutionalized Conflict', *Peace Review* 9, no. 2 (1997): 159–162; Hancock, 'Agency'.

stand against militarism or extremism in their community and attempt to influence others to follow suit:

> Non-violent communities in Ambon and Jos adapted to a rapidly changing conflict environment characterized by the mobilization of vigilantes, criminals, and gangs organized around political actors; deeply polarized ethnic and religious relations; and the formation of militias and a growing militarization of local order. Civilian prevention efforts emerged first through individual leaders who negotiated neutrality within and beyond their communities. Their courageous and high-risk initiatives sparked community-based social movements when ordinary people joined their efforts. Community leaders were guided by *social knowledge* concerning the organization of violence and *lived experience* in other conflict zones prior to the conflicts in Ambon and Jos. Throughout their prevention work, they demonstrated *social learning* with regard to conflict dynamics, imagination of threats and challenges, and continuous *scenario-building* of potential attacks to *anticipate* and mitigate consequences, thus sustaining prevention.[79]

What is clear from this extract—and it resonates with the notion of everyday peace—is the extent to which this form of conflict disruption relies on emotional intelligence and an ability to 'read' a social situation and make a judgement on the feasibility of conflict disruption. Disruptive activity is contingent on circumstances, especially the stage of a conflict and the degree of mobilisation. Conflict disrupters do not only need to understand the local dynamic, they need to be embedded within it. As a result, it is difficult to see how this form of ground-level conflict disruption can be conducted by anyone other than local actors, but it can be supported by external actors. Such a course of action can be dangerous, and such community leaders are often targeted by states and armed groups precisely because of their potential to disrupt the normalisation of conflict and division. The toll of Colombian social entrepreneurs and community activists murdered in the years since the 2016 peace accord is testament to how their activities are regarded as threatening by power holders such as landowners and political elites.[80]

Former gang members have often been most influential in initiatives aimed at calming gang violence or preventing others from joining gangs. They have the contacts and social standing, are knowledgeable of the political economy of gang culture, and are conversant in the gang language. Put simply, they have street

---

[79] Jana Krause, *Resilient Communities: Non-Violence and Civilian Agency in Communal War* (Cambridge: University Press, 2018), 8; italics in original.

[80] Luis Jaime Acosta, 'Murder of Hundreds of Colombian Peace Activists Casts Shadow over Peace Process', *Reuters*, 23 August 2019, https://www.reuters.com/article/us-colombia-peace-feature/murder-of-hundreds-of-colombian-activists-casts-shadow-over-peace-process-idUSKCN1VF0IK.

cred. In Baltimore, for example, a former gang member, Tyree Colion, has been influential in establishing 'No Shoot Zones'. As one profile noted, 'Armed with a vision, a knife for self-defence and a can of spray paint to demarcate the No Shoot Zones, Colion began talking to residents, community leaders, children and gang members. As someone who had served 15 years in prison for gang-related murder, people listened'.[81] His reputation gave him a social credibility that formal institutions lacked. Relations between many African Americans, the Baltimore police, and city officials have suffered for decades, and social capital in many communities has been degraded by long-term drugs use, gang violence, and deprivation.[82] While No Shoot Zones have been trialled in a number of US cities to stem gang violence,[83] what makes the Baltimore experiment different is its bottom-up approach. It is not a top-down prescriptive form of peacemaking that is the product of collaboration between city agencies and NGOs. Indeed, Colion operated at the level below civil society organisations and has met with some opposition from the police for his conflict disruption activity.[84] It relied on positive societalisation, or the acceptance of civil norms by community members and their horizontal spread. A criticism can be made of a No Shoot Zone scheme in that it is a stand-alone initiative and not formally connected with other remedial efforts—perhaps in conjunction with the schools system. Yet such a criticism is probably ungenerous. The number of No Shoot Zones has grown, Colion has mobilised volunteers to establish and monitor No Shoot Zones, and the number of homicides in Baltimore has decreased.[85] It is impossible to say if the No Shoot Zones initiative is responsible for that decline, given other prevailing factors and the official 'Safe Streets' violence reduction initiative.[86]

The promise of conflict disruption is that it creates space in which more significant conflict response activity can take place. It may allow other individuals or groups to emulate or join in, or give them pause for thought. In a good scenario, conflict disruption actions encourage pro-conflict actors to think about

---

[81] Dean Adams, 'How a Rapper Set Up No Shoot Zones to Stop Baltimore's Bloodshed', *Al Jazeera*, 11 October 2018, https://www.aljazeera.com/indepth/features/rapper-set-shoot-zones-stop-baltimore-bloodshed-181001072850663.html.

[82] Background on Baltimore's problems can be found in Andrea Cantora, Seema Iyer, and Lauren Restivo, 'Understanding Drivers of Crime in East Baltimore: Resident Perceptions of Why Crime Persists', *American Journal of Criminal Justice* 41, no. 4 (2016): 686–709.

[83] 'Law Enforcement Approaches to Reducing Gun Violence', *RAND*, 22 April 2020, https://www.rand.org/research/gun-policy/analysis/essays/law-enforcement-approaches-for-reducing-gun-violence.html.

[84] Ethan Mcleod, 'Rapper Tyree Colion Arrested for "No Shoot Zone" Graffiti at Middle River Store Where Teen Was Fatally Shot', *Baltimore Fishbowl*, 3 August 2017, https://baltimorefishbowl.com/stories/rapper-tyree-colion-arrested-for-no-shoot-zone-graffiti-at-middle-river-store-where-teen-was-fatally-shot/.

[85] Adams, 'How a Rapper'.

[86] A. J. Milam et al., 'Changes in Attitudes towards Guns and Shootings Following Implementation of Baltimore Safe Streets Intervention', *Journal of Urban Health* 93, no. 4 (2016): 609–626.

the sustainability of the conflict or their current approach to the conflict. They might be encouraged to scope out ways to lower the costs of the conflict, perhaps through a negotiated process or by moderating their stance. In an optimal scenario, we would see temporary suspensions of the normal rules and hierarchies that sustain conflict and division. We might see the development of liminal spaces and the emergence of new socio-material understandings or a new communitas in which there might be pro-peace and pro-social possibilities.[87] There are no guarantees that conflict disruption is the beginning of a linear process that ends in pacific outcomes. Conflict disruption can be counterproductive and encourage parties to a conflict to redouble their efforts to pursue warlike or antagonistic strategies. But it can be the factor that encourages a pause or a reassessment of violent approaches. It can be an initiation agent that has an impact larger than the original transgressive act or stance.

Conclusion

The essential aim of this chapter has been to consider the wider potential of everyday peace. The concept of conflict disruption has proved to be a useful conceptual vehicle to think through how small acts and small intergroup ties can, potentially, have a wider impact. They encourage us to think foremost about scaling out as well as scaling up. People-to-people dynamics can expand, thus puncturing the notion of a totalising conflict supported by fully mobilised and hegemonic communities. Conflict disruption allows us to see the possibility of outliers and alternatives. People-to-people activities can spread horizontally and become a visible rebuke to political and militant leaders. As such, they adopt a vertical potential as well and become more than highly localised deeds, stances, and relationships. They become the embodiment and enactment of conflict transformation whereby individuals and groups of individuals embark on a journey of personal education about themselves, the other, and identity construction. Lest any of this sound somehow ethereal or romanticised, it should be remembered that many of the examples in this book come from the 'hard cases' of the world wars and ongoing violent conflicts. In these seemingly unpromising contexts, individuals and small groups of individuals took risks, broke moulds, thought differently, were unconvinced of official narratives, and did not follow the herd. These individuals and groups displayed sociality, reciprocity,

---

[87] Siiri Pöyhönen, 'Room for Communitas: Exploring Sociomaterial Construction of Leadership in Liminal and Dominant Spaces', *Leadership* 14, no. 5 (2018): 586. See also Victor Turner, 'Frame, Flow and Reflection: Ritual and Drama as Public Liminality', *Japanese Journal of Religious Studies* 6, no. 4 (1979): 465–499.

and solidarity in making and maintaining intergroup links or in resisting the notion that violent conflict must be totalising.

In some cases, these transgressive stances and acts humanised violent conflict or societal division but did not change the meta-outcome of the violent conflict. Showing kindness and mercy to POWs, for example, did not change the status of the prisoners or the overall outcome of the violent conflict. Yet we should not underestimate the impact of humane acts and stances in the here and now. It is important to recognise, and indeed celebrate, when lives are saved and improved. It is a bonus if these acts and stances inspire others and have a multiplier effect. In some cases, small 'everyday' acts can have a more significant impact than that found in the here and now. Depending on circumstances and the nature of the circuit or assemblage, the everyday peace act or stance can have system-wide impacts. In an optimal scenario, the weak ties of intergroup association can have qualitative significance on the extent to which civility and tolerance can be accepted.[88] These weak ties might even develop in density, and so stances and practices become normalised. They have the possibility of acting as 'bridges' to something more significant than the initial tie.

---

[88] Mark Granovetter, 'The Strength of Weak Ties: A Network Theory Revisited', *Sociological Theory* 1, no. 1 (1983): 229.

Conclusion

This book has been concerned with the connections and disconnections between what might be called 'big peace' and 'small peace'. Big peace refers to top-down, institutionalist peace that might involve organised political and military units such as states, political parties, military groups, and international organisations. This form of peace is often recognised and codified through peace processes, peace accords and constitutions, monitoring missions, and other trappings of formality and legalism. It is also often supported by international organisations, elements of the 'international community', and the caravan of INGOs that follow major peace accords and transitions. It is often based on the notion of 'trickle-down' peace, or the assumption that if elite or meta-level peace is reached, then this will create a context in which other levels of society can experience peace. This model of peace assumes a hierarchy: that elite-level peace comes first and enables peace that occurs at 'lower' levels.

The primary focus of this book has been on localised, informal non-elite approaches to peace that occur at the level of individuals and small groups of individuals. This 'small peace' is relatively under-researched. In part, the relative neglect of localised everyday peace is because of the overwhelming attention devoted to the top-down peace of conflict resolution and conflict management by states, international organisations, and militaries. In part, it is because everyday peace is difficult to see. It often occurs in the shadows and on the margins. It might be deliberately concealed lest it attract unwanted attention. The everyday peace or small peace that has been the focus of this book occurs at a level below civil society organisations and peace movements. It does not take the form of protest marches, lobbying, or empowerment and awareness strategies. Instead, it takes place in everyday places of intergroup encounter: the apartment block stairwell, the workplace corridor, the queue for coffee or a bus. In the view of this book, these venues provide a natural frame of reference for the study of peacebuilding. Crucially, it is a form of peace that is embodied and lived through the actions, stances, and words of so-called ordinary people in their daily tasks in conflict-affected contexts. As a result, this book has tried to move beyond 'the monoculture of Eurocentric scientific knowledge' and at least acknowledge a world beyond states and formal institutions.[1]

---

[1] Sipamandla Zondi, 'Decolonising IR and Its Theory: A Critical Conceptual Meditation', *Politikon* 45, no. 1 (2018): 16.

While the 'big peace' of peace accords, symbolic gestures by political elites, and pro-peace interventions by international actors may do much to set the meta-context, this peace is only part of the story. For peace to be meaningful beyond elites and headlines, it needs to be manifest and embedded in the everyday lives of conflict-affected populations. This means that peace needs to be reflected in the full range of activities that constitute everyday life. Thus, to be meaningful, peace must be reflected in, and be part of, the minutiae of life. While much of policy, academic, and journalistic attention might be on the 'big peace' of peace accord signing ceremonies or the fate of political elites, it is the contention of this book that we need also to train our attention on the routes that people take to work, their social interactions in the workplace corridor, or their retail habits. These details are the stuff of life and peace in conflict-affected societies. In this view, coexistence, tolerance, sociality, and a range of other stances that might be categorised under the broad label of 'peace' are enacted and embodied through routine and everyday actions.

While much of this book has conceptualised the notion of everyday peace, it has also been anxious to demonstrate that everyday peace has the capacity to be more than a declaratory aim. Examples from EPI project research, as well as other research in Lebanon and material from war memoirs and personal diaries, show that everyday peace has taken root in sometimes very unpromising spaces and has had real impacts. A key point in this book is that pacific micro-activities are significant and can have multiplier, imitative, and inspiration effects. The saving and improving of lives—even at the most local of levels and smallest of scales—are important in that they challenge a number of systems on which violent conflict thrives. For example, it can help challenge Newtonian notions of conflict that suggest that conflict is inevitable if supposed precursors are in place.

Perhaps the most obvious demonstration of everyday peace comes in the form of a survey of societies that have emerged from violent conflict and have not slipped back into mass-scale violence. These societies, for example, Bosnia and Herzegovina or northern Uganda, are by no means perfect and face very many structural problems and legacies of violent conflict. Yet there are multiple examples visible in everyday life of how segments of society are moving on, have developed systems of civility and tolerance, and are definitely 'post'-conflict. So-called ordinary people have constructed a social infrastructure that makes life liveable. In some cases, this social infrastructure has included minorities and out-group members and thus gives the society a texture that revolves around more than a single identity. Importantly, and as well illustrated in Séverine Autesserre's work, communities are rarely sitting around waiting for international peacebuilding assistance.[2] Often they simply have to get on with

---

[2] Autesserre, *Peaceland*.

the stuff of everyday life. They have to get the kids to school and put food on the table and, if possible, live a life with cultural pursuits. These everyday processes often involve tolerance towards out-group members. These everyday actions create a society.

Four Questions

Our consideration of everyday peace has led to a number of questions:

1. Is the everyday peace described in the book really peace? Or is it merely tolerance or a grudging agreement to inhabit the same space?
2. Just how significant can everyday peace be? Can we think of scaling up or scaling out everyday peace?
3. Given the marginal and often 'hidden' nature of everyday peace, how can researchers capture it?
4. How can we connect peace that occurs at the everyday and local levels with peace on the national, international, and transnational levels?

The bulk of this concluding chapter answers these questions.

In relation to the first question (the extent to which everyday peace is actually peace), this book is clear that it can, in many cases, be legitimately classed as 'peace'. It is useful to remind ourselves of the contexts covered in the book: deeply divided societies marked by chronic conflict and dysfunction, civil wars, and mass-scale international warfare. In these contexts, it seems unrealistic to think of a celestial peace. Instead, peace is likely to be partial, contested, suspicious, experimental, incremental, non-linear, conditional, and highly political. This lowering of the bar of what constitutes peace should not be taken as a defeatist narrowing of peace to the bare minimum. It is, instead, a recognition of the low baseline experienced in many contexts in which the other side is regarded with disdain, contempt, or worse. In such a context, even minor signs of intergroup sociality or common humanity have a worth. As many of the examples in this book will attest, apparently minor actions and stances of everyday peace can be signifiers of something more meaningful. Everyday peace acts, stances, and speech have the capacity to be the first and last peace. It can be the first peace in the sense of a minor step that punctures warlike stances and opens the possibility of more significant intergroup encounters. It can be the last peace in the sense that it may be a reminder that intergroup civility can survive a more general worsening of intergroup relations. This first and last peace has the potential to puncture narratives favoured by political and military elites and perhaps narratives that are mainstreamed within the in-group. Everyday peace has the potential to reveal that support for conflict or division is not complete. It can be a space in which alternatives are discussed and enacted, and forms of peace are forged through daily routines, encounters, and interactions.

> *Often, when I am hiking, I spot the last tree. This is the last tree on a hillside before the soil becomes too poor, the winds too strong, and the altitude too high to support trees. The last trees on hillsides are often stunted and gnarled—testament to the harsh conditions. Of course, on the way down, the last tree becomes the first tree—a sign that I am entering a more temperate area, with better land and more shelter. As I trudge towards it, I often think of the first/last tree as a lonely outpost. To survive, the last tree probably needs a good deal of luck and resilience. Iain Sinclair's phrase 'the tough fecundity of the margin' comes to mind, whereby some species are able to survive against the odds.[3] In terms of peace and conflict, we can think of this tree as those in the community who retain intergroup friendships as a society descends towards violence, or those who show the first signs of intergroup civility in a period of calm.*

The notion of everyday peace encourages us to re-evaluate what we might mean by peace. It encourages us to move away from ideas of peace as being formal, institutionalised, overwhelmingly male, and associated with the ceremonialism of signing ceremonies, summits, and photo opportunities. Instead, in this view, peace can be embedded in everyday tasks. It is 'acted out' via activities that might be regarded as so minor and humdrum that they are overlooked by scholars and other analysts. Thus, for example, the routine inclusion of a Catholic in the Friday-morning coffee routine of a group of Protestant moms in Northern Ireland may be unremarkable for many. Even among those who measure Northern Ireland's peace process, and the implementation of the peace accord, this sort of everyday indicator of peace is not captured. By broadening our understanding of peace to include intergroup coffee dates, the quietly convivial corridor conversation between Bosnian and Croat workmates and the civility shown to a Christian shopper by a Muslim stallholder in a Nigerian market both count as peace. Given the contexts of division, these acts are important in themselves. But they also have the capacity to be more than single acts of sociality, reciprocity, and solidarity. They can also be statements and acts of conflict disruption that challenge the normalisation of conflict and division. The accretion of everyday speech acts, thinking, and stances can change the conflict landscape. Two examples from this book stand out. The first involves the mutinies that occurred towards the end of WWI, especially among Russian, German, and French

---

[3] Iain Sinclair, quoted in Richard Mabey, *The Unofficial Countryside* (Beaminster, UK: Little Toller, 2014), 2.

troops who had lost faith in their leaders and were reacting to the dreadful conditions they had been expected to endure. The second example is the small group of Sudanese soldiers who stepped in to protect protesters from a pro-regime militia. In both cases, it was not clear that the small acts that constituted the mutinies and the protection of the protesters would have any wider significance. Yet, with hindsight, we can see that the actions disrupted the conflict norm and had wider repercussions that were pro-social and pro-peace. The 'peace' that emerged from both examples was incomplete, uneven, and guarded. Yet this book is resolute in recognising that this is a form of peace. It is not the peace of unicorns frolicking under rainbows. It is likely to be an agonistic peace in which conflict continues but is reframed and reframed again through iterative everyday processes of positive societalisation.[4] Everyday peace is, however, a peace that allows lives to be saved and improved. It allows interpersonal and intergroup relationships to be recalibrated to be less dysfunctional. It might allow for a reconsideration of power relationships and a shift away from 'power over' to 'power to', 'power from', and 'power with'. Everyday peace might be dismissed as only effective in less violent contexts. Certainly, many everyday peace activities and stances require a minimal level of security. But as this book has shown, even in the most adverse situations, individuals and groups of individuals are able to use guile, entrepreneurialism, creativity, and dissembling to carve out spaces for pro-peace and pro-peace dissent and transgression. This may not look terribly like peace, but in creating a different kind of social infrastructure, then space for normalisation, accommodation, and conciliation may be found.

The second question asked just how significant everyday peace could be, especially if is restricted to marginal spaces. Crucially, can it be scaled up and scaled out from the grassroots? Certainly, it can be significant at the micro-level. The snap decision of a soldier on the battlefield to spare the life of an adversary can have a huge impact at the level of individuals. Rather than being killed, a young man becomes a POW and, with luck, might survive that ordeal, be released, and become integrated into a society, perhaps becoming a father, businessperson, teacher, or social entrepreneur. The soldier who makes the snap decision might be spared post-traumatic stress disorder—a very real phenomenon impacting huge numbers of serving and former military personnel. The lives saved and improved at an individual level can add up to be significant numbers and illustrate the importance of jus in bello laws and conventions that seek to civilise warfare.

---

[4] SungYong Lee, 'Local Resilience and the Reconstruction of Social Institutions: Recovery, Maintenance and Transformation of Buddhist Sangha in Post-Khmer Rouge Cambodia', *Journal of Intervention and Statebuilding* 14, no. 3 (2020): 362.

Certainly, many activities and stances that constitute everyday peace, tolerance, and coexistence occur on the margins. In many cases, it would be too dangerous for an individual or small group of individuals to be too public in their dealings with the out-group. As the remarkable friendships covered in chapter 7 demonstrated, some individuals are brave enough to persevere with intergroup relationships in the face of opprobrium from their own group. The promise of everyday and non-elite peace is that the instances of everyday peace coalesce and multiply, leading to a widening normalisation of intergroup civility. For example, in the immediate aftermath of the Yugoslavian civil war, it may have been remarkable for a Bosnian small-town entrepreneur to employ a Croat. For everyday peace to take root, this action needs to be replicated and become less remarkable through positive societalisation. Yet if we look at the longue durée of history, we can observe societies that have had conflict and violence but have also had long periods of coexistence, tolerance, and peace. In the long periods of accommodation, tentative conciliation between groups and individuals and between institutions and people may develop into something more substantive.[5] This peace was manifest in everyday actions and stances, for example, through intermarriage between identity groups and divisions becoming less marked. The history of Yugoslavia and its predecessor territories is full of violent conflict. But it is also full of long lulls between violent conflict, when individuals and families from different identity groups coexisted and cooperated. Significant here is what Granovetter calls 'the strength of small ties'[6] and what Moore sees as an everyday civility[7] that is embedded in the practices and norms of society. As has been discussed in the book, everyday peace has the potential to both scale up and scale out. It can scale up in the sense of giving life and form to top-down peace. It can inhabit spaces that are created by ceasefires and peace accords. Local-level everyday peace, for example, in the form of a growing number of everyday encounters between people of different backgrounds in a society moving out of conflict, can encourage political or security elites to make changes. In an ideal scenario, a virtuous circle develops with top-down and bottom-up peace encouraging each other. Grassroots peace can often outstrip more cautious political leaders in terms of the speed with which it is willing to change. Everyday peace can also scale out in the sense of horizontal spread whereby the everyday peace acts and stances of some individuals inspire others to show sociality, reciprocity, and even solidarity to those from an out-group. The accretion of these multiple small acts can change a society and transform peace from being a declaration

---

[5] Louis Kriesberg, 'Reconciliation: Aspect, Growth and Sequences', *International Journal of Peace Studies* 12, no. 1 (Spring/Summer 2007): 2.
[6] Mark Granovetter. 'The Strength of Weak Ties', *American Journal of Sociology* 78, no. 6 (1973): 1360–1380.
[7] Moore, *Peacebuilding*.

into something that is enacted and embodied. The task facing everyday peace is to upscale neighbour-to-neighbour civility so that it becomes community-to-community. In an optimal scenario, there will be positive societalisation whereby ideas and practices of civility and sensibility spread horizontally. In such a case, they are internalised by community members rather than imposed from above. Here we go back to chapter 7 and the role that charismatic community leaders and remarkable siblings or spouses can play in outreach and what Lederach terms 'middle out'.[8] Often this outreach (or leadership) has a double effect. It is first outreach in the sense of intergroup sociality, reciprocity, or solidarity. But it is outreach in a second sense in that an everyday peace stance or speech act can inspire others in the in-group.

It is worth noting that scaling up, in particular, may require some form of political protection. In order for the expansion of everyday peace to be more than simply horizontally expanding micro-activities, individuals and groups of individuals may need protection from political elites. This protection might come in the form of verbal support, directing the security forces to behave in appropriate ways, or erecting legal protections that enable the visibility and expansion of everyday peace. This brings us back to the issue of power and how any scaling up of everyday peace amounts to a political project (inevitably in societies in which politics is contested and sometimes violent). A key issue is the extent to which everyday peace challenges existing structures of interests or can persuade structures and interests to protect and promote everyday peace. In a sense, in order to scale up, everyday peace needs to 'break cover' and move from the margins to the mainstream. Along with protection, this requires leadership—from those everyday peace activists on the margins and from mainstream political leaders who are able to cede space and authority.

The third question occupying this section is how researchers can capture everyday peace given that it is often marginal, hidden, or so embedded in mundane everyday functions that it is difficult to see. Certainly, those engaged in showing sociality, reciprocity, or solidarity to out-group members may wish to conceal their activities from fellow in-group members. They may be seen as being disloyal or traitorous to their own group. Even the physical spaces where a lot of everyday peace activity might take place can be hard to access. Here the epistemological stances and methodological skills offered by sociology, anthropology, feminism, and sociolinguistics come into play. These disciplines promise more people-centric perspectives and are able, if practiced with care, to access the ground level. Aside from the practical challenges, there are ethical concerns,

---

[8] John Paul Lederach, *Building Peace: Sustainable Reconciliation in Divided Societies*. (Washington, D.C.: United States Institute of Peace Press, 1997), p. 40.

too, as ground-level research can be intrusive and, if conducted in insecure environments, can place both the researcher and the researched at risk.

This book has sought to access the everyday through a number of techniques: the EPI project, interview material from Lebanon and Chad, and the memoirs and personal diaries of those involved in war. These techniques are by no means perfect or exhaustive, but they have been able to help us 'get closer' to the everyday and the networks, routines, and spaces in which people enact and embody their everyday lives. What has become clear in writing this book is that no single academic discipline can hold the answer to complex social problems. Many of the examples that run through this book show the intersectionality of lives: they are complex, messy, and networked, with one aspect of life leaching into other aspects of life. This places a responsibility on researchers to step outside of disciplinary silos (easier said than done, given the gatekeeping of journal editors and tenure committees) and investigate the added value to be found at the interstices between disciplines.

The fourth question is concerned with how we can connect the hyperlocal level that has occupied much of this book with other levels of analysis: the municipal, national, international, transnational, and all levels in between. The book adopted a number of ways to seek to transcend the notion of a vertical linearity whereby the local is at the bottom of the pile and other levels are regarded as somehow being above them. Crucial here was the idea of circuits, or an understanding of peace and conflict and all things in between as being part of a system or a series of systems. These assemblages contain multiple actors operating on multiple levels. Importantly, the notion of circuits reminds us of the connectivities between the different actors and levels. More than this, all actors help to construct—consciously or unconsciously—a whole. It is not the case that the national, international, and institutional construct the local. Instead, the local is part of that construction process. The notion of circuits, and especially messy, developing circuits, allows us to think of circuits within circuits and how micro-circuits help constitute much wider circuits and systems.

This book can be seen as a corrective to exclusively top-down commentaries on peace and conflict that might be prone to exaggerating the agency of the national and the international. It is worth reminding ourselves that whatever concept we deploy—community, local, national, and so on—is always going to be an abstraction. Yet in order to communicate, we do have to use a shorthand, albeit one that risks losing accuracy along the way. Terminological issues aside, a core aim of this book has been to take issues of scale seriously. To be an effective intellectual endeavour, the 'local turn' has to do more than merely recognise that agency operates at the substate level. It needs to situate the local within wider levels of analysis in order to ensure a more accurate reading of the multiplicity of factors that construct systems of peace and conflict. It is here that the value of circuitry can be seen and that peace and conflict can be seen as operating in, and constituting, complex adaptive systems that are based on the circulation of people, norms, ideas, legitimacy, and material. What is clear is that peace and conflict constitute complex systems or ecospheres and that as scholars and practitioners, we need to be aware of their multi-scalar nature.

Final Words

The overall tenor of this book has been optimistic. The examples in the book illustrate the ability of so-called ordinary people to engage in activities, stances, and speech acts that can disrupt violent conflict. This is not to underestimate the structural and proximate threats faced by would-be conflict disrupters. Nor is it to overlook the many so-called ordinary people who do not display intergroup sociality, reciprocity, and solidarity. After all, war, division, and exclusion rely on elites and their supporters who prioritise a single identity over views of humanity based on cosmopolitanism and generosity. Despite the significant factors militating against sociality, reciprocity, and solidarity, it is worth maintaining our focus on the potential of so-called ordinary people to take risks, resist the exhortations of those in favour of violence and exclusion, and engage in actions that do not fit the 'script' of their own community. The overall trend in peacebuilding is towards stabilisation and moving away from expensive and long-running peace-support missions. There is little appetite for extensive liberal internationalism, for now, at any rate. As a result, communities often have little choice but to fall back on their own resources and initiatives to make peace. There are obvious risks inherent in national-level peacebuilding, not least a majority imposing its will on a minority and the lack of external oversight in terms of rights or monitoring. But it is not the case that communities are sitting back waiting for international assistance. Individuals and groups in Syria and Yemen have to get on with life now, and so there may be opportunities for intergroup exchange and initiatives. Moreover, it is often the case that actors in a peace process are left to themselves after a peace accord is reached. Peace support cannot go on forever, and so again, individuals and communities have to rely on their own resources and initiatives. It is here that social entrepreneurs, charismatic individuals, and risk-takers might come to the fore, making a 'small peace' through everyday, incremental, and often cautious actions and stances.

Accessing this 'small peace' requires us to step back from many of the traditional vantage points favoured by peace and conflict studies. Instead, everyday peace (or tolerance, coexistence, humanity, etc.) can be found in the everyday activities of people. In this view, *peace* is a verb as well as a condition. It is enacted and embodied through apparently mundane or everyday actions. Rather than something that can be found in the text of a peace accord or through a pact made between political elites, peace in this sense can be found at kitchen tables, in micro-interactions at the counter of the grocery store, and in the staff room in the workplace. In this view, peace becomes a practice and so is closer to the conflict transformation frame than the frames provided by conflict resolution or conflict management. In order to properly 'see' this interactional and embodied type of peace, we need to go beyond the 'security-scapes' provided by many orthodox views of peace and conflict and instead recentre our analyses on people and communities. This means a concentration on interactional and transversal spaces. It does not mean that we approach the everyday or the local in a romanticised way. Instead, it means examining the logics of society and how this manifests itself in everyday tactical agency and the multiple 'moves' that Goffman suggests we engage in to navigate through life.[9] It means noticing the grammar of institutions and communities and how apparently monolithic entities (for example, states or identity groups) often contain diversity, unevenness, and space for dissent.

As argued in this book, the practice of everyday peace is often context-dependent and is not always consistent. It encourages us to think of peace in terms of people. Individuals and their personalities do matter. Institutions matter, too. This does not only apply to the formal institutions of the state or religious organisations that may be able to provide security or public goods such as education or healthcare. It also applies to the institutions forged by people in their everyday interactions. This social infrastructure seems crucial to the notion and practice of everyday peace. It is not necessarily the civil society of civil society organisations. It is the civil society of societal culture and the extent of networks that cross the intergroup boundaries in that society. Here it is worth mentioning reciprocity. Holding a door open for someone else is not just about hoping that the recipient of your generosity will hold a door open for you on another occasion. It is about making a statement on the type of society you would like to live in.[10] Thus, sociality, reciprocity, and solidarity are larger than individual actions and stances. They are statements about, and contributions to, a hope for a generalised civility. In a deeply divided and conflict-affected society, these small-scale and highly localised (indeed, individualised) everyday actions can matter. They can attain a significance that goes beyond the particular action.

It is worth closing on the issue of power and how many orthodox treatments of peace and conflict concentrate on rather obvious types of power, perhaps linked to the ballot box or military organisations. Those types of power are not to be underestimated. Yet they operate alongside less visible and difficult-to-quantify

---

[9] Goffman, *The Presentation of the Self*.
[10] Simon Rabinovitch, 'What Is Wrong with Tolerance', *Aeon*, 18 June 2018, https://aeon.co/essays/reciprocity-not-tolerance-is-the-basis-of-healthy-societies.

types of power. These types of power are crucial to conflict disruption and everyday or hyperlocal peace. They often rely on the character of an individual or the discourses within a family. As we have seen in previous chapters, everyday peace often takes the form of a mode of thinking as well as manifesting itself in actions or speech acts. It often takes the form of a stance, or the orientation of the individual or group of individuals. The notion of stance has been underexplored in peace and conflict studies (though not elsewhere). The stances taken by an individual might not be consistent, and they are difficult to gauge. They may be a spontaneous moral reaction or part of a long-term stance. They can be purposively hidden or be part of a strategy of dissembling. In order to adopt or maintain a particular stance in a conflict-affected context, an individual or group may have to mobilise and exercise power. This power is likely to be of a very different order from the power that states, militaries, and other institutionalised actors can mobilise. Potentially, that is what makes it transgressive and disruptive to conflict systems that have normalised exclusion and violent conflict. According to circumstances, this everyday peace power (EPP) can manifest itself in spaces that lie outside regular surveillance, and it can construct spaces that allow for alternative actions and logics. It can create a communitas and a socio-material set of stances and relationships that might not always be visible to outsiders and those within a framework of formal institutions. This book recommends EPP and the disruptive potential of so-called ordinary people as areas for renewed research efforts. The 'peace-scapes' that we might find at the everyday and hyperlocal levels might seem far removed from the 'peace' of peace accords and declarations by political leaders, but they are part of the same multi-scalar peace system.

Bibliography

Abdallah, Stéphanie Latte, and Cédric Parizot, eds. *Israelis and Palestinians in the Shadows of the Wall: Spaces of Separation and Occupation*. Farnham, UK: Ashgate, 2015.

Acosta, Luis Jaime. 'Murder of Hundreds of Colombian Peace Activists Casts Shadow over Peace Process'. *Reuters*, 23 August 2019. https://www.reuters.com/article/us-colombia-peace-feature/murder-of-hundreds-of-colombian-activists-casts-shadow-over-peace-process-idUSKCN1VF0IK.

Adams, Dean. 'How a Rapper Set Up No Shoot Zones to Stop Baltimore's Bloodshed'. *Al Jazeera*, 11 October 2018. https://www.aljazeera.com/indepth/features/rapper-set-shoot-zones-stop-baltimore-bloodshed-181001072850663.html.

Adams, Iain. 'A Game for Christmas? The Argylls, Saxons and Football on the Western Front, December 1914'. *International Journal of the History of Sport* 32, nos. 11–12 (2015): 1395–1415.

'Afghanistan's Ghani Declares Eid Ceasefire with Taliban'. *Al Jazeera*, 19 August 2018. https://www.aljazeera.com/news/2018/08/afghanistan-ghani-declares-eid-ceasefire-taliban-180819143135061.html.

Aggestam, Karin, Fabio Cristiano, and Lisa Strömbom. '"Towards Agonistic Peacebuilding: Exploring the Antagonism-Agonism Nexus in the Middle East Peace Process'. *Third World Quarterly* 36, no. 9 (2015): 1736–1753.

Åhäll, Linda. 'Affect as Methodology: Feminism and the Politics of Emotion'. *International Political Sociology* 12, no. 1 (2018): 36–52.

Åhäll, Linda. 'Confusion, Fear, Disgust: Emotional Communication in Representations of Female Agency in Political Violence'. In *Gender, Agency and Political Violence*, edited by Linda Åhäll and Laura J. Shepherd, 169–183. Basingstoke, UK: Palgrave, 2012.

Åhäll, Linda. 'The Dance of Militarisation: A Feminist Security Studies Take on "the Political"'. *Critical Studies on Security* 4, no. 2 (2016): 154–168.

Åhäll, Linda, and Thomas Gregory. *Emotions, Politics and War*. London: Routledge, 2015.

Ahmadi, Belquis, and Sadaf Lakhani. 'Afghan Women and Violent Extremism: Colluding, Perpetrating, or Preventing?' USIP Special Report 396. Washington, DC, 2016.

Åkebo, Malin. *The Politics of Ceasefires: On Ceasefire Agreements and Peace Processes in Aceh and Sri Lanka*. Umeå, Sweden: Umeå University Department of Political Science, 2013.

Alexander, Christine, and Mason Kunz, eds. *Eastern Inferno: The Journals of a German Panzerjager on the Eastern Front 1941–1943*. Philadelphia: Casemate, 2010.

Alexander, Jeffrey C. 'Frontlash/Backlash: The Crisis of Solidarity and the Threat to Civil Institutions'. *Contemporary Sociology* 48, no. 1 (2019): 5–11.

Alexander, Jeffrey C. 'The Societalization of Social Problems: Church Pedophilia, Phone Hacking, and the Financial Crisis'. *American Sociological Review* 83, no. 6 (2018): 1049–1078.

Alexievich, Svetlana. *The Unwomanly Face of War*. London: Penguin, 2017.

Alfred, Taiaiake. *Peace, Power and Righteousness: An Indigenous Manifesto*. Don Mills, ON: Oxford University Press, 1999.

Al-Ghanim, Kaltham A., and Abdallah M. Badahdah. 'Gender Roles in the Arab World: Development and Psychometric Properties of the Arab Adolescents Gender Roles Attitude Scale'. *Sex Roles* 77 (2017): 169–177.
Al Qurtuby, Sumanto. *Religious Violence and Conciliation in Indonesia: Christians and Muslims in the Moluccas*. London: Routledge, 2011.
Amin, Ash. 'Ethnicity and the Multicultural City: Living with Diversity'. *Environment and Planning A* 34 (2002): 959–980.
Amoore, Louise. 'Algorithmic War: Everyday Geographies of the War on Terror'. *Antipode* 41, no. 1 (2009): 49–69.
Anderson, Gordon L. 'The Elusive Definition of Peace'. *International Journal on World Peace* 2, no. 3 (1985): 101–104.
Anderson, Royce. 'A Definition of Peace'. *Peace and Conflict* 10, no. 2 (2004): 101–116.
André, Kevin, and Anne-Claire Pache. 'From Caring Entrepreneur to Caring Enterprise: Addressing the Ethical Challenges of Scaling Up Social Enterprises'. *Journal of Business Ethics* 133 (2016): 659–675.
Ansborg, Nadine. 'How Does Militant Violence Diffuse in Regions? Regional Conflict Systems in International Relations and Peace and Conflict Studies'. *International Journal of Conflict and Violence* 5, no. 1 (2011): 174–187.
Appiah-Mensah, Seth. 'The African Mission in Sudan: Darfur Dilemmas'. *African Security Studies* 15, no. 1 (2006): 1–19.
Arenas, Ivan. 'Assembling the Multitude: Material Geographies of Social Movements from Oaxaca to Occupy'. *Environment and Planning D: Society and Space* 32 (2014): 433–449.
Arnd-Linder, Sarah, Ayelet Harel-Shalev, and Shir Daphna-Tekoah. 'The Political Is Personal—Everyday Lives of Women in Israel'. *Women's Studies International Forum* 69 (2018): 76–84.
Ashworth, A. E. 'The Sociology of Trench Warfare 1914–18'. *British Journal of Sociology* 19, no. 4 (1968): 407–423.
Autesserre, Séverine. *Peaceland: Conflict Resolution and the Everyday Politics of International Intervention*. Cambridge: Cambridge University Press, 2014.
Baaz, Maria Eriksson, and Maria Stern. *The Complexity of Violence: A Critical Analysis of Sexual Violence in the Democratic Republic of Congo (DRC)*. Stockholm: SIDA Working Paper, 2010.
Babchenko, Arkady. *One Soldier's War in Chechnya*. London: Portobello, 2008.
Bachmann, K. M. *The Prey of an Eagle: A Personal Record of Family Life Written throughout the German Occupation of Guernsey 1940–45*. St. Peter Port, UK: Guernsey Press, 1972.
Baker, Joanne. 'Young Mothers in Late Modernity: Sacrifice, Respectability and the Transformative Neo-liberal Subject'. *Journal of Youth Studies* 12, no. 3 (2009): 275–288.
Balaam, A. J. *Bush War Operator: Memoirs of the Rhodesian Light Infantry, Selous Scouts and Beyond*. Solihull, UK: Helion, 2014.
Baranova, Olga. 'Nationalism, Anti-Bolshevism or the Will to Survive: Collaboration in Belarus under the Nazi Occupation of 1941–1944'. *European Review of History* 15, no. 2 (2008): 113–128.
Barkawi, Tarak. 'Culture and Combat in the Colonies: The Indian Army in the Second World War'. *Journal of Contemporary History* 41, no. 2 (2006): 325–355.
Barkawi, Tarak. *Soldiers of Empire: Indian and British Armies in World War Two*. Cambridge: Cambridge University Press, 2017.
Barkawi, Tarak, and Keith Stanski, eds. *Orientalism and War*. London: Hurst, 2012.

Barker, Memphis, and Sami Yousafzai. 'Isis Claims Deadly Suicide Bombings as Afghans Celebrate Taliban Ceasefire'. *Guardian*, 16 June 2018. https://www.theguardian.com/world/2018/jun/16/isis-claims-deadly-suicide-bombing-as-afghans-celebrate-taliban-ceasefire.

Barthas, Louis. *Poilu: The World War I Notebooks of Corporal Louis Barthas, Barrelmaker 1914–1918*. New Haven, CT: Yale University Press, 2014.

Bartmann, Erwin. *Für Volk and Führer: The Memoir of a Veteran of the 1st SS Panzer Division Leibstand SS Adolf Hitler*. Solihull, UK: Helion, 2013.

Baxter, Archibald. *We Will Not Cease*. Christchurch, New Zealand: Caxton, 1968.

Beattie, Peter. 'The Road to Psychopathy: Neoliberalism and the Human Mind'. *Journal of Social Issues* 75, no. 1 (2019): 89–112.

Beeson, Mark. 'Geopolitics and the Making of Regions: The Fall and Rise of East Asia'. *Political Studies* 57, no. 3 (2009): 498–517.

'Belfast City Hall Opens Its Doors after "Goth Invasion"'. *BBC Newsbeat*, 23 July 2015. http://www.bbc.co.uk/newsbeat/article/33626947/belfast-city-hall-opens-its-doors-after-goth-invasion.

Bell, Christine. 'Text and Context: Evaluating Peace Agreements for Their "Gender perspective"'. UN Women, 2015. http://www.unwomen.org/-/media/headquarters/attachments/sections/library/publications/2017/textandcontext-evaluating-peace-agreements-en.pdf?la=en&vs=2652.

Bellamy, Bill. *Troop Leader: A Tank Commander's Story*. Stroud, UK: Sutton, 2005.

Belloni, Roberto. 'Shades of Orange and Green: Civil Society and the Peace Process in Northern Ireland'. In *Social Capital and Peace-Building: Creating and Resolving Conflict with Trust and Social Networks*, edited by Michaelene Cox, 5–21. London: Routledge, 2009.

Benard, Stephen. 'Cohesion from Conflict: Does Intergroup Conflict Motivate Intragroup Norm Enforcement and Support for Centralized Leadership?' *Social Psychology Quarterly* 75, no. 2 (2012): 107–130.

Bentham, Jenny. *Peacemaking in the Middle Ages: Principles and Practice*. Manchester, UK: Manchester University Press, 2011.

Berents, Helen, and Siobhan McEvoy-Levy. 'Theorising Youth and Everyday Peace (Building)'. *Peacebuilding* 3, no. 2 (2015): 115–125.

Bhattacharya, Joyati. 'Gender, Peacemaking and the Case of Northeast India'. *Indian Journal of Political Science* 71, no. 1 (2010): 233–239.

Bielenberg, Christabel. *The Past Is My Life*. London: Chatto and Windus, 1968.

Billig, Michael. *Banal Nationalism*. Thousand Oaks, CA: Sage, 1995.

Bin Ali, Mohamed, and Sabariah Mohamed Hussin. 'Countering Violent Extremism: Role of Women and Family'. *RSIS Commentary* 179, 28 September 2017.

Binswanger, Hans P., and Swaminathan S. Aiyar. 'Scaling Up Community Driven Development: Theoretical Underpinnings and Programme Design Implications.' *World Bank Policy Research Working Paper* 3039 (May 2003).

Bishop, Alan, and Mark Bostridge, eds. *Letters from a Lost Generation: First World War Letters of Vera Brittain and Four Friends*. London: Little, Brown, 1998.

Bissell, David. 'Passenger Mobilities: Affective Atmospheres and the Sociality of Public Transport'. *Environment and Planning D: Society and Space* 28 (2010): 270–289.

Bjarnegård, Elin, and Erik Melander. 'Disentangling Gender, Peace and Democratization: The Negative Effects of Militarized Masculinity'. *Journal of Gender Studies* 20, no. 2 (2011): 139–154.

Björkdahl, Annika, Martin Hall, and Ted Svensson. 'Everyday International Relations: Editors' Introduction'. *Cooperation and Conflict* 54, no. 2 (2019): 123–130.

Blackburn, George C. *The Guns of War*. London: Robinson, 2000.

Blakemore, Erin. 'The Secret Student Group That Stood Up to the Nazis'. *Smithsonian Magazine*, 22 February 2017. https://www.smithsonianmag.com/smart-news/the-secret-student-group-stood-up-nazis-180962250/.

Blum, Matthias. 'War, Food Rationing, and Socioeconomic Inequality in Germany during the First World War'. *Economic History Review* 66, no. 4 (2013): 1063–1083.

Boggero, Marco. 'Darfur and Chad: A Fragmented Ethnic Mosaic'. *Journal of Contemporary African Studies* 27, no. 1 (2009): 21–35.

Boesten, Jelke, and Marsha Henry. 'Between Fatigue and Silence: The Challenge of Conducting Research on Sexual Violence in Conflict'. *Social Politics: International Studies in Gender, State and Society* 25, no. 4 (2018): 586–588.

Borderlines Project. *Borderlines: Personal Stories and Experiences from the Border Counties*. N.p.: Borderlines, 2006.

Borger, Julian. 'US Deploys Aircraft Carrier and Bombers after "Credible Threat" from Iran'. *Guardian*, 6 May 2019. https://www.theguardian.com/world/2019/may/06/us-deploys-aircraft-carrier-and-bombers-after-troubling-indications-from-iran.

Borgerson, Janet, and Daniel Miller. 'Scalable Sociality and "How the World Changed Social Media": Conversation with Daniel Miller'. *Consumption Markets & Culture* 19, no. 6 (2016), 520–533.

Boscawen, Robert. *Armoured Guardsmen: A War Diary June 1944–April 1945*. Barnsley, UK: Leo Cooper, 2001.

Bosi, Lorenzo. 'Explaining the Emergence Process of the Civil Rights Protest in Northern Ireland (1945–1968): Insights from a Relational Social Movement Approach 1'. *Journal of Historical Sociology* 21, nos. 2–3 (2008): 242–271.

Böttger, Arnim. *To the Gate of Hell: The Memoir of a Panzer Crewman*. Barnsley, UK: Frontline, 2012.

Boulding, Kenneth E. *Three Faces of Power*. London: Sage, 1990.

Bourdieu, Pierre. *Distinction: A Social Critique of the Judgement of Taste*. London: Routledge, 1984.

Bourdieu, Pierre. 'The Essence of Neoliberalism'. *Le Monde Diplomatique*, December 1998. https://mondediplo.com/1998/12/08bourdieu.

Brenner, David. 'Ashes of Co-optation: From Armed Group Fragmentation to the Rebuilding of Popular Insurgency in Myanmar'. *Conflict, Security & Development* 15, no. 4 (2015), 337–358.

Brett, Roddy. *The Origins and Dynamics of Genocide: Political Violence in Guatemala*. Basingstoke, UK: Palgrave Macmillan, 2016.

Brett-James, Antony. 'Ball of Fire: The Fifth Indian Division in the Second World War'. Wikia.org, 1951. https://military.wikia.org/wiki/Battle_of_the_Admin_Box.

Brewer, John. *Peace Processes: A Sociological Approach*. Cambridge: Polity, 2010.

Brewer, John D., 'Towards a Sociology of Compromise'. In *The Sociology of Compromise after Conflict*, edited by John D. Brewer, 1–29. Basingstoke, UK: Palgrave Macmillan, 2018.

Brewer, John D., Bernadette C. Hayes, Francis Teeney, Katrin Dudgeon, Natascha Mueller-Hirth, and Shirley Lal Wijesinghe. *The Sociology of Everyday Life Peacebuilding*. Basingstoke, UK: Palgrave Macmillan, 2018.

Brigg, Morgan. 'Relational and Essential: Theorizing Difference for Peacebuilding'. *Journal of Intervention and Statebuilding* 12, no. 3 (2018): 352–366.

Brittain, Vera. *Testament of Youth: An Autobiographical Study of the Years 1900–1925*. London: Fontana, 1979.

Brooke, Erika J., and Jacinta M. Gau, 'Military Service and Lifetime Arrests: Examining the Effects of the Total Military Experience on Arrests in a Sample of Prison Inmates'. *Criminal Justice Policy Review* 29, no. 1 (2015): 24–44.

Broome, Frank. *Dead before Dawn: A Heavy Bomber Tail-Gunner in World War II*. Kindle ed. Barnsley, UK: Pen and Sword, 2012.

Brown, Michael E. 'The Causes and Implications of International Conflict'. In *Ethnic Conflict and International Security*, edited by Michael E. Brown, 3–26. Princeton, NJ: Princeton University Press, 1993.

Bruce, Steve. *Paisley: Religion and Politics in Northern Ireland*. Oxford: Oxford University Press, 2007.

Brune, Peter. *Descent into Hell: The Fall of Singapore—Pudu and Changi—the Thai-Burma Railway*. London: Allen & Unwin, 2014.

Bruni, Luigino. 'The Happiness of Sociality. Economics and Eudaimonia: A Necessary Encounter'. *Rationality and Society* 22, no. 4 (2010): 383–406.

Burleson, Cindy. 'The Ancient Olympic Truce in Modern Day Peacekeeping: Revisiting Ekecheiria'. *Sport in Society* 15, no. 6 (2012): 798–813.

Callahan, Kevin J. 'The International Socialist Peace Movement on the Eve of WWI Revisited: The Campaign of "War against War" and the Basle International Socialist Congress in 1912'. *Peace and Change* 29, no. 2 (2004): 147–176.

Cammett, Melani. 'Sectarianism and the Ambiguities of Welfare in Lebanon'. *Current Anthropology* 56, S11 (2015): S76–S87.

Cantora, Andrea, Seema Iyer, and Lauren Restivo. 'Understanding Drivers of Crime in East Baltimore: Resident Perceptions of Why Crime Persists'. *American Journal of Criminal Justice* 41, no. 4 (2016): 686–709.

Capasso, Matteo. 'Sketches of the Everyday'. *Middle East Critique* 27, no. 3 (2018): 221–229.

Capdevila, Luc, and Daniele Voldman, *War Dead: Western Societies and the Casualties of War*. Edinburgh: Edinburgh University Press, 2006.

Carius, Otto. *Tigers in the Mud: The Combat Career of German Panzer Commander Otto Carius*. Kindle ed. Mechanicsburg, VA: Stackpole, 2003.

Carreiras, Helena. 'Gendered Culture in Peacekeeping Operations'. *International Peacekeeping* 17, no. 4 (2010): 471–485.

Casey, Nicholas. 'Peacetime Spells Death for Colombia's Activists." *New York Times*, 13 October 2018.

Chabal, Patrick. *The End of Conceit: Western Rationality after Postcolonialism*. London: Zed, 2012.

Chandler, David. 'The Limits of Peacebuilding: International Regulation and Civil Society Development in Bosnia'. *International Peacekeeping* 6, no. 1 (1999): 109–125.

Chandrasekaran, Rajiv. *Imperial Life in the Emerald City: Inside Baghdad's Green Zone*. London: Bloomsbury, 2007.

Chang, Xiangqun. 'Recipropriety (lishang-wanglai): A Chinese Model of Social Relationships and Reciprocity—State and Villagers' Interaction 1936-2014'. *Journal of Sociology* 52, no. 1 (2016): 103–117.

Chinn, Peggy L., and Adeline Falk-Rafael. 'Peace and Power: A Theory of Emancipatory Group Process'. *Journal of Nursing Scholarship* 47, no. 1 (2015): 62–69.

Chiu, Yvonne. 'Conspiring with the Enemy and Cooperating in Warfare: "Live and Let Live" as a Representative Element of War'. Institute for Advanced Study, 2014. https://www.ias.edu/ideas/2014/chiu-war.

Christiansen, Lene Bull. 'Versions of Violence: Zimbabwe's Domestic Violence Law and Symbolic Politics of Protection'. *Review of African Political Economy* 37, no. 126 (2010): 421–435.

Chulov, Martin, and Kareem Shaheen. 'Fighting Resumes in Eastern Ghouta Despite "Humanitarian pause"'. *Guardian*, 27 February 2018. https://www.theguardian.com/world/2018/feb/27/russia-humanitarian-pause-eastern-ghouta-syria-enclave.

Clampin, David. *Advertising and Propaganda in WWII: Cultural Identity and the Blitz Spirit*. London: I.B. Tauris, 2014.

Clarke, Liam. 'Moderates Playing Hardball to Stop Chuckle Brothers' Fun'. *Sunday Times*, 9 December 2007.

Clarke, Liam, and Kathryn Johnston. *Martin McGuinness: From Guns to Government*. Edinburgh: Mainstream, 2001.

Cockburn, Cynthia. 'When Is Peace? Women's Post-Accord Experiences in Three Countries'. *Soundings* 53 (2013): 143–160.

Cockett, Olivia. *Love and War in London*. Stroud, UK: History Press, 2008.

Coker, Christopher. *The Warrior Ethos: Military Culture and the War on Terror*. London: Routledge, 2007.

Collins, Patricia Hill, and Sirma Bilge. *Intersectionality*. Cambridge: Polity, 2016.

Collins-Dogrul, Julie. 'Tertius Iungens Brokerage and Transnational Intersectoral Cooperation'. *Organization Studies* 33, no. 8 (2012): 989–1014.

Connolly, Kevin. 'The Friendship That Grew out of War'. *BBC News*, 27 September 2015. https://www.bbc.co.uk/news/magazine-34346621.

Cooley, Alexander. *Logics of Hierarchy: The Organization of Empires, States and Military Occupations*. Ithaca, NY: Cornell University Press, 2005.

Coppard, George. *With a Machine Gun to Cambrai: A Story of the First World War*. London: Cassel, 1999.

Corns, Cathryn, and John Hughes-Wilson. *Blindfold and Alone: British Military Executions in the Great War*. London: Cassell, 2005.

Cortland, Clarissa I., Maureen A. Craig, Jenessa R. Shapiro, Jennifer A. Richeson, Rebecca Neel, Noah J. Goldstein, and Kerry Kawakami. 'Solidarity through Shared Disadvantage: Highlighting Shared Experiences of Discrimination Improves Relations between Stigmatized Groups'. *Journal of Personality and Social Psychology* 113, no. 4 (2017): 547–567.

Cottrell, Fred. 'Men Cry Peace'. In *Research for Peace*, 99–164. Oslo: Institute for Social Research, 1954.

Council on Foreign Relations. 'Women's Participation in Peace Processes', 31 July 2018. https://www.cfr.org/interactive/womens-participation-in-peace-processes/explore-the-data.

Cox, Joseph M. 'Negotiating Justice: Ceasefires, Peace Agreements, and Post-Conflict Justice'. *Journal of Peace Research* 57, no. 3 (2020): 466–481.

Cox, Robert W. 'Social Forces, States and World Orders: Beyond IR Theory'. *Millennium* 10, no. 2 (1981): 126–155.

Cozzolino, Alessio, Gianmario Verona, and Frank T. Rothaermel. 'Unpacking the Disruption Process: New Technology, Business Models, and Incumbent Adaptation'. *Journal of Management Studies* 55, no. 7 (2018): 1166–1202.

Crager, Kelly E. *Hell under the Rising Sun: Texan POWs and the Building of the Burma-Thailand Railway*. College Station: Texas A&M University Press, 2008.

Cragin, Kim, Melissa A. Bradley, Eric Robinson, and Paul S. Steinberg. 'What Factors Cause Youth to Reject Violent Extremism? Results of an Exploratory Analysis in the West Bank'. RAND, 2015. https://www.rand.org/pubs/research_reports/RR1118.html.

Cramer, Judd, and Alan B. Krueger. 'Disruptive Change in the Taxi Business: The Case of Uber'. *American Economic Review* 106, no. 5 (2016): 177–182.

Crocker, Chester H., Fen Osler Hampson, and Pamela Aall, eds. *Herding Cats: Multiparty Mediation in a Complex World*. Washington, DC: United States Institute of Peace Press, 1999.

Croft, Stuart. 'Constructing Ontological Insecurity: The Insecuritisation of Britain's Muslims'. *Contemporary Security Policy* 33, no. 2 (2012): 219–235.

Crotty, Patrick. 'The Context of Heaney's Reception'. In *The Cambridge Companion to Seamus Heaney*, edited by Bernard O'Donoghue, 37–55. Cambridge: Cambridge University Press, 2009.

Crowe, David, M. 'War Crimes and Genocide in History, and the Evolution of Responsive International Law'. *Nationalities Papers* 37, no. 6 (2009): 757–806.

Cudworth, Ericka, and Stephen Hobden. 'Anarchy and Anarchism: Towards a Theory of Complex International Systems'. *Millennium* 39, no. 2 (2010): 399–416.

Currier, Joseph M., Jason M. Holland, and Jesse Malott. 'Moral Injury, Meaning Making and Mental Health in Returning Victims'. *Journal of Clinical Psychology* 71, no. 3 (2014): 229–246.

Dalum, Bent, Christian Ø. R. Pedersen, and Gert Villumsen. 'Technological Life-Cycles: Lessons from Cluster Facing Disruption'. *European Urban and Regional Studies* 12, no. 3 (2005): 229–246.

Damousi, Joy. 'Private Loss, Public Mourning: Motherhood, Memory and Grief in Australia during the Inter-War Years'. *Women's History Review* 8, no. 2 (1999): 365–378.

Danchev, Alex, and Daniel Todman, eds. *War Diaries 1939–1945: Field Marshal Lord Alanbrooke*. London: Phoenix, 2002.

Daragahi, Borzou. 'Clashes between Rival Sudan Armed Forces Risk "Civil War", Protesters Warn'. *Independent*, 10 April 2019. https://www.independent.co.uk/news/world/africa/sudan-civil-war-omar-al-bashir-khartoum-bouteflika-a8863881.html.

Darby, John, and Roger Mac Ginty, eds. *Contemporary Peacemaking: Conflict, Violence and Peace Processes*. Basingstoke, UK: Palgrave, 2003.

Darby, John, and Roger Mac Ginty, eds. *The Management of Peace Processes*. Basingstoke, UK: Macmillan, 2000.

Das, Veena, ed. *Violence and Subjectivity*. Berkeley: University of California Press, 2000.

Davey, Ray. *The War Diaries: From Prisoner of War to Peacemaker*. Belfast: Brehon, 2015.

David, Anthony. *An Improbable Friendship: The Remarkable Lives of Israeli Ruth Dayan and Palestinian Raymonda Tawil and Their Forty-Year Peace Mission*. New York: Arcade, 2015.

Davis, K. D. 'The Neural Circuitry of Pain as Explored with Functional MRI'. *Neurological Research* 22, no. 3 (2000): 313–317.

Dawson, Jeff. 'Builder of Bridges: The Moving True Story of a British POW on the Death Railway Who Forgave His Torturer Is Now a Film'. *Sunday Times*, 22 December 2013, 14.

Dayan, Moshe. *Story of My Life*. London: Weidenfeld & Nicolson, 1976.

D'Costa, Bina. 'Once Were Warriors: The Militarized State in Narrating the Past'. *South Asian History and Culture* 5, no. 4 (2014): 457–474.

De Certeau, Michael. *The Practice of Everyday Life*. Berkeley: University of California Press, 1984.

De Coning, Cedric. 'Complexity Thinking and Adaptive Peacebuilding'. *Accord*, no. 28 (2019). https://www.c-r.org/accord/inclusion-peace-processes/complexity-thinking-and-adaptive-peacebuilding.

De Coning, Cedric. 'From Peacebuilding to Sustaining Peace: Implications of Complexity for Resilience and Sustainability'. *Resilience* 4, no. 3 (2016): 166–181.

De Fazio, Gianluca. 'Civil Rights Mobilisation and Repression in Northern Ireland: A Comparison with the US Deep South'. *The Sixties* 2, no. 2 (2009): 163–185.

Defonseca, Misha. *Misha: A Memoire of the Holocaust Years*. Boston: Mount Ivy, 1997.

Dekel, Rachel, and Dan Solomon. 'The Contribution of Maternal Care and Control to Adolescents' Adjustment following War'. *Journal of Early Adolescence* 36, no. 2 (2016): 198–221.

Demetriou, Olga. 'Counter-conduct and the Everyday: Anthropological Engagements with Philosophy'. *Global Security* 30, no. 2 (2016): 218–237.

Denov, Myriam, and Atim Angela Lakor. 'When War Is Better Than Peace: The Post-Conflict Realities of Children Born of Wartime Rape in Northern Uganda'. *Child Abuse & Neglect* 65 (2017): 255–265.

Department of Education (Northern Ireland). 'Integrated Schools'. https://www.education-ni.gov.uk/articles/integrated-schools.

Dichter, Melissa E., and Steven C. Marcus. 'Intimate Partner Violence Victimization among Women Veterans: Health, Health Care Service Use, and Opportunities for Intervention'. *Military Behavioral Health* 1, no. 2 (2013): 107–113.

'Disrupting Mr Disrupter'. *Economist*, 26 November 2015. https://www.economist.com/business/2015/11/26/disrupting-mr-disrupter.

Donati, Pierpaolo, and Margaret S. Archer. *The Relational Subject*. Cambridge: Cambridge University Press, 2015.

Donovan, Paula. 'JISB Interview: Immunity, Sexual Scandals and Peacekeeping'. *Journal of Intervention and Statebuilding* 9, no. 3 (2015): 408–417.

Dorner, Lisa M. 'The Life Course and Sense-Making: Immigrant Families' Journeys toward Understanding Educational Policies and Choosing Bilingual Programs'. *American Educational Research Journal* 49, no. 3 (2012): 461–486.

Douncher, David. 'The Just War Tradition and Its Modern Legacy: Jus as Bellum and Jus in Bello'. *European Journal of Political Theory* 11, no. 2 (2012): 92–111.

Downham, Peter, and Edward Roe, *Diary of an Old Contemptible: From Mons to Baghdad 1914–1919*. Kindle ed. Barnsley, UK: Pen and Sword, 2015.

Downing, David. *Leading Lives: Yasser Arafat*. London: Heinemann, 2012.

Downing, W. H. *To the Last Ridge: The World War One Experiences of W H Downing*. London: Grub Street, 2005.

Duek, Nechama. 'Dayan's Widow, Arafat's Mother-in-Law Talk Peace'. *Ynetnews*, 22 October 2017. https://www.ynetnews.com/articles/0,7340,L-5032028,00.html.

Duffett, Rachel. 'A Taste of Army Life'. *Cultural and Social History* 9, no. 2 (2012): 251–269.

Dugan, Maire A. 'A Nested Theory of Conflict'. *A Leadership Journal: Women in Leadership* 1: 9–20.

Duneier, Mitchell, and Les Back. 'Voices from the Sidewalk: Ethnography and Writing Race'. *Ethnic and Racial Studies* 29, no. 3 (2006): 548–549.

Dunn, J. C. *The War the Infantry Knew 1914–1919*. London: Abacus, 2003.
Dupuis, Ann, and David C. Thorns. 'Home, Home Ownership and the Search for Ontological Security'. *Sociological Review* 46, no. 1 (1998): 24–47.
Edmond, Rod. '"It's Your Submission We Want Baxter!" We Will Not Cease: The Autobiography of a Conscientious Objector'. *Journal of New Zealand Literature* 33, no. 2 (2015): 142–159.
Edwards, Ruth Dudley. 'Martin McGuinness'. *Spectator* 278, no. 8807 (1997): 22.
Egerton, David. *Britain's War Machine: Weapons, Resources and Experts in the Second World War*. London: Penguin, 2012.
Eisikovits, Nir. *A Theory of Truces*. Houndmills, UK: Palgrave, 2016.
Eklund, Lisa, and Navtej Purewal. 'The Bio-Politics of Population Control and Sex-Selective Abortion in China and India.' *Feminism & Psychology* 27, no. 1 (2017): 34–55.
Elish, M. C. 'Remote Split: A History of US Drone Operations and the Distributed Labor of War'. *Science, Technology and Human Values* 42, no. 6 (2017): 1100–1131.
Ellis, Ray. *Once a Hussar: A Memoir of Battle, Capture and Escape in the Second World War*. Kindle ed. Barnsley, UK: Pen and Sword, 2013.
Elshtain, Jean Bethke. 'Women, the State, and War'. *International Relations* 23, no. 2 (2009): 289–303.
Enloe, Cynthia. *Bananas, Beaches and Bases: Making Feminist Sense of International Politics*. Berkeley: University of California Press, 1990.
Ereira, Alan. *The Invergordon Mutiny*. London: Routledge & Kegan Paul, 1981.
'Eric Lomax: Tortured PoW Who Confronted His Japanese Nemesis—but Chose Reconciliation over Retribution'. *Daily Telegraph*, 10 October 2012.
Evans, Matt, and Selcan M. Kaynak. 'Media Framing in Religious and Secular Conflict in Turkey and Israel'. *International Political Science Review* 36, no. 2 (2015): 139–152.
Evatt, Herbert V. 'Risks of a Big-Power Peace'. *Foreign Affairs* 24 (1946): 195–209.
Everett. Joyce E., J. Camille Hall, and Johnnie Hamilton-Mason. 'Everyday Conflict and Daily Stressors: Coping Responses of Black Women'. *Affilia: Journal of Women and Social Work* 25, no. 1 (2010): 30–42.
Everyday Peace Indicators. 'About'. https://everydaypeaceindicators.org/about/.
Fagan, Kristina. 'Aboriginal Nationalism in Taiaiake Alfred's *Peace, Power and Righteousness: An Indigenous Manifesto*'. *American Indian Quarterly* 28, nos. 1–2 (2004): 12–29.
Farrell, J. G. *The Singapore Grip*. London: Weidenfeld & Nicolson, 1978.
Farrell, Michael. *Northern Ireland: The Orange State*. London: Pluto, 1976.
Fassin, Didier. *Enforcing Order: An Ethnography of Urban Policing*. Cambridge: Polity, 2011.
Feldman, S. Shirley, and Daniel A. Weinberger. 'Restraint as a Mediator of Family Influences on Boys' Delinquent Behaviour: A Longitudinal Study'. *Child Development* 65, no. 1 (1994): 195–211.
Fennell, Desmond. *Whatever You Say, Say Nothing: Why Seamus Heaney Is No. 1*. Dublin: ELO, 1991.
Ferrer, Marlen. 'State Formation and Courtly Culture in the Scandinavian Kingdoms in the High Middle Ages'. *Scandinavian Journal of History* 37, no. 1 (2012): 1–22.
Fielding-Smith, Abigail, Payenda Sargand, and Jack Serle. 'The Anatomy of an American Airstrike'. *Newsweek*, 18 February 2016. https://www.newsweek.com/anatomy-american-air-strike-afghanistan-drones-united-nations-nato-427918.
Filar, Ray. 'Why I'm an Anti-Zionist Jew'. *OpenDemocracy*, 16 April 2016. https://www.opendemocracy.net/transformation/ray-filar/why-i-am-antizionist-jew.

Firchow, Pamina, and Roger Mac Ginty. 'Including Hard-to-Access Populations Using Mobile Phone Surveys and Participatory Indicators'. *Sociological Methods and Review* 49, no. 1 (2020): 133–160.

Firchow, Pamina, and Roger Mac Ginty. 'Indivisibility as a Way of Life: Transformation in Micro-Processes of Peace in Northern Uganda." In *From Transitional to Transformative Justice*, edited by Paul Gready and Simon Robbins, 261–280. Cambridge: Cambridge University Press, 2019.

Fisk, Robert. *Pity the Nation: Lebanon at War*. Oxford: Oxford University Press, 1990.

Fjelde, Hanne, and Desirée Nilsson. 'The Rise of Rebel Contenders: Barriers to Entry and Fragmentation in Civil Wars'. *Journal of Peace Research* 55, no. 5 (2018): 551–565.

Fluri, Jennifer L., and Amy Piedalue. 'Embodying Violence: Critical Geographies of Gender, Race, and Culture'. *Gender, Place & Culture* 24, no. 4 (2017): 534–544.

Foot, William Whyte. *Street Corner Society: The Social Structure of an Italian Slum*. 4th ed. Chicago: University of Chicago Press, 1993.

Francis, Diana. *People, Peace and Power: Conflict Transformation in Action*. London: Pluto, 2002.

Fraser, George MacDonald. *Quartered Safe Out Here: A Recollection of the War in Burma*. London: HarperCollins, 2000.

Fraser, Giles. 'Against the War: The Movement That Dare Not Speak Its Name in Israel'. *Guardian*, 7 July 2014.

Freedom House. 'Freedom in the World 2018—Saudi Arabia'. https://freedomhouse.org/country/saudi-arabia/freedom-world/2018.

Freeman, Shirley E., and Helen Ormiston Smith. 'War and International Humanitarian Law'. *Medicine, Conflict and Survival* 13, no. 2 (1997): 116–124.

Fukuyama, Francis. 'The End of History?' *National Interest* 16 (1989): 3–18.

Galbraith, John H. *The Anatomy of Power*. Boston: Houghton Mifflin, 1983.

Garber, Bryan G., Mark A. Zamorski, and Rahesh Jetly. 'Mental Health of Canadian Forces Members while on Deployment to Afghanistan'. *Canadian Journal of Psychiatry* 57, no. 12 (2012): 736–744.

Gardner, Peter M. 'Respect for All: The Paliyans of South India'. In *Keeping the Peace: Conflict Resolution and Peaceful Societies around the World*, edited by Graham Kemp and Douglas P. Fry, 53–71. New York: Routledge, 2004.

Gardner, Ralph, Jr. 'A Long Friendship amid an Old Conflict'. *Wall Street Journal*, 4 October 2015. https://www.wsj.com/articles/a-long-friendship-amid-an-old-conflict-1444005954.

Garrity, Lyn. 'Five Fake Memoirs That Fooled the Literary World'. *Smithsonian Magazine*, 20 December 2010. https://www.smithsonianmag.com/arts-culture/five-fake-memoirs-that-fooled-the-literary-world-77092955/.

Gaskill, Malcolm. 'Plot 6, Row C, Grave 15'. *London Review of Books* 40, no. 21, 18 November 2018. https://www.lrb.co.uk/the-paper/v40/n21/malcolm-gaskill/plot-6-row-c-grave-15.

Getnet, Kindie, and Charlotte MacAlister. 'Integrated Innovations and Recommendation Domains: Paradigm for Developing, Scaling-Out, and Targeting Rainwater Management Innovations'. *Ecological Economics* 76 (2012): 34–41.

Ghisleni, Maurizio. 'The Sociology of Everyday Life: A Research Program on Contemporary Sociality'. *Social Science Information* 56, no. 4 (2017): 536–537.

Gibbs, Deborah A., Sandra L. Martin, and Ruby E. Johnson. 'Child Maltreatment and Substance Abuse among US Army Soldiers'. *Child Maltreatment* 13, no. 3 (2008): 259–268.

Gibson, Stephen. 'Supporting the Troops, Serving the Country: Rhetorical Commonplaces in the Representation of Military Service'. In *Representations of Peace and Conflict*, edited by Stephen Gibson and Simon Mollen, 143–159. Basingstoke, UK: Palgrave Macmillan, 2012.

Giddens, Anthony. *The Constitution of Society: Outline of the Theory of Structuration*. Cambridge: Polity, 1986.

Giessmann, Hans-Joachim, and Roger Mac Ginty, eds. *The Elgar Companion to Post-Conflict Transition*. Cheltenham, UK: Edward Elgar, 2018.

Gill, Douglas, and Gloden Dallas. 'Mutiny at Etaples Base in 1917'. *Past & Present* 69, no. 1 (1975): 88–112.

Gill, Nick, Deirdre Conlon, Dominique Moran, et al. 'Carceral Circuitry: New Directions in Carceral Geography'. *Progress in Human Geography* 90, no. 2 (2016): 183–204.

Gilligan, Chris, and Jonathan Tonge. *Peace or War? Understanding the Peace Process in Northern Ireland*. London: Routledge, 2019.

Givens, Seth A. 'Liberating the Germans: The US Army and Looting during the Second World War'. *War in History* 21, no. 1 (2014): 33–54.

Goffman, Erving. *The Presentation of the Self in Everyday Life*. London: Penguin, 1990.

Goldenberg, Myrna. 'Lessons Learned from Gentle Heroism: Women's Holocaust Narratives'. *Annals of the American Academy of Political and Social Science* 548, no. 1 (1996): 78–93.

Goldhagen, Daniel. *Hitler's Willing Executioners*. New York: Knopf, 1996.

Goldstein, Joshua S. *War and Gender: How Gender Shapes the War System and Vice Versa*. Cambridge: Cambridge University Press, 2004.

Goode, J. Paul, and David R. Stroupe. 'Everyday Nationalism: Constructivism for the Masses'. *Social Science Quarterly* 96, no. 3 (2015): 717–739.

Goodsell, Charles T. 'The Architecture of Parliaments: Legislative Houses and Political Culture'. *British Journal of Political Science* 18, no. 3 (1988): 287–302.

Gopin, Marc. *Bridges across an Impossible Divide: The Inner Lives of Arab and Jewish Peacemakers*. Oxford: Oxford University Press, 2012.

Gouliamos, Kostas, and Christos Kassimeris, eds., *The Marketing of War in the Age of Neomilitarism*. London: Routledge, 2012.

Goyal, Namrata, and Joan G. Miller. 'The Importance of Timing in Reciprocity: An Investigation of Reciprocity Norms among Indians and Americans'. *Journal of Cross-Cultural Psychology* 49, no. 3 (2017): 381–403.

Graham, David, A. 'The Strange Friendship of Martin McGuinness and Ian Paisley'. *Atlantic*, 21 March 2017.

Granovetter, Mark. 'Economic Action and Social Structure: The Problem of Embeddedness'. *American Journal of Sociology* 91, no. 3 (1985): 481–510.

Granovetter, Mark. 'The Strength of Weak Ties'. *American Journal of Sociology* 78, no. 6 (1973): 1360–1380.

Granovetter, Mark. 'The Strength of Weak Ties: A Network Theory Revisited'. *Sociological Theory* 1, no. 1 (1983): 201–233.

Grant, Richard, and Martin Oteng-Ababio. 'Mapping the Invisible and Real "African" Economy: Urban E-Waste Circuitry'. *Urban Geography* 33, no. 1 (2012): 1–21.

Gray, J. Glenn. *The Warriors: Reflections of Men in Battle*. Lincoln, NE: Bison, 1998.

Gruenewald, Mary Matsuda. *Looking Like the Enemy: My Story of Imprisonment in Japanese-American Internment Camps*. Troutdale, OR: NewSage, 2005.

Guzzini, Stefano. 'Max Weber's Power'. In *Max Weber and International Relations*, edited by Richard Ned Lebow, 97–118. Cambridge: Cambridge University Press, 2017.

Gvion, Liora. *Beyond Hummus and Falafel: Social and Political Aspects of Palestinian Food in Israel.* Berkeley: University of California Press, 2012.

Haddad, Fanar. 'Sectarian Relations and Sunni Identity in Post–Civil War Iraq'. In *Sectarian Politics in the Persian Gulf*, edited by Lawrence G. Potter, 67–116. Oxford: Oxford University Press, 2014.

Hadziristic, Tea. 'Is Bosnia the Worst Place in Europe to Be a Woman?' *OpenDemocracy*, 2016. https://www.opendemocracy.net/can-europe-make-it/tea-hadziristic/women-in-bosnia.

Hafner-Burton, Emillie M., Miles Kahler, and Alexander H. Montgomery. 'Network Analysis for International Relations'. *International Organization* 63, no. 3 (2009): 559–592.

Halperin, Eran. 'Emotion, Emotion Regulation, and Conflict Resolution'. *Emotion Review* 6, no. 1 (2014): 68–78.

Halperin, Eran, and James J. Gross. 'Emotion Regulation in Violent Conflict: Reappraisal, Hope and Support for Humanitarian Aid to the Opponent in Wartime'. *Cognition and Emotion* 25, no. 7 (2011): 1228–1236.

Hamilton, Ralph G. A. *The War Diary of the Master of Belhaven 1914–1918.* London: Endeavour, 2016.

Hampson, Norman. *Not Really What You'd Call a War.* Caithness, UK: Whittles, 2001.

Hancock, Landon E. 'Agency and Peacebuilding: The Promise of Local Zones of Peace'. *Peacebuilding* 5, no. 3 (2017): 255–269.

Hansen, Hans Krause. 'Numerical Operations, Transparency Illusions and the Datafication of Government'. *European Journal of Social Theory* 18, no. 2 (2015): 203–220.

Harding, Cynthia. 'Refugee Determination: Power and Resistance in Systems of Foucauldian Power." *Administration and Society* 35, no. 4 (2003): 462–488.

Harris, Anita. 'Youthful Socialities in Australia's Urban Multiculture'. *Urban Studies* 55, no. 3 (2018): 605–622.

Harris, William. 'Investigating Lebanon's Political Murders: International Idealism in the Realist Middle East'. *Middle East Journal* 67, no. 1 (2013): 9–27.

Hart, Alan. *Arafat: A Political Biography.* New York: Wiley, 1989.

Hartinger, Andreas. *Until the Eyes Shut: Memories of a Machine Gunner on the Eastern Front, 1943–45.* Zurich: Andreas Hartinger, 2019.

Hartzell, Caroline A. 'Settling Civil Wars: Armed Opponents' Fates and the Duration of the Peace'. *Conflict Management and Peace Science* 26, no. 4 (2009): 347–365.

Hartzell, Caroline A., and Andreas Mehler, eds. *Power Sharing and Power Relations after Civil War.* Boulder, CO: Lynne Rienner, 2019.

Harvey, David. 'The Geography of Capital and Accumulation: A Reconstruction of Marxian Theory'. *Antipode* 7, no. 2 (1975): 9–21.

Hassan, Mai, and Ahmed Kodouda. 'Sudan's Uprising: The Fall of a Dictator'. *Journal of Democracy* 30, no. 4 (2019): 83–103.

Hasson, Nir. "'The Last Jewish Community Holding Out against Zionism'. *Haaretz*, 18 August 2017. https://www.haaretz.com/israel-news/.premium.MAGAZINE-the-last-jewish-community-holding-out-against-zionism-1.5443981.

Havers, R. P. W. *Reassessing the Japanese Prisoner of War Experience: The Changi POW Camp, Singapore, 1942–5.* London: RoutledgeCurzon, 2012.

Hawdon, James, and John Ryan. 'Social Relations That Generate and Sustain Solidarity after a Mass Tragedy'. *Social Forces* 89, no. 4 (2011): 1363–1384.

Hayward, Clarissa, and Steven Lukes. 'Nobody to Shoot? Power, Structure, and Agency: A Dialogue'. *Journal of Power* 1, no. 1 (2008): 5–20.

Heaney, Seamus. 'Whatever You Say, Say Nothing'. 1975. https://www.blueridgejournal.com/poems/sh-what.htm.

Heron, Timothy A. '"Alternative Ulster": The First Wave of Punk in Northern Ireland (1976–1983)'. *Études Anglaises* 71, no. 1 (2018): 67–84.

Herzer, Dierk, and Sebastian Vollmer. 'Rising Top Incomes Do Not Raise the Tide'. *Journal of Policy Modelling* 35, no. 4 (2013): 504–519.

Hewison, W. S. *This Great Harbour: Scapa Flow*. Stromness, UK: Orkney, 1985.

Hillbladed, Thorolf. *Twilight of the Gods: A Swedish Waffen-SS Volunteer's Experiences with the 11th SS-Panzergrenader Division 'Nordland', Eastern Front 1944–45*. Warwick, UK: Helion, 2004.

Hills, Alice. 'What Is Policeness? On Being Police in Somalia'. *British Journal of Criminology* 54 (2014): 765–783.

Hills, Melissa. 'Last Hero of the WWII Battle of Gazala in Libya Dies at Age 94'. *Daily Express*, 24 February 2014. https://www.express.co.uk/news/uk/461440/Last-hero-of-the-WWII-Battle-of-Gazala-in-Libya-dies-at-age-94.

Hills, Stuart. *By Tank into Normandy: A Memoir of the Campaign in North-West Europe from D-Day to VE Day*. London: Cassell, 2003.

Hirschfeld, Katherine. 'Rethinking "Structural Violence"'. *Society* 54, no. 2 (2017): 156–162.

Hodgson, Natasha. 'Honour, Shame and the Fourth Crusade'. *Journal of Medieval History* 39, no. 2 (2007): 220–239.

Hoek, Lotte, and Ajay Gandhi. 'Provisional Relations, Indeterminate Conditions: Non-Sociological Sociality in South Asia'. *South Asia: Journal of South Asian Studies* 39, no. 1 (2016): 64–72.

Höglund, Kristine, and Marcus Wennerström. 'When the Going Gets Tough...Monitoring Missions and a Changing Conflict Environment in Sri Lanka, 2002–2008'. *Small Wars & Insurgencies* 26, no. 5 (2015): 836–860.

Holmes, Colin. *Searching for Lord Haw-Haw: The Political Lives of William Joyce*. London: Routledge, 2016.

Horne, John. 'End of a Paradigm? The Cultural History of the Great War'. *Past & Present* 242, no. 1 (2019): 155–192.

Howard, Michael. *The Invention of Peace*. Princeton, NJ: Princeton University Press, 2000.

Howell, Alison. 'Forget "Militarization": Race, Disability and the "Martial Politics" of the Police and of the University'. *International Feminist Journal of Politics* 20, no. 2 (2018): 117–136.

Hunt, Charles T. 'Beyond the Binaries: Towards a Relational Approach to Peacebuilding'. *Global Change, Peace and Security* 29, no. 3 (2017): 209–227.

Human Rights Watch. 'Saudi Arabia', 2018. https://www.hrw.org/middle-east/n-africa/saudi-arabia.

Human Rights Watch. 'Sudan, Events of 2019'. 2020. https://www.hrw.org/world-report/2020/country-chapters/sudan.

Idris, Iffat, with Ayat Abdelaziz. 'Women and Countering Violent Extremism'. *GSDRC Helpdesk Report*, 4 May 2017.

Innovation Enterprise. *Positive Disruption in Company Strategy: Disruptive Innovation in the Enterprise*. Bristol, UK: Innovation Enterprise, 2013.

Inter-Parliamentary Union. 'Women in National Parliaments', 2018. http://archive.ipu.org/wmn-e/classif-arc.htm.
Ismailbekova, Aksana. 'Constructing the Authority of Women through Custom: Bulak Village, Kyrgyzstan'. *Nationalities Papers* 44, no. 2 (2016): 266–280.
Ismailbekova, Aksana. 'Coping Strategies: Public Avoidance, Migration, and Marriage in the Aftermath of the Osh Conflict, Fergana Valley'. *Nationalities Papers* 41, no. 1 (2013): 109–127.
Israel, Adrienne. 'Measuring the War Experience: Ghanaian Soldiers in WWII'. *Journal of Modern African Studies* 25, no. 1 (1987): 159–168.
Jabri, Vivienne. *The Post-Colonial Subject: Claiming Politics/Governing Other in Late Modernity*. London: Routledge, 2003.
Jaffe-Gill, Ellen. 'Sisterhood across High Barriers'. *Jewish News*, 6 November 2015. http://www.jewishnewsva.org/sisterhood-across-high-barriers/.
Jahanbegloo, Ramin. *The Gandhian Moment*. Cambridge, MA: Harvard University Press, 2013.
Jellen, Jolanda, and Matthew J. Hornsey. 'Deviance and Dissent in Groups'. *Annual Review of Psychology* 65 (2014): 461–485.
Jennings, Kathleen M. 'Unintended Consequences of Intimacy: Political Economies of Peacekeeping and Sex Tourism'. *International Peacekeeping* 17, no. 2 (2010): 229–243.
Jennings, Kathleen M., and Morten Bøås. 'Transactions and Interactions: Everyday Life in the Peacekeeping Economy'. *Journal of Intervention and Statebuilding* 9, no. 3 (2015): 281–295.
Jeong, Ho-Won. *Understanding Conflict and Conflict Analysis*. Thousand Oaks, CA: Sage, 2008.
Johnen, Wilhelm. *Duel under the Stars: The Memoir of a Luftwaffe Night Pilot in World War II*. Barnsley, UK: Greenhill, 2018.
Jojarth, Christine. *Crime, War and Global Trafficking: Designing International Collaboration*. Cambridge: Cambridge University Press, 2009.
Jones, Alasdair. "Everyday without Exception? Making Space for the Exceptional in Contemporary Sociological Studies of Street Life'. *Sociological Review* 66, no. 5 (2018): 1000–1016.
Jones, Brian Glyn. 'The Slaughter of a Wedding Party in Yemen: Anatomy of a Bad Drone Strike." *HuffPost*, 14 January 2014. https://www.huffingtonpost.com/brian-glyn-williams/the-slaughter-of-a-weddin_b_4595274.html?guccounter=1.
Jones, Heather. *Violence against Prisoners of War in the First World War: Britain, France and Germany, 1914–1920*. Cambridge: Cambridge University Press, 2013.
Jones, Reece. 'Categories, Borders and Boundaries'. *Progress in Human Geography* 33, no. 2 (2009): 174–189.
Jünger, Ernst. *A German Officer in Occupied Paris: The War Journals, 1941–1945*. New York: Columbia University Press, 2018.
Jünger, Ernst. *Storm of Steel*. London: Penguin, 2004.
Kaiser, Fernand. *We Will Not Go to Tuapse: From the Donets to the Order with the Legion Wallonie and the 5th SS Volunteer Assault Brigade 'Wallonien' 1942–45*. Solihull, UK: Helion, 2016).
Kaldor, Mary. *New and Old Wars*. 3rd ed. Cambridge: Polity, 2012.
Kalyvas, Stathis, N. *The Logic of Violence in Civil War*. New Haven, CT: Yale University Press, 2006.

Kantola, Johanna. 'The Gendered Reproduction of the State in International Relations'. *British Journal of Politics and International Relations* 9, no. 2 (2007): 270–283.

Karakus, Dogukan Cansin, and Isak Svensson. 'Between the Bombs: Exploring Partial Ceasefires in the Syrian Civil War, 2011–2017'. *Terrorism and Political Violence* 32, no. 4 (2020): 681–700.

Karam, Karam. 'The Ta'if Agreement: New Order, Old Framework'. *Accord* 24 (2012): 36–39.

Karaman, Emine Rezzan. 'Remember, S/He Was Here Once: Mothers Call for Justice and Peace in Turkey'. *Journal of Middle East Women's Studies* 12, no. 3 (2016): 382–410.

Karlberg, Michael. 'The Power of Discourse and the Discourse of Power'. *International Journal of Peace Studies* 10, no. 1 (2005): 1–25.

Kaufman, Stuart J. *Modern Hatreds: The Symbolic Politics of Ethnic War*. Ithaca, NY: Cornell University Press, 2001.

Kavalski, Emilian. 'Waking IR from Its "Deep Newtonian Slumber"'. *Millennium* 41, no. 1 (2012): 137–150.

Kay, Sean. 'Globalization, Power and Security'. *Security Dialogue* 35, no. 1 (2004): 9–25.

Kee, Robert. *A Crowd Is Not Company*. London: Phoenix, 2000.

Keen, David. *Complex Emergencies*. Cambridge: Polity, 2008.

Keeton, Rebecca Gutierrez. 'Sueños y Valor: Dreams and Courage'. In *Roads Taken: Women in Student Affairs at Mid-Career*, edited by Kristen A. Renn and Carole Hughes, 23–34. Sterling, VA: Stylus, 2004.

Kempowski, Walter. *Swansong 1945: A Collective Diary of the Last Days of the Third Reich*. New York: Norton, 2015.

Kennedy, Paul. *The Rise and Fall of the Great Powers: Economic Change and Military Conflict from 1500 to 2000*. London: Fontana, 1989.

Kerr, Michael. *Imposing Power-Sharing: Conflict and Coexistence in Northern Ireland and Lebanon*. Dublin: Irish Academic Press, 2016.

Khan. Abdul Ghaffar. *My Life and Struggle: Autobiography of Badshah Khan*. New Delhi: Hind Pocket, 1969.

Kimberley, John R. 'Disruption on Steroids: Sea Change in the Worlds of Higher Education in General and Business Education in Particular'. *Journal of Leadership & Organizational Studies* 23, no. 1 (2016): 5–12.

King, Sophie, and Sam Hickey. 'Building Democracy from Below: Lessons from Western Uganda'. *Journal of Development Studies* 53, no. 10 (2017): 1584–1599.

Kinnvall, Catarina. 'Feeling Ontologically (In)secure: States, Traumas and the Governing of Gendered Space'. *Cooperation and Conflict* 52, no. 1 (2017): 90–108.

Kinnvall, Catarina. 'Globalisation and Religious Nationalism: Self, Identity and the Search for Ontological Security." *Political Psychology* 25, no. 5 (2004): 741–767.

Kinnvall, Catarina, and Jennifer Mitzen. 'An Introduction to the Special Issue: Ontological Securities in World Politics'. *Cooperation and Conflict* 52, no. 1 (2017): 3–11.

Kleinreesink, L. H. E., and Joseph M. M. L. Soeters. 'Truth and (Self) Censorship in Military Memoirs'. *Current Sociology* 64, no. 3 (2016): 373–391.

Klinenberg, Eric. *Palaces for the People: How Social Infrastructure Can Help Fight Inequality, Polarization and the Decline in Civic Life*. New York: Crown, 2018.

Knappe, Siegfried, and Ted Brusaw. *Soldat: Reflections of a German Soldier 1936-1949*. New York: Orion, 1992.

Knaus, Gerald, and Felix Martin. 'Lessons from Bosnia and Herzegovina: Travails of the European Raj'. *Journal of Democracy* 14, no. 3 (2003): 60–74.

Knuth, Sarah. 'Green Devaluation: Disruption, Divestment and Decommodification for a Green Economy'. *Capitalism, Nature, Socialism* 28, no. 1 (2016): 98–117.
Koenig-Archibugi, Mathias. 'International Electoral Assistance'. *Peace Review* 9, no. 3 (1997): 357–364.
Kolers, Avery H. 'Dynamics of Solidarity'. *Journal of Political Philosophy* 20, no. 4 (2012): 365–383.
Koller, Christian. 'Representing Otherness: African, Indian and European Soldiers' Letters and Memoirs'. In *Empire and First World War Writing*, edited by S. Das, 127–142. Cambridge: Cambridge University Press, 2011.
Komter, Aafke. 'Gifts and Social Relations: The Mechanisms of Reciprocity'. *International Sociology* 22, no. 1 (2007): 93–107.
Kopelev, Lev. *No Jail for Thought*. London: Secker & Warburg, 1975.
Koschorrek, Günter K. *Blood Red Snow: The Memoirs of a German Soldier on the Eastern Front*. Barnsley, UK: Frontline, 2011.
Kotkin, Stephen. 'One Hand Clapping: Russian Workers and 1917'. *Labor History* 32, no. 4 (1991): 604–620.
Kovatch, Bonnie. 'Sexual Exploitation and Abuse in UN Peacekeeping Missions: A Case Study of MONUC and MONUSCO'. *Journal of the Middle East and Africa* 7, no. 2 (2016): 157–174.
Krause, Jana. *Resilient Communities: Non-Violence and Civilian Agency in Communal War*. Cambridge: Cambridge University Press, 2018.
Krause, Jana, Werner Krause, and Piia Bränfors. 'Women's Participation in Peace Negotiations and the Durability of Peace'. *International Interactions* 44, no. 6 (2018): 985–1016.
Kriesberg, Louis. 'Reconciliation: Aspect, Growth and Sequences'. *International Journal of Peace Studies* 12, no. 1 (Spring/Summer 2007): 1–21.
Kroc Institute for International Peace Studies. 'Building Sustainable Peace: Ideas, Evidence, and Strategies'. Conference, November 2019. https://kroc.nd.edu/news-events/events/building-sustainable-peace-ideas-evidence-and-strategies/.
Krystalli, Roxanne, and Kimberly Theidon. 'Here's How Attention to Gender Affected Colombia's Peace Process'. *Washington Post*, 9 October 2016. https://www.washingtonpost.com/news/monkey-cage/wp/2016/10/09/heres-how-attention-to-gender-affected-colombias-peace-process/?noredirect=on&utm_term=.b5185d1a80bf.
Kumar, Ruchi. 'Selfies with the Taliban: Afghan Women Buoyed by Ceasefire Snaps'. *Guardian*, 6 July 2018. www.theguardian.com/global-development/2018/jul/06/selfies-with-the-taliban-afghan-women-buoyed-eid-ceasefire-photos-viral.
Laanela, Therese. 'Crafting Sustainable Electoral Processes in New Democracies'. *Representation* 36, no. 4 (1999): 284–293.
Laine, Jussi P. 'The Multiscalar Production of Borders'. *Geopolitics* 21, no. 3 (2016): 465–482.
Lamb, Charles. *War in a Stringbag*. London: Cassell, 2001.
Larson, Jennifer, and Janet I. Lewis. 'Ethnic Networks'. *American Journal of Political Science* 61, no. 2 (2017): 350–364.
Larson, Reed W., and David M. Almeida. 'Emotional Transmission in the Daily Lives of Families: A New Paradigm for Studying Family Process'. *Journal of Marriage and Family* 61, no. 1 (1999): 5–20.
Last, Nella. *Nella Last's War: A Mother's Diary 1939–45*. London: Sphere, 1983.
'Law Enforcement Approaches to Reducing Gun Violence'. *RAND*, 22 April 2020. https://www.rand.org/research/gun-policy/analysis/essays/law-enforcement-approaches-for-reducing-gun-violence.html.

Lawson, George, and Robbie Shilliam. 'Sociology and International Relations: Legacies and Prospects'. *Cambridge Review of International Affairs* 23, no. 1 (2010): 69–86.
Leah, Gordon. 'Forgiveness, Pardon and Justice: Critical Reflections on Eric Lomax's *The Railway Man*'. *Theology* 121, no. 5 (2018)): 341–347.
Lederach, John Paul. *Building Peace: Sustainable Reconciliation in Divided Societies*. Washington, DC: United States Institute of Peace Process, 2002.
Lederach, John Paul. *The Little Book of Conflict Transformation*. Intercourse, PA: GoodBooks, 2003.
Lederach, John Paul. *The Moral Imagination: The Art and Soul of Building Peace*. Oxford: Oxford University Press, 2005.
Lederach, John Paul. *Preparing for Peace: Conflict Transformation across Cultures* Syracuse, NY: Syracuse University Press, 1995.
Lee, Dong-Hoo. 'Smartphones, Mobile Social Space, and New Sociality in Korea'. *Mobile Media & Communication* 1, no. 3 (2013): 269–284.
Lee, SungYong. 'Local Resilience and the Reconstruction of Social Institutions: Recovery, Maintenance and Transformation of Buddhist Sangha in Post-Khmer Rouge Cambodia'. *Journal of Intervention and Statebuilding* 14, no. 3 (2020): 349–367.
Lee, SungYong, and Roger Mac Ginty. 'Context and Postconflict Referendums'. *Nationalism and Ethnic Politics* 18, no. 1 (2012): 43–64.
Lelourec, Lesley. 'The Bad and the Ugly: Good Guys after All: Representations of Martin McGuinness and Ian Paisley in the English Press'. *Estudios Irlandes* 4, no. 4 (2009): 32–44.
Leonard, Madeleine. 'Parochial Geographies: Growing Up in Divided Belfast'. *Childhood* 17, no. 3 (2010): 329–342.
Leonard, Madeleine. *Teens and Territory in 'Post Conflict' Belfast: If Walls Could Talk*. Manchester, UK: Manchester University Press, 2017.
Leonardsson, Hanna, and Gustav Rudd. 'The "Local Turn" in Peacebuilding: A Literature Review of Effective and Emancipatory Local Peacebuilding'. *Third World Quarterly* 36, no. 5 (2015): 825–839.
Lepp, Eric. 'Division on Ice: Shared Space and Civility in Belfast'. *Journal of Peacebuilding & Development* 13, no. 1 (2018): 32–45.
Levine, Kenneth J., Robert A. Muenchen, and Abby M. Brooks. 'Measuring Transformational and Charismatic Leadership: Why Isn't Charisma Measured?' *Communication Monographs* 77, no. 4 (2010): 576–591.
Levinson, Hugh. 'How the Long Walk Became the Way Back'. *BBC News*, 4 December 2010. http://www.bbc.co.uk/news/world-11900920.
Lewis, Norman. *Naples '44*. New York: Carroll and Graf, 2005.
Lewis, Tim. 'Between the Social and the Selfish: Learner Autonomy in Online Environments'. *Innovation in Language Learning and Teaching* 7, no. 3 (2013): 198–212.
Li, Peter. 'The Asian Pacific War, 1931–1945: Japanese Atrocities and the Quest for Reconciliation'. *East Asia* 17, no. 1 (1999): 108–137.
Lie, John Harald Sandie. 'Challenging Anthropology: Anthropological Reflections on the Ethnographic Turn in International Relations'. *Millennium* 41, no. 2 (2012): 201–220.
Liebow, Elliot. *Tally's Corner: A Study of Negro Street Corner Men*. Boston: Little, Brown, 1967.
Lingo, Elizabeth Long, and Siobhan O'Mahoney. 'Nexus Work: Brokerage on Creative Projects'. *Administrative Science Quarterly* 55 (2010): 47–81.
Linklater, Andrew. 'Process Sociology in International Relations'. *Sociological Review* 59, no. 1 (2011): 48–64.

Lister, Andrew. 'Markets, Desert, and Reciprocity'. *Politics, Philosophy & Economics* 16, no. 1 (2017): 47-69.
Livny, Adi. 'Conscientious Objection and the State'. *Armed Forces and Society* 44, no. 4 (2018): 666-687.
Lloyd, Katrina, and Gillian Robinson. 'Intimate Mixing—Bridging the Gap? Catholic–Protestant Relationships in Northern Ireland'. *Ethnic and Racial Studies* 34, no. 12 (2011): 2134-2152.
Logue, Danielle M., and Stewart R. Clegg. 'Wikileaks and the News of the World: The Political Circuitry of Labelling'. *Journal of Management Inquiry* 24, no. 4 (2015): 394-404.
Lomax, Eric. *The Railway Man*. London: Vintage, 2014.
Lombardo, Gabriele. 'The Responsibility to Protect and the Lack of Intervention in Syria between the Protection of Human Rights and Geopolitical Strategies'. *International Journal of Human Rights* 19, no. 8 (2015): 1190-1198.
Lopez, Anthony C., and Dominic D. P. Johnson. 'The Determinants of War in International Relations'. *Journal of Economic Behavior and Organization* 178 (2020): 983-997.
Lopez-Reyes, Raymon. 'Establishing Salvadorian Zones of Peace'. *Peace Review* 9, no. 2 (1997): 225-231.
Lynch, E. P. F. *Somme Mud: The Experiences of an Infantryman in France, 1916-1919*. London: Bantam, 2008.
Lyth, Peter J. 'Traitor or Patriot? Andrey Vlasov and the Russian Liberation Movement 1942-45'. *Journal of Strategic Studies* 12, no. 2 (1989): 230-238.
Mabey, Richard. *The Unofficial Countryside*. Beaminster, UK: Little Toller, 2014.
MacDonald, Charles B. *Company Commander: The Classic Infantry Memoir of WWII*. London: Endeavour, 2015.
MacGill, Patrick. *The Great Push: An Episode of the Great War*. London: Caliban, 1984.
Mac Ginty, Roger. 'Between Resistance and Compliance: Non-participation and the Liberal Peace'. *Journal of Intervention and Statebuilding* 6, no. 2 (2012): 167-187.
Mac Ginty, Roger. "Circuits, the Everyday and International Relations: Connecting the Home to the International and Transnational'. *Cooperation and Conflict* 54 no. 2 (2019): 234-253.
Mac Ginty, Roger. 'Everyday Peace: Bottom-Up and Local Agency in Conflict-Affected Societies'. *Security Dialogue* 45, no. 6 (2014): 548-564.
Mac Ginty, Roger. 'Everyday Social Practices and Boundary-Making in Deeply Divided Societies'. *Civil Wars* 19, no. 1 (2017): 4-25.
Mac Ginty, Roger. 'Indigenous Peacemaking versus the Liberal Peace'. *Cooperation and Conflict* 43, no. 2 (2008): 139-163.
Mac Ginty, Roger. *International Peacebuilding and Local Resistance: Hybrid Forms of Peace*. Basingstoke, UK: Palgrave, 2011.
Mac Ginty, Roger. *No War, No Peace: The Rejuvenation of Stalled Peace Processes and Peace Accords*. Basingstoke, UK: Palgrave, 2006.
Mac Ginty, Roger. 'Political versus Sociological Time: The Fraught World of Timelines and Deadlines'. In *Building Sustainable Peace: Timing and Sequencing of Post-Conflict Reconstruction and Peacebuilding*, edited by Arnim Langer and Graham K. Brown, 15-31. Oxford: Oxford University Press, 2016.
Mac Ginty, Roger. 'Where Is the Local? Critical Localism and Peacebuilding'. *Third World Quarterly* 36, no. 5 (2015): 840-856.

Mac Ginty, Roger, and John Darby. *Guns and Government: The Management of the Northern Ireland Peace Process*. Basingstoke, UK: Palgrave, 2002.

Mac Ginty, Roger, and Pamina Firchow. 'Top-Down and Bottom-Up Narratives of Conflict'. *Politics* 36, no. 3 (2016): 308–323.

Mac Ginty, Roger, and Oliver P. Richmond. 'The Local Turn in Peace Building: A Critical Agenda for Peace'. *Third World Quarterly* 34, no. 5 (2013): 763–783.

Mackenzie, Donald. 'Just How Fast?' *London Review of Books* 41, no. 5 (2019): 23–24.

Maclean, Fitzroy. *Eastern Approaches*. London: Penguin, 2009.

Maeger, Herbert. *Lost Honour, Betrayed Loyalty: The Memoir of a Waffen-SS Soldier on the Eastern Front*. London: Frontline, 2019.

Magliveras, Simeon. 'The Ontology of Difference: Nationalism, Localism and Ethnicity in a Greek Arvanite Village'. PhD diss., Durham University, 2010.

Magone, Claire, Michael Neuman, and Fabrice Weissman, eds. *Humanitarian Negotiations Revealed: The MSF Experience*. London: Hurst, 2011.

Makdisi, Ussama Samir. *The Culture of Sectarianism: Community, History, and Violence in Nineteenth Century Ottoman Lebanon*. Berkeley: University of California Press, 2000.

Maktabi, Rania. 'The Lebanese Census of 1932 Revisited: Who Are the Lebanese?' *British Journal of Middle East Studies* 26, no. 2 (1999): 219–241.

Malešević, Siniša. *The Sociology of War and Violence*. Cambridge: Cambridge University Press, 2012.

Malloy, Kerri. 'In Plain Sight: Healing in Northwestern California'. Paper presented at Building Sustainable Peace conference, Kroc Institute, University of Notre Dame, 7–10 November 2019.

Maloney, Ed, and Andy Pollak. *Paisley*. Dublin: Poolbeg, 1986.

Manatschal, Anita. 'Reciprocity as a Trigger of Social Cooperation in Contemporary Immigration Societies?' *Acta Sociologica* 58, no. 3 (2015): 233–248.

Mandelbaum, Michael. *The Ideas That Conquered the World: Peace, Democracy and Free Markets in the Twenty-first Century*. New York: Public Affairs, 2004.

Marcus, Jonathan. 'An Obituary of the Age of Intervention?' *BBC News*, 17 September 2017. https://www.bbc.co.uk/news/uk-politics-37372597.

Martinez, Robert. 'Punk Rock, Thatcher and the Elsewhere of Northern Ireland: Rethinking the Politics of Pop Music'. *Journal of the Midwest Language Association* 48, no. 1 (2015): 193–219.

Marvin, Laurence. 'War in the South: A First Look at Siege Warfare in the Albigensian Crusade, 1209–1218'. *War in History* 8, no. 4 (2001): 373–395.

Marx, Karl. *Capital: A Critique of Political Economy*, Vol. I, Book One, *The Processes of Production of Capital*. New York: International Publishers, 1887.

Masters, Cristina. 'Bodies of Technology: Cyborg Soldiers and Militarised Masculinities'. *International Feminist Journal of Politics* 7, no. 1 (2005): 112–132.

Mather, Carol. *When the Grass Stops Growing: A War Memoir*. Barnsley, UK: Pen and Sword, 1997.

May, Theresa. 'PM's Speech at Farnborough International Airshow: 16 July 2018'. https://www.gov.uk/government/speeches/pms-speech-at-farnborough-international-airshow-16-july-2018.

McBride, Herbert W. *A Rifleman Went to War*. Kindle ed. London: Endeavour Compass, 2015.

McCann, Eamonn. *War in an Irish Town*. London: Pluto, 1980.

McCrum, Robert. *Wodehouse: A Life*. New York: Norton, 2004.
McDonald, Henry. 'Belfast's City Hall Attacked by Loyalist Demonstrators over Union Flag Vote'. *Guardian*, 3 December 2012. https://www.theguardian.com/uk/2012/dec/03/belfast-city-hall-flag-protest.
McDonald, Henry. 'Ian Paisley, the Dr No of Ulster Politics, Dies Aged 88'. *Guardian*, 12 September 2014. https://www.theguardian.com/politics/2014/sep/12/ian-paisley-dies-aged-88-northern-ireland.
Mcleod, Ethan. 'Rapper Tyree Colion Arrested for "No Shoot Zone" Graffiti at Middle River Store Where Teen Was Fatally Shot'. *Baltimore Fishbowl*, 3 August 2017. https://baltimorefishbowl.com/stories/rapper-tyree-colion-arrested-for-no-shoot-zone-graffiti-at-middle-river-store-where-teen-was-fatally-shot/.
Mcloone, Martin. 'Punk Music in Northern Ireland: The Political Power of "What Might Have Been"'. *Irish Studies Review* 12, no. 1 (2004): 29–38.
McVitty, E. Amanda. 'False Knights and True Men: Contesting Chivalric Masculinity in English Treason Trials, 1388–1415'. *Journal of Medieval History* 40, no. 4 (2014): 458–477.
Medie, Peace A. 'Fighting Gender-Based Violence: The Women's Movement and the Enforcement of Rape Law in Liberia'. *African Affairs* 112, no. 448 (2013): 377–397.
Mees, Ludger. 'The Basque Peace Process, Nationalism and Political Violence'. In *The Management of Peace Processes*, edited by John Darby and Roger Mac Ginty, 154–193. Basingstoke, UK: Macmillan, 2000.
Mellors, Colin, and John McKean. 'Confronting the state: Conscientious Objection in Western Europe'. *Bulletin of Peace Proposals* 13, no. 3 (1982): 227–239.
Mendel, Yonatan. 'Diary'. *London Review of Books*, 15 August 2019.
Mendel, Yonatan. 'A New Nationalistic Political Grammar'. In *From the River to the Sea: Palestine and Israel in the Shadow of 'Peace'*, edited by Mandy Turner, 159–177. Lanham, MD: Lexington, 2019.
Metz, Thaddeus. 'Jus Interruptus Bellum: The Ethics of Truce-Making'. *Journal of Global Ethics* 13, no. 1 (2017): 6–13.
Mies, Maria. *Patriarchy and Accumulation on a World Scale: Women in the International Division of Labour*. 2nd ed. London: Zed, 2014.
Milam, A. J., S. A. Buggs, C. D. M. Furr-Holden, et al. 'Changes in Attitudes towards Guns and Shootings Following Implementation of Baltimore Safe Streets Intervention'. *Journal of Urban Health* 93, no. 4 (2016): 609–626.
Millar, Gearoid. 'For Whom Do Local Peace Processes Function? Maintaining Control through Conflict Management'. *Cooperation and Conflict* 52, no. 5 (2017): 293–308.
Millar, Gearoid. 'Our Brothers Who Went into the Bush: Post-Identity Conflict and the Experience of Reconciliation in Sierra Leone'. *Journal of Peace Research* 49, no. 5 (2012): 717–727.
Millar, Joanne, and John Connell. 'Strategies for Scaling Out Impacts from Agricultural Systems Change: The Case of Forages and Livestock Production in Laos'. *Agricultural and Human Values* 27 (2010): 213–225.
Miller, Alan J. M. *Over the Horizon, 1939–1945*. Finavon, UK: Finavon Print & Design, 1999.
Ministry of Finance (Sierra Leone). 'Mathew Dingie Due Diligence Mission to Georgia on the Introduction of Electronic Cash Registers'. 13 February 2019. https://mof.gov.sl/2019/02/13/matthew-dingie-due-diligence-mission-to-georgia-on-the-introduction-of-electronic-cash-registers/.

Mishra, Pankaj. *From the Ruins of Empire: The Revolt against the West and the Remaking of Asia*. London: Allen Lane, 2012.

Mitchell, Audra. 'Quality/Control: International Peace Interventions and "the everyday"'. *Review of International Studies* 37, no. 4 (2011): 1623–1645.

Mitchell, Christopher, and Susan Allen Nan. 'Local Peace Zones as Institutionalized Conflict'. *Peace Review* 9, no. 2 (1997): 159–162.

Mitchell, Jacqueline. *Blitz Spirit*. Oxford: Osprey, 2010.

Moledijk, Tine. 'Moral Injury in Relation to Public Debates: The Role of Societal Misrecognition in Moral Conflict-Colored Trauma among Soldiers'. *Social Science and Medicine* 211 (2018): 314–320.

Monroe, Cameron J. 'Power and Agency in Precolonial African States'. *Annual Review of Anthropology* 42 (2013): 17–35.

Mookherjee, Nayanika. 'Gendered Embodiments: Mapping the Body-Politic of the Raped Women and the Nation in Bangladesh'. *Feminist Review* 88 (2008): 36–53.

Moore, Adam. *Peacebuilding in Practice: Local Experience in Two Bosnian Towns*. Ithaca, NY: Cornell University Press, 2013.

Moorhead, Joanna. 'The Railway Man's Secret Daughter on How the Movie Has Helped Her Find Peace'. *Sunday Mail*, 5 January 2012, 20.

Moran, Mary H. 'Gender, Militarism and Peace-Building: Projects of the Postconflict Moment'. *Annual Review of Anthropology* 39 (2010): 261–274.

Moss, Paul. 'Northern Ireland: A Year without Devolved Government'. *BBC News*, 8 January 2018. https://www.bbc.co.uk/news/uk-northern-ireland-politics-42608322.

Mukasa, Norman. 'War-Child Mothers in Northern Uganda: The Civil War Forgotten Legacy'. *Development in Practice* 27, no. 3 (2017): 354–367.

Mukhina, Lena. *The Diary of Lina Mukhina: A Girl's Life in the Siege of Leningrad*. Basingstoke, UK: Macmillan, 2012.

Münch, Philipp, and Alex Veit. 'Intermediaries of Intervention: How Local Power Brokers Shape External Peace and State-Building in Afghanistan and Congo'. *International Peacekeeping* 25, no. 2 (2018): 266–292.

'A Murder Too Far'. *Economist*, 17 July 1997. http://www.economist.com/node/151703.

Myers, Emily. 'Gender and Countering Violent Extremism'. Alliance for Peacebuilding, Washington, DC, 2018.

Mylan, Josephine, and Dale Southerton. 'The Social Ordering of an Everyday Practice: The Case of Laundry'. *Sociology* 52, no. 6 (2018): 1134–1151.

Nadarajah, Suthaharan, and David Rampton. 'The Limits of Hybridity and the Crisis of the Liberal Peace'. *Review of International Studies* 41, no. 1 (2015): 49–72.

Narain, Seema. 'Gender in International Relations: Feminist Perspectives of J. Ann Tickner'. *Indian Journal of Gender Studies* 21, no. 2 (2014): 179–197.

Narotzky, Susana, and Paz Moreno. 'Reciprocity's Dark Side: Negative Reciprocity, Morality and Social Reproduction'. *Anthropological Theory* 2, no. 3 (2002): 281–305.

NATO. 'Defence and Related Security Capacity Initiative'. 12 July 2018. https://www.nato.int/cps/en/natohq/topics_132756.htm.

NATO. 'Trust Funds: Supporting Demilitarization and Defence Transformation Projects'. 21 June 2016. https://www.nato.int/cps/en/natolive/topics_50082.htm.

Neitzel, Sönke, and Harald Welzer. *Soldaten: On Fighting, Dying and Killing: The Secret Second World War Tapes of German POWs*. London: Simon & Schuster, 2012.

Ní Aoláin, Fionnuala. 'Counter-Terrorism Committee: Addressing the Role of Women in Countering Terrorism and Violent Extremism'. *Just Security*, New York University

School of Law, 2015. https://www.justsecurity.org/25983/counter-terrorism-committee-addressing-role-women-countering-terrorism-violent-extremism/.

Ní Aoláin, Fionnuala, Dina Francesca Haynes, and Naomi Cahn. *On the Frontlines: Gender, War and the Post-Conflict Process*. Oxford: Oxford University Press, 2011.

Nicolson, Juliet. *The Great Silence 1918–1920: Living in the Shadow of the Great War*. London: John Murray, 2009.

Niemann, Derek. *A Nazi in the Family: The Hidden Story of an SS Family in Wartime Germany*. London: Short, 2015.

Nikolić-Ristanović, Vesna. 'War, Nationalism and Mothers'. *Peace Review* 8, no. 3 (1996): 359–364.

Noble, Greg. 'Cosmopolitan Habits: The Capacities and Habits of Intercultural Convivialities'. *Body and Society* 19, nos. 2–3 (2013): 162–185.

Northern Ireland Council for Integrated Education. *Annual Report 2016–17*. Belfast: NICIE, 2017.

Northern Ireland Life and Times Survey. https://www.ark.ac.uk/nilt/1998/Community_Relations/SMARRRLG.html; http://www.ark.ac.uk/nilt/2006/Community_Relations/SMARRRLG.html; http://www.ark.ac.uk/nilt/2018/Community_Relations/SMARRRLG.html.

Norton-Taylor, Richard. 'I Was Not a Nazi Collaborator, PG Wodehouse Told MI5'. *Guardian*, 26 August 2011.

'No Surrender: Ian Paisley (Obituary)'. *Economist* 412, no. 8905 (20 September 2014): 86.

'Not at Home: Lebanon's Mixed Marriages." *Economist* 392, no. 8647 (5 September 2009): 46.

Nye, Joseph S. 'Public Diplomacy and Soft Power'. *Annals of the American Academy of Political Science* 616, no. 1 (2008): 94–109.

'Obituary: Martin McGuinness Died on March 21st'. *Economist*, 23 March 2016. https://www.economist.com/obituary/2017/03/25/obituary-martin-mcguinness-died-on-march-21st.

O Dochartaigh, Niall. *From Civil Rights to Armalites: Derry and the Birth of the Irish Troubles*. 2nd ed. Basingstoke, UK: Palgrave Macmillan, 2005.

Oesterheld, Joachim. 'The Last Chapter of the Indian Legion'. *South Asian Chronicle* 5 (2015): 120–143.

Omissi, David, ed. *Indian Voices of the Great War: Soldiers' Letters 1914–1918*. Basingstoke, UK: Macmillan, 1999.

Ó'Muelleoir, Máirtín. *Belfast's Dome of Delight: City Hall Politics 1981–2000*. Belfast: Beyond the Pale, 2000.

O'Reilly, Maria. *Gendered Agency in War and Peace: Gender Justice and Women's Activism in Post-Conflict Bosnia-Herzegovina*. Basingstoke, UK: Palgrave Macmillan, 2018.

Oriola, Temitope B. '"Unwilling Cocoons": Boko Haram's War against Women'. *Studies in Conflict and Terrorism* 40, no. 2 (2017): 99–121.

Ormerod, Katherine. *Why Social Media Is Ruining Your Life*. London: Cassell, 2018.

Orwell, George. *Homage to Catalonia*. London: Penguin, 1989.

Osiel, Mark J. *Obeying Orders: Atrocity, Military Discipline and the Law of War*. Piscataway, NJ: Transaction, 2001.

Ossewaarde, Marinus. 'Living off Dead Premises: The Persistence of Enlightenment Mentalities in the Making of Social Sciences'. *European Quarterly of Political Attitudes and Mentalities* 4, no. 4 (2015): 1–14.

Owen, Frank. *The Fall of Singapore*. London: Joseph, 1960.

Paffenholz, Thania, N. Ross, S. Dixon, A. L. Schluchter, and J. True. *Making Women Count—Not Just Counting Women: Assessing Women's Inclusion and Influence on Peace Negotiations*. New York: UN Women, 2016.
Pain, Rachel. 'Everyday Terrorism: Connecting Domestic Violence to Global Terrorism'. *Progress in Human Geography* 38, no. 4 (2014): 531–550.
Paisley, Ian. Text of a Speech by Ian Paisley, Leader of the Democratic Unionist Party, to the DUP Annual Conference, 1995. http://cain.ulst.ac.uk/issues/politics/docs/dup/ip_1995.htm.
Parashar, Swati. 'Interview—Swati Parashar'. *E-International Relations*, 8 March 2020. https://www.e-ir.info/2020/03/08/interview-swati-parashar/.
Parashar, Swati. "This Is a War on Women." *Indian Express*, 3 December 2019. https://indianexpress.com/article/opinion/columns/this-is-a-war-on-women-rape-sexual-violence-6148420/.
Peeples, Matthew A., and W. Randall Haas Jr. 'Brokerage and Social Capital in the Prehispanic U.S. Southwest'. *American Anthropologist* 115, no. 2 (2013): 232–247.
Pelz, William, A. *A People's History of Modern Europe*. London: Pluto, 2016.
Peniston-Bird, Corinna. 'War and Peace in the Cloakroom: The Controversy over the Memorial to the Women of World War II'. In *Representations of Peace and Conflict*, edited by Stephen Gibson and Simon Mollan, 263–284. Basingstoke, UK: Palgrave, 2012.
Pennisi, Elizabeth. 'Tracing Life's Circuitry'. *Science* 302, no. 5651 (2003): 1646–1649.
Pérez, Michael Vicente. 'The Everyday as Survival among Ex-Gaza Refugees in Jordan'. *Middle East Critique* 27, no. 3 (2018): 275–288.
Persson, Andres. 'Shaping Discourse and Setting Examples: Normative Power Europe Can Work in the Israeli-Palestinian Conflict." *Journal of Common Market Studies* 55, no. 6 (2017): 1415–1431.
Peruzzotti, Enrique. 'The Societalization of Horizontal Accountability'. In *Human Rights, State Compliance and Social Changes: Assessing National Human Rights Institutions*, edited by Ryan Goodman, 243–269. Cambridge: Cambridge University Press, 2011.
Phelps-Roper, Megan. *Unfollow: A Journey from Hatred to Hope, Leaving the Westboro Baptist Church*. London: Riverrun, 2019.
Philpott, Daniel. 'Peace after Genocide'. *First Things* (2012): 39–46.
Picq, Manuela L. 'Critics at the Edge? Decolonizing Methodologies in International Relations'. *International Political Science Review* 34, no. 4 (2013): 444–455.
Pilling, David. 'Sudan's Army Clashes with Security Forces over Protests'. *Irish Times*, 8 April 2019.
Pöppel, Martin. *Heaven and Hell: The War Diary of a German Paratrooper*. Staplehurst, UK: Spellmount, 2000.
Potter, Antonia. 'Women, Gender and Peacemaking in Civil Wars'. In *Contemporary Peacemaking: Conflict, Peace Processes and Post-war Reconstruction*, 2nd ed., edited by John Darby and Roger Mac Ginty, 105–119. Basingstoke, UK: Palgrave Macmillan, 2008.
Poulos, Christopher. *Accidental Ethnography: An Inquiry into Family Secrecy*. Walnut Creek, CA: Left Coast, 2009.
Powell, Jonathan. *Great Hatred, Little Room: Making Peace in Northern Ireland*. London: Vintage, 2009.
Pöyhönen, Siiri. 'Room for Communitas: Exploring Sociomaterial Construction of Leadership in Liminal and Dominant Spaces'. *Leadership* 14, no. 5 (2018): 585–599.

Prince, Simon. *Northern Ireland's '68: Civil Rights, Global Revolt and the Origins of the Troubles*. Dublin: Irish Academic Press, 2007.
Purdy, Martina. 'Ian Paisley Says DUP Told Him to Quit as Leader'. *BBC News*, 20 January 2014. https://www.bbc.co.uk/news/uk-northern-ireland-25801295.
Quester, George H. 'Wars Prolonged by Misunderstood Signals'. *Annals of the American Academy of Political and Social Sciences* 392, no. 1 (1970): 30–39.
Rabinovitch, Simon. 'What Is Wrong with Tolerance'. *Aeon*, 18 June 2018. https://aeon.co/essays/reciprocity-not-tolerance-is-the-basis-of-healthy-societies.
Rafanell, Irene, and Hugo Gorringe. 'Consenting to Domination? Theorising Power, Agency and Embodiment with Reference to Caste'. *Sociological Review* 58, no. 4 (2010): 604–622.
Rafiq, Haras. 'Testimony before Terrorism, Non-Proliferation, and Trade Subcommittee'. Committee on Foreign Affairs, United States House of Representatives, 27 February 2018.
Rajput, A. B. *Maulana Abul Kazam Azad*. Lahore: Lion, 1957.
Ramsbotham, Oliver, Tom Woodhouse, and Hugh Miall. *Contemporary Conflict Resolution*. 3rd ed. Cambridge: Polity, 2012.
Ranfurly, Hermoine. *To War with Whitaker: The Wartime Diaries of the Countess of Ranfurly*. London: Bello, 2014.
Rashid, Syeda Rozana. 'Bangladeshi Women's Experiences of Their Men's Migration: Rethinking Power, Agency and Subordination'. *Asian Survey* 53, no. 5 (2013): 883–908.
Rawicz, Slavomir. *Long Walk: The True Story of a Trek to Freedom*. New York: Lyons, 2010.
Razavi, Shahrashoub. 'Families Can Drive Gender Equality, but Only if We Help Them Evolve'. *Conversation*, 15 May 2017. https://theconversation.com/families-can-drive-gender-equality-but-only-if-we-help-them-evolve-77546.
Read, Róisín, and Roger Mac Ginty. 'The Temporal Dimension in Accounts of Violent Conflict: A Case Study from Darfur'. *Journal of Intervention and Statebuilding* 11, no. 2 (2017): 147–165.
Reader, W. J. *At Duty's Call: A Study in Obsolete Patriotism*. Manchester, UK: Manchester University Press, 1998.
Reeves, Richard. *Infamy: The Shocking Story of the Japanese-American Internment in WWII*. New York: Henry Holt, 2015.
Regan, Patrick M. 'Bringing Peace Back In: Presidential Address to the Peace Science Society'. *Conflict Management and Peace Science* 31, no. 4 (2014): 345–356.
Rehfeldt, Hans Heinz. *Mortar Gunner on the Eastern Front*, Vol. 1, *From the Moscow Winter Offensive to Operation Zitadelle*. Barnsley, UK: Greenhill, 2019.
Reicher, Steve, C. Cassidy, I. Wolpert, N. Hopkins, and M. Levine. 'Saving Bulgaria's Jews: An Analysis of Social Identity and the Mobilisation of Social Solidarity'. *European Journal of Social Psychology* 36 (2006): 49–72.
Render, David (with Stuart Tootal). *Tank Action: An Armoured Troop Commander's War 1944–45*. London: Weidenfeld & Nicolson, 2016.
Reporters without Borders. 'World Press Freedom Index'. https://rsf.org/en/ranking.
'Resilient Cities, Networks and Disruptions'. *Environment and Planning B: Planning and Design* 40 (2013): 571–573.
Rice, Laura. 'African Conscripts/European Conflicts: Race, Memory and the Lessons of War'. *Culture Critique* 45 (2000): 109–149.

Richards, Frank. *Old Soldiers Never Die*. Cardigan, UK: Parthian, 2016.

Richmond, Oliver, P. 'Devious Objectives and the Disputants' View of International Mediation: A Theoretical Framework'. *Journal of Peace Research* 35, no. 6 (1998): 707–722.

Richmond, Oliver P. *Failed Statebuilding: Intervention, the State and the Dynamics of Peace Formation*. New Haven, CT: Yale University Press, 2014.

Richmond, Oliver P. 'The Green and the Cool: Hybridity, Relationality and Ethnographic Biographical Responses to Intervention'. *Mediterranean Politics* 23, no. 4 (2018): 479–500.

Richmond, Oliver P. 'Peace in Analogue/Digital International Relations'. *Global Change, Peace and Security* 32, no. 3 (2020) 1–20.

Richmond, Oliver P. 'The Problem of Peace: Understanding the "Liberal Peace"'. *Conflict, Security & Development* 6, no. 3 (2006): 291–314.

Richmond, Oliver P. *The Transformation of Peace*. Basingstoke, UK: Palgrave Macmillan, 2005.

Richmond, Oliver P., and Roger Mac Ginty. 'Where Now for the Critique of the Liberal Peace'. *Cooperation and Conflict* 50, no. 2 (2014): 171–189.

Rimmer, Susan Harris. 'Barriers to Operationalising the 'Women, Peace and Security' Doctrine in United Nations Peacekeeping'. *Journal of International Peacekeeping* 20, nos. 1–2 (2016): 49–68.

Rintamaki, Lance S., et al. 'Persistence of Traumatic Memories in WWII Prisoners of War'. *Journal of the American Geriatrics Society* 57, no. 12 (2009): 2257–2262.

Rittner, Carol, and Sondra Myers. *The Courage to Care: Rescuers of Jews during the Holocaust*. New York: New York University Press, 1986.

Roberts, David. 'Beyond the Metropolis: Popular Peace and Postconflict Peacebuilding'. *Review of International Studies* 37, no. 5 (2011): 2535–2556.

Roberts, David. *Liberal Peacebuilding and Global Governance: Beyond the Metropolis*. London: Routledge, 2001.

Robertson, Cheryl Lee, and Laura Duckett. 'Mothering during War and Postwar in Bosnia'. *Journal of Family Nursing* 13, no. 4 (2007): 461–483.

Rogers, Kim Lacy. *Righteous Lives: Narratives of the New Orleans Civil Rights Movement*. New York: New York University Press, 1995.

Rogne, Leah. 'The Greatest Generation Revisited: Conscientious Objectors and the Great War'. *Humanity and Society* 34, no. 1 (2010): 3–38.

Roland, Charles G. 'Allied POWs, Japanese Captors and the Geneva Convention'. *War & Society* 9, no. 2 (1991): 83–101.

Roquen, Jeff. 'International Law and "Humanity" in the Making and Unmaking of European Solidarity, 1830–1915". *European Review of History: Revue Européenne d'Histoire* 24, no. 6 (2017): 889–904.

Rose, Richard. *Northern Ireland: A Time of Choice*. Basingstoke, UK: Macmillan, 1973.

Rosen, Richard Freiherr von. *Panzer Ace: The Memoirs of an Iron Cross Panzer Commander: From Barbarossa to Normandy*. Barnsley, UK: Greenhill, 2018.

Roux, Dominique, and Valérie Guillard. 'Circulation of Objects between Strangers in Public Space: An Analysis of Forms of Sociality among Disposers and Gleaners'. *Recherche et Applications en Marketing* 31, no. 4 (2016) 28–46.

Rudel, Hans Ulrich. *Stuka Pilot*. London: Black House, 2011.

Rudloff, Peter, and Michael G. Findlay. 'The Downstream Effects of Fragmentation on Civil War Reoccurrence'. *Journal of Peace Research* 53, no. 1 (2016): 19–32.

Rushton, Amy S. 'A History of Darkness: Exoticising Strategies and the Nigerian Civil War in *Half of a Yellow Sun* by Chimamanda Ngozi Adiche.' In *Exoticising the Past in Contemporary Historical Fiction*, edited by E. Rousslet, 178–195. London: Palgrave Macmillan, 2014.

Rydstrøm, Helle. 'Gendered Corporeality and Bare Lives: Local Sacrifices and Sufferings during the Vietnam War'. *Signs* 37, no. 2 (2012): 275–299.

Sabaratnam, Meera. 'Avatars of Eurocentrism in the Critique of the Liberal Peace'. *Security Dialogue* 44, no. 3 (2013): 259–278.

Sabaratnam, Meera. *Decolonising Intervention: International Statebuilding in Mozambique*. New York: Rowman & Littlefield, 2017.

Said, Edward. *The End of the Peace Process*. London: Granta, 2000.

Salifu, Uyo, and Irene Ndung'u. 'Preventing Violent Extremism in Kenya: Why Women's Needs Matter'. Institute for Security Studies East Africa Report 13, May 2017.

Salla, Michael Emin. 'Integral Peace and Power: A Foucauldian Perspective'. *Peace and Change* 23, no. 3 (1998): 312–332.

Santiago, Vinícius, and Marta Fernández. 'From the Backstage of War: The Struggle of Mothers in the Favelas of Rio de Janeiro'. *Contexto Internacional* 39, no. 1 (2017): 35–52.

Sareen, T. R. 'Subhas Chandra Bose, Japan and British Imperialism'. *European Journal of East Asian Studies* 3, no. 1 (2004): 69–97.

Sarna, Igal. 'The Prisoner President'. *Financial Times*, 21 February 2004, 16.

Schaffer, Bradley J. 'Homeless Military Veterans and the Intersection of Partner Violence'. *Journal of Human Behavior in the Social Environment* 22, no. 8 (2012): 1003–1013.

Schanzer, Jonathan. *State of Failure: Yasser Arafat, Mahmoud Abbas, and the Unmaking of the Palestinian State*. New York: Palgrave Macmillan, 2013.

Schatzki, Theodore R. 'A New Societist Social Ontology'. *Philosophy of the Social Sciences* 33, no. 2 (2003): 174–202.

Schiederbauer, Armin. *Adventures in My Youth: A German Soldier on the Eastern Front 1941–45*. Solihull, UK: Helion, 2013.

Schlögel, Karl. *Moscow 1937*. Cambridge: Polity, 2012.

Scholl, Inge. *The White Rose: Munich 1942–1943*. Middletown, CT: Wesleyan University Press, 1983.

Schuck, Andreas R.T., et al. 'Who's Afraid of Conflict? The Mobilising Effect of Conflict Framing in Campaign News'. *British Journal of Political Science* 46, no. 1 (2016): 177–194.

Schumpeter, Joseph A. *Capitalism, Socialism and Democracy*. London: Taylor & Francis, 2003.

Scott, James C. *Decoding Subaltern Politics: Ideology, Disguise and Resistance in Agrarian Politics*. London: Routledge, 2013.

Scott, James C. *Domination and the Art of Resistance: Hidden Transcripts*. New Haven, CT: Yale University Press, 1990.

Sekerka, Leslie E., and Roxanne Zolin. 'Professional Courage in the Military: Regulation Fit and Establishing Moral Intent'. *Business and Professional Ethics Journal* 24, no. 4 (2005): 27–50.

Sen, Amartya K. 'Democracy as a Universal Value'. *Journal of Democracy* 10, no. 3 (1999): 3–17.

'Service to Mark 19th Anniversary of Omagh Bomb'. *Ulster Herald*, 12 August 2017. http://ulsterherald.com/2017/08/12/service-mark-19th-anniversary-omagh-bomb/.

Severloh, Hein. *WN62: A German Soldier's Memories of the Defense of Omaha Beach, Normandy, June 6, 1944*. Garbsen, Germany: HEK Creativ, 2007.

Sewell, Brian. *Outsider: Always Almost, Never Quite: An Autobiography*. London: Quartet, 2012.

Shaban, Abdur Rahman Alfa. 'Ugandans Believe Police Are 75% Corrupt—Report'. *AfricaNews.com*, 23 June 2016. http://www.africanews.com/2016/06/23/ugandans-believe-police-are-75-percent-corrupt-survey//.

Shankar, Shakini. "'Metaconsumptive Practices and the Circulation of Objectifications'. *Journal of Material Culture* 11, no. 3 (2006): 293–317.

Sharrock, David. 'One Final Show for the "Chuckle Brothers"'. *Times*, 9 May 2008.

Sheffield, Gary. *Forgotten Victory: The First World War: Myths and Realities*. London: Headline Review, 2002.

Sheffield, Gary, and John Bourne, eds. *Douglas Haig: War Diaries and Letters 1914–1918*. London: Weidenfeld & Nicolson, 2005.

Shepherd, Laura J. *Gender, Peacebuilding and the Politics of Space: Locating Legitimacy*. Oxford: Oxford University Press, 2017.

Shepherd, Laura, J. 'Power and Authority in the Production of United Nations Security Council 1325'. *International Studies Quarterly* 52, no. 2 (2008): 383–404.

Silber, Irina Carlota. 'Mothers/Fighters/Citizens: Violence and Disillusionment in Post-War El Salvador'. *Gender & History* 16, no. 3 (2004): 561–587.

Simić, Olivera. 'Does the Presence of Women Really Matter? Towards Combating Male Sexual Violence in Peacekeeping Operations'. *International Peacekeeping* 17, no. 2 (2010): 188–199.

Singer, David J. 'The Level of Analysis Problem in International Relations'. *World Politics* 12, no. 3 (1961): 453–460.

Singh, Gurinder. 'A Decade of Ceasefire in Nagaland'. *Strategic Analysis* 31, no. 5 (2007): 815–832.

Sinha, Samrat. 'The Strategic Use of Peace: Non-State Armed Groups and Subnational Peacebuilding Mechanisms in Northeastern India'. *Democracy and Security* 13, no. 4 (2017): 273–303.

Sjoberg, Laura. 'Gender, the State and War Redux: Feminist International Relations across "Levels of Analysis"'. *International Relations* 25, no. 1 (2011): 108–134.

Sjoberg, Laura. 'Scaling International Relations Theory: Geography's Contribution to Where IR Takes Place'. *International Studies Review* 10, no. 3 (2008): 472–500.

Sjoberg, Laura, and Sandra Via, eds. *Gender, War and Militarism: Feminist Perspectives*. Santa Barbara, CA: Praeger, 2010.

Slim, Hugo. *Killing Civilians: Method, Madness and Morality in War*. London: Hurst, 2007.

Slim, Hugo. 'Wonderful Work: Globalizing the Ethics of Humanitarian Action'. In *The Routledge Companion to Humanitarian Action*, edited by Roger Mac Ginty and Jenny H. Peterson, 13–15. London: Routledge, 2015.

Sluzki, Carlos E. 'The Pathway between Conflict and Reconciliation: Coexistence as an Evolutionary Process'. *Transcultural Psychiatry* 47, no. 1 (2010): 55–69.

Smirl, Lisa. *Spaces of Aid: How Cars, Compounds and Hotels Shape Humanitarianism*. London: Zed, 2015.

Smith, Andrew. 'Rethinking the "Everyday" in "Ethnicity" and Everyday Life'. *Ethnic and Racial Studies* 38, no. 7 (2015): 1137–1151.

Smith, Colin. *Singapore Burning: Heroism and Surrender in WWII*. London: Penguin, 2006.

Smith, Leonard V. *Between Mutiny and Obedience: The Case of the French Fifth Infantry Division during World War I*. Princeton, NJ: Princeton University Press, 1994.
Smith, Linda Tuhiwai. *Decolonising Methodologies: Research and Indigenous Peoples*. London: Zed, 2012.
Smith, Roger. 'Technology Disruption in the Simulation Industry'. *Journal of Defense Modelling and Simulation* 3, no. 1 (2006): 3–10.
Smoker, Paul. 'Small Peace'. *Journal of Peace Research* 18, no. 2 (1981): 149–157.
Smyth, Lisa, and Martina McKnight. 'Maternal Situations: Sectarianism and Civility in a Divided City'. *Sociological Review* 61, no. 2 (2013): 304–322.
Soussi, Alasdair. 'Life after the Army: Israel's Conscientious Objectors'. *Al Jazeera*, 12 February 2018. https://www.aljazeera.com/news/2018/02/life-army-israel-conscientious-objectors-180211121020314.html.
Spiegel, Steven. 'Regional Security and the Levels of Analysis Problem'. *Journal of Strategic Studies* 26, no. 3 (2003): 75–98.
Srivavasta, J., and A. Sharma. 'International Relations Theory and World Order: Binaries, Silences and Alternatives'. *South Asian Survey* 21, nos. 1–2 (2014): 20–34.
Srnicek, Nick. 'Conflict Networks: Collapsing the Global into the Local'. *Journal of Critical Globalisation Studies* 2 (2010): 30–64.
Stafford, Philip. 'Trading Monitoring Goes into Seconds'. *Financial Times*, 24 February 2011. https://www.ft.com/content/ce35dd98-3ffa-11e0-811f-00144feabdc0.
Starr, Harvey, and Stanley Dubinsky. *The Israeli Conflict System: Analytic Approaches*. London: Routledge, 2015.
Steans, Jill. 'Engaging from the Margins: Feminist Encounters with the "Mainstream" of International Relations'. *British Journal of Politics and International Relations* 5, no. 3 (2003): 428–454.
Stedman, Stephen J., Donald Rothchild, and Elizabeth M. Cousens, eds. *Ending Civil Wars: The Implementation of Peace Agreements*. Boulder, CO: Lynne Rienner, 2002.
Steele, Brent J. 'Organisational Processes and Ontological Security: Torture, the CIA and the United States'. *Cooperation and Conflict* 52, no. 1 (2017): 69–89.
Stevenson, David. '1918 Revisited'. *Journal of Strategic Studies* 28, no. 1 (2005): 107–139.
Stevenson, Katie. 'Contesting Chivalry: James II and the Control of Chivalric Culture in the 1450s'. *Journal of Medieval History* 33, no. 2 (2007): 197–214.
Stockholm International Peace Research Institute. Sustainable Peace. 2019. https://www.sipri.org/research/peace-and-development/sustainable-peace.
Stovel, Katherine, and Lynette Shaw. 'Brokerage'. *Annual Review of Sociology* 38, no. 1 (2012): 139–158.
Strachan, Hew. 'Introductory Essay: The Changing Character of War'. In *Conceptualising Modern War*, edited by Karl Erik Haug and Ole Jørgen Maaø, 1–25. New York: Columbia University Press, 2011.
Studdert, David. 'Sociality and a Proposed Analytic for Investigating Communal Being-ness'. *Sociological Review* 64, no. 4 (2016): 622–638.
Sturma, Michael. 'The Limits of Hate: Japanese Prisoners on Board US Submarines during the Second World War'. *Journal of Contemporary History* 51, no. 4 (2016): 738–759.
'Sudan Approves 22% Pay Raise for Military'. *Sudan Tribune*, 9 May 2013. http://www.sudantribune.com/spip.php?article46520.
'Sudan Protests: Soldier "Killed while Protecting Activists" as Clashes Break Out'. *Sky News*, 8 April 2019. https://news.sky.com/story/sudan-protests-soldier-killed-while-protecting-activists-as-clashes-break-out-11687949.

'Sudan Protest: Clashes among Armed Forces at Khartoum Sit-in'. *BBC News*, 8 April 2019. https://www.bbc.co.uk/news/world-africa-47850278.
Sumter, Sindy Resita, Caroline L. Bokhurst, and P. Michiel Westenberg. 'The Robustness of the Factor Structure of the Self-Restraint Scale: What Does Self-Restraint Encompass?' *Journal of Research in Personality* 42 (2008): 1082–1087.
Sutton, Tara E. 'The Lives of Female Gang Members: A Review of the Literature'. *Aggression and Violent Behaviour* 37 (2017): 142–154.
Svirsky, Gila. 'Local Coalitions, Global Partners: The Women's Peace Movement in Israel and Beyond'. *Signs* 29, no. 2 (2004): 543–550.
Swaab, Jack. *Field of Fire: Diary of a Gunnery Officer*. Stroud, UK: Sutton, 2007.
Swärd, Anna. 'Trust, Reciprocity, and Actions: The Development of Trust in Temporary Inter-organizational Relations'. *Organization Studies* 37, no. 12 (2016): 1841–1860.
Tainter, Joseph A. *The Collapse of Complex Societies*. Cambridge: Cambridge University Press, 2003.
Tamayama, Kazou, and John Nunneley. *Tales by Japanese Soldiers*. London: Cassell, 2001.
Taylor, Frederick. *Coventry, Thursday, 14 November 1940*. London: Bloomsbury, 2015.
Taylor-Robinson, S. D. 'Operation Lifeline Sudan'. *Journal of Medical Ethics* 28 (2002): 49–51.
Temby, Owen. 'What Are Levels of Analysis and What Do They Contribute to International Relations Theory?' *Cambridge Review of International Affairs* 28, no. 4 (2015): 721–742.
Tepe, Fatma Fulya. 'Turkish Mother Citizens and Their Homefront Duties: The Cold War Discourse of the *Türk Kadını* Magazine'. *Feminist Formations* 29, no. 1 (2017): 25–52.
Terkel, Studs. *The Good War: An Oral History of World War Two*. London: Penguin, 1985.
Thirlway, Frances. 'Everyday Tactics in Local Moral Worlds: E-Cigarette Practices in a Working Class Area of the UK'. *Social Science and Medicine* 170 (2016): 106–113.
Thompson, Elizabeth. *Colonial Citizens: Republican Rights, Paternal Privilege and Gender in France, Syria and Lebanon*. New York: Columbia University Press, 2000.
Tickner, Ann B. 'Core, Periphery and (Neo)imperialist International Relations'. *European Journal of International Relations* 19, no. 3 (2013): 627–646.
Tillmann, Lisa M. 'Coming Out and Going Home: A Family Ethnography'. *Qualitative Enquiry* 16, no. 2 (2010): 116–129.
Tilly, Charles. *Coercion, Capital and European States, AD 990–1992*. London: Wiley-Blackwell, 1992.
Tittenbrum, Jacek. 'Social Capital: Neither Social, nor Capital'. *Social Science Information* 53, no. 4 (2014): 453–461.
Toktamis, Kumru. F. 'A Peace That Wasn't: Friends, Foes and Contentious Re-entrenchment of Kurdish Politics in Turkey'. *Turkish Studies* 19, no. 5 (2018): 697–722.
Tonge, Jonathan. *The Democratic Unionist Party: From Protest to Power*. Oxford: Oxford University Press, 2014.
Toorn, Jojanneke, Naomi Ellemers, and Bertjan Doosje. 'The Threat of Moral Transgression: The Impact of Group Membership and Moral Opportunity'. *European Journal of Social Psychology* 45, no. 5 (2015): 609–622.
Traboulsi, Fawwaz. *A History of Modern Lebanon*. London: Pluto, 2007.
Tschunkert, Kristina, and Roger Mac Ginty. 'Legitimacy in Lebanon'. In *Local Legitimacy and International Peacebuilding*, edited by Oliver P. Richmond and Roger Mac Ginty, 240–260. Edinburgh: Edinburgh University Press, 2020.

Turner, Victor. 'Frame, Flow and Reflection: Ritual and Drama as Public Liminality'. *Japanese Journal of Religious Studies* 6, no. 4 (1979): 465–499.

Uganda Legal Information Institute. Oaths Act, schedule 1 (1995). https://ulii.org/ug/legislation/consolidated-act/19.

UK Research and Innovation. 'Making Peacekeeping Data Work for the International Community'. https://gtr.ukri.org/project/494E4AD1-F7A2-4AD3-B474-FEAC43CA18B8.

United Nations. 'Report of the Secretary-General: Peacebuilding and Sustaining Peace. New York, 18 January 2018. https://www.un.org/peacebuilding/content/report-secretary-general-peacebuilding-and-sustaining-peace.

United Nations Peacekeeping. 'Summary of Troop Contributions to UN Peacekeeping Operations by Mission, Post and Gender', 2018. https://peacekeeping.un.org/sites/default/files/7_gender_report_5.pdf.

UN Women. 'Peace and Security', 2018. http://www.unwomen.org/en/what-we-do/peace-and-security.

Valdez, Carmen R., Tom Chavez, and Julie Woulfe. 'Emerging Adults' Lived Experience of Formative Family Stress: The Family's Lasting Influence'. *Qualitative Health Research* 23, no. 8 (2013): 1089–1102.

Van Doren, Didi, Peter Driessen, Hens Runhaar, and Mendel Giezen. 'Scaling-Up Low-Carbon Urban Initiatives: Towards a Better Understanding'. *Urban Studies* 55, no. 1 (2018): 175–194.

Van Emden, Richard, ed. *Sapper Marin: The Secret Great War Diary of Jack Martin*. London: Bloomsbury, 2009.

Van Leynseele, Yves. 'White Belonging and Brokerage at a South African Rural Frontier'. *Ethnos* 83, no. 5 (2018): 868–887.

Varshney, Ashutosh. *Ethnic Conflict and Civic Life: Hindus and Muslims in India*. New Haven, CT: Yale University Press, 2002.

Veenkamp, Ivo, and Sara Zeigler. *Countering Violent Extremism: Program and Policy Approaches to Youth through Education, Families and Communities*. Amsterdam: IOS, n.d.

Venn, Couze. 'Post-Enlightenment Cosmopolitanism and Transmodern Socialities'. *Theory, Culture & Society* 19, no. 1–2 (2002): 65–80.

Visoka, Gëzim. 'Metis Diplomacy: The Everyday Politics of Becoming a Sovereign State'. *Cooperation and Conflict* 54, no. 2 (2019): 167–190.

Vogt, Wendy A. 'Crossing Mexico: Structural Violence and the Commodification of Undocumented Central American Migrants'. *American Ethnologist* 40, no. 4 (2013): 764–780.

Voss, Johann. *Black Edelweiss: A Memoir of Combat and Conscience by a Soldier of the Waffen SS*. Kindle ed. N.p.: Aberjona, 2013.

Wacker, Albrecht. *Sniper on the Eastern Front: The Memoirs of Sepp Allerberger, Knights Cross*. Kindle ed. Barnsley, UK: Pen and Sword, 2008.

Wade, John E. 'The Wartime Curriculum'. *Journal of Educational Sociology* 16, no. 7 (1943): 403–406.

Wallace, Rick. *Merging Fires: Grassroots Peacebuilding between Indigenous and Nonindigenous peoples*. Halifax: Fernwood, 2013.

Wallace, Tina, Fenella Porter, and Mark Ralph-Bowman, eds. *Aid, NGOs, and the Realities of Women's Lives: A Perfect Storm*. Rugby, UK: Practical Action, 2013.

Wallensteen, Peter. *Understanding Conflict Resolution*. 4th ed. Los Angeles: Sage, 2015.

Wallensteen, Peter, and Margareta Sollenberg. 'An End to International War? Armed Conflict, 1989-1995'. *Journal of Peace Research* 33, no. 3 (1996): 353-370.

Wallis, Roy, Steve Bruce, and David Taylor. 'Ethnicity and Evangelism: Ian Paisley and Protestant Politics in Ulster'. *Comparative Studies in Society and History* 29, no. 2 (1987): 292-313.

Waltz, Kenneth. *Man, the State, and War: A Theoretical Analysis*. New York: Columbia University Press, 2001.

Wang, Jin Jun. 'Questions and the Exercise of Power'. *Discourse and Society* 17, no. 4 (2006): 529-548.

Warr, T. 'Circuitry', *Performance Research* 6, no. 3 (2001): 8-12.

Watson, Sophie. 'The Magic of the Marketplace: Sociality in a Neglected Public Space'. *Urban Studies* 46, no. 8 (2009): 1577-1591.

Watt, D. C. 'Summits and Summitry Reconsidered'. *International Relations* 2, no. 8 (1963): 493-504.

Weiss, Carol H. 'The Circuitry of Enlightenment: Diffusion of Social Science Research to Policymakers'. *Knowledge: Creation, Diffusion, Utilization* 8, no. 2 (1986): 274-281.

Weiss, Erica. 'Beyond Mystification: Hegemony, Resistance, and Ethical Responsibility in Israel'. *Anthropological Quarterly* 88, no. 2 (2015): 417-443.

Weitz, Yechiam. 'The Founding Father and the General: David Ben-Gurion and Moshe Dayan'. *Middle Eastern Studies* 47, no. 6 (2011): 845-861.

Whelpton, P. K. 'Why the Large Rise in the German Birth-Rate?' *American Journal of Sociology* 41, no. 3 (1935): 299-313.

White, Peter, *With the Jocks: A Soldier's Struggle for Europe 1944-45*. Stroud, UK: Sutton, 2004.

Whyte, John. *Interpreting Northern Ireland*. Oxford: Clarendon, 1990.

Wiess-Wendt, Anton. *Eradicating Differences: The Treatment of Minorities in Nazi-Dominated Europe*. Cambridge: Cambridge Scholars, 2010.

Williams, Kevin. 'War Correspondents as Sources for History'. *Media History* 18, nos. 3-4 (2012): 341-360.

Williamson, Anne. *Henry Williamson and the First World War*. Stroud, UK: Sutton, 2004.

Wittel, Andreas. 'Towards a Network Sociality'. *Theory, Culture & Society* 18, no. 6 (2001): 51-76.

'Women and Preventing Violent Extremism: The US and UK Experiences'. CHR & GJ Briefing Paper, New York University School of Law.

Wood, Elisabeth Jean. 'The Ethical Challenges of Field Research in Conflict Zones'. *Qualitative Sociology* 29, no. 3 (2006): 373-386.

Woodward, Rachel and Neil Jenkins. *Bringing War to Book: Writing and Producing the Military Memoir*. Basingstoke, UK: Palgrave, 2018.

Woollcombe, Robert. *Lion Rampant: The Memoirs of an Infantry Officer from D-Day to the Rhineland*. Edinburgh: Black and White, 2014.

World Bank. 'Military Spending (% of GDP)'. Washington, DC, 2019. https://data.worldbank.org/indicator/MS.MIL.XPND.GD.ZS.

Wright, Quincy. 'Criteria for Judging the Relevance of Researches on the Problems of Peace'. In *Research for Peace*, 3-98. Oslo: Institute for Social Research, 1954.

Yamashita, Karen Tei. *Letters to Memory*. Minneapolis: Coffee House, 2017.

Ylonen, Aleski. 'Conflict Diamonds "Alive and Well": Failing Controls and the Changing Landscapes of Global Diamond Landscape'. *African Security Review* 21, no. 3 (2012): 62-67.

Yusupova, Guzel. 'Cultural Nationalism and Everyday Resistance in an Illiberal Nationalising State: Ethnic Minority Nationalism in Russia'. *Nations and Nationalism* 24, no. 3 (2018): 624–647.

Yuval-Davis, Nira, Georgie Wemyss, and Kathryn Cassidy. 'Everyday Bordering: Belonging and the Reorientation of British Immigration Legislation'. *Sociology* 52, no. 2 (2018): 228–244.

Zahar, Marie-Joëlle. 'Peace by Unconventional Means: Lebanon's Ta'if Agreement'. In *Ending Civil Wars: The Implementation of Peace Agreements*, edited by Stephen John Stedman, Donald Rothchild, and Elizabeth M. Cousens, 567–597. Boulder, CO: Lynne Rienner, 2012.

Zartman, I. William, and J. Lewis Rasmussen, eds. *Peacemaking in International Conflict: Methods and Techniques*. Washington, DC: United States Institute of Peace Press, 1997.

Zondi, Sipamandla. 'Decolonising IR and Its Theory: A Critical Conceptual Meditation'. *Politikon* 45, no. 1 (2018): 16–31.

Zonsheine, David. 'The Conscientious Objectors Threatening the Israeli System'. *Haartez*, 18 March 2018. https://www.haaretz.com/opinion/.premium-the-conscientious-objectors-threatening-the-system-1.5449772.

Zunes, Stephen. 'Questions of Strategy'. In *Understanding Nonviolence*, edited by M. C. Hallward and J. M. Norman, 73–97. Cambridge: Polity, 2015.

Index

For the benefit of digital users, indexed terms that span two pages (e.g., 52-53) may, on occasion, appear on only one of those pages.

Afghanistan, 88-89, 162-63, 164-65, 206
agency, 1, 8-9, 27, 43, 53, 82, 97-98
anthropology, 2-3, 27, 31-32, 82
Autessere, Séverine, 2-3, 172-73, 213-14

Basque Country, 68-69
Belfast, 95, 204
Boer War, 116
Bosnia, 10-11, 169-70
Boulding, Kenneth, 81-82, 83, 91-92, 93-94
Brewer, John, 8-9
business, 66, 205-6

ceasefire, 48, 106, 126-33, 143, 145, 146-50, 151-52, 206
circuitry, 5-6, 7-8, 14-15, 18-19, 23, 25-26, 34-45, 52, 57-58, 81-83, 90-91, 99-101, 105-6, 114-15, 125-26, 134-35, 140, 145-46, 147-48, 150, 156, 159, 161-62, 173-74, 186, 199-200, 207, 219
civilians, 120
civil society, 11-12, 14-15
civil society organisations, 2-3, 11-12, 47, 95-96, 109, 163, 208-9
Colombia, 177-78, 208
colonialism, 113-14
compassion, 2-3
complex adaptive systems, 21-22, 27-28, 35, 36-37, 38, 47-48, 55-56, 92-93, 105-6, 219
confidence-building measures, 11-12, 127-28
conflict disruption, 2-3, 4, 5, 6, 8, 9-10, 20-21, 24, 34-35, 43, 53, 136, 137-38, 144, 158-60, 190-211, 220
conflict transformation, 83, 97, 130, 148, 201-3, 210-11

Darfur, 56, 165-67, 171-72
Dayan, Ruth, 197-99
Democratic Unionist Party, 192, 193-94
disruption. *See* conflict disruption
drone, 57-58, 164-65

economics, 66
everyday, 15-16, 18-19, 20, 27-34, 40-41, 190, 213-14, 219, 220-21

Everyday Peace Indicators, 1, 6-7, 15-16, 17, 31-32, 61, 62, 67-68, 177, 213
extremism, 179-80, 183

family, 11-12, 14-15, 16, 20, 28, 31, 39-40, 105, 161, 163, 164-65, 173-82
Firchow, Pamina, 17
friendship, 9, 11-12, 19-21, 34, 41-42, 93, 190-202, 215, 217-18

gender, 13-14, 16, 17, 20, 30-31, 109-10, 125, 138-39
gender studies, 2-3, 29-30, 31-32, 161-89
Germany, 114, 119, 124-25, 152-53, 183

Hitler, Adolf, 83-84
Holocaust, 112, 113
home, 7-8, 10, 15, 17, 29-30, 31-32
humanitarianism, 126-27

identity, 32-33, 40, 54, 58-59, 60-61, 67-68, 71-72, 73, 88-89
India, 128, 153
indigenous, 96-97
international humanitarian law, 130-32
international relations, 27, 35-36, 37, 45-46, 49, 82, 90-91, 107-8, 161, 175, 186-87
Irish Republican Army, 192, 193-95
Israel-Palestine, 9, 59-60, 69-70, 72, 79, 197-99, 203-4

Japan, 114, 153, 195-97

Kyrgyzstan, 184, 188-89

Lebanon, 54-55, 173-74, 180-82, 184, 185, 200-1
Lederach, John Paul, 2-3, 26, 48, 77-78, 93-94, 159-60, 162-63, 217-18
local, 14-15, 17, 23, 28
local turn, 13-14, 31-32, 219
Lomax, Eric, 195-97
Lord's Resistance Army, 1, 58-59, 68, 80-81, 100-1

Martin, McGuinness, 192–95
memoirs and diaries, 15–16, 18, 104–5, 106, 107–15, 138–39, 164
militarism, 104, 116–17, 133, 134–35, 158–59, 167–68, 197–98
military elites and leaders, 108, 149–50, 156, 210–11
mutiny, 41, 43, 154, 155–56, 207, 215–16
Myanmar, 63, 128–29

Nazis, 70, 85–86, 112, 118–19, 151–52, 156–57, 175–76
New Zealand, 155
Northern Ireland, 33–34, 55, 60, 68–69, 76, 91–92, 98, 181, 184, 187–88, 192–95, 204, 215–16

Paisley, Ian, 192–95
peace, 4
    agonistic peace, 4
    liberal peace, 83n.8, 87–88
    peace accords, 13–14, 16–17, 128, 129–30, 167–68, 169
    peace and conflict studies, 15–16, 18, 22–23, 25–26, 28–29, 31–32, 45–46, 107–8, 158, 161, 202–3
    peacebuilding, 47, 171, 172–73
    peacekeeping, 17–18, 171, 172
    peace processes, 76, 128, 129–30, 161, 167–69, 194
    sustainable peace, 69–70
    top-down peace, 13–14
Phelps-Roper, Megan, 200
political elites and leaders, 12–13, 18–19, 41, 43, 106–7, 118–19, 167–68, 200–1, 203, 210–11
power, 5, 6–7, 16, 19–20, 28, 30–31, 40, 41–42, 80–103, 105, 114–15, 125–27, 133, 134, 138, 140, 145–46, 158–59, 161, 173, 183, 199, 204, 205–6, 215–16, 221–22
    everyday peace power, 5, 6–7, 8, 19–20, 80, 133, 134, 136, 161–62, 173, 188–89, 199, 221–22
    power-sharing, 88–89
prisoners and prisoner of war, 111, 113, 115, 120–23, 131–32, 139, 140, 141, 154, 159–60, 195–97, 211, 216

radicalisation, 20
reciprocity, 4, 6–7, 19, 40, 53–54, 65–67, 71–75, 136–37, 144–52, 178–79
reconciliation, 4, 11–12, 13–14, 51–52, 201–2
religion (and faith), 45, 59, 66–67, 71, 72, 73, 74–75, 77, 192, 200, 201

Richmond, Oliver, 2–3, 64–65
Russia, 112, 113, 118–19, 124–25

Saudi Arabia, 85
scale, 18–19, 31–32, 39–40, 43–44, 76, 105–6, 115, 190
scaling up, 1–3, 4, 5–6, 7–8, 14–15, 18–19, 26, 34–35, 45–49, 75–79, 105–6, 144, 159–60, 162–63, 190, 216, 218
Schumpeter, Joseph, 204–5
sexual and gender based violence, 57, 124–25, 165–66, 171
social entrepreneurs, 48
sociality, 6–7, 19, 40, 43–44, 53–54, 61–65, 71–75, 114–15, 125–26, 136–37, 139–44
societialisation, 7–8, 26, 78–79, 105–6
sociology, 2–3, 17, 27, 28, 31–32, 37–38, 82
solidarity, 4, 6–7, 19, 40, 54, 67–70, 71–75, 114–15, 136–37, 152–58
South Africa, 62, 64, 65–66, 67–68, 174–75
Soviet Union. *See* Russia
spoilers, 128, 129–30
states, 84–86, 89–91, 99, 114–15, 130–31, 154–55, 221
Sudan, 1–2, 7–8, 37–38, 39–40, 44–45, 50, 126–27, 215–16
Syria, 71–72, 132

Takashi, Nagase, 196–97
Tawil, Raymonda, 197–99
time and timing, 64, 68–69, 78–79, 102, 110–11, 158
total war, 105, 106–7, 115–26, 137–39, 158–59
truce. *See* ceasefire
trust, 66–67
Turkey, 175–76

Uganda, 1, 62, 68, 100–1, 176–77
United Kingdom, 78–79, 84–85, 139, 152, 192–93, 194, 196
United Nations, 17–18, 56, 132, 171, 172
United States, 36, 57–58, 123, 152, 154–55, 208–9

Wodehouse, P.G., 152
World War I, 8–9, 41, 43, 54, 105–6, 115–26, 136–37, 144, 148–49, 155, 207, 215–16
World War II, 2, 69, 109–10, 114, 115–26, 149–50, 183, 185, 195–97

Zimbabwe, 31–32, 67–68
zones of peace, 154–55